American Culture

Contributions from *Ethnology*

American Culture

>>> <<<

Essays on the Familiar and Unfamiliar

Leonard Plotnicov

Editor

University of Pittsburgh Press
in cooperation with Ethnology

Published by the University of Pittsburgh Press, Pittsburgh, Pa. 15260
Copyright © 1990, University of Pittsburgh Press
All rights reserved
Baker and Taylor International, London
Manufactured in the United States of America

The essays in this volume are reprinted by arrangement with the editors of *Ethnology* and have appeared in the following issues of that journal: "Atomistic Order and Frontier Violence" and "Filipino Hometown Associations in Hawaii," vol. 22 (October 1983): 327–39 and 341–53; "Persistence and Change Patterns in Amish Society," vol. 3 (April 1964): 185–98; "Relations of Modes of Production in Nineteenth Century America" and "The Cultural Evaluation of Wealth," vol. 26 (January 1987): 1–16 and 37–50; "The Family Reunion," vol. 5 (October 1966): 415–33; "Jewish Ethnic Signalling," vol. 17 (October 1978): 407–23; "Nicknames and the Transformation of an American Jewish Community," vol. 26 (April 1987), 73–85; "The Samoan Funeral in Urban America," vol. 9 (July 1970): 209–27; "Brokerage, Economic Opportunity, and the Growth of Ethnic Movements," vol.18 (October 1979): 399–414; "The Rock Creek Auction," vol. 26 (October 1987): 297–311; "Culture and Conceptualization," vol. 1 (July 1962): 374–86; "Political Kinship Alliance of a Hasidic Dynasty," vol. 23 (January 1984): 49–62; "Ritual in the Operating Room," vol. 20 (October 1981): 335–50.

Library of Congress Cataloging-in-Publication Data

American culture: essays on the familiar and unfamiliar / Leonard
    Plotnicov, editor.
        p. cm.
    Includes bibliographical references.
    ISBN 0-8229-1157-4
    ISBN 0-8229-6092-3 (pbk)
    1. Ethnology—United States—Case studies. 2. United States—
Social conditions—Case studies. 3. Minorities—United States—
Case studies. 4. United States—Social life and customs—Case
studies. I. Plotnicov, Leonard. II. Ethnology.
GN560.V6A53 1990
306'.0973—dc20   89-16638
                                                                CIP

Contents

Acknowledgments vii

Introduction ix

Worlds of Order and Disorder   3

Atomistic Order and Frontier Violence:
Miners and Whalemen in the Nineteenth-Century Yukon   7
  Thomas Stone

Persistence and Change Patterns in Amish Society   25
  John A. Hostetler

Relations of Modes of Production in Nineteenth-Century
America: The Shakers and Oneida   41
  Matthew Cooper

The Search for Roots   63

The Family Reunion   67
  Millicent R. Ayoub

Jewish Ethnic Signalling: Social Bonding in
Contemporary American Society   89
  Leonard Plotnicov and Myrna Silverman

Nicknames and the Transformation of an American
Jewish Community: Notes on the Anthropology of
Emotion in the Urban Midwest   111
  Jack Glazier

Strangers Who Settle Among Us   129

The Samoan Funeral in Urban America   135
  Joan Ablon

Filipino Hometown Associations in Hawaii   159
  Jonathan Y. Okamura

Brokerage, Economic Opportunity, and the Growth of
Ethnic Movements 179
Miriam J. Wells

Seeing and Understanding 197

The Cultural Evaluation of Wealth: An Agrarian Case Study 201
Elvin Hatch

The Rock Creek Auction: Contradiction Between
Competition and Community in Rural Montana 223
Frederick Errington

Culture and Conceptualization: A Study of Japanese and
American Children 241
Mary Ellen Goodman

Pollution and Purity 255

Political Kinship Alliances of a Hasidic Dynasty 259
Rhonda Berger-Sofer

Ritual in the Operating Room 279
Pearl Katz

Acknowledgments

The editor is grateful for the years of pleasurable collaboration with his associates, Dolores Donohue, Richard Scaglion, and Arthur Tuden, whose excellent judgment in the adventure of *Ethnology* and for the present volume is without measure. Gratitude is also extended to the authors of the essays that follow for making this volume possible. As several contributors have changed their institutional affiliations since their articles were first published in *Ethnology,* they and their current institutions or addresses are listed below:

    Joan Ablon, University of California, San Francisco
    Millicent R. Ayoub (deceased)
    Rhonda Berger-Sofer, University of Haifa
    Matthew Cooper, McMasters University
    Frederick Errington, 46 Orchard Street, Amherst, MA 01002
    Jack Glazier, Oberlin College
    Mary Ellen Goodman (deceased)
    Elvin Hatch, University of California, Santa Barbara
    John A. Hostetler, Temple University
    Pearl Katz, 13804 Rippling Brook Drive, Silver Spring, Md 20906
    Jonathan Y. Okamura, University of Hawaii, Hilo
    Leonard Plotnicov, University of Pittsburgh
    Myrna Silverman, University of Pittsburgh
    I. Thomas Stone, State University of New York, Potsdam
    Miriam J. Wells, University of California, Davis

The editors of *Ethnology* also express their appreciation to the University of Pittsburgh Press and its director, Frederick A. Hetzel, for making this publication possible.

Introduction

THIS BOOK is intended for a general audience, people interested in or curious about anthropology and Americans—actually, the anthropology of Americans. It may seem incongruous to speak of the anthropology of Americans, for anthropology has the reputation of exploring exotic societies and cultures. That is true, as those who have experienced college introductory courses in cultural anthropology will affirm. But what animates anthropology is not just a fascination with the strange and sometimes titillating customs of "savages" or "primitive" people. Knowing others is a means of understanding ourselves.

Anthropologists have recognized this since the discipline's birth well over a century ago, and the premise has inspired the titles of introductory or general texts such as *Mirror for Man* and *To See Ourselves*. Anthropologists insist that their domain of enquiry encompasses all known examples of human society and culture for the ultimate aim of scientifically understanding human nature as expressed in all social institutions and behaviors. Thus, a knowledge of non-Western or tribal societies has direct relevance for the understanding of modern and complex societies, and the opposite also applies. The two-way reflective process is never ending.

Anthropology's interest in studying modern society and culture has been present for a long time, but in the past such endeavors were peripheral interests of scholars whose main activities lay in fieldwork with the strange folk. Our distinguished anthropological ancestors—such as Benedict, Boas, Herskovits, Kluckhaven, Kroeber, Linton, Lowie, Malinowski, Mead, and Radin—and their notable offspring—including Firth, Goldschmidt, and Steward—all dabbled on the side with research into contemporary or advanced or industrial society. With other forebears, like Lewis, the Lynds, Powdermaker, Spiro, and Warner, this concern was salient and central to their work.

But not until the present generation of anthropologists has there been a concerted effort to direct research at modern society and one's own culture. This has established a field of study within the discipline, a core of central interest to a body of researchers, and the beginning of a scholarly tradition, all of which are apparent in the emergence of specialized anthropological journals that deal principally with modern conditions, and in the rising number of articles treating similar subject matter in the traditional journals of the profession.

The chapters that form this volume first appeared in *Ethnology* a journal of general social and cultural anthropology published through the University of Pittsburgh since its founding in 1962. What distinguishes this group of articles is the concern with things American, the attempt to depict and understand the familiar from the perspective of the exotic. Some of the subject matter may appear quite ordinary, even mundane. Other subjects do have a touch of the exotic about them, like the "strangers" among us, whether they are the relatively recent newcomers like the Samoans in California or the venerable and inward-looking Amish of Pennsylvania. Even the ordinary becomes exciting, however (and sometimes strange), when we regard it in a new way, as when the modern hospital operating theater and the activities within it are compared with what anthropologists have come to understand about religious ritual.

Indeed, one of the objectives of traditional social and cultural anthropology is to help us become familiar with the exotic so that we can appreciate how ordinary and mundane is most human behavior, even that of the most exotic people. Much of cultural anthropology explores the ordinary. People everywhere must find ways of surviving, ways of relating to others, ways of entertaining themselves, and ways of making sense of their world. These ordinary modes of human expression interest anthropologists most and inform the articles selected for reappearance here.

The articles have been grouped into five sections, each section determined by a theme common to the group. The clusters are arbitrary, of course, and readers probably could organize these selections in various combinations that are equally rational, as each article can have different aspects highlighted. Indeed, I feel certain that many of the authors, if given the opportunity, would place a different emphasis on their work than what I have chosen. The issue is not a matter of correctness but one of taste. I have arranged the articles by the way each has stimulated me and how it has enhanced my knowledge of anthropology and of the human condition. In short, I view these essays on America and Americans as a means of wider understanding.

The first section, Worlds of Order and Disorder, contains articles about frontiersmen, the Amish, and the nineteenth-century religious, utopian communities, the Shakers and Oneida. Common to each of these societies is a concern with constructing a moral order, with particular focus placed on whether social relations will be governed by pragmatic or ideal means. The different codes of conduct and social control chosen by these groups result, as we may expect, in very different consequences for the quality of life within the society and the group's stability.

INTRODUCTION xi

The next group of readings, The Search for Roots, implies that Americans, in an impersonal and rapidly changing society, feel a need for belonging or closeness with others to share a sense of community and common history. This theme applies equally to other readings—for example, those on immigrants—which could have been included in this section. Two articles here are about Jews, but other groups could serve just as well for the analytical principles derived from these examples. Ethnic groups have been regarded as primordial communities; the first article in this cluster presents a variation on this grouping principle. It deals with people who may not share the same ethnicity or religion but who feel themselves a part of an important group through ties of blood and marriage. They are relatives, most of them only remotely related, but being related is significant enough for the members to make great efforts to maintain ritual solidarity. This is no strange cult. It is the common phenomenon of American relatives getting together for annual reunions.

Strangers Who Settle Among Us, the third cluster of readings, is about immigrants. Two of the immigrant groups, Samoans and Filipinos, are relatively recent arrivals in the United States. Another group, Hispanic-Americans, has been present in this country for centuries, long before the appearance of most European immigrants. Despite being old settlers, they are often treated as and perceive themselves to be immigrants. Might the same be said of American Indians? Of African-Americans? All these groups, like immigrants elsewhere, share similar concerns about adjustment in a society where they are strangers and, for a time, live a cultural world apart. The strategies they devise for accommodating to their conditions are often typical for immigrant groups; namely, fraternal associations and benevolent societies. Sometimes the modes of adjustment are culture-specific, employing techniques that are within the group's heritage. The Chicanos, described by Wells, exemplify this. Upon moving to Wisconsin for employment, they initially placed their security in a traditionally structured patron-client relationship. Ultimately, that proved nonviable.

Seeing and Understanding, the next section, has two readings on ranchers and one on schoolchildren. The latter compares Americans with their Japanese counterparts to determine whether their different cultural upbringings influence their cognitive processes. They do, but not as we might expect. Among other things, what we learn from the articles on ranchers is that we perceive and make sense of our conditions not so much subjectively or objectively as culturally. This is an old saw in social science, but it is nice to be reminded of it by seeing how unfamiliar is the familiar.

The final group of readings, headed Pollution and Purity, apposes two topics that apparently could not be further apart. One is the modern hospital operating room with its procedures to avoid infection. The other is a genealogical study of the rabbinical leadership of an extremely Orthodox sect. We can sense more readily the connections between these when considering, for instance, that hospital staff use strict procedures to maintain asepsis, and that the Hasidic Jews follow equally strict rules of marriage to maintain the charismatic purity of succession to leadership. There are other suggestive analogies. The operating room layout and procedures may be apperceived as fundamentally religious and ritualistic, and the marriage and leadership patterns of the Lubavitch Hasidim as fundamentally political. It is part of the beauty of anthropology to be able to analytically make sacred and profane worlds their obverse. Here are the fruits of *Ethnology*. Enjoy.

American Culture

Worlds of Order and Disorder
>>> <<<

Most Americans are at best only dimly familiar with that part of their nation's history concerning religious communities that flourished during the nineteenth century but ultimately failed. The Shakers, of course, had the cards of viability stacked against them partly because they were sexually abstemious and required the infusion of recruits from without to replace departed members. But some Shaker traditions live on, memorialized in a sense, in certain classic hymns and in the fine quality of furniture they bequeathed us. Similarly, we remember and appreciate the Oneida and Amana communities, associating them with silverware and refrigerators respectively. This is far from the goals intended by the founders of these utopian movements, or from what they envisioned as their fate. It is ironic and sad that the principles and ideals that served to form and give strength to these groups should also carry the seeds of their demise, as Cooper relates.

Cooper's essay is an economic analysis of the Shaker and Oneida communities and rightly focuses on their organization of production, which was fundamental to their religious ideals. The economic innovations at the heart of their endeavors were perceived by them both as a criticism of the society developing under American capitalism and as a clear expression of their utopian vision. Their economic organization was an example of how people could live righteously yet comfortably. However, Cooper also shows how these groups had to relate their activities to a growing and encompassing industrial society, and how they negotiated market forces and economic opportunities in a manner that was advantageous financially but destructive ideologically.

Like the Amish, who are considered in the following chapter, and the Hutterites, the Oneida and Shakers began as agriculturalists. Farming was the means to figuratively transform Earth into Heaven. While the Amish and Hutterites persisted with an agrarian economy that forswore modern innovations and did not require a reliance on hired labor, the Shakers and Oneida embraced technological and financial innovation, including hired labor, all of which propelled them unwittingly into manufacturing, trade, and captialist enterprise. What began as communist ideals of joy and egalitarianism in work evolved into the rationalization that innovations in production, more efficient manufacturing operations, and profitable financial ventures freed the members for higher spiritual pursuits. Hired labor, however, came to be viewed and treated in a framework of management-worker relations, and as the communites became successful capitalist enterprises, to that extent did they diverge from their original objectives. Their histories end with the Shakers reduced to a few elderly ladies and the Oneida transformed into a joint-stock corporation.

The Amish are a large, conservative Christian sect that attempts to live in an eighteenth-century manner in a twentieth-century world. They prefer to be left alone, but must relate politically, commercially, and socially to others within the wider American communities in which they reside. Most of what they produce, like tobacco in Lancaster, Pennsylvania, is not intended for subsistence but for market. Their appearance and customs attract the curiosity of tourists who regard them as quaint, like living cultural fossils. They dislike this, but even worse, from the Amish insular perspective, they are constrained by the same laws and regulations that govern their neighbors. The outside world is a threat to their integrity, and for several centuries they have largely avoided the penetration of polluting influences from without.

Amish do not like being the object of attention, whether by tourists or anthropologists. Thus much of our intimate knowledge of them comes not from movies like *Witness* but from former members, like Hostetler. For readers who relate Amish society and culture with halcyon old ways of (despite the smell) organic farming and horse-and-buggy transportation, and see Amish life as as idyllic oasis protected from the stresses and social forces of modern times, Hostetler's account is revealing. Amish are not immune from internal strains, personal dissatisfactions, or rebellious youth, and even show an astonishingly high rate of suicide. But we should not take such uninvited observations merely as the means to declare titillating revelations. The imperfections disclosed by our intrusion backstage also affirm the humanity shared by Amish with all of us. They are remarkable Americans who merit our admiration not only for their farming and husbandry skills, their productivity and material self-sufficiency, but above all for the extent to which they have succeeded in determining their cultural destiny.

A commonly held view of human nature, articulated by Thomas Hobbes in the seventeenth century, presumes that if left to their own devices, most people will put self-interest above community well-being, even when the latter condition is rationally in their personal best interest; thus an external authority is required to control the selfish impulses of the masses, forcing them to cooperate for the good of the community and society. Hobbes thought that, at some point in the human past, people evolved sufficiently so as to recognize the inherent evil in human nature, and therefore created what we know as the "social contract," giving power and authority to government in order to curb egocentricity and avoid anarchy.

This myth does not explain how state government actually arose. Anthropologists have provided numerous examples showing that people in "simple" societies can live at peace and have institutionalized mechanisms for managing conflict. But in some circles the view persists that within all humans there beats a savage heart, kept in check only by fears of government and religious sanctions. The paradigm of inherent aggression makes for good fiction. In *Lord of the Flies*, by William Golding, a group of schoolboys, shipwrecked on an island and lacking adult restraints, reverts to viciousness. The same paradigm is implicit in Hollywood films of the Old West: set men loose on the frontier, out of reach of the law, and the bullies will run rampant.

Are there any experiments we could devise that would answer the question about the fundamental nature of human beings? The laboratory will not serve for this, as human subjects arrive already culturally conditioned. There is a way, however. Anthropologists use "natural laboratories" where, in a manner of speaking, the experimental conditions are provided by different natural settings. This "controlled comparison" is how Stone utilizes historical data on nineteenth-century North American frontier communities of gold miners and whalers.

Compared with the whalers, the communities of the miners appear unstructured and thereby ripe for the appearance of treachery and conflict brought on by greed. Their conditions seem ideal to nourish social atomism; there is, as Stone puts it, "an absence of bases of social collaboration other than *ad hoc*, individual discretion." The whalers, on the other hand, were organized as ships' crews, each under the hierarchical command of its officers, who were not reluctant to dispense punishment and to use arms as necessary force. Despite the tight disciplinary structure, the occurrence of conflict and violence was far greater among the whalers than among the miners.

There are several reasons for this. One is that the miners instituted a system of third party adjudication that was "forward looking" and concerned more with "protecting the community against what [a man] might do in the future" than with punishment. Conflict management decisions were communal, took personal character into account, and reduced the possibility for violence by separating and keeping adversaries apart.

The whalers, on the other hand, were motley crews comprised in part of Pacific Islanders, Cape Verde Africans, and waterfront drifters who were sometimes shanghaied into service. The ships' officers viewed them as social scum whom they were forced to associate with until the whaling expedition had been satisfactorily completed. How frequently violence and thefts among crew members occurred is uncertain because those who might have recorded such events contemptuously overlooked them. But thefts of a ship's stores, or of the officers' personal effects, met with harsh reprisal. The exercise of brutal punishment on erring crew members did little to deter them from repeated offenses and served only to perpetuate a vicious circle of bitter antagonisms. Readers may infer from this analysis a moral applicable to the failing criminal justice system in contemporary America.

nineteenth century. The effects of community organization on the nature and functioning of systems of public justice in these two populations, and the effects of these systems of public justice, in turn, on conflict management, fail to confirm the forgoing conventional wisdom. In what follows, I explore the reasons for this, drawing on current theory which suggests that a community's system of public justice will influence levels of internal violence primarily through its effects on opportunities for resort to nonviolent forms of conflict management (Koch 1974; Nader and Todd 1978; Black 1983). In particular, the levels of intracommunity violence which emerge in these two populations appear to be consistent with the proposition that systems of public justice will influence the potential for internal violence primarily through their impact on the availability and use of both third-party resolution and separation, inasmuch as these constitute major, recognizably significant alternatives to the kind of continuing dyadic confrontation which may foster or escalate violence (Koch 1974:26–35, 159–175; Roberts 1979:83–86; Black 1983).

Contrasting Communities in the Nineteenth Century Yukon

In the closing years of the nineteenth century, an American invasion of what was shortly to become the Yukon Territory took place on two fronts. Beginning in the 1870s, gold prospectors moved into the region and their numbers increased substantially following significant strikes on the Stewart (1885) and Fortymile (1886) Rivers. By 1894, a settlement at the junction of the Yukon and Fortymile had grown to a town of some 150 log buildings which served as the center for a mining district where close to 1,000 miners were working. In the meantime, American whalemen had entered the Beaufort Sea and in 1890 were wintering their ships at Herschel Island, on the present-day Yukon's arctic coast. The early success of these first wintering whalers led increasing numbers of ships to follow suit. By 1895, the population of the wintering community of whalemen, frozen in with their ships at the island for ten months, had grown to 500 or more (Goodrich 1897; Ogilvie 1913; Wright 1976; Bockstoce 1977). In 1894 the North West Mounted Police reconnoitered the interior Yukon and they appeared in force in 1895; in 1903 they extended their operations north to the whalemen and established a post at Herschel Island. But before their arrival, the developing communities of miners and whalemen were left to rely on their own devices when it came to handling conflict and maintaining social order; there was no immediate local access to the established Canadian and American institutions of law and government.

In certain respects, the small expatriate communities which the miners and the whalemen established in the Yukon were much alike. First, they were composed almost wholly of transients; neither group thought of the Yukon region as a permanent home. In addition to their transient character, the whaling and mining communities also shared a similar feature in their annual cycles of population dispersal and concentration. Summer was a season of population dispersal and high mobility, and it was also the time when the numbers of whalemen and miners in the area were largest. The long winter period, for whalemen and miners alike, brought with it a reduction in population as many moved "outside" for the season, and those who stayed tended to become concentrated in a few population centers where they remained, largely immobilized, until the return of the warm weather. Nonetheless, in spite of these similarities, the organization of the whaling and mining populations could hardly have provided a more striking lesson in contrasts.

On the one hand, the miners arrived in the Yukon district as an almost wholly unorganized mass of independent adventurers. Whatever relationships they formed once they were in the territory were characteristically ad hoc, fluid, highly transitory and egalitarian in character. Even the most basic social bond of the miner's society—the partnership—was a highly unstable alliance. As men recurrently collected in groups and then dispersed in the course of their traveling, prospecting, mining and wintering, partnerships were likely to be reshuffled; as a result, during successive periods of dispersal, men were not likely to be working with the same companions. Men who continued to work in the region, of course, came to be known to one another either from acquaintance or by reputation. But for much of his time in the territory a miner never knew whom he might end up ing with, and many of those to whom he became linked in some common enterprise were likely to be strangers to him (Snow 1896–1925; McQuesten 1952; Goodrich 1897; Ogilvie 1913; Stone, in press).

At all levels, from a pair of miners working on an isolated creek to the largest wintering community assembled around a trading post, the partnerships or groups which the miners formed lacked any formal positions of leadership or authority. The relationships which emerged among them were always consensual, negotiated as expedient on an ad hoc basis. When men came to disagree on plans or strategies, or other conflict arose among them, they simply parted company and linked up with new associates who, for the time being or the purpose in question, appeared to be more kindred souls. This is not to deny, of course, the existence of leadership nor the appearance of singularly prominent figures among the mass of men moving through the territory. Significant leaders did emerge to often exert their influence. These men were traders or other old-timers in the region who stood out with respect to the control of two essential resources: supplies and knowledge of the local region. But they exercised their considerable influence informally and wholly by the consent of those who were willing to listen to them, rather than through their position in any explicit organizational structure (Snow 1896–1925; McQuesten 1952; Goodrich 1897; Ogilvie 1913; Stone, in press).

The whalemen, for their part, enjoyed none of the individual autonomy and independence of the miners. From the point of their departure for the north and throughout their time in the arctic they remained tightly organized as members of a particular ship's company, firmly bound by the status—and status distinctions—which membership in that particular organization entailed. Here, the units involved in the annual pattern of population concentration and dispersal were not individuals, but ships. Summer found them off at sea, on the whaling grounds or en route to or from the arctic with only occasional and brief calls at the whaling station on Herschel Island. With the coming of winter, the ships then gathered at Herschel (or, occasionally, at sites further east) where they remained frozen in for ten months. Here, aside from occasional hunting forays away from the island, their crews formed a stable and concentrated population. But even during this long winter sojourn, the ships retained the same organization as at sea, with the same profound and rigid distinctions of authority and status which separated officers from the crews (Cook 1926; Bodfish 1936; Stevenson 1968; Bockstoce 1977).

During the long winter season at the island, the work involved in securing sufficient supplies of water, wood, and food often brought the men of different ship's companies together, but the basic division of authority between officers and men remained very much in effect. Even in the various forms of community recreation which emerged at the island, the status distinctions implicit in the structure of the whaleship were never very deeply submerged. Masters were sometimes accompanied by their wives and families and they, together with other officers, introduced a number of social events and activities in an effort to reconstruct as much as possible of the character of polite New England society. These events, which included theatrical performances, dinner and whist parties, and "grand balls," either involved ordinary seamen not at all or in some clearly subordinate capacity. The men ranking below officer status were left to seek their amusement primarily in drinking, cards, and the company of native women (Cook 1926; Bodfish 1936; Stevenson 1968; Bockstoce 1977; Stone 1981).

To all intents and purposes, the organization of the whaling community was established at the beginning of the whalemen's voyage, when they entered (voluntarily or otherwise) into a contract which rigidly defined their rights and obligations for the duration. These social arrangements remained in effect as the various ships came into association for the winter at the island, and the maintenance of these established status relationships took precedence over any ad hoc organizational arrangements which emerged as a result of the winter association of crews. The result was a rigidly and sharply stratified, segmental community structure, divided in one dimension by ships' companies, in another by the line of authority separating officer and crews.

The concept of social atomism, understood in Ruth Benedict's original sense of the absence of bases of social collaboration other than ad hoc, individual discretion (Maslow and Honigmann 1970:323), highlights the essential contrast in the organization of the miners' and whalers' communities in the Yukon. It would be hard to find a better example of atomistic structure as Benedict defined it than the one provided by the miners, whose social life was almost entirely ordered by individual, transient, ad hoc, discretionary alliances. Among the whalemen, on the other hand, community organization was dominated by the recognition and acceptance of rights and obligations attaching to social position within rigid, permanently constituted group structures, the kind of organization which for Benedict was a hallmark of non-atomistic, corporate society (Maslow and Honigmann 1970:323–324).

The idea that societies which "recognize only individual allegiances and ties" beyond the elementary family and "lack the social forms necessary for group action" are prone to generate high levels of internal aggression was endorsed by Benedict in the 1940s (Maslow and Honigmann 1970:325–326) and later became enshrined in the concept of the "atomistic society" as formulated in the 1960s (Munch and Marske 1981:158–161). More recently, however, this view of the social consequences of atomistic structure has come under challenge. Providing data from the island of Tristan Da Cunha as a case in point, for example, Munch and Marske (1981:168–169) contend that atomistic social structure may give rise to its own distinctive mechanisms for maintaining social order, through "normatively prescribed behavior patterns" which "aim to minimize the chances of individual conflict and to limit individual aggression, either by selective cooperation or separation of interests..." (Munch and Marske 1981:161).

A comparison of the mining and whaling communities lends some support to this later view. The systems of public justice in these communities diverged sharply in their impact on resort to third-party mechanisms and separation, as opposed to escalating dyadic confrontation, in response to intracommunity conflict. And this difference was reflected, in turn, in the way responses to conflict worked to limit the potential for intracommunity violence among the miners and enhance it among the whalemen.

Public Justice, Conflict and Violence: The Miners

Although each community remained without local access to the legal institutions of Canada and the United States before the Mounted Police arrived on the scene, in each there emerged institutionalized sources of local authority serving to publicly define, identify, and sanction limits to permissible conduct. Like the communities themselves, the nature and functioning of these institutions of public justice was a study in contrasts.

In the Yukon mining camps, the principal institution for the administration of public justice was the "miner's meeting" (Stone 1979:84–95), simply an ad hoc assembly of all those in a particular locale who chose to attend when an assembly was called. Anyone in the locality in question was entitled to call a meeting to consider any grievance or question which he wanted to bring to it. The jurisdiction which the miners' meeting assumed was, accordingly, wide ranging: it provided a forum for the disposition of private disputes, it prosecuted crimes, it established mining regulations, and could establish by-laws relating to almost any conceivable matter of public concern which might emerge within the camp. After a particular issue was argued, the decision of the meeting was rendered by a simple majority of all those present. In cases where it was considered necessary, a committee might be elected from the assembled miners to act on behalf of the meeting in executing its decision.

Two of the hallmarks of the justice dispensed by the miners' meeting were an emphasis on a norm of generalized reliability in the miners' dealings with one another and a correlative concern with personal character. These features of the miners' system of local justice were in turn directly rooted in the transient, atomistic character of the population. The miners' ability to rely on one another for support in unplanned (and even anonymous) social encounters was essential to their well being, even to the point of their very survival. In the work involved in prospecting and mining, in traveling, in meeting needs for information, in emergencies, in all of these circumstances and more, there were situations which might arise where success or survival could depend on gaining the ad hoc support of some erstwhile stranger who was willing to put himself out on your behalf even if at some cost to himself. By the same token, the person who thought only of his own advantage in a situation and acted accordingly, even when dealing with strangers, posed a positive threat to the community.

There was good reason, then, given the conditions of life in the Yukon district for the miners' meeting to resort to what Colson (1974:54) has termed a "forward-looking" style of justice, concerned less with punishing a man for what he had done than with protecting the community against what he might do in the future. Not surprisingly, both a concern with personal character and a selection of sanctions designed primarily to secure the future order of life in the community stand out in the accounts of the adjudications of the miners' meetings (Walden 1928:52; Ogilvie 1913:50, 271; Constantine 1895:81; Bompas 1893; Brown 1895). Both in the decisions taken in these meetings and in independent actions in confronting situations of serious conflict, the miners' "forward-looking" style of justice favored the separation of conflicting parties as a means for reducing the potential for continuing (or escalating) confrontation. The nature of the existing, atomistic social order facilitated resort to this form of conflict management without posing any threat to the organizational requirements of the community, its constituent groups, or their activities. The patterns of mobility and group "flux" which were so prominent in the organization of the miners' society were characterized by a tendency for affiliations at any level to persist only so long as they were viewed as mutually supportive, the miners uniting and dividing in groups and joining and separating their interests in ad hoc fashion to suit their individual predilections (Stone, in press).

While the miners' meeting reflected public values which were rooted in the atomistic nature of the miners' community, it also provided an opportunity for resort to a forum which could function as an institutionalized third-party mechanism of conflict management. A necessary condition for the viability of any such forum is its ability to define problems and remedies in ways that are acceptable to participants and potential participants (Conn 1977:218–219). The flexibility of the miners' meeting, and its potential for responsiveness to the personal concerns and interests of its clientele, easily satisfied this criterion. The meetings' jurisdiction was not limited by an enumeration of specific kinds of offenses which came within its competence; an assembly could be called for any reason that any member of the local community thought justifiable. By the same token, the meeting was not an instrument of social control which could, on its own initiative and for reasons external to the perceived needs and wants of members of the local community, undertake to impose some external system or standards of justice. The system of justice it provided was one which was both potentially and in fact highly flexible in responding to differing and changing perceptions regarding needs for support and threats to security as circumstances warranted. The meeting was thus an institution which was totally responsive to the personal needs of its public.

The effect of all this was to reduce rather than exacerbate the potential for violence in those instances where serious conflict did arise. Appeal to a miners' meeting rather than a resort to personal retaliation, coupled with the sanction of banishment, worked to dampen the potential for further violence resulting from serious aggravation or an initial violent incident. In one well known incident of this sort, after Frank Leslie had attempted to poison and then shoot his partners on the Stewart River in the winter of 1886–1887, they brought him a number of miles downriver to the Stewart post to hand him over to the judgment of a miners' meeting, rather than retaliating themselves on the spot. Leslie was forthwith banished from the camp (Ogilvie 1913:42–50; Sonnikson manuscript in Snow 1896–1925; Buteau 1967:98–99). Another aggrieved miner also showed a noteworthy measure of restraint in a case of theft described by Arthur Walden. On one occasion during Walden's time at Circle City, a miner on his way into the post broke into another man's cache, took supplies sufficient for his immediate needs, and left the rest where they could be destroyed by animals. He then traveled to Circle and kept the theft a secret; he neither sought to replenish the cache himself nor report his use of it so someone else might do so. A short time later the owner returned to the cache, found it raided, and without supplies barely managed to reach town. The trail left by the thief from the cache to the point of his arrival in town was followed by the owner, and gave the thief away. The owner nonetheless waited several days to give the thief a chance to own up and when he didn't, called him before a miners' meeting. The thief acknowledged his guilt to the meeting and was banished (Walden 1928:53–55).

Such restraint was not always exercised by an antagonized party, but in cases where it wasn't, the response of the community could still forestall escalation. In an incident at the Fortymile post in the winter of 1893–1894, in the course of a drunken argument at his cabin a miner by the name of Wickham stabbed George Matlock in the back. Not being incapacitated by the wound, Matlock left to get a gun from his own cabin and returned to fire at Wickham's silhouette through the cabin window. Wickham was injured, but not fatally. In response to the incident, a miners' meeting was called and a decision was handed down to banish both men if any further trouble occurred between them; the men patched things up and became friends without further incident (Buteau 1967:113; Bompas 1893; Constantine 1895:81). A similar case is recorded from Circle in 1896 where a miners' meeting ruled that if either of two men who had been involved in a shooting match killed the other, or if one even died under suspicious circumstances, the survivor would be hung without trial (Walden 1928:52).

An incident with the clear potential for a homicidal outcome which took place in the Tanana region in 1888 shows the same pattern of response (Davis 1967: 59–60). During the summer prospecting season of that year, Henry Davis and his partner picked up a man named King (a stranger to them) as a third companion, after he asked to join them in a prospecting trip up the Tanana from the post at Nuklukayet. En route upriver, they encountered John Folger who alerted Davis to "watch out" for King as he was "no good." A short time later in the course of an argument over which side of the river it would be best to row up, King leveled his rifle at Davis. When the boat came close to shore Davis managed to grab the rifle and he and his partner put King ashore with a frying pan, some flour, and his blankets. They left his gun and axe on the next point downriver.

When Davis and his partner at length returned to Nuklukayet for the winter, they were told by others who had already come in that King was there and had threatened to kill Davis. Davis immediately found King and confronted him, gun in hand, telling him "one more squawk out of you and I'll shoot." King walked away and told the others he would leave and cause no more trouble. The miners had "told him if anybody talked any more about shooting in the camp, out he would go. That settled it." (Davis 1967:60).

One case in which homicide was not prevented is recorded for Circle City in 1896.[1] A miner reported to have been involved in earlier shooting incidents at Fortymile (Buteau 1967:113) and Circle (Walden 1928:52) threatened the bartender of a Circle saloon with a gun and the bartender shot him. The miner was killed, and the bartender himself immediately called a miners' meeting, and he was quickly tried and acquitted for shooting in self defense (Buteau 1967:113; Walden 1928:53). Otherwise, the record for homicide among the miners during this early period before the establishment of police control is sparse.[2] There is no way of knowing, of course, how many unrecorded cases may have occurred. But there were not likely to have been many; where cases of serious conflict do appear in the sources, they often appear in several places, suggesting that such incidents gained a measure of notoriety: they were talked about and considered noteworthy enough to record.

But the point to be emphasized is that when serious conflict did erupt, it typically brought a response which had the effect of forestalling or reducing the potential for further violence. Disorder in the form of violent conflict was far from being totally absent from the miners' community, but it was hardly a chronic state of affairs or serious social problem, and this fact was a reflection of the presence and effective operation of social mechanisms which could work to dampen it.

Public Justice, Conflict and Violence: The Whalemen

The whaling community at Herschel Island might at first glance appear to be better equipped to forestall violent internal conflict than were the miners to the south. The presence of shared organizational affiliation and positions of superordinate authority have been widely cited as structural facilitators of resort to third-party conflict management rather than coercive (and perhaps violent) forms (Roberts 1979:163, 165; Koch 1974:166–171). The whaling community provided both of these structural facilitators. The major segments of the community—the companies of the various wintering vessels—were internally united in a common group structure under a common authority. These segments of the community were in turn linked to one another by a cross-cutting division of the community based on class and authority, and the captains collectively constituted a level of authority capable of making decisions binding on the community as a whole, regardless of crew affiliation. In the miners' community, in contrast, neither positions of superordinate authority or shared organizational affiliation were elements of the social structure.

But among the whalemen, neither the resort to third-party conflict management nor the separation of parties in conflict in fact emerged as genuine alternatives to what amounted to dyadic confrontation when serious conflict arose. The structure of the whaling community served, rather, to generate both conflict and responses to conflict which worked to foster internal violence, in noteworthy contrast to the dampening effects of the organization and responses of the miners.

At Herschel Island, the virtually absolute authority of the masters over their crews provided the institutionalized basis for the administration of public justice. Throughout the winter season, just as at sea, each captain remained responsible for his own ship and crew. The unity of authority which existed for the wintering community as a whole was achieved by way of the voluntary (and only occasional) assembly of a captain's council, where the masters might take some collective decision or agree to join in some unified course of action in a matter which concerned them all. But even in such councils it was the captains, of course, who decided for the community, and carried through these decisions on the basis of cise of their authority over their own crews. In matters of public justice, it was up to the captains alone to decide whether wrongs had been committed, to determine matters of guilt or innocence, and to dictate the character of sanctions or other actions which might be called for.

The primary concerns of the captains were two: maximizing the chances for the economic success of the whaling voyage and maintaining the viability of the organization upon which, in their view, the success of their enterprise necessarily rested. These goals, the system of authority supporting them, and the social stratification of the whaling community worked together to virtually guarantee that the most significant conflicts in the community would arise where there was no genuine "third party" mechanism to deal with them.

The American whaling industry in the late 19th century united men of widely disparate classes in the formation of the typical whaling crew. If organizations can be said to provide the primary setting where different classes are likely to meet on a continuous basis (Stinchcomb 1965:181), then the late 19th century whaleship carried this feature of organizational life to its extreme. The social gap separating officers and crews was profound, due in no small measure to the difficulty of securing labor for the industry and resulting methods of recruitment. Crew members were often virtually shanghaied from among a population of waterfront drifters, and Blacks from the Cape Verde Islands as well as Pacific Islanders were commonly a component of a ship's company. In the particular case of the arctic fishery, the crews also included Eskimos.

The substantial complement of green, unwilling, or otherwise unruly hands led, in its turn, to a feeling on the part of many masters that only a measure of brutality could ensure the obedience and performance required from a crew (Hohman 1928:48–62; Williams 1964:271–272; Stackpole 1953:470–471). The harsh treatment which the exigencies of an economically successful voyage might be thought to demand could be meted out with little guilt; the crews were widely regarded by their officers as representing the very dregs of society. While many of the excesses in the exercise of their authority which led Morison (1961:324) to characterize the whaling masters as "cold-blooded, heartless fiends on the quarterdeck" had been tempered by the 1890s, the authority of the captains was likely to be mobilized only where they were themselves party to a conflict, and their own response was at some point likely to involve a resort to violence.

Public mechanisms for dealing with conflict were, therefore, not only more limited at Herschel than among the miners, coming into play in the former case for the most part only on those occasions where the interests of the captains were implicated in a conflict. They also contrasted with the miners' system with respect to the effects of their mobilization on the incidence of violent confrontation. Given the position and attitude of the whaling masters and the fact that their own interests were typically at stake where their authority was mobilized in the context of a dispute, a violent outcome was hardly surprising. Rather than serving as a mechanism for forestalling violence as it did among the miners, public justice at the island simply constituted one arena where conflicts (engendered by the position of officers vis-à-vis crews) were played out in an often violent fashion.

Both the types of offenses which were publicly prosecuted and the sanctions which were employed at the island reveal these contrasts with the miners' meeting. There is little indication, for example, that thefts between seamen, if such took place, came to the attention of captains, or at least, concerned them enough to warrant mention in the various sources available. Thefts from ships stores or from officers, however, were another matter; they received frequent mention and drew punishment ranging anywhere from a disrating through a period of hard labor to confinement in irons and beating. (Bodfish 1936:65, 156–157, 233–234, 253; Cook 1926:251; Leavitt 1902:15–20 November entries; *William Baylies* 1894:26 Nov., 28 Dec. entries; *Karluk* 1906:2 July entry). Serious injury or the threat of it in fights between crewmen led the captains to intervene and administer some sort of punishment in these affairs (Leavitt 1896:27 May entry; *William Baylies* 1895:12 April entry; *Karluk* 1905:7 April entry; Bodfish 1936:121 –122, 133, 221–222, 250), but assault on an officer was regarded as doubly serious because of the challenge to the established authority structure which it represented. Punishment in such cases appears to have been more than anything aimed at securing a public statement of contrition and submission (Bodfish 1936: 159–160; Cook 1926 279–282), but incidents of insubordination could lead to a rapidly escalating sequence of assaults.

A dramatic incident of this sort took place in 1896 when the second mate of the Beluga "had trouble" with a crewman and hit him. The crewman responded by seizing a handspike and attacking while others in the crew urged him to go ahead and kill the officer. The mate escaped, and reported the incident to the captain, Hartson Bodfish, who immediately went after the crewman in question, "laying him out without any delay," but the affray escalated when one of the crewman's supporters jumped in and stabbed Bodfish. Bodfish, undeterred by his wound, grabbed a squegee and continued the fight, decking his attackers and some others before the fight ended (Bodfish 1936:159–160). Bodfish had his attacker put in irons and "triced up" in the rigging for twenty minutes, by which time "he had experienced genuine contrition and promised to behave himself." Bodfish then let him go and claims to have had no more trouble with his crew on that voyage (Bodfish 1936:160).

More common than assaults upon officers were assaults between crewmen themselves. In 1894, Bodfish (1936:112) notes a "knifing affair" aboard the *Newport* and in 1895, Thomas Martin stabbed George Hughes of the *Alexander* in the course of an argument over laying out a baseball diamond (*William Baylies* 1895:12 August entry; Bodfish 1936:121–122). In 1896, the second mate of the *Jeanette* got drunk and shot a sailor through the leg (Leavitt 1896:27 May entry; Bodfish 1936:138) and Hartson Bodfish recorded how he "kicked the cook this morning for threatening the Steward with a cleaver, and also to keep my promise to do so if there was any more trouble in the galley" (Bodfish 1936:133). In 1902, a fight on board Bodfish's ship resulted in a dislocated shoulder which was "repaired with difficulty" (Bodfish 1936:201) and the following year he reports how four crewmen "hectored" a fifth to the point where he turned on them and knifed one of his antagonists, delivering "eight cuts on his body, one near the collar bone and another in the upper arm being very serious" along with another "along his lower ribs that was ten inches long" (Bodfish 1936:221). In April 1905, an argument between a seamen named Nugent and another member of the *Karluk* crew at a pond over loading ice resulted in Nugent stabbing the other man, wounding him severely. Nugent was put in irons, and while he was still in irons in June a petition from the crew was submitted requesting that he be kept that way because he had threatened several of their lives (*Karluk* 1905:7 April and 16 June entries).

Such instances of assault at the island might in part be blamed on the failure of the existing system of public justice to deal with conflicts in such a way as to forestall violent confrontations. But they could also be taken to reflect the absence of separation as a viable mechanism for conflict management. Among the miners the expedient of separation was available and readily used as a means to handle or avoid conflict (Stone, in press) and accordingly reduce the potential for resort to more violent forms of conflict management. At Herschel Island, however, not only was this alternative less readily available and resorted to, but when (perhaps in desperation) it was attempted, such an attempt was likely in its own right to lead to an escalation of conflict and the potential for violence. Separation—in the form of desertion—posed a threat to the structured organization of the community which often generated its own violence in response.

The frequency with which desertions were attempted at the island provides eloquent testimony to the seamen's dissatisfaction with their lot and their lack of institutionalized means to deal effectively with their grievances. The attitude which may have characterized many deserters is illustrated in a passage from Captain George Leavitt's journal, where he notes how a deserter from William Mogg's ship, whom one of Leavitt's men had encountered in "badly frozen" condition, had told him that "if he had Captain Mogg there he would shoot him then shoot himself" (Leavitt 1904:29 March entry).

It should not be forgotten, either, that desertions were taking place here under very difficult conditions. Herschel was no south sea island, and from the beginning, in the winter of 1890–1891, the precedent of considerable suffering with little hope of success was firmly established and continually reinforced for those who chose to desert. In many instances, certainly, a desertion in the face of the severe arctic environment could hardly be viewed as anything other than an act of desperation. From the standpoint of the seamen, there simply existed no public authority capable of handling conflicts which involved them with the ship's officers. In the absence of such authority and of the power to coerce a satisfactory remedy, they resorted to a time-honored form of conflict management: they attempted to terminate the social relationship which was the source of the problem by separation and withdrawal.

Although desertions are the most commonly mentioned offense which commanded the captains' attention, few men actually succeeded in their attempts to escape the ships. Pursuit parties (aided by natives reporting the whereabouts of deserters and assisting in their capture) either brought them in or, more commonly, the deserters themselves returned voluntarily after facing the privations of an arctic environment with which they were hardly prepared to cope. The ravages of frostbite often left deserters permanently maimed; while few appear to have frozen to death before returning or being captured, amputations were common (Leavitt 1893:23–28 October entries; *William Baylies* 1894:November 3, 5, December 27 entries; 1895:January 1, 9, 14 entries; *Karluk* 1905: 19 March entry; Bodfish 1936:104, 119, 133; Cook 1926:61–62, 86–87, 282–283). A primary concern of the captains, in any case, was the potential loss of hands and the jeopardy this posed to the success of a whaling season in a setting where lost crewmen could not easily be replaced. Captain William Hegarty, for example, after the loss of five men in an 1898 desertion incident, managed to save a season's whaling only by convincing a party of gold-seekers who were prospecting in the vicinity of the island to sign on as replacements for the lost hands (Mason 1910:87–88). The goal of the captains was to forestall successful desertions by any possible means in order to sustain the performance capabilities of their crews (Bodfish 1936:135; Stevenson 1968:28). And in any event, a desertion was inevitably an act of defiance with as much potential for precipitating violent conflict as for forestalling it, and its potential in this respect did not go unrealized.

The potential for violent confrontation which desertions posed was apparent in an incident in October 1893. Two men deserted from the Beluga and broke into a storehouse on shore for supplies, rifles, and ammunition. The pair was pursued by Captain James Tilton, who apprehended them but was forced to let them go because "he was covered by rifles" (Leavitt 1893:24 October entry). They later sent a cartridge to Tilton as a message of defiance, but ultimately returned voluntarily due to the cold (Leavitt 1893:23, 24, 28 October entries; Bodfish 1936:104).

It was in 1896, however, that the potential for gunplay evident in the *Beluga* incident was realized. In January of that year, a number of men from the fleet deserted together and robbed a storehouse. The captains responded by organizing a patrol of the fleet and storehouses and dispatching a pursuit party. The party reached the deserters, but was forced back by gunfire. A week later another pursuit party was more successful, bringing back four of the deserters, one with badly frozen feet (Bodfish 1936:133; Cook 1926:86–87).

In March, twelve more men deserted; a pursuit party was again dispatched and again "held up" by the deserters, who this time took two sleds and dog teams as well as supplies from their pursuers. A few days later a pursuit party of officers again reached the deserters, but were driven back twice in attempts to shoot it out with them and again they returned empty handed. Ten days after the initial desertion, natives reported being robbed by the deserting crewmen, and a third party was sent out, this one led by Captain James Leavitt of the *Hume* and including other officers and a native guide. A pitched battle again took place when the party reached the deserters' camp; this time the officers returned with six of the deserters, one of them shot to death in the gun battle and another badly wounded. The survivors were put in irons and chained to the decks for a month (Bodfish 1936:134, 136; Cook 1926:90–94; Stevenson 1968:28; Whittaker, n.d.).

These desertions in 1896 may have been the largest, but they were not the only ones to end in violence. In 1898 four men attempted to desert from the *Hume* in the face of warnings from the captain; in the ensuing pursuit, the ships engineer (one of the pursuit party) and two of the deserters were killed in a gun battle; two of the deserters escaped (Mason 1910:86–87).

The structured organization of the whaling community was thus not only a source of strain which contributed to the motives for desertion; by the nature of its highly structured character, the loss of men through desertion posed such a threat to the viability of the enterprise which brought the whaling captains to the island that these attempts could easily lead to further violent confrontations.

Conclusions

Among the Yukon miners described here, an informal system of popular frontier justice, rooted in a highly atomistic social order, proved compatible with an emphasis on both third-party adjudication and separation in response to conflict. The result was that the potential for continuing, escalating dyadic confrontation, leading to prolonged or escalating violence within the community, was curtailed. Social disorder in the form of high levels of intracommunity violent conflict was hardly a prominent feature of this particular frontier population of independent, fortune seeking, migrant adventurers.

In contrast to the miners, the whalemen arrived at Herschel Island as members of an established, continuing, and highly structured corporate organization, which constrained their individual independence of action in the frontier setting. The corporate structure which served to unite the whalemen in their collective economic enterprise, however, proved to be the source of serious conflicts, and at the same time, rendered the community incapable of providing effective mechanisms of separation or genuine third-party resolution when conflicts emerged. Continuing and potentially escalating dyadic confrontation, often with a violent outcome, was the result.

The lesson here is that on the frontier (as elsewhere) there is not necessarily any simple correlation between popular as opposed to authoritarian forms of local justice and the potential for community disorder, even when the former is linked to the atomization of a community and the latter is linked to the presence of strong corporate structures which bind their members in collective enterprise. What matters is the way in which local systems of public justice and the community context in which they are embedded work to influence the availability and use of particular, non-violent forms of conflict management. If the links between community organization, forms of public justice, and intracommunity violence are to be better understood, then the communities which emerged on the North American frontier merit continuing attention. There is the opportunity as well as the need here for more comparative study of the impact of particular institutions of public justice on conflict and conflict management in the particular frontier settings where these institutions appeared.

NOTES

1. Although the North West Mounted Police had arrived in the Yukon district by this date, Circle City remained outside their jurisdiction, across the international boundary in Alaska.

2. With one exception, additional homicides recorded for the Yukon region during this period involved conflicts between whites and Indians (Davis 1967:55–58; Bettles 1967:121–122; Anonymous 1967:119–124). The exception is the murder of a priest by a member of his own traveling party; the murderer in this case traveled to St. Michael and was subsequently sent to Sitka for trial (Buteau 1967:100–101; Heller 1967:84).

BIBLIOGRAPHY

Anonymous. 1967. A Sequel to Mrs. Bean's Murder. Sourdough Sagas, ed. H. Heller, pp. 123–124. Cleveland.

Bettles, G. C. 1967. Some Early Yukon River History. Sourdough Sagas, ed. H. Heller, pp. 119–122. Cleveland.

Black, D. 1983. Crime as Social Control. American Sociological Review 48:34–45.

Bockstoce, J. R. 1977. Steam Whaling in the Western Arctic. New Bedford.

Bodfish, H. H. 1936. Chasing the Bowhead. Cambridge, Mass.

Bompas, W. 1893. Bompas to Minister of Interior, 9 December 1893. Constantine Papers, MG 30/E55, Vol. 3, File 4, Public Archives of Canada. Ottawa.

Brown, C. 1895. Report to Constantine from S/Sgt. Brown, 9 February 1895. Records of the Royal Canadian Mounted Police, RG 18, Vol. 1344, File 190–1895. Public Archives of Canada. Ottawa.

Brown, R. M. 1976. The History Vigilantism in America. Vigilante Politics, eds. H. Rosenbaum, and P. Sederberg, pp. 79–109. Philadelphia.

Buteau, F. 1967. My Experience in the World. Sourdough Sagas, ed. H. Heller, pp. 93–118. Cleveland.

Colson, E. 1974. Tradition and Contract: The Problem of Order. Chicago.

Conn, S. 1977. The Extralegal Forum and Legal Power: The Dynamics of the Relationship—Other Pipelines. The Anthropology of Power, eds. R. D. Fogelson and R. N. Adams, pp. 217–224. New York.

Constantine, C. 1895. Report of Inspector Constantine, 10 October 1894. Report of the Commissioner of the Northwest Mounted Police Force, 1894, pp. 70–85. Ottawa.

Cook, J. A. 1926. Pursuing the Whale. Boston.

Davis, H. 1967. Recollections. Sourdough Sagas ed. H. Heller, pp. 28–84. Cleveland.

Goodrich, H. B. 1897. History and Condition of the Yukon Gold District to 1897. Geology of the Yukon Gold District, Alaska, ed. J. E. Spurr, pp. 103–133. Washington.

Gough, B. 1975. Keeping British Columbia British: The Law-and-Order Question on a Gold Mining Frontier. Huntington Library Quarterly 38:269–280.

Heller, H., ed. 1967. Sourdough Sagas. Cleveland.

Hohman, E. P. 1928. The American Whaleman. New York.

Howard, D. M. 1907. Report of Inspector D. M. Howard, Herschel Island. Report of the Northwest Mounted Police, 1906, pp. 128–132. Ottawa.

Karluk. 1905. Log (ms.). Providence Public Library. Providence, R.I.
———. 1906. Log (ms.). Providence Public Library. Providence, R.I.
Koch, K. F. 1974. War and Peace in Jalemo. Cambridge, Mass.
Leavitt, G. B. 1893. Journal (ms.). Baker Library, Harvard University, Cambridge, Mass.
———. 1896. Journal (ms.). Baker Library, Harvard University, Cambridge, Mass.
———. 1902. Journal (ms.). Baker Library, Harvard University, Cambridge, Mass.
———. 1904. Journal (ms.). Baker Library, Harvard University, Cambridge, Mass.
Maslow, A. H., and J. J. Honigmann. 1970. Synergy: Some Notes of Ruth Benedict. American Anthropologist 72:320–333.
Mason, W. S. 1910. The Frozen Northland. Cincinnati.
McQuesten, L. N. 1952. Recollections. Dawson City, Yukon.
Morison, S. E. 1961. The Maritime History of Massachusetts, 1783–1860. Boston.
Munch, P. A., and C. E. Marske. 1981. Atomism and Social Integration. Journal of Anthropological Research 37:158–171.
Nader, L., and H. L. Todd, Jr. 1978. The Disputing Process: Law in Ten Societies. New York.
Ogilvie, W. 1913. Early Days on the Yukon. New York and London.
Reid, J. 1977. Paying for the Elephant: Property Rights and Civil Order on the Overland Trail. Huntington Library Quarterly XLI:37–64.
Roberts, S. 1979. Order and Dispute. New York.
Sharp, P. 1955. Whoop-up Country: The Canadian-American West, 1865–1885. Norman.
Snow, G., comp. and ed. 1896–1925. Snow Papers of the Yukon. Dartmouth College Library (microfilm). Hanover, NH.
Stackpole, E. A. 1953. The Sea Hunters. Philadelphia.
Stevenson, A. 1968. Whaler's Wait. North 15:24–31.
Stinchcomb, A. L. 1965. Social Structure and Organizations. Handbook of Organizations, ed. J. G. March, pp. 142–193. Chicago.
Stone, T. 1979. The Mounties as Vigilantes: Perceptions of Community and the Transformation of Law in the Yukon, 1885–1897. Law and Society Review 14:83–114.
———. 1981. Whalers and Missionaries at Herschel Island. Ethnohistory 28:101–124.
———. (In press). Flux and Authority in a Subarctic Society: The Yukon Miners in the 19th Century. Ethnohistory (forthcoming).
Trimble, W. 1972 (orig. 1914). The Mining Advance into the Inland Empire. New York.
Walden, A. T. 1928. A Dog Puncher on the Yukon. Boston.
Whittaker, C. n.d. Memoranda of the Mission to the MacKenzie River Eskimos (ms.). Archives of the Anglican Church of Canada. Toronto.
William Baylies. 1894. Journal (ms.). Providence Public Library. Providence, R.I.
———. 1895. Journal (ms.). Providence Public Library. Providence, R.I.
Williams, H. 1964. One Whaling Family. Boston.
Wright, A. A. 1976. Prelude to Bonanza. Sidney.

Persistence and Change Patterns in Amish Society

John A. Hostetler

THE STUDENT of human society finds explicitly developed moral postulates in human institutions which Malinowski (1944: 52) calls the "charter." The charter is "the system of values for the pursuit of which human beings organize." It is "an organized system of purposeful activities." In Amish society behavior is oriented to absolute values, involving a conscious belief in religious and ethical ends entirely for their own sake and independent of any external rewards. This orientation to *Wert-rational*, or absolute values, as Max Weber (1947: 305–306) states it, requires of the individual unconditional demands. Regardless of personal considerations the members are required to put into practice what is required by duty, honor, personal loyalty, and sacrifice. Behavior is tradition-directed by unwritten norms. In Amish society there is an almost automatic reaction to habitual stimuli which guides behavior in a course which has been hallowed by the habit of long experience.

The consistency of "charter" in Amish society has been noted by a number of social scientists. Gillin (1948: 209–220), for example, has termed the Amish culture "remarkably compatible with the various components of its situation." Kollmorgen (1942: 105) observed that the integrative aspects of the culture "must have qualities that make for survival." Huntington (1956: introduction) states that in Amish society "Each community is integrated, but not self contained." Freed (1957: 55) has noted the absence of class differences in Amish society as a factor in the acceleration of change.

The generalization that the Amish are a stable people, consistent in their moral values, has led to several misconceptions and over-statements about Amish social organization. One recent source (Schreiber 1962: 58), for example, states that "juvenile delinquency is unknown among the Amish." Consistency of major points in the charter does not mean that Amish life is relatively free from stress, sustained personal conflicts, or rebellious behavior.

It will be the purpose of this paper to develop five elements in the Amish charter which demonstrate a high degree of consistency. They are formulated from careful observation in a number of contemporary communities, from the original documents (Gascho 1937), and from personal experience as a participating member of the culture. Second, evidence for sustained personal conflicts in this seemingly "remarkably compatible" culture will be presented. The evidence is based upon depth interviews with Amish and former Amish persons and reveals stress patterns of the following character: thwarted motivations for higher education, the practice of marginal occupations, the presence of suicidal behavior, and rowdyism. Third, it will be shown how persons with unresolved personal conflicts make meaningful contacts with outgroups by means of acculturation agents.

The Charter

Separation from the World. The doctrine of separation is an expression of the Amish view of reality, which is one of "nonconformity to the world." The conception of reality is conditioned by a dualistic view of human nature. Although the natural, "created" world is amoral, the world of man is categorically divided into the pure and impure, light and darkness, and the powers of good and of evil. Separation from the world is based upon this dualistic conception of reality, and it is expressed in life situations, in ecology, and social organization. Separation is furthermore based upon explicit scriptural passages which validate the practice: "Be not conformed to this world . . ." and "Be ye not unequally yoked together with unbelievers." The ark of safety for the member is within the community, and not outside of its beliefs and customs. This doctrine forbids marriage with outsiders, it prohibits members from establishing business partnerships or sustained associations with outsiders, and it keeps intimate human associations within the ceremonial community.

Biblical Tradition. The whole of the Old and New Testaments, in the German language, and to some extent the Apocrypha as well, constitute the sacred writings for the Amish. The codifications and moral principles have their basis in the teachings of Christ and his proclamation of a kingdom. The Amish have perpetuated the teachings of the sixteenth century Anabaptists from whom they are direct descendants, having been an offshoot of the Swiss Brethren in the late eighteenth century. Some of their teachings and practices are taken literally from scriptural texts, e.g., the refusal to retaliate or bear arms, to swear oaths, or to hold public office, the observance of adult baptism, the foot-washing ceremony, and mutual concern for the aged and poor. They refuse to accept or to pay social security on the grounds that it is insurance; they pay taxes without qualms of conscience, but compulsory insurance is another matter. The vow of baptism involves not only confession of faith in the Trinity but the promise to remain in the narrow path of "obedience" to the rules of the believing community.

The Ordnung *or Rules of Order.* The rules of order of the church are clearly understood by all baptized members, and the individual is committed not only to obedience but to active maintenance of the rules. Marriage, always occurring after baptism and not before, admits the individual to even greater responsibility for promoting and "building the church." The body of rules and traditions which govern behavior are rarely specified in writing; they are essentially a body of sentiments and taboos intimately shared among the members. The rules are taken for granted, and it is usually only the questionable or borderline issues which are specified in the "examination" service preceding the semi-annual communion service. A change in the rules, either toward relaxation or formalization, requires a members' meeting where each person is asked to give assent to the unanimous recommendations of the ordained functionaries. The bishop is, of course, the spokesman. The rules are not strictly the same in all communities. Those which are most nearly universal in the twenty states where the Old Order Amish live are the following: no electricity, telephones, automobiles, central heating systems, or tractors with pneumatic tires; beards but no moustaches for all married men; long hair (which must be parted in the center if parted at all); hooks-and-eyes on dress coats; and the use of horses for farming and for travel within the community. No formal education beyond grade eight is also a rule of life.

Meidung *or Shunning.* Shunning is a technique of keeping the fellowship "clean" or purged from habitual transgressors. Although a means to an end, it is so important in the total life of the society that it becomes prominent in the charter. Shunning is applied after the offender has been formally excommunicated from the fellowship by vote of the assembly. In such a state the transgressor cannot enjoy normal relations with other members of the church. He may not eat at the same table in the home. Married couples may not sleep in the same bed, and church members may not receive gifts or favors from one who is under "the ban." The offender can be restored if he so desires after a period of shunning by confessing violation of the taboos and by expressing repentance. A member can be excommunicated not only for lying or for adultery but also for buying an automobile, for possessing a driver's license, or for cutting the hair too short. Persons who voluntarily leave the church to join more relaxed groups, such as factions who drive automobiles or Mennonite groups, are excommunicated and shunned for life. They are regarded as "vow-breakers" and apostates. Members are in duty bound to regard them in this way, and any member who sides with the offender is also excommunicated. Shunning is regarded by the "strict" Amish as absolutely essential as a disciplinary measure. That it should continue to be rigidly practiced was one of the main issues on which the Amish separated from the Swiss Brethren.

Agrarianism. The Amish world view is conditioned by first-hand experience with nature. The ordered seasons, celestial objects such as the moon and stars, and the world of growing plants and animals provide the Amish with a sense of order and destiny. Hard work with the soil, where muscles and limbs ache from daily toil, provides human satisfaction. All family heads are required to limit their occupation to farming or to closely related activities such as operating a sawmill, carpentering, or masonry. Hard work, thrift, and social concern for the believing community find sanction in the Bible. The city by contrast is held to be the center of worldly progress, of laziness, of nonproductive spending, and often of wickedness. Man occupies his right place in the universe when he is caring for the things in "the garden," that is, the plants and animals created by God. The Amish agrarian experience for several centuries has been conducive to isolation characteristic of the ideal-typical folk society (Redfield 1947: 293–308), which greatly strengthens their religious outlook on life.

The above five elements of the Amish charter demonstrate a high degree of consistency and integration. Contradictions of belief appear to be at a minimum. Agrarianism, for example, is compatible with the doctrine of separation from the world. Conformity to absolute values is expressed by adherence to the Biblical formulations as interpreted by the functionaries. Powerful social controls are exercised through institutionalized rules (*Ordnung*) and shunning (*Meidung*) of offenders.

Higher Education: The Forbidden Fruit

Despite the internal consistency of the charter, an increasing number of Amish persons find meaningful and satisfying experiences outside of the Amish society. As the American rural community becomes more urban the Amish, with their small familistic type of society, are less and less able to satisfy the psychological and social needs of their individual members. When individuals find personal fulfillment outside of the Amish community the relationship to the traditional community is altered. As marginal persons they frequently experience great personal stress; the individual is no longer sure of himself or of the values which he has traditionally held. Problem areas then arise within the society which threaten elements within the charter. Families who live on the fringe of the larger settlements of Amish appear to be exposed to greater stress than those living in "solid" communities.

One of the areas of internal conflict is the desire of young people to obtain education beyond the elementary grades. Attendance at high school is prohibited by the Old Order Amish, and such ambitions are blocked. The increased emphasis on education in American society as a prerequisite for adult living makes learning very attractive to the Amish boy or girl. The following life-history documents reflect the rewarding experiences of outside learning and show how such satisfying behaviors are legitimized to other members of the Amish society.

Our first case is that of an ex-Amish person whom we shall call Sam. Sam recalls his early interest in schooling, leading to his decision to enter college:

> I always loved school from the day I started. My parents didn't start me until I was seven so I wouldn't have to go to high school. They thought I couldn't learn very well, and I wanted to show them I could. When my mother was young she taught school. She wanted to go on to school but never had a chance. I sort of caught this desire from my mother. It made me mad when my father kept me home for a day's work. Sometimes, when I was to stay at home, I would switch into my school clothes at the last minute and get on the bus.

Sam was adept in making friends at school and during his last grades in school, he said, "I hated that I came from such a backward family." His animosity over his backwardness grew as he learned to know his classmates and especially a certain non-Amish girl.

> We were always the top two in the class. I could beat her in arithmetic, but she always beat me in reading. It was always tit for tat between us. We were always together in those early years. I always hated that I was an Amishman. My older brother was a "good boy" and listened to daddy but was always getting into trouble. Sunday after Sunday I would go to church, and all we would do after church was sit out in the buggies and tell filthy stories. I was the cockiest guy, I guess, as I was more or less the leader of our group of boys. My, how I used to get whippings from my father. I hear other people brag how they thank the Lord for their whippings, but mine just did not make sense.

With the completion of grade school Sam wanted to go to high school but could not. "I felt there was nothing to do but stay home and work for Dad till I was twenty-one. My life was terribly lean during those years." Sam was baptized in the Amish church. After he reached legal age he was exposed to a wider association of friends, most of them Mennonites. Following his release from service he entered a Mennonite college. Although for some years he attempted to retain his Amish affiliation, eventually he became a member of the Mennonite Church.

Another case is that of Rebecca, who turned from her Amish background at the age of eighteen without having been baptized.

> I read a great many books and anything I could get my hands on. I tried to persuade my father to let me go to high school. But he would not. After grade school I was Amish for another six years, and this was a very difficult time in my life. My dissatisfaction began to show in physical ways. I had no energy. I was anaemic. Nothing interested me. I didn't fit in with the Amish young people, and I sort of despised them for their lack of learning. I made attempts to be popular among the Amish and dated a few times, but I didn't like it very much. I was pretty lonely, and it was a very miserable time for me. I was the oldest of eight, and mother kept on having children. This tied me down, and I was constantly resenting this. I was always running away to read, and I hid books. When mother was not watching I would read everything I could.
>
> When I was eighteen, I thought mother had reached the age when she could have no more children. Finally, I thought I could begin to see daylight, have a little more time to myself, and keep the house neat without working so hard. Then I learned that mother was pregnant again, and this was the last straw. I simply could not face this. I went to the basement and just cried. I told father that I had had enough, I was leaving. While I was packing my suitcase, mother became upset. Father knew that mother needed my help. So we worked out a compromise. Father said if I would stay until the baby was born, the next year I could go to Bible school. This was enough for me; then I could get away and go where there was a library and read.

A third case is that of a lad whom I shall designate as Chris.

> I wanted to go to high school so badly that I remember crying about it, trying to persuade my parents. They gave us county-wide achievement tests after grade eight, and I found out I was the highest in the county. I competed from grade one through grade eight very closely with a girl who went on and became valedictorian. In the accumulative tests which included all eight grades I had all A plusses except two. My principal talked to my father several times and told him, I had possibilities. I was only fourteen, so my father made me repeat the eighth grade the next year. After getting all A plusses in grade eight I barely got As the second

> time. I was very athletic, though, and even though I was not going on to high school the principal let me go all out for athletics. All the time the kids and neighbors (non-Amish) wanted me to go on to high school. In my second year in the eighth grade I quit when April came because it was time to start plowing. I went home, and I remember how terrible I felt.

With all his chums now in high school, the lad returned to the principal and explained his painful experience. The principal gave him ninth grade books, and Chris promised that he would study them and appear for the semester tests.

> I hardly touched the books, but I took the first semester test and got all As and Bs. But I finally gave up and returned the books. But I knew I would never stay Amish because the principal convinced me the Amish should not keep their children home from school. He told me I had brains. He told me I could be more than a farmer.

Such experiences frequently result in a reconsideration of the basic provision of the Amish charter which unilaterally forbids any formal training beyond the elementary grades. The Amish leaders know that they must consider the problem of finding teachers for their own private schools in areas where school consolidation has been put into effect. So long as the one-room public school served the Amish, they did not need to face the problem of securing teachers. Presently there are about 150 privately operated schools whose teachers are Amish, most of them offering no more than an elementary education. The realization that education is needed to prepare teachers for their own schools has helped to legitimize the teacher role. A few members have entered college for preparation without bringing upon themselves the sanctions of *Meidung*. The role of these persons as agents of change within the Amish society may have the effect of modifying the charter in the future.

Marginal Occupations

The Amish charter requires that persons aspire to be laborers on farms and eventually farm owners. Investigation of current occupations reveals exceptions to this rule. Old Order Amish girls who have taken training as nurses have not remained Amish. There are no Amish physicians, and this role appears not to be a likely one. One unusual occupation is that of an Amish girl who is employed as a registered technician. She completed high school by correspondence, and by borrowing books from a local high school she qualified for a high school certificate. She had always anticipated the vocation of nursing. Upon counseling with a Director of Nursing, she learned that a professional uniform would be required for a trained nurse and that no exception could be made. She knew that she could not remain loyal to the Amish church if she followed this vocation, so she began training for work as a technician. She commuted to a college and completed the required courses. As a registered technician she is not required to wear white shoes or white stockings, and she may wear a white coat over her Amish uniform while on duty. The hospital officials have been very cooperative in helping the girl find security in her new vocation. Safeguards were taken not to give publicity which would jeopardize her relationship to the Amish church. When photographs of her graduating class appeared in the papers, for example, hers was omitted. Her Amish friends believe that, if she keeps the *Ordnung* otherwise, she may be able to continue her profession.

Sickness, incapacity, or chronic illness of a family head may lead to marginal occupations of a nontraditional type. Daniel, a man in his fifties, always loved farming. According to a neighbor, "He has been in many things." As a result of an accident in his youth, "he had surgery done on his head and has suffered many headaches since. He has taken many pills from different doctors, which now affects his heart." Besides being a sales agent for seeds, which allows him to travel in many Amish settlements, he also has been engaged in dynamite blasting as custom work. In this business he served as a supplier of dynamite for hardware stores in his region of the state. He ordered the dynamite by carload lots and stored it in a stone quarry on his farm. This occupation was perhaps more compatible with farming than many.

The question may be raised why Amish persons who are really marginal remain within the Amish community. One young Amishman, after many years of trying to remain loyal to the Amish faith, gave up, saying, "I would rather be a conservative Mennonite than a liberal Amishman." But many who are allowed to exercise a small degree of marginality prefer to remain with their kin and community. A marginal occupation may be tolerated by the community so long as it does not constitute a direct threat. However, when a person takes his marginal occupation seriously and wishes to excel, as in nursing, teaching, or business, the stresses created tend to exceed the limits of toleration.

Marginal persons who persist in their deviation, as in the cases above, frequently become effective agents of change. They create favorable attitudes toward behaviors usually forbidden. An Amish father who invokes no sanction against his son for buying an automobile becomes an innovator. Family heads who merely refrain from taking negative sanctions against violators are in a favorable position for introducing change, especially if they are from families of high status. Agents of change may accept the goals of their society but use other than institutional means for achieving the goals.

Suicide

The frequency of suicides, even in the face of strong Biblical injunctions against taking life, suggests the presence of unresolved personal conflicts. While most common among single unmarried Amish males, suicide also occurs among adults who occupy key positions (Hostetler 1963: 283). Two well-informed persons in one community could recall fifteen suicides, fourteen of whom were males and most of them under the age of 22. This period in life appears to be the most crucial for acceptance or rejection of the basic values of the culture. Persons "without values" (Durkheim 1951) to direct a course of action revert to apathy and despair. Anomic suicides reflect one aspect of personal disorganization. Religious functionaries who are charged with maintaining the *Ordnung* are subjected to extraordinary role stress. The threat of strong negative sanctions for suggesting alternative courses of action contributes to anxiety and conflict in persons charged with maintaining the norms.

One of the most dramatic instances of suicide was that of a very prominent leader who hanged himself to the surprise of the entire Amish community. The reason for his sudden "disgraceful act" remained a mystery to his kin and his close friends. Upon close examination of the case it is clear that the ordained man was caught between contradictory expectations.

The rate of suicide among the Amish may be higher than that of the rural United States population in general—possibly even as high as that for rural Michigan (Schroeder and Beegle 1953), which exceeds that of the urban population. This impression derives from a survey based on the memory of informants in one large community, but we shall not know conclusively until a complete investigation has been made. The Amish would need to have but four suicides per year to approximate the rate for the United States at large (10.3 per 100,000).

Rowdyism

"Running wild" is tolerated in the normal life of the young unmarried adult male. The number of young persons who defect permanently varies considerably with each community. After marriage the individual generally conforms to the rules of the community and accepts seriously the norms of its culture. Before marriage, however, there is a great deal of rowdyism and other forms of antisocial behavior in reaction against the traditional norms. This has become especially manifest in the largest Amish settlements, where it is associated with the relaxation of traditional controls.

The geographic boundaries of the community have expanded beyond the limits encompassed by a horse and buggy. This poses no problem for the adult ceremonial community, which has explicit recognized boundaries. But for the young people of courting age there are no geographic boundaries. One result has been the development and differentiation of informal special-interest groups, especially in connection with the institution of Sunday evening "singings." Sharp differentiations are expressed in the names and modal behavior of the various "singings." According to one young man:

> The Groffies are the most liberal, then the Ammies, and then the Trailers. Each has a number of subgroupings and interests, and under the Groffies, for instance, there are the Hillbillies, Jamborees, and Goodie-goodies. The Hillbillies occupy the hill country, the Jamborees are the most unruly, and the Goodie-goodies are so called because they are the Christians.

These groups maintain social distance and display various forms of antagonism. "There are times when one gang has cut the harness of another to pieces, or they have unhooked the horses of the others and let them run off." Differentiation is also expressed in patterns of smoking, entertainment, dating, and the use of automobiles.

Indulgence in antisocial acts, within the religious community as well as outside of it, occurs with greater frequency as individuals experience problems of stress. Stealing chickens or grain and selling these products, or trading them for a dance floor for a night, is not unknown. One juvenile said: "We used to see who could do the best job of swearing and being the biggest blow gut. If there was anything daring to be done, I had to show the boys I had the nerve to do it." Problems associated with drinking alcoholic beverages have come to the attention of the wider community. There have been a number of arrests of Amish for violation of the liquor laws. After complaints from neighbors, the police conducted several raids on Sunday night singings. On one occasion, officers reported more than a dozen cases of empty beer bottles, and several youths were arrested for drunkenness. Although parents are concerned about the mischief of the boys, they appear helpless. After one arrest at a singing, an Amish father said: "What can I do, I know it's wrong for minors to drink beer, but the boys would get down on me if I didn't allow it."

Outsiders are not welcome at Amish singings and are chased off the grounds if not invited. One outsider, who was a farm hand but had worked for an Amish family, decided to attend a nearby singing. He was surrounded by a score or more of Amish boys and was accused of wanting their women and of spying. He did not escape without a beating. Just as the staunch Amish are wary of the outsider who wants to write a book about them, so the young too are suspicious of the stranger as a possible intruder.

Acculturation Agents

After a period of permissive "wildness" the typical Amish young man returns to a state of conformity, for baptism and marriage, and to serious observance of the moral postulates of the society. Those who cannot or will not be induced to accept the basic elements in the charter usually make successful linkages with outsiders who bridge the gap between the Amish and the surrounding alien culture.

Acculturation agents are those non-Amish persons outside the Amish society but adjacent to it who are in unique positions to assist the marginal Amish person, e.g., members of nearby churches, physicians, businessmen, officers of the law, and neighboring farmers. They are the middlemen who mediate between the small and the great society.

To obtain a valid driver's license (forbidden by the *Ordnung*) an Amish youth must have some kind of assistance before he applies for a permit at the police headquarters. Usually he will have learned how to drive an automobile from a friend or relative in the Amish Mennonite religious group, or in some cases from an employer if, for instance, he has been employed by a non-Amish construction firm. Amish youth who wish to qualify for college entrance frequently fulfill their high school requirements by taking special examinations administered by the state. Assistance in applying for the proper forms and in acquiring the knowledge and tutorial instruction necessary to pass the examinations is often obtained from a school principal or a non-Amish friend.

Owing to their ignorance of the ways of the outside world, the Amish are sometimes exploited by outsiders, e.g., by charging an exorbitant price for an automobile. Automobile salesmen, salesmen of musical instruments, insurance salesmen, and issuers of driver's licenses do business secretly with young Amish people so that their parents and the public do not discover such activities and the special procedures involved. When Amish youths are arrested or convicted, their names are often withheld from the newspapers if they request it. Frequently a postman or mail carrier will hold certain mail until he sees the recipient personally, so that parents will not be aware that a family member has received a forbidden item such as an insurance policy or a driver's license.

Young Amish men who have been stopped for speeding, or for legal charges having to do with the condition of an automobile, e.g., a faulty muffler, are known to have been released because a police officer "favored" or was in sympathy with them. Many have passed driver's examinations with a little bribery. Some examining officers have the reputation among Amish youth for passing them easily on driver examinations. Even persons under the legal age have been issued licenses, as well as trustworthy youths who have not had adequate driver training. In return for pies, rolls of bologna, and home-cured hams these "agents" provide licenses under conditions which Amish youths can meet.

There are gasoline service stations which permit Amish boys to park their automobiles with them. One used-car salesman allows boys to keep their autos on his lot when they are not driving them on the understanding that they will buy the automobiles from and service them with his firm. A number of service stations receive much Amish patronage on weekends.

Increasing numbers of Amish youths, minors included, patronize bars and liquor stores because they are trusted and favored by many outsiders and rarely cause trouble. In general, the Amish young people enjoy an excellent reputation among outsiders because they are usually honest and industrious. There appear, however, to be a few outsiders who cooperate with the elders and parents to keep the young people "in line."

For those who leave the group, making the initial break with the culture takes place in a number of ways and is usually an adjustment to stress. Some run away from home without making a successful contact with outside reference groups. A boy aged sixteen suddenly disappeared one Saturday afternoon. The first sign of his leaving was the discovery of his Amish hat a mile away from home. The father was alarmed but could do nothing but wait hopefully. The next day a neighbor received a phone call from a large city stating the exact place where the runaway boy could be picked up. The boy had discarded his Amish clothing, had his hair cut in a barber shop, and traveled to the city, then became despondent and gave up. Unknown to any of the family members the boy had entertained the notion of running away for many months as a result of an unhappy encounter with his father.

Four Pennsylvania boys, two of whom were members, made their departure after midnight by walking and thumbing their way to Ohio. The first sign of their leaving was the discovery of their long shorn hair in an upstairs bedroom. Within two weeks all were back in their native community, though not all returned to their homes. Two of them joined the army, and the other two soon married girls outside the Amish faith. A former Amish father, when asked why boys sometimes run away, said:

Who wouldn't? All the teaching they get is *Attnung* [*Ordnung*] and the command from their parents *"Du bliebst Deitsch"* [You must stay Dutch]. Parents are too rigid in their demands and punishment. My brother ran away from home last year, and I can tell you why. Dad was awful rough with him. He gave us boys one licking after another. Even when I was eighteen he tried to lick me, but that's when I said, "It's enough." I didn't let him.

Slipping outside the Amish community with intent to return appears to be more common now than in former years. As outside pressures exert themselves on small neighborhoods, and as young members have more and more knowledge about outside affairs, "having a fling" with the world and returning has become institutionalized. Thirty or forty years ago it was not uncommon for two or more Amish persons to go west and work their way with the harvest from Texas to North Dakota. They usually returned and after marriage settled down as members in the Amish community.

Two brothers purchased an automobile "to see the world." One of them said:

> We traveled all over the United States and visited practically all the states. We just cut a huge figure eight all over the United States. We were interested in traveling, and we told our parents, and then bought a car. We each had a half share and after returning I sold my share.

The boys left in the spring and returned in the fall.

Another type of exodus is typified by a boy who left as usual on Monday morning for work on a nearby non-Amish farm.

> I did not want to leave this way, but I decided I would write my parents a letter after I was away so they wouldn't need to worry about me. I stayed away several weeks. Then, because I was not of legal age, I got a warning from the courthouse. I told my boss I did not think the warning meant anything because I was sure my father would not go to law. Then in a few days I got a phone call from my dad, and he asked if I am coming home. I told him I would come home to visit but I didn't feel too welcome. I said I could not stay home. So he said he would have to go to the courthouse. Then I knew he was not kidding. My boss went to the courthouse to find out what would happen. He found out they could only take me home, but they could make it bad for him as my employer. So I left his place and on the advice of a friend went to Florida. While down there I also got a warning from the courthouse, so I went to see them about it. They said Florida authorities could do nothing, but the Pennsylvania authorities could come and get me, but it would cost them a lot of money and they probably would not. After they heard my story, they told me not to worry.

Another young man gave the following account:

> I did not run away at night. After my father accused me of something I had not done, I just put on my old straw hat and walked down the road. I wanted to join the army but was too young. I worked for an English farmer not far away who hated the Amish. My father saw me in town one day and asked me why I don't come home. I said, "I'm not coming home now nor will I ever come home."

The young man then joined a traveling medicine show which visited his home town.

> They needed a boy to help. Of course I was interested. I had read a lot about circuses, so I joined the show. We traveled all over the state. I ran the popcorn machine, took the tent down, and cleaned up the papers and mess afterwards. The show did not get into any of the Amish communities. I would sell tickets at the door, and if the ropes needed tightening I did that. On my birthday the recruiting officer got in touch with me. I left and joined the service.

Conclusion

The Amish charter embodies elements which tend to be consistent with each other. But consistency does not assure conformity. Amish life is not free from personal stress and sustained conflict. The experiences related in the above case materials reveal problems of thwarted motivation and problems of socialization common to marginal persons. The role of "agents of change" within Amish society and of "acculturation agents" outside the society gives rise in multiple ways to meaningful personal contacts in the larger American society. Alterations of behavior patterns occur, forcing a reevaluation of the charter. Unless the charter is reinterpreted, inconsistencies develop between doctrine and practice, and these may lead to anomie, fragmentation, and demoralization. The central doctrines remain essentially the same, but the applications change. Separation from the world, for example, remains a central doctrine, but slight modifications in dress, in mechanization, and in other living habits occur in the process of solving the existential problem and of coping successfully with the environment.

The Amish response to change, especially when it threatens the charter, characteristically takes the form of fragmentation and division over what appear to the outsider as hair-splitting issues. Divisions are rarely peaceful or the result of deliberations. Instead, the relations between different ceremonial groups are commonly characterized by *Meidung* and animosity. Some settlements have as many as five different kinds of Amish, with different symbolic behavior systems, who practice ritual avoidance in relation to all others. These subsystems function so as to prevent further change. Each group expells its marginal persons and controls marriage and intergroup associations. The large number of small and extinct communities of Amish is evidence of such fragmentation (Mook 1955; Umble 1933).

But extinct settlements do not mean failure of the community—only failure of its spatial dimension. The Amish take their social institutions with them to other areas where group fulfillment can be successfully resolved. Complete disintegration is rare, for staunch families generally migrate if they dislike their community or the conditions in it. Migration is frequently the only alternative for those Amish who wish to shun all progress. Amish who cannot put up with change frequently sell their farms and move to other settlements, often across state lines. Those who moved from Pennsylvania to Ontario in recent years said: "We want to go back fifty years; things are going too fast there." Thus a father faced with the possible threat of the automobile or the tractor may write to an uncle or a distant relative in another state and ask, "How are things there?" In prospecting for a new location, the strictness of *Ordnung* there is as important to him as the price of land.

Migration, for the Amish, is one of the most important factors in resisting acculturation. Freed (1957: 55) has observed that specialists and class differences are essential to the maintenance of the Jewish shtetl of Eastern Europe. By contrast, the Old Order Amish, who have no occupational class differences and no specialists, are able to survive by migration. Had they not migrated from Europe to America they would have become extinct long ago. Indeed, those who remained in Europe have coalesced with other Protestant sects or with Catholics (Hostetler 1955). Migrations are normally directed to new localities rather than old ones, but there is also constant family mobility between communities.

All cultures exert pressures on the individual, and in Amish culture, as in that of French Canada (Hughes 1943: 216), such pressures generate feelings of resentment. Like the French Canadians, the Amish have not had to absorb their own "misfit people," their own "toxic by-products." Their misfits and marginal persons, following their excommunication by the Amish, are absorbed by neighbors of other religions. Discontent finds expression in a variety of complaints, and rowdyism has exceeded institutionalized boundaries and become a serious problem. Marginal personalities have emerged among individuals who have identified themselves with the dominant outgroup but have encountered relatively "impermeable barriers" (Kerckhoff and McCormick 1955: 54).

Amish communities, like other separatist communities, find themselves in a problematic situation. Amish society is faced with the problem of community self-realization and personal fulfillment for each new generation of members born into it. The problem must be solved within the range of its limited potentialities and by means of its available natural and human resources and its own unique local heritage. The constant striving to achieve the goals of the charter has given rise to distinctive patterns of deviancy and stress.

BIBLIOGRAPHY

Durkheim, E. 1951. Suicide. Chicago. (Original edition, 1897).
Freed, S. A. 1957. Suggested Type Societies in Acculturation Studies. American Anthropologist 59: 55–68.
Gascho, M. 1937. The Amish Division of 1693–1697 in Switzerland and Alsace. Mennonite Quarterly Review 22: 235–266.
Gillin, J. P. 1948. The Ways of Men. New York.
Hostetler, J. A. 1955. Old World Extinction and New World Survival of the Amish: A Study of Group Maintenance and Dissolution. Rural Sociology 20: 212–219.
———. 1963. Amish Society. Baltimore.
Hughs, E. C. 1943. French Canada in Transition. Chicago.
Huntington, G. E. 1956. Dove at the Window: A Study of an Old Order Amish Community in Ohio. Unpublished Ph.D. dissertation, Yale University.
Kerchoff, A. C., and T. C. McCormick. 1955. Marginal Status and Marginal Personality. Social Forces 34: 48–55.
Kollmorgen, W. M. 1942. The Old Order Amish of Lancaster County, Pennsylvania. United States Department of Agriculture, Rural Life Studies 4: 1–105.
Malinowski, B. 1944. A Scientific Theory of Culture and Other Essays. Chapel Hill.
Mook, M. A. 1955. A Brief History of Former, Now Extinct, Amish Communities in Pennsylvania. Western Pennsylvania Historical Magazine 38: 33–46.
Redfield, R. 1947. The Folk Society. American Journal of Sociology 52: 292–308.
Schreiber, W. I. 1962. Our Amish Neighbors. Chicago.
Schroeder, W. W., and J. A. Beegle. 1953. Suicide: An Instance of High Rural Rates. Rural Sociology 18: 45–56.
Umble, J. S. 1933. The Amish Mennonites of Union County, Pennsylvania. Mennonite Quarterly Review 7: 71–96, 162–190.
Weber, M. 1947. The Theory of Social and Economic Organization. Glencoe.

Relations of Modes of Production in Nineteenth-Century America: The Shakers and Oneida[1]

Matthew Cooper

>>> <<<

NINETEENTH CENTURY AMERICAN utopian societies often developed rather extensive economic relations with the society they opposed. Yet utopians, whether religious or secular, were wary of worldly contamination and the danger it posed to their attempts to build radically different societies. Why then did such relations develop? Did certain kinds of economic relations develop rather than others? How did they affect the internal economies and social structures of such communities?

Here I will compare the Shakers and the Oneida Community in respect of their modes of production and the pattern of economic relations that developed between them and the wider society. The Oneida and the Shakers are among the best studied of such groups and exhibit interesting similarities and differences. The comparison will show that successful societies with communal modes of production when embedded in a larger society with a capitalist mode of production will, under certain conditions, achieve stable forms of articulation or else ultimately become capitalist themselves. It will also suggest that American utopian societies provide important cases for thinking about the relations of modes of production, different from the cases usually considered. Following Wolf (1982: 75), a mode of production is defined as "a specific, historically occurring set of social relations through which labor is deployed to wrest energy from nature by means of tools, skills, organization, and knowledge." Such a definition "allows us to understand how the technical transformation of nature is conjoined with the organization of human sociality" (Wolf 1982: 74).[2]

The approach taken here analyzes modes of production in relation to goals and belief systems. Individual action plays an important part in the analysis, both on general, theoretical grounds and because in these cases the obvious strength of community leaders makes such consideration imperative. Economic dealings with the outside world are analyzed as reflecting the needs and wants of the utopian society as conceived by its members, including the consequences of prior extracommunity relations. The actions of external actors and general conditions of the wider social economy also play an important part. In this approach there is no mechanical compulsion, no interaction of disembodied, abstractly conceived structures following the "needs" determined by their internal logics or laws (cf. Foster-Carter 1978; Brenner 1977). Rather, there are people acting together and apart under conditions not entirely of their own making in light of their goals, understandings, emotions, and needs, trying to create more satisfying communities in which to live. But they do so in the context of a surrounding society that both constrains them and offers them opportunities.

The approach taken here differs from several recent attempts to understand the relations of small collective economies with an environing society. In her major comparative sociological study of utopian societies, Kanter (1972) deals in detail with relations between utopian communities and the wider society but her focus is on individual "commitment mechanisms" rather than on economic relations. Barkin and Bennett (1972) show how Israeli kibbutzim and Hutterite colonies strive to balance the requirements of the external system and their need to develop and maintain their own institutions. While otherwise useful, their approach has two serious defects. First, it treats culture and structure as exogenous factors, individual choice being the key element. Second, their analogical use of opportunity cost is circular and vacuous; any perceived cost or reward can explain anything. Erasmus (1977) provides a wide-ranging study of utopian experiments throughout Western history but the work suffers from an inadequate conceptualization of the relations between the utopian communities and their encompassing societies.

At a theoretical level, the perspectives of these authors are essentially individualistic, based as they are on an analysis of the opportunity costs of alternatives for Barkin and Bennett (1972) and on the structure of incentives ("humanistic behaviorism") for Erasmus (1977). Neither approach provides an adequate account of structure. Yet utopian settlements above all else are attempts to change structures and thereby to change the conditions under which individuals act and live. The advantage of the approach taken here is that it allows us to see structure and action as mutually determining, neither reducible to the other, both essential to understanding specific historical trajectories. Analysis of change must be "simultaneously structural and historical: structural in its identification of the underlying patterns of social and economic relations that explain observed events; historical in its tracing of those patterns to the human actions that brought them about" (Starr 1982: 8).

Most studies of the relations of modes of production have been concerned with the transition from feudalism to capitalism in early modern Europe (e.g., Sweezy 1976) or the penetration of capitalism into the noncapitalist periphery in more recent times (e.g., Wolpe 1980). But American utopian societies formed, grew, prospered, and/or failed within a developing capitalist social economy. In these cases one cannot argue that the noncapitalist modes were functional for capitalism (cf. Wolpe 1980) except in a minor way, as escape hatches for frustrated idealists and malcontents. These utopian societies were resistance movements but of the most optimistic sort; they stood as potent cultural critiques of nineteenth century American society. In their attempts to build more humanly satisfying societies they exposed, through propaganda and example, the faults they saw in American life.

In the end, either such societies became capitalist or developed stable ways of articulating with the surrounding capitalist economy. But the transformation of their modes of production did not follow from the appropriation of their land and other means of production, as has often happened with peasants reduced to semi- or wholly proletarian status or from exchange under exploitive terms of trade. Nor did the societies become suppliers of labor power for noncommunity capitalists. Rather, they became successful industrialists and merchants, employers of labor themselves. External relations grew increasingly important, one might think, because the utopian society could not adequately supply the full range of goods and services its members needed or came to want. But for the Shakers and Oneida, external relations initially followed from ideological imperatives. Later, the very success of their modes of production, based on communal property and attempts to improve labor-saving technology, made such ties stronger. Because they produced good quality, often innovative goods at relatively low cost, demand for the goods grew outside the society. The group then expanded production to meet demand, sometimes hiring outside labor to do so. The Oneida Community employed labor in the interests of capital accumulation while the Shakers appear to have aimed at simple, rather than expanded, reproduction. Members realized that it made sense economically to specialize in certain goods, acquiring other things from the outside. At Oneida, especially, members began using their own labor power in more remunerative ways. Thus, gradually the modes of production were transformed from within. As the process continued, individual members often came to see and understand their experience differently, which affected their commitment to the earlier ways, and created pressure for further change in economy, social relations, and ideology.

These cases show how the opportunities provided by a dynamic capitalism can transform other modes of production and may at times be more important than the constraints it places upon them. They also show how essential it is to understand the role of culture and belief systems in studying the relations of modes of production. Finally, these examples require one to take seriously individual action as a crucial element in structural change.

In the discussion that follows, I have organized the materials in parallel so as to facilitate comparison. First, a short history of the group is given, then an account of its system of beliefs (especially as that relates to economic goals and the relations of production, exchange, and consumption), and third, a brief discussion follows of the society's actual economic system as it developed which leads, finally, to external economic relations.

The Shakers

Founded in England as an outgrowth of the Quakers, the Shakers appeared in New York in the late 1770s. Mother Ann Lee, their prophet and first charismatic leader, settled near Albany and began the work of proselytizing. By 1790, the society had begun to expand to places in New England, often gaining converts during regional religious revivals. A general plan of organization was worked out and the basic beliefs of the group were clarified by 1795. Shortly thereafter, expansion began again, this time in the West, so that by 1826 there were some 25 Shaker settlements, each divided into a number of "families" of 30 to 100 individuals. After 1860, the society entered a long period of decline; today, a few elderly women living in Maine and New Hampshire are the last survivors of the more than 17,000 recorded members (Hayden 1976: 66).

The Shakers believed themselves to be the "Church of the Last Dispensation" or the "Millennial Church," according to their division of history into four cycles. The day of judgment began with the establishment of their church and would be completed by its spread and development (Nordhoff 1965: 133). Four pillars, or basic principles, upheld the Church; "Virgin Purity, Christian Communism, Confession of Sin, and Separation from the World" (Hinds 1908: 39). They also developed a comprehensive theology that included, among other tenets, the belief that God was both male and female, Jesus having represented on earth the male aspect and Mother Ann Lee the female. A comprehensive set of statutes and ordinances, the Millennial Laws, regulating almost every aspect of life evolved and was issued to the member societies in 1845 (Andrews 1963: 243–289 reproduces the laws).

Shaker economic ideology rested on their belief, as expressed in written covenants signed from 1795 onwards, "that there could be no Church in Complete order, according to the Law of Christ, without being gathered into one Joint Interest and union, that all the members might have an equal right and privilege, according to their Calling and needs, in things both Spiritual and temporal" (quoted in Andrews 1963: 61–62). That is, full members relinquished all personal and other property to the Church and received "Just and Equal rights an privileges, according to their needs, in the use of all things in the Church" (Andrews 1963: 62). All work should be "done plain and decent, according to the order and use of things, neither too high nor too low, according to their order and use" (Andrews 1963: 60). Work was a service dedicated to the community and to God, thus to be done joyously, as a pleasure. Cultivation of the land was "a part of the grand scheme to deliver the world from its evils. Waste, neglect, and misuse of God's blessings aroused the Shaker soul" (Andrews 1963: 117). Simplicity and functionality were inscribed in many of the rules governing the design and production of goods, as well as of course in those dealing with consumption. "Order and use", "needs," not "superfluities." These words expressed how organization and activity must reflect the essential and fixed nature of the world as God had created it and as was shown in the Bible and the revelations of Mother Ann and subsequent Shaker leaders. The mode of production developed in these communities thus was based on an ideology of Christian communism, believed to reflect the practices of the primitive church.

The basic unit of Shaker economic organization was the "family," several of which might make up one society. "Families [might] differ in their temporal conditions, from fortuitous circumstances, such as location, the business they chose to adopt, the ability to conduct affairs, the number of members, and from many other causes of a temporal or spiritual nature" (Andrews 1972: 36). The community at New Lebanon, New York, (whose economic affairs have been studied in some detail by Andrews [1972]) when completely established by the early 1820s consisted of eight families, each of about 30 to 100 persons. There were several levels or "orders" of families, originally an "inner court" of those most highly developed spiritually and free from debt and family involvements, a second "court" of those who still retained such involvements, and a third consisting of children, the elderly, and those selected to carry on business relations with the world. Each family was led by Elders and Deacons and Deaconesses (who were trustees), the latter having the authority (eventually spelled out in great detail in the Millennial Laws) to control virtually every aspect of economic life, although they could be removed at any time by the central ministry (Andrews 1963: 257–260). Families, thus, were divided into two groups; one governing by virtue of institutional authority delegated by the society (although still required to engage in manual labor), the other entirely involved in productive labor. Although the governing groups clearly controlled the means of production, they should not be seen as appropriating the surplus produced by ordinary members. Males and females formally were equal but were kept separate in occupation as in most other areas of life. Members generally engaged in such work as they had done before joining the society, but the Shakers believed that "variety of occupation is a source of pleasure" and in some lines practiced a system of rotation of labor (Andrews 1972: 31, 117), especially in the women's tasks. Labor was allocated flexibly to the different branches of production, allowing communities to adapt to changing circumstances. Thus, the social relations of production may be characterized as communist; all property belonged to the community, an administrative elite controlled most economic decision making but did not personally appropriate surplus, the distribution of income was essentially equal and based on the principle of "to each according to his needs."

Agriculture, including stockbreeding, served as the foundation of Shaker community economies but from almost the very beginning, the Shakers also developed small manufacturing industries. In his study of the economy of the New Lebanon society, Andrews (1972) groups the latter into several categories: garden seeds, dried sweet corn and apples, medicinal herbs, blacksmithing and machine shop work, miscellaneous carpentry and milling trades, tanning, broom and brush making, the manufacture of items such as baskets, boxes, barrels, sieves, wool cards, etc., clothing and dyeing, and (of course) the chair industry. While many of these lines aimed at community self-sufficiency, they also provided goods for exchange with other Shaker groups and for sale to outsiders. The Shakers were widely known for the quality of their products and for the many inventions and labor-saving devices they developed. Andrews (1972: 39–45) lists 39 inventions but, in addition, there were important innovations in the organization of production as well as in hygiene and other areas related to the quality of life. Such innovativeness reflected in part the necessity to solve problems set for them by their ideology and adopted social organization.

> [E]very improvement relieving human toil ... [gives] time and opportunity for moral, mechanical, scientific and intellectual improvement and the cultivation of the finer and higher qualities of the human mind.
>
> We are not called to labor to excel, or be like the world: but to excel them in order, union and peace, and in good works—works that are truly virtuous and useful to man, in this life. (Both quoted in Andrews 1963: 114, 115)

Both labor and innovations to save labor showed the sacred commitment to redeem the world and by so doing transform earth into heaven. At a somewhat less lofty level, an improved washing machine, for example, allowed women to deal quickly and efficiently with the laundry of a family with 30 to 100 members. The Round Barn of the Church Family at Hancock, Massachusetts (built 1826 by Daniel Goodrich) was deemed a gift of God because, among other virtues, it allowed 52 cattle, housed in radiating stalls, to be fed by a single hand (Hayden 1976: 92). Frugality, hard work, and invention produced rewards in worldly terms as well. By 1839, when the Shakers' property at New Lebanon was assessed, their holdings had grown to 2,292 acres, valued (including buildings) at $68,225 (Andrews 1972: 46). Contemporary observers felt that the Shaker standard of living compared very favorably with that of average mechanics, laborers, and farmers of the time (for example, Hinds 1908, Nordhoff 1965, and other authors cited in Andrews 1963: 129–135), but the colonies were not so wealthy as envious outsiders thought them to be.

Business dealings with "the world" played an important part in Shaker economies from an early date. In order to insulate members from outside influences, the Shakers appointed a few brethren, two of whom were to be Deacons or trustees, to conduct trading for each family. The ministry closely regulated and supervised all transactions and other activities engaged in by these emissaries; the Deacons and trustees were not to communicate the details of their dealings to the ordinary members, except that they could tell them the market prices of articles bought or sold. Regular routes were laid out for the travellers. Some goods were left on consignment to be sold on commission by established agencies, some were wholesaled through distributors in larger business centers, while some manufactures were retailed through local community stores. Within a short time, the market for the products of this single society extended throughout the Hudson River Valley and beyond (Andrews 1972: 49). Probably the best known of these products were the Shaker chairs, production of which began before 1800. After 1852, the chair industry at New Lebanon developed on a large scale thanks to the efforts of Robert Wagan, a "man of unusual mechanical skill and executive ability" (Andrews 1972: 243). Thousands of chairs were sold all over the country, especially through large urban furniture dealers, leading the Shakers to build an additional factory in 1872, introduce new designs, and even to apply for a trademark to protect their business against imitators; similar chairs were manufactured for sale at many of the other Shaker societies (Andrews 1972: 229–248). The success of this business and most of their other enterprises reflected the Shakers' insistence on well-designed, consistently high quality products and scrupulously honest dealing, for which they were well known. The use of credit ran contrary to the

Society's principles, so most transactions were on a cash basis, though some involved barter. The proceeds from this trade were used to buy corn, wheat, rye, and other grains "in great quantity," wool, hides for tanning, herbs and roots for their medicinal herb industry, and so forth (Andrews 1972: 65, 92). But larger surpluses often were used to purchase additional lands. Because the Shakers were celibate and because it became increasingly difficult for them to recruit new members, especially young men, in the latter part of the nineteenth century, the population of the societies began to decline. With fewer brethren, many of the small industries were given up; the New (now Mount) Lebanon society focused increasingly on agriculture and on the sisters' handicraft industries. As the twentieth century proceeded, more and more of the farm labor was done by hired hands.

For the Shakers, economic relations with the outside world remained almost entirely at the level of exchange. Certain goods were made mainly for sale; transactions followed the norms and practices of nineteenth century American capitalism. But capitalist forms of organization did not appear in the productive process, except when hired hands came to be used because of a shortage of male labor. The communist mode of production proved advantageous for the societies because ideology and comprehensive forms of social control helped to hold down individual consumption, thus communities rather than individuals accumulated capital.

Little overt pressure came from "the world" to try to force the Shakers to change their ways. In a series of legal cases that tested the validity of Shaker covenants, especially in regard to the claims of former members to a portion of community property and recompense for wages foregone, the courts consistently ruled in favor of the Shakers (Andrews 1963: 204–212; Weisbrod 1980). An investigation by a committee appointed by the New York State Assembly in the late 1840s into the principles and practices of the sect proved sympathetic, rejecting allegations that the Shakers had prospered so much that they were monopolizing the available land and thus constituted a danger to the wider society (Andrews 1963: 217–221).

More subtle but more important pressures affected the Shakers in two major ways. First, growth of the American economy, westward expansion, and the apparent decline of religious utopianism as a widespread form of protest after the Civil War (cf. Fogarty 1975 for an opposing view) made it more difficult for the Shakers to obtain recruits, particularly young males. Second, changing relations with the outside world led members to reexamine some of the sect's tenets. As Andrews (1972: 235) says, the problem "inherent in the whole concept of separation, was where to draw the line between worldliness and sainthood. . . . If certain conveniences were condoned, who could say what ones should be denied? ... Committed to the principle of scientific progress, how could the order totally insulate itself from the materialism of the industrial age?" Reflection on such questions in light of their experience both of the society and of the world lead some Shaker Elders to quite different positions. Internal disunity grew as liberal, conservative, and moderate factions developed. As well, in some communities in the late nineteenth century, more worldly tendencies crept in, allowing members to enjoy music, newspapers, magazines, and pictures, for example. Changing technology, forms of economic organization and practices, beliefs, attitudes, and desires, all were filtered through the lens provided by the members' own experience in a complex process that is not simply summarized by cataloguing the alternatives open to members or the incentives they faced.

Adequate supplies of labor were crucial to the Shakers' economic success. When such labor could no longer be obtained either through recruitment because of changes in the wider society or through natural increase because of their celibacy, the Shakers went into a long period of decline. They retained their own mode of production but only by virtue of being able to hire labor and having properties from which they received income. In a sense, the existence of a capitalist economy beyond their villages had become a condition of their success in accumulating property. For without external trade and the profits it generated they could not have acquired as much land as they did nor could they have survived so long. Yet the excessive accumulation of land itself contributed to their decline, particularly when they could no longer cultivate it themselves. The Shaker experience in the United States shows, among other things, how a noncapitalist mode of production may benefit from the opportunities provided by capitalism, at least until the opportunities taken themselves begin seriously to constrain action. It also shows the crucial role played by ideology in such relations and that ideology cannot be reduced simply to material interest. After all, had the Shakers not practised celibacy their labor problem would not have been so severe.

The Oneida Community

The Oneida Community grew out of earlier experiments in community living by its founder and charismatic leader, John Humphrey Noyes. Having been converted during the Second Great Awakening in 1831, Noyes studied theology at the Andover Theological Seminary and Yale before becoming a licensed preacher. By 1834 he began to espouse Perfectionism, a doctrine that claimed people could attain a state of inner perfection in this life. Ostracised by church and friends, he wandered through New England and New York preaching his new faith. Between 1838 and 1848, he and a small group of followers lived together in Putney, Vermont, where they adopted the principle of holding property in common and also the institution for which they became famous, or rather, notorious, complex marriage. In a Statement of Principles (November, 1846), they pledged that "All individual proprietorship of either persons or things is surrendered and absolute community of interests takes the place of the laws and fashions which preside over property and family relations in the world" (quoted in Robertson 1970: 10).

With warrants out for the arrest of several members on grounds of adultery and rumors of imminent mob attacks on the commune, members of the community left Putney and by 1848 had settled at Oneida, in central New York. There they began building utopia.

Over the next 30 years the Community constructed communal living quarters, workshops, and factories to house approximately 250 members and their growing businesses. As Hayden (1976: 219) suggests, design, planning, and construction constantly were occurring on different scales and with the participation of the entire community. From the buildings and grounds community history could be read. They also developed further the social institutions of "Bible Communism." All members were united in a group or complex marriage, and exclusive personal attachments were frowned upon. The group itself (that is, its "central members," who had ascended highest towards spiritual perfection) regulated sexual relationships, including the sexual initiation of boys and girls. To allow women to escape the burden and dangers of continual childbearing, Noyes (1966) introduced the practice of "male continence." Later, he developed a eugenic theory ("stirpiculture," based on the principle of ascending spiritual fellowship) that informed the allowed matings for procreative purposes. The Oneida Community raised its children collectively, providing them with excellent educational opportunities for the time. In theory, at least, men and women were equal, although in practice women may not have been as important as decision makers. Administration of the group's affairs fell to the lot of 21 standing committees and 48 functional departments concerned with almost every aspect of life (Nordhoff 1965: 279), but major decisions were taken at general meetings. Noyes (1966) also developed the practice of "mutual criticism," in which members could be criticized publicly for their failings, spiritual and practical, including illness. In the 1870s, several area clerics launched crusades against the Community on grounds of immorality. By this time, John Humphrey Noyes largely had withdrawn from active leadership of the group and internal factional disputes became important. In 1879, when legal action against them was threatened, Noyes moved to Canada and the Community decided to abandon its practice of complex marriage. Shortly thereafter, they also gave up communal property holding, forming a joint-stock company to manage their now extensive business enterprises and effectively rejoined the wider society. "Without faith in Noyes's divine sanction, without a united belief in Perfectionism, and without complex marriage, Oneida lost its justification for existence. It had neither the leaders nor the heart to tackle the drastic reorganization necessary to preserve utopia" (Carden 1971: 104).

Like the Shakers, the Oneida Perfectionists believed that the kingdom of Heaven could be established on earth in this life.[3] But unlike the Shakers, who elaborated more and more detailed rules covering every aspect of life, at Oneida "legality" was frowned upon. Carden (1971: 23) points out that Noyes directed the group's affairs according to general principles, two of which dominated Community life, individual perfection and communal good. The first implied the need for individuals constantly to bring their outer behavior into line with that state of inner perfection they professed through moral, spiritual, and intellectual improvement. Such concerns, for Noyes, took precedence over material needs. The second principle, to be fully achieved, required that all selfish interests, all possessiveness, be relinquished. Striving always to balance individual self-realization and communal good, the Community saw itself as a family adapting, evolving. Perfection was not a state but a process.

Oneida economic ideology followed easily from these general principles. The goal of economic life was to provide the material abundance that made possible realization of their spiritual ideals. Initially, they focused their efforts on horticulture but when this proved inadequate to support the Community various lines of manufacturing and commerce were taken up. The point was to adapt as circumstances required yet always in the service of Community ideals. Later, Noyes (1966: 19) generalized from the Oneida experience in writing about the history of American socialist communities:

> Judging by our own experience we ... think that this fondness for land, which has been the habit of Socialists, had much to do with their failures. Farming is about the hardest and longest of all roads to fortune; and it is the kind of labor in which there is the most uncertainty as to modes and theories, and of course the largest chance for disputes and discords in such complex bodies as Associations. ... Socialism, if it is really ahead of civilization, ought to keep near the centers of business, and at the front of the general march of improvement. We should have advised [other groups to] ... put their strength as soon as possible into some form of manufacture. Almost any kind of a factory would be better than a farm for a Community nursery.

The group encouraged members to invent new ways of producing goods and providing services so as to enhance efficiency and to reduce necessary labor time. Work was to be a joy. "Loving companionship in labor, and especially the mingling of the sexes makes labor attractive" (Noyes 1966: 636). Work rotation including managerial jobs and rejection of the usual sexual division of labor would make work a "free-will offering; there was no pressure exerted to demand it of the members" (Robertson 1970: 22). Criticism of work in the trap shop made in 1856 illustrates some of their beliefs. Foremen did not attend sufficiently to the spiritual interests of the shop; in selecting the workers, there was not a "true combination of old and young, spiritual and unspiritual, and the commingling of the sexes. . . ."; there was too much reference to the immediate results of labor; it was not made sufficiently attractive to women to join in the work (quoted in Robertson 1970: 222). Work bees, or "unitary industry," were a "good promotor of the family spirit" and helped them "to make good music in all our work" (quoted in Robertson 1970: 61). When outside labor was hired, the workers were to be treated fairly and generously. Carden (1971: 83) points out that Noyes promoted enlightened labor practices for the time, even providing an evening school for the young employees. "The old vicious hireling system of the world was quite distasteful to the Community people, they said" (quoted in Robertson 1970: 215).

Just as all property belonged to the Community, goods and services were to be equally available to all. Many were consumed collectively (food, most notably) and consumption levels were decided upon by the group. The Oneida Community did not disapprove of indulgence so long as it was communal; after all, such consumption reflected the increasing perfection of their way of life. Thus, eventually, they enjoyed steam heat throughout their Mansion, food equivalent to that of a good hotel, a Turkish bath, a photographic studio, a library of perhaps 5,000 volumes, a chemical laboratory, elaborate properties for theatrical performances, musical instruments for their orchestra and even a summer cottage on Oneida Lake several miles away (Carden 1971: 44–45). As Nordhoff (1965: 288), who visited them in 1874, pointed out, their religious theory called for no internal struggles and little self-denial.

The economy of Oneida began, as noted above, with a focus on horticulture. But the Community became solvent only after it had established itself in manufacturing and commerce. By 1857, after nine years of operation and the investment of almost $108,000 by members, Community assets were worth (at all branches) only $67,000 through a combination of inexperience, bad luck, poor decisions, and so forth (Noyes 1966: 644). The road to solvency opened initially through the leadership of two men, John R. Miller and Sewell Newhouse. Miller pioneered Oneida commercial activities after observing that local settlers depended upon itinerant merchants for many commodities; he promoted the Oneida effort to sell preserved fruit from its farm, traveling bags they manufactured, and notions of all sorts they bought for resale. When Newhouse joined the Community he brought with him the animal traps he had invented. As demand for the traps increased, other Community members added their efforts and the industry was flourishing by the mid-1850s (Carden 1971: 38–41). Other lines of industry sprang up from members' abilities, ingenuity, and their perception of demand, including broom making, foundry work (such as various kinds of castings, wagon fixtures, etc.), silk weaving, the production of machinery for the trap and silk works, making rustic furniture and other wooden articles, and, finally, producing silverware. Eventually, four main industries emerged: traps, silk, fruit-preserving, and silverware (Robertson 1970: 20–21). Cyclical demand for some of the Community's products, especially traps, forced them in the mid-1860s to take a close look at their use of capital and labor, to find ways to diversify, to sell off unproductive assets at bargain prices, and to reduce their accumulated debt. After this they continued to prosper, earning respectable profits on sales each year. Over the ten years to 1870, net earnings averaged $18,058, while over the period 1867–1872 they rose from $21,416 to $71,011 (reports quoted in Robertson 1970: 229–262).

Community members performed all work in the early period, based to a considerable degree on individual preferences and prior experience. A creative tension always existed between the community goal of efficiency in production and labor as a means towards personal and social perfection. The actual organization of work fell to the lot of the various committees and departments; committee memberships as well as particular jobs were rotated, although in practice some individuals retained certain jobs and supervisory positions for long periods. Frequent job changes were "among the many advantages arising from Communism" (quoted in Robertson 1970: 86) not only because it relieved boredom but also because it promoted inventiveness by encouraging recognition of analogous design problems (Hayden 1976: 197). As discussed previously, members sought constantly to improve the methods of production through inventions, the adoption of outside innovations, and the reorganization of work, always with a view to increasing efficiency and quality while reducing the labor time required. By the late 1860s, when outside labor had become quite important, it appears that the balance had tipped towards efficiency rather than the social goals of labor. Noyes (1966: 643) estimated for 1868 the returns to Community labor, a notional profit of

33¢ per day per member. As he pointed out, "[W]ere it possible for a skillful mechanic to live in co-operation with others, so that ... his family could secure the economies of combined households, their wages at present rates would be more than double the cost of living." But by the early 1860s, with increasing prosperity, the Community began to employ outside labor. At first, a few local people were engaged to help with outside work but soon hired labor began to replace members in all menial tasks, whether in farming, the manufactory, or domestically. In 1865 they had 27 hired men and women, in 1866, 49 (Robertson 1970: 215). By 1874 they were employing 20–35 farm laborers and "a number" of fruit pickers in season plus 201 fulltime workers at Oneida, 103 of whom were women; 75 of the women worked in the silk factory while 67 of the men worked in the trap works, foundry, and machine shops. At their Wallingford branch the silk works employed 35 hired women and girls (Nordhoff 1965: 263). Increasingly, members served as superintendents while outsiders performed the less attractive and menial tasks. Somewhat defensively, a Community member wrote in 1871, "[T]his has been brought about not because we have felt above manual labor, but because all our own help has been absorbed in more remunerative employments pertaining to manufacturing. We have not allowed ourselves to get lily-fingered, and have always stood ready ... to do with cheerful zeal anything that our circumstances seem to call for (quoted in Robertson 1970: 89–90). Nordhoff (1965: 263), a sympathetic but critical observer, wrote that the hired laborers liked their employers who paid good wages, treated their servants kindly, "looking after their physical and intellectual well-being, building houses for such of them as have families and need to be near at hand, and in many ways showing interest in their welfare." Yet it is clear that by the 1870s Community members, although owning their property in common and enjoying equality of wealth and income amongst themselves, stood as capitalists in relation to their labor force. Their prosperity, and the reproduction of their own mode of production, had come to depend ever more heavily on capitalist relations of production.

It should be obvious from the foregoing that the Oneida Community had many and various relations with the wider society. John Humphrey Noyes came to think that such relations were essential to the success of socialist communities, which would benefit from the "general march of improvement" and the profits obtainable in trade. Carden (1971: 83) states that the Community "secured local support by contributing substantially to the local economy." In outline, the external economic relations of the Oneida Community fall into several broad categories; purchase of raw materials and items for resale, credit, hired labor, training of members, adoption of new technology, sale of products, and entertaining of tourists.

From the mid-1850s onward, these relations became increasingly important to the Community's success. As with any small, open economy bound to a much larger one, this one had constantly to try to adapt to changes—especially of factor prices and levels of demand—in the more powerful system. But because the Oneida mode of production was communal, economic adaptation often involved extensive community discussion in which alternatives were evaluated explicitly in terms of community principles (see the various extracts from Community publications quoted in Robertson 1970: 218–264).

There were five major downturns in the business cycle between the mid-1850s and the late 1870s, including the major depressions that began in 1857 and 1873 (Lebergott 1984: 396) that affected demand for the Community's products, the cost and availability of credit, and the ability of customers to pay for their purchases from the Community. In 1873, the *Oneida Circular* remarked,

> Financial panics, like fire, try men's works and not unfrequently discover a hollow interior, when all was solidity to outward view. ... the unpleasant sensation of finding ourselves liable to sympathetic cramp when Wall Street is undergoing a convulsion; of worrying for a few thousand dollars when ten times as much is due us from prompt paying customers, leads us to renew our resolution of getting at once in a situation to pay as we go. Then, if the whole country becomes bankrupt, the worst that can happen to us will be a temporary cessation of manufacturing; but having no debts to pay we can live on mush and applesauce and wear our old clothes till better times. Our cause is too precious to risk in the arena with the bulls and bears. (Quoted in Robertson 1970: 262–263).

On the positive side, new opportunities sometimes appeared, such as the increased demand for traps following the end of the Civil War, the U.S. purchase of Alaska, and the completion of the transcontinental railroad (Robertson 1970: 213, 257). As the financial reports reproduced by Robertson (1970) show, the Community managed to weather the succession of financial storms and increase its income and net worth through the 1870s.

In a balance sheet of the consequences for the Oneida Community of its relations with the wider society, three areas stand out: capital accumulation, the transformation of the social relations of production, and the gradual taking on of outside standards. In 1857 the Community's assets were valued at about $67,000; by the time the Community became a joint-stock company in 1879 its holdings had grown to more than $600,000. "Association," and the economies of scale it allowed, paid off but perhaps the growth of external demand for its products and its ability to produce relatively efficiently through the adoption of labor-saving technology was more important. The increasing use of hired labor turned the Oneida communists into capitalists. Although the Community apparently was a progressive employer for the time, its structural position required it to develop ways of treating its workers—such as a piece-work system—that were antithetical to its own principles but that allowed members to live increasingly comfortably at the expense of their employees.

Erasmus (1977: 157–159) argues that economic integration with the wider society forced utopian societies to take on increasingly the goals and values of the world and that those goals inevitably became more immediate, short term, and individualistic. For Oneida this process involved a growing concern with calculating the returns to alternative uses of its resources, demonstrated, for example, in improvements to bookkeeping methods and in a constant willingness to drop a line of business if it became less profitable. Although members were aware of the potential dangers to the Community from economic integration, they preferred to take opportunities that promised tangible, measurable rewards. Thus, in the service of a mode of production that promised rewards based on need, the Oneida Community developed a form of capitalist rationality that allowed it to make commodities of things, time, and persons. In 1875 Nordhoff (1965: 393) concluded that "Oneida is in reality more a large and prosperous manufacturing corporation, with a great number of partners all actively engaged in the work, than a commune in the common sense of the word." Four years later it became legally what it already had become in fact.

Comparisons

These two utopian societies became deeply involved economically, as well as in other ways, with the surrounding society. Why?

For the Shakers, the short answer is that they developed because production for sale and trading allowed profits that could be invested in land. This accumulation of land was ideologically motivated, it was done to redeem God's earth and transform it into Heaven. How did these commercial activities lead to profits for the Shakers? First, note that trading did not apparently lead to lower unit costs of production. Because their industries were artisanal, increasing output did not normally lead to increased productivity; that is labor costs were not affected. On the other hand, clearly the Shakers did aim to reduce labor costs through mechanization and improved organization of production. But was this a result of large scale production for the market? Again, the impetus seems rather to have come from the ideology. Even though work was a sacred activity and meant to be joyous, reduced labor time freed members to improve themselves spiritually which, after all, was their chief goal. Although I have no evidence of it, materials costs may have been reduced through volume purchases. In general, however, it seems that profits accrued mainly because of the expansion of demand for the Shakers' products, on the one hand, and the community controls on consumption that lowered the reproduction costs of labor, on the other.

For Oneida, the impetus for external relations also was clear. The Community engaged in business to make possible reaching its "Perfectionist" goals. Deepening and widening the relations Oneida had with the wider society had allowed the Community to prosper, initially through trading and later through the surpluses generated in production, and thus had underwritten the group's experimental social practices. Although much technical innovation that led to increased productivity, and thus reduced costs occurred within the Community, it was stimulated and aided by the flow of information from outside, including the training enjoyed by some members in factories and universities. In the case of Oneida, it seems clear that commercial success encouraged the hiring of additional outside labor that, in a factory system, allowed for higher levels of productivity through the reorganization of production and attempts to motivate workers to produce more; and thereby increased profits. After 20 years of experience at Oneida, J. H. Noyes concluded that utopian societies should develop manufactures and locate near the centers of business activity rather than accumulate land and focus on agriculture. Interdependence benefitted them, he thought, while farming in more or less isolated regions not only promoted dissension but also made it difficult for societies to achieve more comfortable levels of living.

The trend in both cases was for external relations to grow over the years and for relations at the level of exchange to predominate at first. But, as described above, both later came to rely on hired labor for help in production. For the Shakers, such labor was employed mainly in farming (not in their manufacturing activities) because of the shortage of young males in the society, while the Oneida Communty increasingly turned to hired labor for its growing manufacturing industries. Also, both societies developed stronger ties with wholesalers, retailers, and freight haulers in order to market their goods more widely and to buy more cheaply. The Shakers avoided credit, on ideological grounds, while the Oneida Community used it extensively, eventually reducing its debts; but for pragmatic reasons.

How did these relations affect internal structures? For the Shakers, until at least the 1860s, the external exchange relations appear to have strengthened their social structure. The highly centralized, almost military, social structure made it possible for external contacts by individuals and the uses of trading profits to be strictly controlled and contamination from "the world" contained. The very success of their enterprises provided further resources with which leaders could reinforce their power. The success of their products in outside markets and their reputation for honesty, excellent design, and craftsmanship may have helped to attract new members. Trading profits allowed Shaker societies to accumulate greater amounts of land. It did not make them dependent on the world, at least not during the early period.

On the other hand, in the periods of decline and contraction, external relations became increasingly important. The Shakers relied on hired labor for subsistence production and on rents for a portion of their income, especially as the membership became predominantly older and female. Without these relations, especially based on the earlier accumulation of land, the Shakers could not have continued as communal property holders or retained a system of distribution based on need. In the end, the costs of external dependence could be contained, perhaps because their use of hired labor aimed at the simple reproduction of their productive means and because the strength and completeness of their ideology gave them resources with which to ward off the fatal attractions of the world. Thus, using the resources of the surrounding capitalist economy made retention of their own mode of production possible.

The Oneida Community, at an early point in its existence, came to depend more heavily on the surrounding economy than did the Shakers. Above we noted that the major consequences of external economic relations for Oneida came in capital accumulation, the growth of capitalist relations of production, and replacement of "Perfectionist" goals and standards by those of the world. As these processes went forward, mediated by its relatively decentralized and egalitarian power structure and pragmatic ideology, Oneida came to resemble more closely the surrounding society. Oneida community members, as a class, appeared as capitalists vis-à-vis their workers, they owned the means of production, organized and supervised production, and appropriated the profits. Ultimately, of course, Oneida became a joint-stock corporation rather than a community based on communal property holding. Thus, for Oneida, the benefits reaped from taking the opportunities open to them in the surrounding capitalist economy entailed costs it could not contain.

Discussion

Interactions of economy, ideology, and the action of individuals shaped the historical courses of Oneida and the Shakers. They are only two of a much larger number of utopian societies that arose in nineteenth century America. Comparison of such cases, taking regional and temporal variation in American society and economy into account more seriously than was possible here, would reveal a range of phenomena different in some respects from those generally considered in the literature on the relations of modes of production. It would also contribute to the ongoing project that seeks to make culture and action crucial elements in the study of modes of production.

Most writings on the articulation of modes of production have been concerned with the transition to capitalism from feudalism or from other noncapitalist modes of production. As Ruccio and Simon (1986: 213) argue, several different models have been used to try to understand how different capitalist and noncapitalist modes can be combined in a single social formation. All the models employ two major variables; the form of interaction, and the degree of dominance by one mode of production over the others. Generally it is assumed that capitalism comes to dominate the others by determining their ability to reproduce themselves over time. As well, the ability of the noncapitalist modes to satisfy the postulated needs of capitalism is taken to hinder or to enable the development of the capitalist mode of production.

Differences from the more usual cases emerge in studying the Shakers and Oneida, especially in regard to the question of dominance. Nineteenth century utopian societies were attempts to resist an already or soon to be dominant capitalism and ultimately to replace it. For the Shakers and Oneida this meant, among other things, that their critique of capitalist practices was based on experience as well as religious ideology and their plans had to take into account the existence and dominance of the wider society. Thus, the utopians had to create for themselves new ways of conceptualizing and valuing goods, labor, and time.[4] They had to make those new ways powerfully expressive and motivating for people whose earlier experience had been of the practices of nineteenth century American capitalism. Generally, utopians saw their settlements not as refuges but as exemplars. By offering living proof of the possibility of perfect communities they would bring about the complete reform of America through replication of the successful models (Fellman 1973). In the end, however, capitalism did determine the conditions that allowed them to reproduce their own modes of production, partly because of the opportunities they had already taken advantage of.

Other differences have to do with the form of the relations. At first, relations took the form of exchange, as usually has been the case historically in the periphery (Rey 1973). Later, in some utopian societies, capitalism took root in the communal mode of production but this occurred without the extraeconomic sanctions often employed in those peripheral societies to bring this result about. The utopians seem to have chosen the paths that allowed for the growth of capitalist relations of production; for example, rather than having been pushed or led down them. In these cases, the presence of the noncapitalist modes cannot reasonably be argued to have been functional for the development of capitalism. Utopian societies did not serve as reservoirs of cheap labor subsidizing the labor costs of capitalist industry. If anything, especially for Oneida, the relationship was just the opposite.

As noted above, these cases also require one to take seriously culture and action in analyzing the relations of modes of production. For example, the relatively stable form of articulation developed by the Shakers was a complex product of the ideological, such as controls on consumption and reproduction, a commitment to transform earth into Heaven, a belief in the sacredness of labor, commitment to values of simplicity and honesty, with the economic exigencies of farming, small-scale manufacturing, and trading in nineteenth century America. Individuals, through the revelations they proclaimed, the creation and interpretation of rules and beliefs in particular circumstances, the creative development of novel technological and organizational solutions to perceived problems played a crucial, irreducible part in charting the Shakers' historical course. The goals and meanings of their economic and social practices are essential to an understanding of the Shakers. The choices of farming as the preferred productive activity, celibacy as a key social practice, and simplicity in consumption underlay both their success and their ultimate failure.

Analogously, in the Oneida case commitment to principles of individual perfection, communal good based on sharing all things, a desire for comfortable levels of living, a belief in progress and the role of reason in it, and a principled dislike for "legality" or (put positively) a preference for creative flexibility helped to shape the economic practices that developed. Putting aside simplicity, they believed that the good things of this world were to be enjoyed, especially if they promoted intellectual and spiritual perfection. By encouraging higher levels of consumption, these factors also provided motives for the growth of industry and commerce. The coincidence between their desires for a richer life and the growing demand for their products lead them to use ever more hired labor which then required extensive supervision. In contrast to the Shakers, Oneida made legitimate the desire of individuals for expanded consumption and decided for purely economic reasons to focus on manufacturing and trade. John Humphrey Noyes, their charismatic leader, was the fount from which flowed most of the peculiar Oneida ideology. But many other individuals opened lines of business, invented new products and production methods, and contributed in diverse other ways. Oneida became capitalist through a series of steps, often debated at length, each of which could itself be justified in terms of the principles of individual perfection and communal good. But, taken together, these decisions undermined the foundations of "Bible Communism" and the community built on it.

NOTES

1. Margaret Rodman provided helpful advice on an earlier draft of this paper.

2. Worsley (1984: 35–36) criticizes Wolf for "designating everything that bears upon, is affected by, or has consequences for the economy as production relations." In practice Wolf's use of the concept is more restricted.

3. Mandelker (1984) argues that in American utopian societies generally, and Oneida in particular, the connections among theology, sacred history, values, prophecy, and the creation and ultimate failure of community organization are essential for understanding the societies. More particularly, he sees the organizational problems faced by the Oneida Community as "expressions of persistent and ultimately irreconcilable tensions between religion and world characteristic of utopian religious experiments in general, and expressed in the Oneida Community's theology and practice" (1984: 7).

4. Hall (1978: 200), writing about contemporary communes, argues that, "In essence, communal worlds differ from one another because the participants . . . constitute time differently . . . and attend to events and action in the lifeworld according to different schemes of relevance."

BIBLIOGRAPHY

Andrews, E. D. 1963. The People Called Shakers (rev. ed.). New York.
———. 1972 (1932). The Community Industries of the Shakers. Philadelphia.
Barkin, D., and J. W. Bennett. 1972. Kibbutz and Colony: Collective Economies and the Outside World. Comparative Studies in Society and History 14:456–483.
Brenner, R. 1977. The Origins of Capitalist Development. New Left Review 104:25–93.
Carden, M. L. 1971 (1969). Oneida: Utopian Community to Modern Corporation. New York.
Erasmus, C. J. 1977. In Search of the Common Good: Utopian Experiments Past and Future. New York.
Fellman, M. 1973. The Unbounded Frame: Freedom and Community in Nineteenth Century America. Westport, Conn.
Fogarty, R. S. 1973. Oneida: A Utopian Search for Religious Security. Labor History 14:202–227.
———. 1975. American Communes, 1865–1914. Journal of American Studies 9:145–162.

Foster-Carter, A. 1978. The Modes of Production Controversy. New Left Review 107:47–77.
Hall, J. R. 1978. The Ways Out: Utopian Communal Groups in an Age of Babylon. London.
Hayden, D. 1976. Seven American Utopias: The Architecture of Communitarian Socialism, 1790–1975. Cambridge, Mass.
Hinds, W. A. 1908 (1878). American Communities and Co-operative Colonies (3rd ed.). Chicago.
Kanter, R. M. 1972. Commitment and Community. Cambridge, Mass.
Lebergott, S. 1984. The Americans: An Economic Record. New York.
Mandelker, I. L. 1984. Religion, Society and Utopia in Nineteenth Century America. Amherst, Mass.
Nordhoff, C. 1965 (1875). The Communistic Societies of the United States. New York.
Noyes, J. H. 1966. Strange Cults and Utopias of 19th-Century America (orig. History of American Socialisms, 1870). New York.
Rey. P.-P. 1973. Les alliances de classes. Paris.
Robertson, C. N. 1970. Oneida Community: An Autobiography, 1851–1876. Syracuse, N.Y.
Ruccio, D. F., and L. H. Simon. 1986. Methodological Aspects of a Marxian Approach to Development. World Development 14:211–222.
Starr, P. 1982. The Social Transformation of American Medicine. New York.
Sweezy, P. M. 1976. The Transition from Feudalism to Capitalism. Atlantic Highlands, N.J.
Weisbrod, C. 1980. The Boundaries of Utopia. New York.
Wolf, E. 1982. Europe and the People without History. Berkeley and Los Angeles.
Wolpe, H. 1980. The Articulation of Modes of Production. London.
Worsley, P. 1984. The Three Worlds: Culture & World Development. London.

# *The Search for Roots*
>>> <<<

Ayoub's article deals with that wider set of relatives anthropologists call the "kindred" and Americans refer to as "family" or, simply, "relatives." Her subject is of special interest to scholars of modernization because it challenges and requires qualifications to the view that modern society is inimical to kinship relations. This view holds that relatives are not in a position to provide the solidarity and material support of kinsmen as occurs with traditional societies. Nowadays, except within the immediate family, we do not interact with relatives primarily or nearly as often as we do with others. Contacts between kin are tenuous and relations are maintained mostly through exchanged greeting cards, telephone calls, and occasional get-togethers. Relatives rarely offer us goods or services at discount prices; we do as well shopping around or relying on friends and other contacts. We do not depend on kin to provide our children with summer employment or assistance to meet college tuition and related costs. Still, Americans believe that relatives may be relied on at times of need.

If relatives are useless or unimportant for instrumental or utilitarian purposes, they remain significant, as Ayoub shows, because they exist. That they are there appears to be their primary raison d'être. We take comfort in the sense of belonging, they to us and we to them. They represent part of our "roots," our origins, and give us a sense of identity more intimate than we get from our other social personas. As much as Americans like to believe in freedom of choice and in establishing social intimacy on the basis of an other's intrinsic qualities and worth, they also recognize that relationships with friends, neighbors, colleagues, and workmates are not as enduring as ties of blood and do not carry the same moral weight. Thus kin are needed, and people drive hundreds of miles to share a day's picnic with distant cousins, some of whose names are unknown or hardly remembered.

Although Ayoub does not extend her conclusions to suggest why Americans desire and maintain wide family connections, it is due very likely, as Plotnicov and Silverman suggest in the chapter following Ayoub's, to the conditions of modern society, with its multiple social institutions, and social and geographical mobility, among other things. Under such conditions, primary group relationships are narrowly circumscribed and are constantly being eroded. As a result, most of our social relationships are not sufficiently stable or personal.

Studies of ethnicity in the United States have tended to emphasize the significance of large-scale social, economic, and political processes to account for the demise or endurance of hyphenated-Americans. It has been shown that, after arriving as immigrants, such groups search out economic opportunities and employ ties of common origin to create or occupy economic niches. This has created some stereotypic impressions, such as the Irish as police, the Greeks operating restaurants, the Welsh digging coal, and the Italians cutting hair and repairing shoes. American urban politics has traditionally stressed the "balanced ticket"—a slate of municipal candidates designed, not to represent varieties of political philosophy, but to draw local ethnic votes. Whereas fifty years ago sociologists were confidently predicting their extinction, American ethnic groups have shown unexpected resilience. Perhaps in response to the success of blacks in the civil rights movement of the 1960s, immigrant groups from Europe have mobilized for political lobbying at all levels of government, a phenomenon aptly referred to as the rise of the unmeltable. Polish jokes to the contrary, it may even be fashionable now to be ethnic and display ethnic pride, as does Garrison Keillor with his homespun humor about Scandinavians in Minnesota.

Few studies of American ethnicity, however, have taken the perspective of the individual in order to learn what is personally derived from ethnic identification. Whatever the reasons for this, intimate views of the inside have largely come through fiction. The articles of Glazier, and of Plotnicov and Silverman, enter the gap and show that even when ethnic solidarity appears to wane, it still has importance for interpersonal relations. Plotnicov and Silverman ask why this is so and suggest that shared ethnic identity offers a primordial sense of belonging in social contexts where people do not know one another as whole persons, and where the basis for their coming together is formed only in terms of the relevant institutional roles they perform.

In contexts like schools, businesses, factories, markets, hospitals, and heterogeneous neighborhoods, references to common ethnicity or other shared characteristics personalize impersonal relationships that otherwise have little in common beyond the fact that the individuals have been thrown together by chance. In such circumstances, people prefer to season their everyday greetings and predictable conversations with an occasional reference to their common ethnic identity because it distinguishes the *we* and *us* from the crowd, highlighting what is shared that the rest lack. As the authors point out, people will focus on anything that establishes a personalizing connection based on some common interests or traits. This is why people at work chit-chat about the progress and prospects of the local athletic team they root for, and why strangers at a social event, or when traveling or vacationing, will search for their common ground and feel more at ease once it has been found.

Americans do not bestow nicknames on everyone, and their full social and historical significance has still to be determined. They are prominent among professional athletes and popular entertainers like jazz musicians, and prevail for boys and young men in urban black ghettoes, yet have disappeared from other neighborhoods, such as that described by Glazier. Some of us are old enough to remember with fond nostalgia the color and richness that nicknames lent to our street lives. If, for example, one's schoolmates and street pals include several "Jacks," rather than use surnames, is it not preferable to distinguish among them with endearments like "Turk," for a large hooked nose, or "Blubber," for generous size and a propensity to whine?

What is in a name, a nickname? Glazier says that it offers personal recognition by calling attention to physical, social, and other attributes. Thus "Cob," apparently, was too poor to afford toilet paper. Nicknames can also bestow honor, for the same Cob is mythologized as the one who could race the length of an entire street without his feet touching the ground (by leaping from roof to roof).

As Glazier reports, the affection and bonding connoted by nicknames make their continued use endearing to older men who have maintained ties with boyhood friends, much to the chagrin and annoyance of their wives. Perhaps these men continue to employ their boyhood nicknames out of habit; perhaps it also evokes a proud past of adventure and daring feats. Perhaps, finally, it is symbolic of their bittersweet success in achieving middle-class status, but at the expense of losing the *gemeinschaft* quality of the first- and second-generation immigrant community in America.

The Family Reunion[1]

Millicent R. Ayoub

>>> <<<

IN RECENT YEARS, anthropologists have begun to look at the nature of kinship in complex industrialized societies and at the theoretical implications of the principle of cognatic or nonunilinear descent (Davenport 1959; Firth 1956; Murdock 1960; Pehrson 1954; Schneider and Homans 1955). The present paper reflects both these developments. It takes a single phenomenon, the regularized reunion of cognatic kinsmen in the United States as a convenient vantage point from which to look at the specific American formulation of this principle of descent.

In the United States, kinsmen who live in different places sometimes assemble for a more or less formal celebration which, in composition and procedure, seems to typify the kinship system for both the observer and the participants themselves. The celebration is termed a "family reunion," or alternatively a "family picnic" or "get-together." The family reunion is a summer event frequent in the rural areas of the Midwest.[2] Our focus is on its occurrence in southwestern Ohio.[3]

The study is based upon three types of material. The more important consists of intensive interviews with some 63 persons native to the area;[4] these interviews were loosely structured, and the informants were encouraged to say whatever they wished about the subject. In addition, with an assistant, I attended and participated in several reunions of each type. Consultation of old and current newspaper files constituted the third source of information.

It is surprising that an event so common to the Amercian Midwest scene has received so little attention from anthropologists, sociologists, social psychologists, and social historians.[5] Writers of regional fiction occasionally pay attention to the more dramatic events, although I have found only three explicit references: Bromfield (1933), Miller (1929), and Seewald (1961). There are few studies of comparable phenomena elsewhere in the United States, with the notable exception of the work of Leichter and Mitchell (1960) on associations of kinsmen formed by urban Jews. Studies of urban people by sociologists, e.g., Dotson (1959), Komarovsky (1946), and Litwak (1960), are relevant, although the associations described lack two prime characteristics of Ohio reunions: periodicity and the basis in kinship.

Family Reunions as a General Class

The family reunion is an annual assembly of approximately 50 persons, more or less, who gather together one day each year on the basis of sharing a cognitive image of descent from the same ancestor or ancestress. The cognatic links which obtain among these people, or between any one of them and the putative ancestor, may be said to be the links of the surviving personal kindred of the apical ancestor.

A family reunion has a number of typical features.[6] It is annual. It takes place out of doors (though with a shelter in case of rain) and hence usually in the summer months. The locale is often standardized within a small arc of freedom, i.e., in one or another state park or on school or church grounds. The date is regularized, e.g., on the first or second Sunday of a summer month, or on the Sunday nearest to the birthday of the posited ancestor. The reunion begins in the morning and ends in the late afternoon. Participants travel to the event by truck or private automobile. The afternoon is marked by a huge buffet meal provided by separate nuclear families but partaken of by everyone. After the meal a business meeting is held; its degree of formality varies with the level of organization of the kin group. Every adult may vote, and all are equally qualified for office. Family officers (president, secretary, and treasurer) are elected and serve for terms of one or two years. The date and place of the next year's reunion are decided upon, unless fixed by custom. After the business meeting, the men and children play games, while the women clear tables and talk to each other. Family relics and records of past reunions are displayed, and may be explained to new members of the group, who are nearly always children and new affines. Before departure, token prizes are awarded to individuals who have excelled in certain competitions. Notice of the event—its date, place, and estimated size and the names of new officers—is given by the secretary to the local newspaper if no reporter is present.

To understand the composition of a reunion, we should look first at its folk image, at what it claims to be. I was repeatedly told that the group sees itself as an assembly of the descendants of a single ancestor (or married pair of ancestors) and the spouses of these descendants. This is the cognitive map which the assembly holds and to which they ascribe their attendance. Hence it is a datum of which the anthropologist should be aware and "accept." The descendants of the focal ancestor have legitimate birthrights to the celebration. Spouses are admitted by courtesy and in their capacity as fathers and mothers of junior descendants, however significant their contribution to the events of the day may be. Attendance at a reunion may be restricted, but it is not compulsory and does not assume attendance in subsequent years. A kinsman is at liberty to participate one year, forego the next, attend again, or cease attending altogether. So long as a reunion group retains a quorum large enough to assemble, it is justified in meeting.

The foregoing remarks raise the issue of the type of kin group (if it is a group at all) which is being described, and with which among the many classifications of social organization this regular assembly of cognatic and affinal kinsmen may be aligned. Its classification must reflect its characteristics, notably its composition, shape, size, and purpose.

I start with the statement by Leach (1962: 132) that a group such as this, though it may be based on the ideology of descent, has only a potential membership: "For in such groups, not only is it the case that membership derives from choice rather than from descent ... the membership is at all times ambiguous." To "ambiguous" I would add "optional." Attendance at a reunion is always optional, and it is from this fact that it derives its ambiguity. Whether a person is or is not a member of the kin group which the reunion represents has to be reaffirmed each year. Although one may be "member" of the personal kindred of the reunion group's claimed forebear *in perpetuum*, such membership signifies the quality of category, not of bounded group. One cannot "belong" to another's kindred in the sense that one can join a club or be a soldier in an army. One is merely ascribed or not ascribed the quality of belonging to a particular kindred as well as to an unlimited number of other similar personal kindreds. Everyone at a reunion (except affines) is kin of everyone else by virtue, at minimum, of his filiation with the posited ancestor, and this connection is the organizing principle of the reunion.

For these reasons, the classification which seems most suitable is that of "occasional kin group" (Firth 1958). In their occasional concurrence at the time of a reunion, in the wide lateral extension of the status of kinsmen throughout the group, in their joint ownership of miscellaneous reunion equipment, and even in their welcome of spouses to the occasion, although not to the group, the appellation "occasional kin group" would seem best to comprehend the amorphous aggregation of people and purposes attendant upon the family reunion.

Types of Reunions

Three kinds of assemblies merit the designation of "family reunion." They differ in numerical size, in genealogical dimensions, and in formality of organization. Each type will be considered separately, beginning with the smallest and shallowest.

Sibling Reunion Type. The Sibling Reunion is the type which I formerly termed the Grandmother Reunion (Ayoub 1959) since it comprises a clustering of adult offspring about the person (or the memory) of their mother. The earlier term seems inappropriate inasmuch as it can also denote a mere dinner given for an extended family. Moreover, the core of what I now term a Sibling Reunion is not a grandmother in person, name, or spirit, but rather an axis of uterine siblings, her offspring. Paternal half siblings may also be reckoned as legitimate members, and commonly attend when the parent has remarried. (The criterion of shared residence during childhood seems to be operative here.)

The Sibling Reunion is a gathering of relatives three or four generations in depth, counting from the founding sibling axis as the first generation. In addition to siblings, it includes lineal kinsmen, commonly the siblings' children and grandchildren. Hence, in the descending generations it includes collaterals who are not siblings but first and second cousins to each other. It is the only one of the reunion types which can conveniently convene in a private home, although it may swell to a size where, as in the case of the other types, such intimacy becomes unwieldy. As long as it convenes in a private residence, this is usually the house of one of the first-generation female siblings or of one of their daughters. The surname of the owner of the house is not relevant to its use.

Rarely are both the father and mother of the siblings still living when the reunion is initiated. This usually occurs after the death of the mother, often several years later. Previously, they would have met as offspring, not as siblings, their primary solidarity being with the mother. Only with the loss of this pivotal figure do the siblings begin meeting in their own right. What is required, apparently, is the impetus of the maturity of the second generation, the siblings' own children, and the belated recognition on the part of the siblings that first cousins do not "know" each other as we, brothers and sisters, did when we were their age.

The Sibling Reunion is not, at least at first, verbalized as a reunion. It begins as "going to (sibling's name)," replacing the previous custom of "going to Mother's." The date of the reunion may coincide with the birthday of the departed parent because the family was accustomed to foregathering on this date. Sometimes it is determined by an outside event such as a national holiday, e.g., Memorial Day, when it was formerly thought that all should appear at the family plot in the town graveyard.

Unlike the other types, the Sibling Reunion has no formal organization. It lacks officers, a business meeting, dues, and record keeping. No speeches are needed to encourage group loyalty. So long as a parent remained in the parental home, the children's obligation to him as parent was sufficient to cement the group. If he or she has moved elsewhere, e.g., to the home of one of the children, the bond is reinterpreted as one of sibling unity in support of the parent-child bond.

Though lacking formal organization, the Sibling Reunion still shares several of the characteristic features of larger reunions. There is, for instance, the same emphasis on quantity of food separately provided but consumed by all, on gossipy talk, on the separation of the sexes after dinner, and on the unstructured games of the men and the children. One important difference may be evident. A Sibling Reunion offers an opportunity for extended family councils to discuss and resolve major problems. Backsliding children may be called to order and reproved. The support of aged parents may be discussed and settled.

The part which the male affine plays at a Sibling Reunion is crucial. His refusal to attend would imply a rejection of his wife, the sibling, not a mere disinclination which might be forgiven at a larger gathering. The Sibling Reunion is too small to tolerate only partial support. It demands personal attendance unless circumstances are truly beyond one's control. The performance of a female affine, a sister-in-law or daughter-in-law, is likewise weighed by her in-laws. They appraise her performances as mother and wife and watch her measure of success in bringing her husband over to her family's side. Should she not appear when her husband does, this may be interpreted as implying a break in their marriage, which is not suggested by a man's nonappearance with his wife.

It is difficult to fix the Sibling Reunion in the flow of time because to do so would call for stopping the clock at precisely the moment when the reunion has passed from the stage of "going to Mother's" and before it has been transformed into what would be more accurately termed a Cognate Reunion. The life span of a Sibling Reunion depends on the vitality of the original female siblings. So long as they live, the gathering remains a Sibling Reunion, but it may terminate on their death unless the cousins in the second generation wish to continue meeting as the descendants of the parents in the focal sibling axis. If they follow the latter course, their meeting is transformed into a Cognate Reunion type. Reunions of the Cognate type can also arise in other ways, e.g., in imitation of other reunions or from the segmentation of a larger Name Reunion group, but spontaneous generation is unlikely, if not impossible, without some prior form of organized sibling unity.

Name Reunion Type. The Name Reunion is also a meeting of persons (and their spouses) who have an ancestor in common. However, the links to this ancestor and with each other are here greatly attenuated and have moved beyond the knowledge of all but a few amateur genealogists.

The most striking feature in this type is its exhibition of a telescoped rather than an expanded pedigree. The figure regarded as the founder of the line is known by name, but his children are either forgotten or specified only vaguely or incompletely. The pathways from the founder's offspring may be remembered and charted, or perhaps one or two may be selected and their background distorted at the pleasure of the descendants or their hired genealogist. This practitioner may sell the family a bowdlerized edition of a family history or a romanticized pedigree which takes the founder back to a particular hearth in Europe. For example, one of the families in this study proudly displays a history book purporting to trace the family's origin back to a Viking raid on the coast of Normandy; the book then moves through several centuries of minor noblemen to an emigrant to the New World. The informant does not say that he believes or rejects this account; he merely claims, with a jolly agnosticism, that some such person living in the twelfth century may have fathered children who in their turn could have been his own ascendants.

A Name Reunion is often too large for most of the farms, churches, or school grounds which offer ample space for a smaller Cognate Reunion, and for its meetings it may consequently rent the fair grounds or utilize space in a state park. Such a reunion normally includes kinsmen at least as distant as fifth cousins. The lineal depth of seven generations which this implies, however, is less significant than its lateral width. Though they value closeness of relationship, the participants stress the tracing of kinship to the widest extent possible.

What is most remarkable is the faithfulness with which the participants sustain the idea of such attenuated connections, even though no one but a professional genealogist would dare attempt to reproduce them. They accept his statement of their pedigrees on faith. It is sufficiently gratifying to associate with several hundred others at a Name Reunion, knowing that the fact of inclusion affirms their kinship, no matter how remote or fragile this maybe.

Often I have heard talk of lines of descent which diverged after the forebear and have observed the emergence of loyalties to new segments of old lines. These junior lines begin holding separate and smaller reunions, perhaps offering a perfunctory nod to the parent group, which continues meeting as before. At first, the new sections are likely to be too shallow in lineal depth and too narrow in lateral spread to lose track of their previous assciations, and they should probably be classed with Cognate Reunion type. The precise time of such swarming is not immediately apparent and must be inferred from its occurrence after the fact.

The proceedings of the Name Reunion resemble those in the model, though greatly magnified in all dimensions—more participants, more food, more noise, more games, and a more formal business meeting, with more obvious competition among the candidates for the posts of family officers. Being an officer in a Name Reunion group may bring political, financial, and social rewards extending beyond the bounds of the family unit.

When the size of the group may be counted in the high hundreds, as is often the case, it begins to take on the complexion of other large, outdoor festivities such as a town Independence Day picnic, a county fair, or a political rally. In the effort to counter this disturbing tendency, the theme of "family" is emphasized. The family is exalted as unique and precious. "It has had a shining past, a splendid and optimistic present, and shall have a glorious future with no end in sight." It is converted, in other words, into an objective entity. Such reification permits individual accomplishments to be lauded by the group. Such laudation is reflexive; by applauding the family, people applaud themselves as its members.

It follows from this that a Name Reunion needs objects to dramatize the family theme. The emphasis is placed, not on a single person or descent line, but rather on the one thing which all may claim to share: the family name. Emphasis on the name distinguishes the reunion from other large assemblies and affiliates it with the smaller family reunions from which it is probably derived. Prominence is given to physical objects which remind the group of its past. A few examples may be cited: a huge family pedigree painted on paper of poster size; a privately printed family history book; an album containing clippings of news stories on the achievements of family members; photographs of the rude houses in which their ancestors lived long ago. Such items are displayed year after year, and their freshness seems to thrive on the new kinsmen who examine and extol them. Children are told: "This is your Great Uncle Lafayette; he used to own half the state." New fiancees are lectured: "This is your Great Aunt Mary; she had ten children, and most of them lived." Young men are shown soldiers in dilapidated uniforms and told of their wartime exploits. Further specification is unnecessary; the kinship terms "uncle," "aunt," and "great" are conveniently susceptible to multiple definition. That such family culture heroes may be sham should not concern us any more than it worries the participants.

A Name Reunion may expand in size and increase in complexity to the point that it acquires a genuine corporate entity. The kin group may own property, even if only the land on which it holds its reunion. It may open a bank account under the group's surname or in some cases be actually incorporated (cf. Mitchell 1959: 126). The president of the family may become the chairman of the board, and other family offices may be established.

When it reaches this stage of development, the Name Reunion has lost all but the charter myth of cognation. The John Smith Reunion becomes the Smith Reunion, and all bearers of the Smith surname are encouraged to attend—an open invitation qualified only by the concurrence of the surname and a geographic region. Since towns and counties often bear the name of the dominant families which have inhabited them, the Name Reunion verges toward a town or county reunion, which might be argued to constitute a fourth major type, although I do not suggest this.

An alternative development of the Name Reunion grown large is to attract or join other kin groups in other regions with whom some kinship connection can be imagined or reconstructed. Thus one of the groups studied in Ohio asserts linkage to people in three adjacent states, in Canada, and in Great Britain. Before learning the possibilities of an international organization in the last decade, the Ohio group met only yearly. Since then it has met biennially in one of the four states or Canada and in so doing has lost the identification (i.e., reunion attendance) of its less cosmopolitan members. These latter now hold new, smaller reunions under a similar name. Two years ago the splinter group sent a single token "delegate" (my word) to the parent reunion. Last year only greetings were sent. This defection is openly resented by members of the larger group, but it is understood and may be imitated. I suggest that one of the effects of overorganization is its opposite—disorganization and fission. In our cognatic kinship culture, only a professional genealogist can command knowledge of a large family's history and present composition. What began as a family reunion in the minds of its organizers has become something different and thus moved beyond the scope of our inquiry.

Cognate Reunion Type. Intermediate between the other two types in numerical size, lineal depth, lateral width, and intricacy of organization is the Cognate Reunion. This name was chosen most reluctantly and reflects the paucity of established terms for groupings of nonunilineal kinsmen. Actually, the participants at a Cognate Reunion are no more cognates than are those at any of the other reunions, since they likewise include affines.

A Cognate Reunion commonly includes from 75 to 200 participants. Its core consists of consanguines, but some of those who attend are the spouses of these kinsmen, and some are the spouses of consanguines who are deceased or not present. Even friends and neighbors, who look upon the event as a picnic, may occasionally attend. Generational depth from the putative founder runs from five to ten generations, as compared with fewer than five at a Sibling Reunion and more than ten at a Name Reunion. It is not the lineal dimension, however, which best distinguishes the Cognate from the Name Reunions, but rather the sense of an obligation to maintain personal acquaintance with all the other participants, which seems to be dissipated with a lateral spread in excess of ten degrees. All pathways of descent from the common forebear are theoretically adjudged equal. Neither the male nor the female line, nor any combination thereof, is deemed the more legitimate, nor does the fact that one's surname is the same as that of the reunion group confer an advantage. Any Smith is as much a Smith if his mother, Mrs. Robert Jones, was born a Smith.

A Cognate Reunion meets in a public park, on school or church grounds, or, if small, on the farm of a participant. Everyone eligible to attend is notified by postcard, unless a traditional date and place have been previously established. The following are quotations from early newspaper accounts:

> The Ogburn family reunion was held at the usual place west of town on Saturday. There were one hundred eighty present.... (*Wilmington Journal*, September 2, 1902)

> The McClellan family reunion and picnic was held yesterday at the Fauber School house about four miles from Xenia. About two hundred members of this large family were present and were treated to a fine dinner and a very enjoyable day, games and social amusements occupying the time. (*Xenia Gazette*, August 13, 1897)

> The twentieth annual reunion of the Corry family was held—a hundred people—of course they were not all Corry by name, most of them conscious of the Corry blood in their veins, but most of them were, and those that were not linked to it by the tie that binds, or attracted there by the good dinner provided social converse by all the men talking about wheat, oats and cattle and their culture and with a little politics thrown to spice it, while the ladies talked—the range was so wide that we give it up. (*Xenia Gazette*, August 13, 1886)

As at all reunions, food is brought in large picnic baskets and hampers. From all descriptions, it is the abundance of the meal which is paramount. Baked hams, fried chickens, and noodle and bean casseroles appear as main dishes; molded gelatin and potato salads are usual; summer dessert is the cook's glory—fruit pies and lofty cakes, luscious berry puddings, and wine-soaked trifles. German and Scottish are the chief ethnic strains, and are reflected in the menu. Some representative quotations follow:

> ... masses of pie and cake, roast turkey and ice cream.... (Bromfield 1933: 135).

> Large and perspiring women bake for days cakes and pies to be consumed ... a sentimental debauch, a grand gorging ... while the heart throbs the stomach is working over-time. (Stearns 1922: 294)

The women who cook food at a Cognate dinner are easily identified by name. At a Sibling Reunion, by contrast, the sisters and sisters-in-law routinely divide the courses, each doing what she and the others agree she does best, and at a Name Reunion there are too many people serving and eating to link any dish with the cook. Only at the Cognate Reunion does a cook have the chance to be praised for her production. As one walks between the tables, he may comment on the food in the hearing of its maker, for example: "Here's Aunt Mary's peach crumble pie. I remember when I used to call it 'peach crummy pie.' Please make it for Francy's wedding, won't you? I'll tell her you'll be doing it."

Before the group disperses, prizes are awarded to individuals for achievement in competitions which by their nature are noncompetitive; the winner is known before the race is run. For example, awards are given to the oldest and youngest persons attending the reunion, to the parent who has brought the most children, and to the kinsman who has traveled farthest to attend the celebration. The peculiar nature of these "competitions" reveals the latent significance of the reunion for its participants. Since achievement is rewarded for winning contests which are paradoxically not contested, everyone knows that no charge of favoritism can be leveled against a winner nor any hint of prejudice against a runner-up. If a mother with nine children loses to someone with ten, she may win the next year. No prizes are awarded for the best food in any category. Only at a county fair, where the contestants are unlikely to be kin, would such personally threatening rivalry be permissible. Where all are relatives and it is this fact which is being celebrated, no one may be adjudged superior in any regard lest the harmony of the reunion group be disturbed.

The charter myth of the occasion is enacted in the distribution of awards. The honor paid to the very young attests the survival of the kin group. The effort of the individual who has made the longest journey demonstrates the intent of the occasion and thereby of the group itself. The honor accorded the parents who have brought the most children is similarly symbolic; they have helped to perpetuate both the reunion and the kin group. Announcements are also made of noteworthy accomplishments by family members, such as winning awards at a county fair in cooking or farm skills and earning a high-school or college letter for athletics. Here the intention is different but not contradictory.

The business meeting held at every Cognate Reunion is enacted as a parody of the formal meeting of any business or association. The president, who officiates, must contend with gibes from the assembly who scoff good-humoredly at the spectacle of a familiar figure appearing in a formal role. The secretary reads the minutes of the last meeting, which are accepted without question. The treasurer—or if there is none, the secretary—notes the amount of the funds in the family treasury. Normal expenditures include the rental of the reunion grounds and the sums spent for coffee and soft drinks and for flowers sent by the group to members in the hospital. If the invalid is in need of blood, an appeal may be made for donors, although these are more often members of the nuclear family.

The term of office is either one, two, or three years, and when tenure has expired new officers are appointed, elected, or chosen by universal acclaim. The president is usually elected, but the posts of secretary and treasurer are often held by a middle-aged spinster who has had some office experience, although she may have to be jokingly induced to accept the appointment by the promise that "when she gets married" another will succeed her. During World War II appeals were made at the business meeting for letters to family members in the armed forces, and answers received were read aloud. Attendance figures may be announced, though sometimes the secretary who gives them to the newspapers estimates the statistics.

After the business meeting, it was formerly customary to hold an informal talent show, at which small children were urged to sing and recite or adolescents to play musical instruments. In recent years, however, this mode of entertainment has declined in frequency for the alleged reason that television and the movies have made such amateur performances seem ludicrous. The sexes now separate—the men for "men talk": their occupations; number of acres plowed this year; number of lambs born; cattle sales; politics; and general gossip—the women for "women talk": housekeeping; number of jars canned and put away; number of babies born; gynecological problems; and gossip. Advice is freely and sometimes gratuitously given. The younger men and boys play ball and pitch horseshoes; the younger women and girls take care of the babies and small children.

An effort may be made to increase attendance the following year through a rallying speech by the president or by a respected elderly member of the family. These speeches stress group unity but do not specify the reasons for its value. Among these, the role of group cohesion in the socialization of children is deemed especially important. What is left unsaid, and is perhaps unrecognized, is that reunions seem to be sustained for the benefit of the more elderly members of the group, with younger kinsmen attending out of respect for their parents and grandparents.

Life Cycle of Family Reunions

Family reunions exhibit a life cycle: their origin; their continuation, with or without interruptions; and their termination or reconstitution. The participants at a reunion may cite the reason for initiating the cycle, e.g., the seventy-fifth birthday of a pivotal figure, but they are usually more concerned with whether or not it should be continued. Should they, next year, expend the effort in leaving home, making preparations, and perhaps traveling a considerable distance for rewards which are at best intangible?

In general, once started, a reunion cycle tends to be perpetuated through cultural inertia unless some new force—either from outside the kin group, like a war, or from within, like a process of fission—intervenes to terminate it or change its direction. Sometimes it may be interrupted for a number of years and then revived by either the former participants or their junior kinsmen. In one recorded case a reunion which had stopped about 1909 was resuscitated in 1960.

It is not unusual at reunions to be told about, or overhear discussion of the possibility of, terminating the cycle. Rarely, however, is a reunion intentionally ended and its demise announced. Gradual erosion is commonly offered as an explanation of why a reunion is no longer being held or attended: "People just left off coming." This may be accompanied by criticism of others. Thus one woman explained the breakup of her family reunion in these words: "My daughters just don't go any more; I used to take my brother's son, but then I thought it was his mother's job." (Note that an affine is accused of failing in the duty of supporting her husband's kin group.)

Names of Reunions

The name given to a reunion is commonly the patronym of the founder or founders of the family or families which it celebrates. It takes one of the following forms: the Smith Family Reunion, the Smith Reunion, the John Smith Reunion, the John and Mary Smith Reunion, the Smith-Jones Reunion, or the Smith-White-Jones Reunion (rare). The form does not indicate either the type of reunion or the stage of the cycle which the group has reached.

Hyphenation, as in the case of a Smith-Jones Reunion, signals that two descent lines are celebrating together. This commonly results from the fact that some pivotal female figure was a member of both groups, one by birth, the other through marriage, but it may also occur when two originally independent pioneer families have become linked through the marriage of the son of one to the daughter of the other. Sometimes people, especially males, resent the secondary position of their name. In the case of the Black-Jones family reunion, for example, one old man complained:

> Like in our family there were too many girls, and they all went and got married, Now there are hardly any Joneses left but me. That's why I nominated Mary Gates to be secretary. Her grandmother was a Jones, you know. The Blacks all came from the Joneses anyway. The first Black married a Jones.

A name like John Smith Reunion does not necessarily connote the reunion of a subgroup within a larger Smith family. In such a case it is more likely that the name will be changed, e.g., to the Smythe Reunion. New spellings of this type are frequent and often signal a past or future cleavage in a kin line. Fissiparousness is typical of the reunion complex. Despite proud boasts to the effect that "this is the fiftieth annual reunion of the X Family," it is probably the fiftieth reunion of only one part of an original X family, the others having broken off, moved away, lost interest, or died out at various times.

A name of obviously non-English origin may be Anglicized so that its spelling will better accord with standard English usage. Thus Wulf or Wolff or Wolfe becomes Wolf, or Kuntz is changed to Coons. Alternatively the idea of a new spelling may connote an alteration in the social-class status of either the whole kin group or one section of it. The greater Wulf family may see itself as having risen above that spelling and decide to alter it to Wolf. Or a subgroup may come to believe itself better—i.e., richer, more fashionable, better educated, more "American"—than its relatives and hence adopt the more British spelling of the name.

The news story of a reunion in the local press may enhance the significance of the event. To see one's name in print, perhaps in a report of the election of family officers, can be gratifying, especially to people who otherwise receive newspaper notice only on life-cycle occasions such as high school graduation, marriage, and death.

Affines at a Reunion

Because family reunions in the United States bring together kinsmen linked by both paternal and maternal bonds, the position of the nonconsanguines who attend merits consideration, particularly in the case of a Cognate Reunion. An individual is privileged to attend a reunion as an affine without necessarily being accompanied by someone who is a genuine member of the group, e.g., his spouse or an offspring of their marriage. The status of affine is in itself sufficient to explain and justify his attendance.

In keeping with the patronymic bias of American society, the status of an in-marrying wife is that of an appendage with little structural significance in the social organization of the reunion, except, of course, in her feminine roles as caterer, scribe, historian, or the like. She figures primarily with respect to her reproductive capacity—as a funnel through which the line may or may not continue.

The in-married husband, on the other hand, presents a problem. He contributes a second patronym. He is the representative or potential founder of another descent line, affiliation with which is as legitimate for his offspring as is that with their mother's line which is featured in the reunion in question. His attendance presents the reunion with the traditional dilemma inherent in the dual statuses of affine in one context and consanguine in another. It compels the group to recognize the fact of his separateness and to attempt a resolution of the problem it poses.

A Cognate Reunion group may counter this threat by stressing the bilaterality of its composition, by treating alike the descendants of all the men who have married female members of the group. It may, for example, emphasize given names rather than surnames, so that John is reckoned as a Smith even though his surname happens to be Jones. Thus one early account (Porterfield 1932: 45) describes "... the annual Porterfield reunion, sixty-five human beings. Everyone a Porterfield at heart even if the marriage of daughters has corrupted the name."

A Cognate Reunion group can function adequately without the presence of kinsmen bearing the name of the reunion, and often does so. The slate of family officers may include only affines or the children of a kinswoman and an outsider. Sometimes a youthful reunion tries to limit its presidency to persons bearing the family name, but after a dozen years or so this ideal is usually surrendered.

At a reunion, males and females behave according to the standard expectations for their sex, regardless of whether they are consanguines or affines. The second-class status of affines becomes evident only in feeble joking during the nominations for family officers or perhaps in reminiscences of other reunions. When the cessation or continuation of the reunion is under consideration, the affines remain silent.

Reasons for Attendance

The decision to attend one reunion is commonly a decision not to attend another reunion. Attendance at one implies at least temporary rejection of another and of the kin group which it represents. Paradoxically, the necessity for making such a decision carries with it the implication that one must act to join a group of which one has been a member since birth.

Since an individual is linked to his various kinsmen through the multiplicity of genealogical pathways which converge on him, it is theoretically legitimate for him to participate in all the reunions which celebrate these converging descent lines. That he does not attend them all, that he chooses some and omits others, is a matter of expediency. He must ration his time and effort; it would commonly be quite impossible to participate actively in all the kin groups to which he has potential entree.

Not all families in the area hold formal family reunions, but all are aware of the practice, and hence the potentiality exists. Each summer an individual is faced with the choice of adherence to one of several lines of descent represented by the several reunions open to him. Filiation presents the field of choices but leaves open the option to be exercised.

When the question "Why do reunions exist?" is posed to a consistent reunion-goer, the typical reply is: "Because we want our children to be known by their relatives." What does this statement say about American kinship?

In the first place, on the negative side, the statement does not say that children should be indoctrinated in the mores of family culture, as may be the case in more primitive societies, nor does it assert that reunions are valued because of the opportunities they provide for the child to become acquainted with his distant kin. In fact, it actually implies the opposite, namely that the virtue of a reunion lies in one's adult relatives, the parents' peers, knowing one's child. As one old woman expressed it: "If we don't have a reunion, then their cousins would not even know the children. They would be lost to each other." As she spoke, she pointed to her own generation on the kinship diagram.

From the parents' point of view, reunions are a means of presenting the child to his relatives, of holding him up to remind them of his existence. Whether or not the child sees the matter in the same light is to them of secondary importance. There is perhaps an analogy to the coming-out party given a debutante to present her to society, that is, to the society composed of her parents' peers. That she is also being presented to her own generation is automatically assumed.

At a Sibling Reunion, unlike a Cognate Reunion, the child does not require such presentation. The group is small, and its kinship bonds are too fresh and immediate to need an explicit reminder. At a Name Reunion the group is much too large for the introduction of a single individual to have real meaning, unless he is a celebrity.

Those who attend a Cognate Reunion are very conscious of the service the celebration performs and argue that their reunion is worthwhile because it reintroduces kinsmen to one another. In effect, it repairs gaps in kinship bonds wrought by miles of distance or years of minimal contact, and none doubts that such repairs are praiseworthy. Reunions institutionalize kin relationships and transmute them into diffuse associations characterized by optative and casual friendship.

The reunion phenomenon makes debatable the oft expressed view that Americans neither know nor believe they should know kinsmen more remote than grandparents or first cousins. It serves as a mechanism for transmitting knowledge of distant kin to anyone who may be concerned. Reunions express and foster what I would call "a sentiment of corporateness." Although the data disclose no evidence of true corporate kinship groups, such as are reported, for example, from Africa, I would contend that family reunions provide Americans with one way of representing an aggregate of kinsmen to the outside and to itself as a unified kin group. Those who attend a reunion are no more a collection of kinsmen; they have been transformed into a kinship group. What concerns us is their conviction of corporateness, not whether or not they are in fact corporate.

Historical Background of the Family Reunion

On the basis of early records of reunions, family histories, and personal accounts by informants, I presume that the phenomenon had its origin early in the second half of the nineteenth century. The earliest newspaper notice encountered dates from 1872: "We had the pleasure of attending on Saturday last, the picnic annually made by these two large and influential families. More than two hundred were present, embracing grey head and many of them are aged men and women; young men and handsome maidens; and children of all sizes and ages" (*Wilmington Journal*, July 15, 1872, p. 5). That the practice is still older, however, is implied by a reference to a family's "twentieth annual reunion" in a newspaper story in 1886.

The family reunion has been called a rural phenomenon, but an argument can be made that it should more rightly be termed an urban phenomenon, despite its outdoor setting and the farmers who attend. This view regards the reunion as an expression of the city man's nostalgia for a youth spent on the farm, of his sentiment for his family's antecedents as farmers. After the Civil War, with the rise of industrialism, the farm population was sharply depleted, and farm living came to be disparaged. With time, however, there came a reaction and a resurgence of romanticism about farm living and farm people. Older people still on the farm made strong efforts to reassemble their city children for a day's token visit and used that day to bring together relatives who lived too far apart for frequent contact. Sentiments clinging to the family's pioneer homestead were reinvoked, and probably reinforced by the inevitable disillusionment with factory work and city dwelling which the farm youth were experiencing.[7]

A farmer's son could return to the farm for a family reunion, knowing it was only for a day and that his job in the town was not endangered. By communion in a pastoral setting with the associates of his youth, he may be reconvinced that there is goodness here and that it has been implanted in him as well. In the fulness of the feast before him he partakes of the body of the family and of the blood of generations dead or yet to be born. An account of one reunion (Porterfield 1932) expresses these sentiments as follows: "Cold ham such as the Republican packing houses know not, butter from cows that never kept late hours; vegetables that grow where men are men and women are content with their gender.... But the wisdom of this gathering! There was not hate hence there was pan-wisdom."

Content Analysis of Reunion Reports

Spontaneous reports of reunions reveal numerous likenesses; similar occasions, similar items of social organization, and similar kinds of people are described over and over. This repetition by its very monotony serves to confirm the general pattern. Nevertheless, certain differences were noted in the reports of adults and children, of males and females. These were isolated by subjecting 63 reports of reunions to content analysis by a modification of the technique described by Berelson (1954). The informants were classed into four groups: 20 men, 27 women, 9 unmarried boys (average age 13.6), and 7 unmarried girls (average age 12.5). Their verbal reports and my field observations were scanned for frequently mentioned subject matter, yielding 32 different topics, some mentioned by many informants, some by few or none. The data are presented in Table 1.

Comparing men with women, we note that men talked more about the formal business meeting, the election of officers, and the collection of money, and that, on the whole, they tended to grumble about the occasion. The women were more concerned with the size of the attendance and the regularity of the date. In addition, they and their daughters were more interested than the males in genealogical data. For the children, the plentitude of food clearly outweighed other subjects. The boys more often mentioned the playing of games and, like their fathers, complained of being forced to attend the celebration. In general, people seem to mention the aspects of the reunion which offer them the most personal gratification.

Reports of the three types of reunions reveal considerable similarity in the conceptualization of the event by the participants. The fixity of the

TABLE 1
CONTENT ANALYSIS OF REPORTS BY 63 PARTICIPANTS AT FAMILY REUNIONS
(in percentages by sex and age categories)

Subject	Men	Women	Boys	Girls
Fixity of location	.95	.67	.89	.57
Fixity of date	.65	.78	1.00	.28
Number of participants	.35	.78	.33	.43
Size of meal	.35	.48	.89	.71
Family officer election	.60	.44	.11	.14
Games for men and children	.50	.30	.44	.29
Criticism of reunion	.40	.11	.17	—
Family treasury report	.30	.26	—	—
General talk	.30	.15	.11	.14
Display of family pedigree	.20	.22	—	.14
Distance traveled by participants	.20	.18	—	—
Entertainment	.15	.15	.11	—
Minutes of past business meetings	.15	.15	—	—
Propaganda for the family	.15	.07	—	—
Saying of devotions	.05	.07	—	—
Opportunity to see the very old	.05	.04	—	.14
News of the sick	.05	.04	—	—
Opportunity to meet one's "cousins"	—	.07	—	—
Talk about people	—	.07	—	—
Prize for oldest participant	—	.04	—	—
Prize for youngest participant	—	.04	—	—
Attendance counted	.05	—	—	—
Talk about sports	—	—	.11	—
Talk about politics	.05	—	—	—
National patriotism	—	.04	—	—

name, date, and place communicates a sense of permanence, despite the always changing composition of the kin group. The meal, as the most tangible feature of the occasion, is always elaborate. The games, the elections, the talk, and the paper sketches of the family pedigree are perishable incidentals. The dependable regularity of reunion events doubtless helps to explain why it is the very old who especially welcome these occasions and why it is said to be for their sake that reunion cycles are sustained.

Discussion and Summary

The family reunion replicates in miniature the American kinship system as a whole in at least these respects. First and most important, the composition of the reunion assembly assumes the equivalence of all lines of descent and thus expresses the ultimate in bilaterality. Second, it exhibits a fissiparous tendency; like many unilinear descent units, the nonunilinear reunion group from time to time splits apart and reforms in new but functionally complete segments. Third, the reunion complex reflects the theme of denial and choice. No individual is able to operate in the total framework of his kinship system, as seems to be assumed, for example, by Parsons (1954). At any one time he must select one or possibly two lines of descent and make good his claim to membership in them. Other equally legitimate lines have perhaps already been sloughed off by his parents, and still others he himself will in turn discard. Alternatively he may choose to dismiss his consanguines entirely and affiliate with the reunion group of his wife. Or he may damn both houses while retaining the kinship idea and found his own descent group.

The reunions an individual attends or avoids and the similar choices made by his near relatives determine the contours of his effective personal kindred and the kindred which his children will inherit. To operate efficiently or even to operate at all, a kinship system, like a language, requires the selection of a few significant units from a wider field of choice. Nature seems to abhor a genuinely multilineal system.

Although Sibling, Cognate, and Name Reunions have been considered as subtypes—possibly sequential ones—of a single general category of "family" reunions, it should be pointed out that only in the case of a Sibling Reunion have the assembled kinsmen constituted at any time an actual family. At Cognate or Name Reunions, the participants do not even pretend ever to have been part of the same family unit. They rather glory in their differences of origin and present residence, arguing that in this dissimilarity lies the strength of the kin group and the particular virtue of the reunion. They make no apology for the jagged outline of their table of organization. They consider themselves as constituting one family only in a mythical sense (cf. the definition of myth in Webster 1944: "A story, the origin of which is forgotten, that ostensibly relates to historical events which are usually of such character as to serve to explain some practice, belief, institution or natural phenomenon").

The bonds of affiliation with a reunion group are ambilineal—in a certain sense even unilineal, since an individual is linked with such a group through only one parent, either his father or his mother. Only in very aberrant cases is a person connected with a reunion group through both parents, owing to the state laws and folk beliefs concerning the mating of close kin.[8]

People speak, for example, of attending a reunion on the "mother's side," and this is how such attendance is conceptualized. Murdock (1960: 11) makes the same point: "Wherever kin-group affiliation is nonexclusive, an individual's plural memberships almost inevitably become segregated into one primary membership."

Long after kinsmen have stopped meeting as a reunion group, or indeed meeting at all, they seem still to preserve the image of themselves as members of a single collectivity. It is as if what has been termed the sentiment of corporateness outlives the group itself.

Finally, my study of the complex of family reunions in the United States suggests that, despite the absence of a formal ancestor cult and of unilineal descent, the charter myth of relationship based on filiation and affinity still succeeds in promulgating the acceptance of the blanket role of kinsmen among people who believe themselves to be so related and are willing to celebrate this premise.

NOTES

1. This investigation was supported in part by Public Health Service research grant MH 02705-04 from the National Institute of Mental Health. The work was done at the Fels Research Institute, Yellow Springs, Ohio. I am indebted to Ethel Nurge of McMaster College, to David M. Schneider of the University of Chicago, and to my husband, Victor F. Ayoub of Antioch College, for constructive criticisms.

2. To give the reader some indication of its frequency, the *Springfield News*, a morning newspaper in Springfield, Ohio, a city with a population of 82,720, printed reports of some nine reunions during the month of July, 1961.

3. Data on family reunions also came to my attention from several other states: Illinois (Jorgensen 1962), Indiana (Roger 1957), Iowa (Wallace's Farmer 1952), Michigan (Seewald 1960), Minnesota (Sister Mary Peters 1951), and West Virginia (Porterfield 1932).

4. The ages of those studied ranged from eight to about 70 years or older. Their occupations were typical of the area: farming; occupations accessory to farming, such as veterinary medicine, manufacture of farm machinery, or publication of farm journals; retail store management in small towns; factory work in nearby cities; the armed services; minor professional work such as school teaching. Their social-class levels would range from upper lower to upper middle.

5. The following sources contain relevant information: Poe 1929; Porterfield 1932; Stearns 1922.

6. The word "typical" is important. Nothing said in this paper is completely true for all family reunions. The modifier "usually" should be read before all statements of general fact. As this caveat is constant, it will not be mentioned again.

7. This interpretation of the origin of reunions was suggested by Louis Filler, Professor of American Civilization, Antioch College.

8. The marriage of first cousins is prohibited in the states of Idaho, Illinois,

Indiana, Kansas, Michigan, Minnesota, Nebraska, North Dakota, Ohio, South Dakota, West Virginia, and Wisconsin. The reason usually given is that it may produce deformed children.

BIBLIOGRAPHY

Ayoub, M. 1959. The Reunions of Large Occasional Kin Groups in the United States. Paper read before the annual meetings of the Central States Anthropological Society, Columbus, Ohio.
Berelson, B. 1954. Content Analysis. Handbook of Social Psychology, ed. Gardner Lindsay, 1: 489–522. Cambridge.
Bromfield, L. 1933. The Farm. New York.
Cooper, J. H. 1951. The Clan MacMillan 1750–1951. Fairborn, Ohio.
Davenport, W. 1959. Non-unilineal Descent and Descent Groups. American Anthropologist 61: 557–572.
Dotson, F. 1959. Voluntary Associations in a Mexican City, American Sociological Review 18: 380–386.
Family Reunions in 1952. 1952. Wallace's Farmer, Iowa Homestead, September 29, 1952, p. 66.
Filler, L. 1961. Personal Communication.
Firth, R. 1956. Bilateral Descent Groups: An Analytical View. Ms.
Freeman, J. D. 1961. On the Concept of the Kindred. Journal of the Royal Anthropological Institute 91: 192–220.
Jorgensen, K. 1962. Kinship Systems in a Middle Western Community. Unpublished dissertation, Ohio State University.
Komarovsky, M. 1946. Cultural Contradictions and Sex Roles. American Journal of Sociology 20: 42–47.
Leach, E. 1962. On Certain Unconsidered Aspects of Double Descent Systems. Man 62: 130–134.
Leichter, H. J., and W. E. Mitchell. 1960. Feuds and Fissions Within the Conjugal Kindred. Paper read at the Fifty-ninth Annual Meeting of the American Anthropological Association, Minneapolis, Minnesota.
Litwak, E. 1960. Occupational Mobility and Family Cohesion. American Sociological Review 25: 9–21.
Miller, N. 1929. Luella May: A Reunion. Detroit.
Mitchell, W. E. 1961. Descent Groups Among the New York City Jews. Jewish Journal of Sociology 3: 121–128.
Moore, J. 1940. All in the Family. American Home 24: August, 33–53.
Murdock, G. P., ed. 1960. Social Structure in Southeast Asia. Chicago.
Parsons, T. 1954. The Kinship System of the Contemporary United States. Essays in Sociological Theory, pp. 177–196. Glencoe.
Pehrson, R. N. 1954. Bilateral Kin Groupings as a Structural Type. Journal of East Asiatic Studies 3: 199–202.
Peters, Sister M. 1951. Farm Reunions. Land 10:70–72.

Poe, C. 1927. Don't You Want a Family Reunion? Progressive Farmer 42: xxxiii, 801.
Porterfield, A. W. 1932. In Patriarchal Fashion. Saturday Review 9: 45–47.
Roger, V. 1957. Personal Communication.
Schneider, D. M., and G. Homans. 1955. Kinship Terminology and the American Kinship System. American Anthropologist 57: 1194–1208.
Seewald, E. 1960. Family Reunion. Ms.
Shuey, D. B. 1919. History of the Shuey Family in America, 1732–1919. Galion, Ohio.
Stearns, H. E. 1922. Civilization in the United States. New York.
Townsend, P. 1957. The Family Life of Old People. Glencoe.
Webster's New International Dictionary of the English Language, 1944. Springfield.

Jewish Ethnic Signalling: Social Bonding in Contemporary American Society[1]

Leonard Plotnicov and Myrna Silverman

>>> <<<

THIS STUDY describes and attempts to explain a common behavioral phenomenon in contemporary society: the effort people make to find and express shared social and cultural attributes in order to enhance the basis for their relationship. This expressive behavior is described here mainly as it occurs among American Jews, with whom it often takes the form of telegraphing the fact of their shared ethnicity—a behavior we refer to as ethnic signalling.[2] This paper, then, has a dual purpose. On the one hand it points out that contemporary Jewish ethnicity carries important behavioral dimensions that have been ignored or unrecognized by social scientists. On the other hand it attempts to demonstrate that this ethnic behavior is but one expression of a general behavioral phenomenon whereby two or more individuals seek out and display cultural or structural elements they mutually share which provide them with an identity as a social unit and which distinguishes them from the institutional basis of their normal interaction.

Jewish Ethnic Identity and Ethnic Signals

Ethnic signalling is a form of ethnic identity, but as the expression "ethnic identity" has been a cover term for a wide range of phenomena, it is useful to explain how signalling differs from conventional usages. Regarding American Jews, the concept of ethnic identity has been conventionally employed by sociologists to provide quantitative measures of the degree to which individuals or sections of the population have maintained an active involvement in formal Jewish institutions (e.g., Dashefsky and Shapiro 1974; Goldstein and Goldscheider 1968; Lazerwitz 1970; Rosen 1965; Segalman 1967; and Sklare and Greenblum 1967). Their concern has been to assess measures of assimilation into American society according to the degree to which individuals manifest such traits as religious observance, formal training in religion and Jewish history, membership in religious and ethnic institutions, positive identification with the state of Israel, and the degree to which their attitudes conform to the ideologies of Jewish ethnic, religious, and national institutions. But we are not concerned here with how Jewish a particular individual is; instead, we wish to examine when, how, and why he uses his Jewishness. With ethnic signalling our focus shifts from these institutionally compartmentalized areas of contemporary social life, and from group behavior per se, to the behavioral components of ordinary social interaction, particularly in those social contexts that are not defined as ethnic or religious.

In another sense, ethnic identity refers to those attributes that are displayed volitionally or involuntarily by markers or significata that indicate an individual's assignment to a population socially defined as an ethnic group. Indicators of ethnic identity may be phenotypic—in some cases, as with Afro-Americans, Chicanos, Orientals, and American Indians, providing salient testimony—but more commonly are manifested in cultural traits like distinctive names, personal adornment, and, particularly in the case of Jews, religious emblems.[3] Some markers of ethnicity are not obviously indicative unless they appear together in recognizable configurations, as when given names and surnames, occupation and place of residence conform to ethnic modal or normative patterns. In addition, individuals display ethnic behavioral characteristics, most saliently in styles of speech, which are so deeply ingrained that they are performed without awareness.

Jews, for example, are unaware generally that they habitually use the greeting, "How's the family?" instead of enquiring about specific family members or using the phrase, "How's your family?" which are more commonly heard. Jews also tend to append to the greeting, "Have a happy new year," the additional phrase "and a healthy one." While American Jews fail to recognize many such traits as culturally distinctive, they are aware that some characteristics, such as the noise level of conversation, certain gestures, proxemic habits,[4] and expressions like "What's new?" or "How are things?" ending with inflexions or preceded by "well" or "so", are idiosyncratically ethnic and refer to these and other more subtle traits as "talking Jewish." Although these speech patterns are usually unconsciously employed they may also be deliberately expressed to signal ethnic identity.

While most identifications can be made with confidence, others remain uncertain, for the clues to a particular individual's ethnic identity are sometimes ambiguous. Whichever the case, whether to confirm an impression or to establish with certainty the identity of a stranger, many Jews tend to avoid the impolite, blatantly direct inquiry in favor of an indirect approach, such as a discreet question or remark that signals their own identification. They expect a stranger, if he or she is Jewish, to acknowledge this in reciprocal behavior. In such cases ethnic signals are mutually communicated.

Ethnic signalling, then, is the intentional display or indication of one's ethnic identification vis-à-vis specific others as part of the course of social interaction. It is not limited to intra-ethnic communication. Across ethnic lines one can, if one wishes, determine that one's own identification will not be misperceived and one can also indicate an awareness of the identity of others. Whether between different ethnic group representatives or within the same group, the expressive connotations conveyed with signalling vary. The intention of the message may be pejorative, positive, or affectively neutral. The examples we deal with here, however, are largely confined to ingroup expressions and most of these convey sentiments of common bonding. In some cases the intent of the bonding is instrumental, in others it is clearly expressive, and in many cases it is both.

For behavior to be regarded as ethnic signalling it, like speech, must be volitional, under conscious control, and aimed at specific targets. By these criteria the phenomenon may be distinguished from other indicators of ethnicity, more aptly called signs. The difference between the two is that signals communicate messages whereas signs merely carry evidence. The latter often require inference or interpretation.[5] Or, in concrete terms, a person may carry signs of Jewish ethnicity but not deliberately advertise the fact.

Some signs of ethnicity, such as phenotype or dialect, are entirely or almost entirely beyond a person's control. Others, such as distinctive dress or the use of ethnoreligious insignia, while deliberate and controlled, are indiscriminately broadcast and, in a sense, are substitutes for indelible markers. Still other signs, such as gesturing and styles of speech, are both involuntary and consciously controlled. We wish to stress that these are analytical distinctions; under empirical conditions it is sometimes difficult to determine whether a particular act is a sign or a signal.

We mentioned earlier that we are examining ethnic signalling in social contexts that are neither ethnic nor religioethnic. This is because ethnic signalling is absent within Jewish institutional contexts, as the setting itself ipso facto provides the identity of the participants. At a *bar mitzvah* or Jewish wedding the burden of properly identifying themselves, if they so wish, rests with the gentile guests. In Jewish ethnic and religious settings the Yiddish and Hebrew expressions and greetings, which in other contexts would be signals, are here prescribed. With synagogue participation, for example, one should greet others with *Gut Shabas* (good Sabbath) or *Gut Yontov* (good Holy day), as the occasion warrants.[6]

These prescriptions extend with diminishing force to the Jewish holidays and the ritual life-cycle rites of passage. On these occasions equivalent English expressions are permitted and are common. So much is this so that when an individual, upon being informed of a marriage, birth, or graduation, responds with *mazel tov* (literally "good luck," but better translated as "congratulations"), we may regard that as an event of signalling.

Thus, signalling should be seen as extraneous to the recognized purpose of a social encounter. Goffman (1974: 210) recognizes this phenomenon in a more general way. "In doings involving joint participation, there is to be found a stream of signs which is itself excluded from the content of the activity but which serves as a means of regulating it, bounding, articulating, and qualifying its various components and phases. One might speak here of directional signals."

Population and Research Methods

When informants are like the people one normally invites to dinner—when we study people who might just as well be studying us (Cassell 1977)—there is difficulty in achieving emotional distance from the subjects and there is the danger of taking for granted the population's cultural assumptions, thus losing the critical perspective of an outsider. One way out of this dilemna may be to measure and quantify, for, as Cassell (1977: 413) notes, "statistics help distance the observer from the observed." She wisely adds, however, that quantifying the unit by survey techniques simply measures what the researcher regards as significant and does not necessarily reveal the intrinsic nature of the population. We therefore chose for this study to employ traditional ethnographic field research methods, with participant observation as a central technique. This allowed us to observe both the regular rhythm of mundane social behavior and the ephemeral occurrence of ethnic signalling.

Indeed, were it not for our being natural members of the research population it is doubtful that we could have gained the kind of data described here. The behavior we are considering is difficult to observe in the conventional sense of participant or field observation, since, while repetitive, the phenomenon is temporally irregular. For the anthropologist to be present in a situation when signalling occurs is more a matter of chance than research design. Linguists concerned with the natural expression of speech face similar but not identical problems (Grimshaw 1971). For linguists the tape recorder and even the structured laboratory setting provide appropriate data. These instruments and techniques were not particularly useful for our purpose.

Our research began with a log of behavioral events that characterized Jewish ethnic identity in the interactions of those we observed and as these involved ourselves. From these observations we developed an interview schedule that probed the significant markers of ethnic identity and the modes used for communicating a shared bond of ethnicity. We conducted open-ended interviews with over 25 adult male and female Jews in Pittsburgh. Informants included people who had converted in and out of Judaism, those who identified with the three major Judaic religious sects, and others who did not identify themselves as Jews except through the accident of birth. All the informants are middle-class. Their occupations include independent businessmen (shopkeeper, manufacturer), professionals (physician, academic), blue collar workers, and managerial and sales positions. Those not employed include students, housewives, and widows. Their educational backgrounds range as widely, and there are approximately as many males as females in the sample.

During the period of research—approximately nine months—we came increasingly to focus on the events of ethnic signalling as they occurred in our own lives and as recounted to us by friends, colleagues, neighbors, and strangers. Whenever possible, we subsequently checked the accuracy of the described events with those involved or with witnesses, and we reviewed our interpretations of the underlying behavioral motivations with them and other informants. We were also sensitive to the issues of ethics and confidentiality that now confront researchers everywhere, and have taken all reasonable measures to conceal the identities of the persons described here and to acquaint them with the manner in which information obtained from them will appear in this report. Perhaps because the subject matter is innocuous, we received no objections.

While the events described here are not replicable, the mode of observation and analysis is. As unstructured as it often must be, it is particularly useful to anthropologists working in their own and, particularly, contemporary society. We agree with Goffman (1971), whose work ours resembles, that

> The method that often is resorted to here—unsystematic, naturalistic observation—has very serious limitations. I claim as a defense that the traditional research designs thus far employed in this area have considerable limitations of their own. In spite of disclaimers, the findings of these studies ... which emerge tend to be creatures of research designs that have no existence outside the room in which the apparatus and subjects are located.

What we have done is no radical departure from the dual perspectives anthropologists attain when conducting field research in alien settings. By including ourselves as informants or subjects for observation we have reversed the traditional fieldwork process. In order to see ourselves from an external point of view we have held up a research mirror that reflects our participation in the society in which we live.[7] This personal involvement is unavoidable as anthropologists move into studies of their own groups but it also has the advantage of revealing in greater depth and clarity those features of social and cultural complexity that otherwise remain nebulous and misunderstood.

Signalling Events

Among American Jews we do not know how many employ ethnic signalling in social encounters or how often they do so. Informants tell us that they do so habitually, and they acknowledge that they are sensitive to the emotionally imbued element of shared ethnicity in their social relations. From our observation the most common way Jews signal their ethnic identity is by using Yiddish and Hebrew words and expressions to season conversation. (As many of these expressions have become part of colloquial American English it is sometimes uncertain whether they are actually being used as signals.) But other forms of ethnic signalling occur and are so varied as to defy categorizing. Some signals are so subtle that they are perceived only by those sufficiently enculturated, their very subtlety permitting them to go unrecognized and unanswered, if that is what the sender or receiver wishes. Here are two such examples deriving from a dinner party.

A woman tells a group of strangers how she experienced a flat tire while driving to the cemetery the previous weekend. What she stresses as significant is that the same thing happened, in almost the same place, exactly a year earlier. She does not explain, however, that these breakdowns occurred on the weekend before *Rosh Hashanah* (the Jewish New Year), a time when Jews traditionally visit the graves of close kin.

Another woman introduces herself as Mrs. Skolnick. Someone asks her if she is related to the "show biz personality." The reference is to Menashe Skulnik, a Yiddish comedian well known to an older generation of American Jews, but virtually unknown to others. In this case the questioner had the option of pretending she meant some Hollywood or Broadway producer if the lady's response indicated she was ignorant of the Yiddish theater of the 1930s and 1940s. As it turned out, she said she was not related to "Menashe," thus reciprocating a signal.

Most cases, however, are less subtle or not subtle at all. As an instance, we were told how Mr. Kapp, a company sales representative, was trying to conclude an agreement. After a lengthy discussion, the potential client, Mr. Kane, asked Mr. Kapp,[8] "What kind of name is Kapp?" "The same kind of name Kane is," was the response, and the contract was signed forthwith. Another informant, also a businessman, said that he uses ethnic signals to close a sale because he feels that this makes customers trust him more. He added that he does this not with people who are his friends or steady customers but only with those with whom commerce and contact are infrequent.

The above examples and other instances suggest that one reason American Jews use ethnic signalling is to enhance a relationship, by bringing a common denominator of presumed importance, ethnicity, to a situation where such primordial sentiments should be irrelevant. While this is generally true, we may be more precise by categorizing the conditions under which signalling occurs into three types:

Type I: Beginning and fleeting relationships;
Type II: Maintaining or intensifying established relationships; and
Type III: Responding to situations of strain or stress.

These are analytical categories; empirical cases often apply to both types I and III and II and III. The typology is also based on function rather than form as the kinds of signalling employed for the different circumstances vary little by type.

Beginning and Fleeting Relationships. Ethnic signalling among Jews bolsters single-stranded, or contractual, relationships and for that reason is commonly associated with sales personnel, merchants, real estate and insurance agents, and lawyers. It is an investment for continued relations and implies a better rate of exchange. The two cases below show this.

After moving to another neighborhood, one of our informants went to the local pharmacy to fill a prescription. The proprietor asked if he were a new resident. That being confirmed, the proprietor welcomed him to the area and in the process of wishing him a happy and healthy stay used the Yiddish terms *gezund* (health) and *glik* (luck). In this case and the one following, the informant is convinced that he extended no signals.

The same informant had several months earlier been trying to buy a home and visited one for inspection with his gentile wife. The owners, an elderly couple, conducted a tour of the house. They gave no indication of their ethnic identity until the informant's wife returned alone to the garden for review. In her absence the owners repeated to our informant their earlier remarks about how well the house was suited for raising a family and living comfortably but this time they injected the terms *nachas* and *simcha* (Hebrew for "pride" and "joy"). It seemed to the informant and to us that the switch in linguistic style was timed with the wife's absence to raise and underscore the common ethnicity between the potential buyer and the owners, and to avoid possibly antagonizing the wife, whose sentiments regarding Jewish ethnicity were unknown and whose co-operation in purchasing the house was necessary. Had the signalling occurred in her presence, she might have been affronted by the impoliteness suggesting she was an outsider.

Thus ethnic encounters may be infused with an expectation for added advantage. Sahlins (1968) suggests there is an economic aspect to all social relationships, the economic nature depending on the closeness of the tie. "Thus from a relative, 'you can get it wholesale', and, from a close relative, perhaps for free" (Sahlins 1968: 81). At least among the Jews of our study, ethnic bonds appear like an extension of kin ties and thereby convey similar expectations for preferential treatment. But Jewish ethnic encounters are far from being exclusively instrumental; signalling is frequently intended to be nothing more than an attempt to be friendly, as the following instances illustrate.

At a summer evening cocktail party where most of the guests are academic, a university colleague chats with one of the authors. The colleague changes the conversation to ask if the author knows someone who can translate scientific Hebrew. She explains she is examining a dissertation and wants to check some references. Several people who have attempted this proved inadequate. The author offers some suggestions, most of which she has already considered.

Her companion, not previously known, volunteers that his knowledge of Hebrew is limited to *Ma nishtanah ha layla ha zeh* (Why is this night different from all other nights of the year?), singing this with the customary melody. It is the first of the four ritual questions asked usually by the youngest capable male child at the opening of the Passover *seder*, and for many American Jews is the only extended Hebrew phrase remembered into adulthood. It is a witty injection into the conversation. The companion has signalled his background and elicited the author's appreciative chuckle; a response which confirms the companion's assessment of the author's ethnicity.

Another instance of signalling for humorous and friendly, rather than instrumental, intent involved two businessmen. Mr. Schwartz, the owner of a manufacturing firm, had long dealt with a particular supplier and its sales representative, Mr. Boynton, who Mr. Schwartz did not know was Jewish. One day Mr. Boynton called Mr. Schwartz regarding an order the latter had placed. In the course of the conversation Mr. Schwartz began to sense that Mr. Boynton, despite his gentile name, might be Jewish and, when a problem arose regarding the suitability of substituting certain items for those which were not available, suggested that Mr. Boynton consult a *maven* (expert). To which the sales representative responded with a chuckle and then added a quip of his own to confirm Mr. Schwartz's suspicion and to provide the latter with the satisfaction of knowing that he had been dealing with a fellow Jew for years without being aware of it. The two ended their conversation with mutual joking.

The injection of ethnic signals in a conversation serves as a bonding agent, but when the signals are accompanied with humor they also ease the strain people experience when entering into a new relationship, as the next example also shows.

At the beginning of a new academic year, a university department held a social gathering. A newcomer to the faculty, a young Jewish man, introduced his Oriental wife to a senior faculty member, also Jewish, and the latter's wife, who clearly is not Jewish. After some small talk, the pauses in the conversation became increasingly long. Finally, the new colleague blurted, "Well?" Smiling, the older colleague responded, "Well?" To which the younger man immediately said, "*Nu?*" The first "well" probably was not intended as a signal but was taken as a sign and as an opportune time for the older colleague to ease the tension with a bit of joking. But the latter's "well" clearly was a signal, as it is a Jewish social trait to answer a question with a question. *Nu* (Yiddish for "well?" or "so?"),[9] indicated that the older colleague's signal was appreciated. In its simplest terms, the underlying message communicated is that the two men shared a common ethnicity. But it is also possible that this basis for additional bonding was enhanced by the fact that both men recognized that they were wed to women who are not Jewish, a matter of some significance with American Jews.

Our observations convince us that people attempt to bring into new relationships various threads that may tighten the bond—common network links, similar professional interests, tastes, and ideologies—and that there may even be a reluctance to signal their shared ethnicity. We sense that some hold back on signalling because they fear it might elicit a counterproductive response, as some people regard the intrusion of the particularism of common ethnicity into a relationship based on universalistic standards as inappropriate to the institutional context. Thus, some Jews resent attempts to involve them in ethnic signalling when they are acting in their professional roles. A case in point is when Jewish students at a university signal in an attempt to establish a preferential link between themselves and a professor and are rebuffed by what appears to them to be an antisemitic Jew.[10]

Maintaining or Intensifying Established Relationships. Ongoing social relationships require periodic infusions of vitality. This is accomplished with symbols expressive of solidarity, which may also be used to help raise the relationship to a new level. Since it is rarely clear which of these purposes is intended we have grouped the two aspects together. It seems reasonable to assume that people are far more concerned with keeping a relationship from weakening than with intensifying it since relatively few of a person's many ties are capable of being strengthened. Goffman (1971: 73) calls these maintenance rites, and they serve "to guarantee the well-being of the relationship. It is as if the strength of a bond slowly deteriorates if nothing is done to celebrate it, and so at least occasionally a little invigoration is called for. Thus our collectively timed ceremonials of Christmas and New Year's function as a reminder of the need for, and an excuse for the performance of, various supportive expressions. Individually timed ritual occasions, such as birthdays and wedding anniversaries, have a similar function."

So it is with American Jews, who have more than the usual number of ritual occasions for providing supportive expressions, including and involving ethnic signals. Signalling under normal circumstances is hardly memorable, being more like background noise; it is therefore not surprising that informants have difficulty recalling signalling events with relationships that have become routinized. Far easier is their recall of instances surrounding relationships being established or those being threatened with disruption. Most often, however, signalling occurs under routine circumstances where one of the parties reminds the other that Jewish identity is something they share, as in the following instance.

One Sunday afternoon, a man took his children to a neighborhood playound. There the children were joined in play by a friendly but unknown little boy who was phenotypically Nordic. He wore a sweatshirt marked "St. Edmund's Academy" and said his name was Andy. A couple came by, neighbors of the man and, like him, Jewish. They engaged in casual conversation and from time to time, the woman called out to Andy, whom she obviously knew. After a while, and for no apparent reason, she turned to the man and remarked, "Would you believe his [Andy's] name is Cohen?"

We earlier mentioned several instances where ethnic signalling took the form of in-group joking. Common with Jews, and probably common with all ethnic groups, in-group joking closely resembles one of the principal social functions of code-switching, as stated by sociolinguists. Bilinguals and multilinguals with the same background "share many common experiences and points of view (or they think they do or pretend they do) and therefore they tend to speak to each other in the language which represents for them the intimacy they share" (Fishman 1965: 70). On the other hand, the same social technique may be employed to maintain formality or social distance (Grimshaw 1971: 437). One need only to switch from one language to another in the reverse direction. Just as switching is a means of regulating social distance so, too, is signalling. If its use is a way of bringing people closer, its deliberate avoidance can have the opposite effect, particularly when bonding through signalling has been part of the background of a relationship and especially since social relationships do not maintain an even keel by themselves but periodically require some righting. This leads us to consider our third category.

Responding to Situations of Strain or Stress. Whether trivial or serious, disturbances are an inevitable intrusion into all social relationships. These vary in severity, of course, and need not necessarily threaten the quality or strength of a relationship. Even if they do, people do not always seek to maintain the relationship's equilibrium, or even to maintain the relationship. Our research indicates that when people invoke ethnic signalling to ease strained relations it is as a palliative against mild irritations and petty annoyances. We are cautious about this generalization, however, for our research was limited to observational opportunities that did not include serious relational ruptures. With fleeting relationships, in which superficial and ephemeral contacts would seem to be sufficiently governed by ordinary rules of politeness, ethnic signalling is manifest when one of the parties has cause to be upset. It is done as a form of stroking in the attempt to redirect the relationship on an amicable course, as we see with the next two examples.

One of our informants received the theater tickets she ordered but they were for the wrong date. She telephoned her complaint to the ticket agency, explaining that the ticket date was not only wrong but inconvenient. After obtaining our informant's name and address, the agency representative said she understood the problem perfectly, the date fell on a Jewish holiday. Then she introduced herself as Mrs. Rosenbaum, and promised to mail suitable tickets that day.

Another informant called a discount house about an appliance she had purchased, the delivery of which continued to be delayed. As he had on previous occasions, the dealer said he would determine and rectify the problem. Later that day, he telephoned to say that delivery would occur the following morning. Then he added, jokingly, "See, it pays to be a *nudge*" (possibly derived from *nudnick*, meaning "nuisance" or "pest").

The attempt to placate someone in an established and ongoing relationship is also frequently attended with ethnic signals, as the following cases illustrate. One informant observed that her husband's old friend, who normally does not employ Yiddish expressions, does so after he and her husband quarrel. Other informants provided similar instances.

One, for example, reported how a Jewish neighboring family and her own were frequently at odds over mutual petty annoyances. Invariably, the informant's complaints to the other family elicited conciliatory responses employing an abundance of Yiddish expressions to reestablish goodwill. A third neighbor of the two families, also Jewish, occasionally gossiped with the informant about the "un-Jewish" behavior of the other family, thereby expressing sympathy with the informant's plight but at the same time employing morality as a device for signalling.

Just as signalling can be used to express sympathy, as in the last example, it can be intended to elicit sympathy,[11] as in the next. One of our informants is a junior faculty member at a university. When he first visited the university to be interviewed for his position, he was coached by his sponsor on how to relate to the other faculty members in terms of their interests and peculiarities. He wanted to convey a good impression and tried to develop with each interviewer those lines of conversation he thought would establish ties of common interest. With a particular senior faculty person he remembered signalling his Jewish identity.

After he was hired, his relationship with the senior colleague developed favorably, but his relationship with his former sponsor deteriorated to a point where he felt that his position was threatened. At times when he felt insecure about this he approached his senior colleague for reassurance. One such time, he said, he went to this colleague to discuss his problem and employed his entire, but frustratingly limited, repertoire of Yiddish expressions in order to convey the depth of his feelings, to ensure a sympathetic hearing, and to solicit political support.

This last case provides examples appropriate to all of our types. The informant signalled at the start of a relationship, raised signals to maintain and strengthen that relationship, and was stimulated to signal when stressed.

Who May Not Signal

The word "may" is intended to be ambiguous to cover two unrelated conditions and two quite different categories of persons. One consists of those persons whom other Jews regard as falsely signalling because they are perceived as not being Jewish. For them to signal would indicate shared ethnicity which, according to the signs they carry or fail to carry, is not the case.

Two gentile women, who are not likely to be mistaken phenotypically for Jews, have become sensitive to these circumstances through having married Jewish men. One, a linguist, reports that she employs Yiddish phrases phonetically correctly and in the appropriate contexts to the consternation of some Jews and the amusement of others. But these are never taken to be genuine signals, or as indications that she defines herself as Jewish. The other tells us that when she first attempted to cook Eastern European Jewish dishes, Jewish tradesmen required her to provide an explanation. (These recipes require special cuts of meat and certain vegetables that can be obtained only in Jewish shops and are not purchased by gentiles who partronize these shops.) When she asked for the purchases by their Yiddish names (because the English terms were unknown or the translation awkward), she invariably was asked to repeat the request, then asked why she wanted the items, and, finally, how she came to know about such things.

Of course it sometimes happens that someone Jewish is mistaken for gentile by other Jews or that signals fall on deaf ears because someone is mistaken for Jewish or someone Jewish pretends not to be. We have among our informants former gentiles who have converted to Orthodox Judaism whose combination of incongruous attributes suggest that their ethnic signals may produce a dissonant reception among other Jews. How such persons are perceived is an intriguing question that, for lack of sufficient data, we cannot answer.

If some people are denied the right to signal because they are not Jewish there are others who, as Jews, choose not to exercise the privilege. From all we have said it might appear that ethnic signalling must emerge inevitably in the social interaction of Jews. This is not so. While signalling may be a right or privilege it is not an obligation. Jews may avoid signalling for many reasons, of which the following seem most important. When someone (1) chooses to dissociate himself from his ethnic identity in general or under social institutional conditions within which he deems the intrusion of ethnicity to be inappropriate; (2) avoids signalling in the company of other Jews out of deference to their presumed wish to avoid it; (3) wishes to be hostile or formal to someone sending signals as a friendly overture; and (4) wishes to communicate that an existing social tie is sufficiently strong so as not to require such external supports. Indeed, for the last point, signalling may be taken as an indication that one of the parties to the relationship is not so confident about its presumed solidarity.

In our attempt to answer the question of why some Jews do not signal, when in most other respects they may be expected to, we reasoned that if ethnic signalling provides indications of solidarity to social relationships then, in its absence, other kinds of signals or signs must do the same. This we think is the case, in support of which we provide the following examples.

One informant's neighbor and good friend does not signal. Relations between their families are excellent; the children play in each other's homes; the wives chat together, shop for each other, and lend and borrow items across the fence adjoining their properties, and dinner invitations are occasionally exchanged. The husbands provide mutual aid in house repairs, gardening, in freely lending and borrowing tools and supplies, and they also enjoy watching sports on television together, sharing special enthusiasm for the local professional football team. Each man has cherished hobbies and each ritually inquires of the other's progress on a particular avocational project. When this is not suitable they speculate upon the performance and progress of their beloved football team. We suggest that it is in the exchange of these social niceties that the two men acclaim their relationship.

We have not been able to isolate those factors that might provide an explanation for why some people shun ethnic signalling altogether. As far as we have been able to determine, nonsignallers do not differ in any socially significant characteristics from those people who normally signal. It appears that sociolinguists have not achieved better results with similar research. Gumperz (1970: 139) states, "While the usual sociological measures of ethnic background, social class, educational achievements, etc., have some correlation with usage rules, they cannot be regarded as accurate predictors of performance in particular instances." Gumperz (1970: 147) does suggest that "language usage patterns seem to depend on family backgrounds," but our data neither support nor refute this.

Ethnic Signalling as Sociolinguistic Behavior

It is apparent that ethnic signalling is a sociolinguistic phenomenon. But of what sort? To answer this we take direction from Gumperz (1964, 1970). It is obvious that people could not perform ethnic signalling unless they controlled cultural information that could form statements that can be correctly identified as signals. Some of these statements are part of an individual's speech repertoire. According to Gumperz (1964: 137–138):

> The verbal repertoire ... contains all the accepted ways of formulating messages. It provides the weapons of everyday communication. Speakers choose among this arsenal in accordance with the meanings they wish to convey.
>
> The verbal repertoire may consist of code-switching, style-shifting or both. Code-switching involves the optional use of two or more languages or dialects. Style-shifting refers to the use of variations within a language

or dialect by commonly agreed-on conventions which serve to categorize speech forms as informal, technical, vulgar, literary, humorous, etc.

Of the two, code-switching and style-shifting, it seems that signalling more closely resembles style-shifting.[12] This does not deny the similarity of intent or purpose between signalling and code-switching, for code-switching encompasses the use of a minority language "for informal, in-group, family interaction, while the majority language serves for communication with outsiders" (Gumperz 1970: 132). But code-switching is the accepted paradigm for bilingualism (Gumperz 1970: 131) and the people we described fall far short of being bilinguals. Their use for signals of a very small number of Yiddish and Hebrew expressions is better described by what linguists call foregrounding. Gumperz (1970: 136) states:

> Foregrounding in the most general sense of the term relies on the fact that words are more than just names for things. Words also carry a host of culturally specific associations, attitudes, and values. These cultural values derive from the context in which words are usually used and from the activities with which they are associated. When a word is used in other than its normal context, these associations become highlighted or foregrounded.

Foregrounding or highlighting, however, may also go unrecognized precisely because words are used in other than their normal context. It also fails to communicate when the signal is so esoteric or peculiarly local that the cultural associations are incompletely shared or not shared at all. In other words, not all ethnic signals are sufficiently universal to be correctly grasped by most members of the group. Those signals that are regionally or class specific or apply only to some social subdivision of the group will carry their message only to appropriate insiders. But even the more universal signals may be misperceived if they come unexpectedly, as in the following example.

One of our informants went to lunch with several Jewish friends at a restaurant. Nothing about the restaurant—its menu, location, or clientele—would suggest that the owner is Jewish, and our informant had no reason to consider that possibility. As the group moved toward their table they greeted mutual friends and paused to chat. Standing nearby, apparently having been conversing with these other diners, was the owner's wife, observing the interaction. During the meal she approached the informant's table and after making the expected inquiries concerning the meal remarked that she and her husband were old friends of the parents of the other diners greeted by the present group. In fact, they were members of the same country club, whose name she mentioned. The informant and her friends knew that this club catered to Jews but did not recognize it by its new name. Thus the signal was not received. They recognized that she was trying to indicate something to them but as they did not expect an ethnic signal in this setting, and as the woman did not appear to be Jewish, even her next attempt at a more universal ethnic signal was also misunderstood. She asked, "Where do you go for the holidays?" meaning "What congregation do you attend for the High Holy Days?" One responded, "We go to the shore." Another, however, correctly assessed the intent and said, "We go to the Temple," thus indicating her Reform affiliation. The owner's wife then mentioned the name of the Conservative synagogue to which she belonged, thereby underscoring the correct frame of reference.

Discussion

If ethnic signalling is a form of ethnolinguistic behavior, then the assertion of Gumperz (1970: 147) that "one of the most important problems in the sociolinguist's study of speech behavior is the fact that there seems to be no direct relationship between ethnic identity and language usage patterns" requires qualification. We do not know whether or to what extent ethnic groups other than Jews practice ethnic signalling, for our survey of the relevant literature has returned little evidence on this point[13] and our field research has concentrated exclusively on Jewish signalling. On theoretical grounds, which we discuss below, the activity can hardly be limited to Jews, and there are sufficient indications to suggest that if it is not a ubiquitous phenomenon it is at least widespread. We came across an instance of ethnic signalling in a fleeting relationship that struck us as being quite familiar, although it did not involve Jews.

A Pittsburgh family was driving to a New Jersey seaside resort area but just before they reached their destination, the car broke down. The proprietor of the garage to which the car was towed, upon cursory examination, estimated repairs to be about $300, and that it would be several days before the necessary parts could be obtained. The Pittsburgh man, recognizing the garage owner's name as Ruthenian, mentioned that he was a stranger about to vacation in the area and asked where the nearest Byzantine church might be. The result, in short, was that the bill came to slightly over $100 and the work was completed the next day.

Signalling, as a form of behavior communicating parochial or other shared social identities may well be a universal feature of modern or complex societies regardless of whether ethnicity is the binding element. Keith Brown (personal communication) reports that the Japanese in Japan display such behavior among themselves. As ethnic and dialect differences play no significant part in distinguishing among Japanese, the emphasis of particularistic ties among strangers is based on common regional or district origins, which can be surmised from peculiar linguistic expressions. Indeed, this is the way Koreans who attempt to pass as Japanese are exposed; they lack a sophisticated knowledge of any regionally distinctive speech idioms and, if they are required to converse long enough, eventually display this ignorance.

Other bounded groups—sexual, social, professional, etc.—most certainly use this type of expressive behavior for conveying particularistic messages of group solidarity or differentiation from the contemporary social millieu of undifferentiated mass. Or signalling may be used as a form of instrumental behavior geared to engage similar others in liaisons, exchanges of services, or the reciprocation of favors reserved for members of one's own group.

Although the nature of the signal may be prescribed by virtue of group membership, it is not the corporate character of the group that compels signalling behavior. Rather, it is the quality of life in modern society, where social lives are compartmentalized, relationships are institutionally defined and functionally specific, and where economic exchanges are based on universalistic standards, that impells people to supplement their social ties with symbols and expressions of commonality that are extraneous to the nature of the relationship. Signalling sets them apart from the institutional matrixes and the accidental circumstances that brought them together. Thus, ethnic signalling should be regarded as but a variant of the normal social bonding rituals and exchange mechanisms that are a regular feature of our mundane lives.

We spend an enormous amount of time in expressive small talk and chitchat, greasing the wheels of social intercourse. However slight and trivial the matter, we are compelled to seek out and express those things we share with others over and above the raison d'etre of the relationship or the purpose of the interaction, sometimes as an extension of the usual social amenities but often as well to place ourselves in a favorable position for future interactions.

By no means are we the first to point out this feature of modern society. Sapir (1949), in his article, "Language," for the 1933 edition of the Encyclopedia of the Social Sciences, observed:

> In between the recognized dialect or language as a whole and the individualized speech of a given individual lies a kind of linguistic unit which is not often discussed by the linguist but which is of the greatest importance to social psychology. This is the subform of a language which is current among a group of people who are held together by ties of common interest. Such a group may be a family, the undergraduates of a college, a labor union, the underworld in a large city, the members of a

club, a group of four or five friends who hold together through life in spite of differences of professional interest, and untold thousands of other kinds of groups. Each of these tends to develop peculiarities of speech which have the symbolic function of somehow distinguishing the group from the larger group into which its members might be too completely absorbed.
... The extraordinary importance of minute linguistic differences for the symbolization of psychologically real as contrasted with politically or sociologically official groups is intuitively felt by most people. "He talks like us" is equivalent to saying "He is one of us." (Reprinted in Mandelbaum 1949: 15–16)

But the recognition of the importance of these supportive interchanges and their relevance for anthropological inquiry seems woefully neglected. Thus we heartily agree with Goffman's (1971: 63–65) view that

In contemporary society rituals performed to stand in for supernatural entities are everywhere in decay.... What remains, in brief, are interpersonal rituals. These little pieties are a mean version of what anthropologists would look for in their paradise. But they are worth examining. Only our secular view of society prevents us from appreciating the ubiquitousness and strategy of their location, and, in turn, their role in social organization [and].... these acts have been surprisingly little studied certainly hardly at all in our Western society, in spite of the fact that it would be hard to imagine a more obvious contemporary application of the analysis recommended by Durkheim and Radcliffe-Brown.

People have considerable latitude in choosing among structural, cultural, and idiosyncratic features to serve as the cement for social bonding. Why, then, should they choose shared ethnicity as the medium? Doubtless, there are many reasons. It may well be that the erosion of primary relationships in modern society and their replacement by identification with occupation or professional affiliation, social class, and educational categories are insufficiently satisfying. People appear to need primordial roots and seek them if they are not readily apparent. It is partly for this reason that ethnicity in contemporary society has failed to lie down and play dead. It plays a vital role in maintaining clearly bounded social identities that are otherwise constantly being eroded. Ethnicity's load of primordial sentiments therefore is especially appropriate for supportive interchanges.

Ethnic signalling also has important functions among those groups who perceive that they are deprived or allowed only limited access to the resources and rewards of the majority society. It allows and justifies particularistic behavior where the principles of equality of opportunity and treatment are regarded as myth and sham. In short, as long as ethnic groups seek recourse in particularism and parochialism ethnic signalling will remain a viable mode of expressive interaction.

If it is now fashionable in the social sciences to recognize the vitality of ethnicity in modern society, there nonetheless remains a tendency to restrict consideration of its importance to manifestations of corporate behavior. From this point of view, ethnic identity is equated with the momentous processes of political action, conflict, and economic competition. If one takes the view that ethnic signalling is a trivial matter, not worth researching, it is an easy step to conclude that the phenomenon is a cultural vestige, one final piece of pluralistic baggage that is discarded before ultimate and total assimilation. Perhaps this is so, but we think that perspective limited and misleading.

It is of interest that ethnic signalling behavior occurs among Jews designated by sociologists as marginal (Sklare 1971: 217) for their lack of religiosity or involvement in ethnic and religious institutions. But the signalling behavior is the same as with those whose active participation in the religioethnic community provides clear and quantifiable measures of ethnic identity. The conventional social science indicators of Jewish ethnic identity have been too limited and must be reassessed. We turn now to this issue.

Generally, the concepts of what comprises Jewish ethnic identity center on religion. Accordingly, many researchers have ascertained Jewish ethnic identity by the degree to which individuals or statistical samples (as by generation or social class) of American Jews affiliate with formal religious institutions or retain traditional rituals and religious practices. But while religion has played a salient role in Jewish life and identity, it is not the sole determinant of Jewish ethnic identification. Whether or not people light Sabbath candles indicates something about change in Jewish culture but it is not the only or even an accurate measure of what ethnicity means to Jews or how Jewish ethnicity has changed. Studies that measure Jewish ethnic identification based on criteria of traditional religious beliefs and behaviors overlook the fact that ethnicity changes qualitatively as well as quantitatively. Younger American Jews have adopted new meanings for their identification that do not coincide with those of older generations. A visit to Israel and learning Hebrew has for many replaced religious activity and speaking Yiddish. Quantitative measures of religioethnic indicators may facilitate research but they are inherently biased toward institutional arrangements that lend ethnicity both a corporate and static character.

If contemporary American Jews show a tendency to employ ethnic signalling among themselves it is not merely because they have relatively little difficulty identifying others as Jews, nor because, due to its ascriptive nature, they cannot easily deny ethnic identity, nor even because there is an impulse to enlarge single-stranded relationships. Rather, it seems clear, most hold the ethnic identity as a positive value. Its ready access makes it convenient for signalling, and its strong moral component makes it admirably suited for expressive interchanges.

Ethnicity, whether Jewish or other, is more than a trait list. It displays itself in subtle forms that often go unrecognized even by the members themselves. But this indicates that there is another kind of importance to ethnicity—not entirely dramatic and grave nor solely lighthearted and frivolous—that is commonplace, mundane, and pervasive. It partakes of the "little pieties and rituals" that govern ordinary social interaction. Like the air we breathe, unnoticed unless befouled, these unremarkable behaviors go unheeded. It is, however, precisely its ubiquitous normality that informs ethnic signalling with significance for anthropological study.

NOTES

1. An earlier version of this paper was presented at the 75th Annual Meeting of the American Anthropological Association, Washington, D.C., November, 1976. We are grateful to the many who have commented on previous drafts and provided helpful criticism, particularly Keith Brown, Don Handelman, Helen Jeroslow, and Authur Tuden.

2. The concepts of signals and signalling have established references in linguistics. Our restricted use of ethnic signalling as a kind of idiom is similar to that of Hockett (1958: 305–306).

3. With Jews, ethnic and religious identity are often confounded. While ultraorthodox Jewish men and women may be readily identified as both ethnically Jewish and extremely religious through distinctive garb and the appearance of hair and/or beard, other Jews who are avowedly agnostic or even atheist may wear a Star of David necklace as a personal display of ethnic identity.

4. As Hall (1966) has made us aware, people are extremely sensitive to the culturally determined distances that define polite confrontation in conversation. Americans stand about an arms-length apart, Eastern European Jews stand much closer (about half-an-arm's-length), and the latter's American descendants stand about midway between these distances.

5. This is not to deny that messages, sometimes ambiguous, may also require interpretation.

6. Some leeway remains in the choice of the precise greeting. For example, people born in Eastern Europe tend to employ traditional Hebrew and Yiddish expressions that mark their sophistication in the idiomatic usage of older generations, while younger-generation American Jews will use greetings like *Shabbat Shalom* or simply *Shalom*. The older Jews employ their local European dialects; the young American Jews use the contemporary Israeli dialect.

7. Although rarely done, researchers utilizing themselves as informants is not without precedent in anthropology. (See, for example, Roberts, Chiao, and Pandey 1975).

8. The actual names are similarly inconclusive as to Jewish ethnic identity.

9. One of our informants volunteered that he consciously employs signalling in his business relationships, saying that he uses "so" (with a rising infection) as a key expression to elicit someone's affirmation of Jewish identity.

10. It would be interesting to know whether there are differences among the professions so that some professionals discourage while others encourage particularizing the relationship with a client through shared ethnicity. But we have insufficient data to hazard a generalization except to note that when a practice is based on an ethnic clientele signalling may be expected to occur.

11. Sympathy itself, implying shared emotion, parallels the functions of shared ethnicity, and the expression or solicitation of sympathy is behaviorally akin to signalling.

12. To be more precise, the ethnic signalling we describe appears to be what Blom and Gumperz (1972) call metaphorical switching, wherein the style shifts in conversation allude to two or more relationship ties among the same set of individuals.

13. There are, however, suggestive morsels in statements such as that many Lithuanians in Los Angeles who prefer to speak English "make sure to sprinkle their conversation with select Lithuanian words" (Baskauskas 1977).

BIBLIOGRAPHY

Baskauskas, L. 1977. Multiple Identities: Adjusted Lithuanian Refugees in Los Angeles. Urban Anthropology 6: 141–154.

Blom, J.-P., and J. J. Gumperz. 1972. Social Meaning in Linguistic Structure: Code-Switching in Norway. Directions in Sociolinguistics: The Ethnography of Communication, ed. J. J. Gumperz and D. Hymes, pp. 407–434. New York.

Cassell, J. 1977. The Relationship of Observer to Observed in Peer Group Research. Human Organization 36: 412–417.

Dashefsky, A., and H. Shapiro. 1974. Ethnic Identification among American Jews: Socialization and Social Structure. Lexington, Mass.

Fishman, J. A. 1965. Who Speaks What Language to Whom and Why? Linguistique 2: 67–88.

Goffman, E. 1971. Relations in Public: Microstudies of the Public Order. New York.

———. 1974. Frame Analysis: An Essay on the Organization of Experience. New York.

Goldstein, S., and C. Goldscheider. 1968. Jewish Americans: Three Generations in a Jewish Community. Englewood-Cliffs.

Grimshaw, A. D. 1971. Some Social Forces and Some Social Functions of Pidgin and Creole Languages. Pidginization and Creolization of Languages, ed. D. Hymes, pp. 435–445. Cambridge.

Gumperz, J. J. 1964. Linguistic and Social Interaction in Two Communities. The Ethnography of Communication, ed. J. J. Gumperz and D. Hymes. Special Publication of the American Anthropologist 66: 137–153.

———. 1970. Verbal Strategies in Multilingual Communication. Georgetown University Round Table on Languages and Linguistics 1970. Washington, D. C.

Hall, E. T. 1966. The Hidden Dimension. New York.

Hockett, C. F. 1958. A Course in Modern Linguistics. New York.

Lazerwitz, B. 1970. Contrasting the Effects of Generation, Class, Sex and Age on Group Identification in the Jewish and Protestant Communities. Social Forces 49: 50–59.

Mandelbaum, D. G., ed. 1949. Selected Writings of Edward Sapir in Language, Culture and Personality. Berkeley.

Roberts, J. M., C. Chiao, and T. N. Pandey. 1975. Meaningful God Sets from a Chinese Personal Pantheon and a Hindu Personal Pantheon. Ethnology 14: 121–148.

Rosen, B. C. 1965. Adolescence and Religion. Cambridge.

Segalman, R. 1967. Jewish Identity Scales: A Report. Jewish Social Studies 29: 92–111.

Sahlins. M. 1968. Tribesmen. Englewood Cliffs.

Sklare, M. 1971. America's Jews. New York.

Sklare, M., and J. Greenblum. 1967. Jewish Identity on the Suburban New Frontier. New York.

Nicknames and the Transformation of an American Jewish Community: Notes on the Anthropology of Emotion in the Urban Midwest[1]

Jack Glazier

>>> <<<

THIS ARTICLE examines the nature of nicknames, their derivation, usage, and functions among Ashkenazic and Sephardic Jews in Indianapolis. While the nicknames themselves are often colorful and amusing, they also provide a window on the past, for they offer considerable insight into an aging urban group of European-born immigrants and, particularly, the first-generation American-born; people now mostly age 50 and older. Once a flourishing phenomenon, conferring nicknames that stick for life has now largely dissipated among the younger generations, yet still lively instances of established nickname usage occur among the older generations. Nicknames are restricted to men, who received them during their youth when they and their families lived in a dense, Jewish immigrant neighborhood on the Southside of the city. While not every man above age 50 is known by a nickname, the nicknaming phenomenon is most closely associated with men in this age category; either those who were born in Europe and emigrated in childhood with their families to the city or those who were born in this country of immigrant parents. Women of comparable age did not usually receive nicknames. A nickname in this context refers to a name conferred by peers and by definition excludes such affectionate names as the common diminutives in Yiddish, Ladino (Judeo-Spanish), or English often bestowed on children within the family.

In documenting an established tradition of urban nicknaming, the present account analyzes its manifestations in what others have regarded as an improbable setting. Compared to its various expressions in the villages of rural Europe, the Middle East, or other nonindustrial, small-scale communities, nicknaming fits less integrally into the complex, fragmented design of urban life. Consequently, a novel approach to this ubiquitous phenomenon is taken through an analysis of the current role of nickname usage in linking past and present; the reasons for the apparent decline of nickname dissemination among younger generations is also discussed. The tradition of nicknaming has, in effect, outlived the particular social conditions that gave rise to it. In exploring nickname survivals in an urban community that has undergone significant social and ecological change, this article further considers the emotional and cognitive response of people seeking to come to grips with the dramatic changes that have buffeted their lives. Accordingly, the distinct role of memory, nostalgia, and sentiment in giving nicknames their contemporary force is also examined through what might simply be termed the anthropology of emotion—the exploration of the sociocultural matrix of mood, feeling, and sentiment, and the manner in which emotion and memory are socially constructed and culturally interpreted.

Nickname usage, in surviving the social context generating it, has effectively come to represent a mnemonic of community; a symbol that readily defines a group with complex, diffuse social bonds evoking generational memories of neighborhood life and its radical alteration. At the same time, this usage constitutes a kind of social anchor that secures identity amid the personal and community dislocations of rapid social change. That is, an important but not sole function of nicknames is their evocative and expressive capacity to call up nostalgic images of the urban community in which these names were conferred and disseminated and to reiterate the generational bonds among those who are socially enclosed by this knowledge. Through the many transformations of the original neighborhood and the social lives of its inhabitants, participation in what might be termed the community of nicknames continually reinforces one's social and psychological moorings.

Nicknames and City Life

Several reasons help to account for the inattention to nicknaming in cities and illustrate important differences between the ways anthropologists have conceptualized rural as opposed to urban life. The neglect of nickname usage in cities is probably not because nicknames simply do not exist in cities but rather because they operate in ways much less implicated in the structural framework of city life. The functions of nicknaming in cities are thus not as obviously consequential for social control or for the maintenance of harmonious or orderly social relations as in rural areas, where anonymity or escape from public scrutiny cannot so readily be achieved.

Anthropological interest in nicknames in nonurban locales has nonetheless prompted many insightful articles analyzing this phenomenon from several perspectives; functional, social structural, demographic, and psychological. Many of these accounts are set in Spain, Italy, or other areas of the circum-Mediterranean, where nicknaming compels the investigators' interest owing to its pejorative quality and unforgiving comment on personal and physical defects. These studies are set within the context of stable village communities and thus, for the most part, do not consider nicknaming in relationship either to dramatic social change or to a specifically urban existence. But two notable articles (Brandes 1975; Barrett 1978) explore the decline of nickname usage in larger populations and under demographic and social conditions associated with urbanization.

Brandes's (1975:146) excellent discussion of nicknaming in Navanogal, Spain, argues that the social organization of city life is inimical to this phenomenon and also suggests that there are upper and lower limits of population size that inhibit nickname usage. In cities, he claims, a critical social prerequisite of nicknaming ("moral unity") is lacking, thus precluding agreement on what is right and wrong. In this view, since the moral consensus supporting nicknaming is missing and the size of cities militates against the "common knowledge" of nicknames, the phenomenon does not develop or at least does not exert social control functions (Brandes 1975:148). Concentrating on these functions, Brandes (1975:146) goes on to say that "this is why we have no record of prominent nicknaming for small communities of the more industrially developed portions of Europe, as well as the United States" and argues that in cities nicknames "can have no significant social impact" (1975:146).

In a similar vein, using data from a northern Spanish village and considering the critical effects of social change on nicknaming, Barrett (1978:103) asserts that modernization (marked by many social patterns normally associated with urbanism) has likewise inhibited the spread of nicknames. Included here are an expanding scale of social relations indicated by extra-village social ties, the breakdown of public life in the village, and a growing self-sufficiency of families. Amid these many changes in village life, the social significance of nicknames has atrophied along with the dense, internal networks of communication on which their establishment depends (1978: 101, 103).

The attenuation of nickname development and dissemination following the decline of the Jewish immigrant neighborhood described in this article lends support to these arguments, as it outlines the social features of a once-flourishing community within a city providing the seedbed from which nicknames sprang. But beyond this familiar strategy of nickname study, it also probes the expressive and mnemonic role of nicknames as social inscriptions of identity, both personal and collective, in a rapidly changing locale. At this point, a distinction thus far implicit in the discussion should be made explicit; namely, that between the usage of established youthful nicknames, on the one hand, and the emergence and spread of new ones, on the other. While many social conditions of the city clearly inhibit the latter, the continuing vitality of the former requires explanation.

The Historical and Ethnographic Setting

The Jewish settlement of Indianapolis, like that of other American cities, assumed its shape through successive waves of immigration from Europe. The predominant migrations began with those of German-speaking Reform Jews in the mid-nineteenth century, whose liberal views of Judaism, strong assimilationist values, and dramatic economic success insured that their membership would include the most prominent Jewish participants in civic life. At the same time, these qualities set them apart from the two subsequent Jewish immigrant groups: Azhkenazim from Eastern Europe, and Sephardim from Greece and Yugoslavia. The former arrived during the years from the 1880s until the restrictive legislation of the 1920s and, with the earlier German-Jewish group, comprised a familiar part of the ethnic landscape of urban America. While both groups of immigrants are well-represented in American cities with any sizeable Jewish population, a third, much smaller group of Sephardic Jews settled in Indianapolis and a few other American cities between the years 1905 and 1925.

Once in Indianapolis, the Sephardim assumed residence in close proximity to the immigrant Ashkenazim in an area approximately one-mile-square located on the Southside of the city. The northern margin of the neighborhood lay about a mile south of the downtown area. This settlement, although only a few miles distant from the wealthy neighborhood of Reform Jews, was culturally and economically much further removed. These settlements, in effect, were two very distinct social worlds. It is the experience of Ashkenazic and Sephardic immigrants and their children during the first five decades of the century that are treated here. Although the area they settled was by no means exclusively Jewish, it nonetheless approximated a community that, if not physically bounded, exclusively Jewish, or autonomous in any significant degree, was characterized by dense networks of friendship, kinship, and affinity strengthened by a common economic struggle to transcend poverty. Also within the neighborhood were religious institutions, including five synagogues, a Hebrew school, kosher butcher shops, Jewish bakeries, other retail outlets, and a community center—all strongly oriented to the needs of Jewish immigrants and their children. The nicknames I collected emerged from this fertile ground, and I will later look in some detail at the social features promoting this development. Each name clearly marks a portion of its bearer's life history shaped by early experience in the immigrant settlement.

The Jewish neighborhood on the city's Southside slowly began to dissolve in the 1920s when some families improved their lot and moved to more prestigious neighborhoods lying northward. This process accelerated over the years and by the 1950s few Jewish residents remained in the original settlement. Economic success brought additional residential shifts to suburban areas and a growing familial atomization, or what Bott calls individuation. By this term, she means "that the elementary family is separated off, differentiated out as a distinct, and to some extent autonomous, social group" (1971:101). Individuation thus brings a reduction in both social density and the diffuse, varied bonds that are the classic hallmark of communities.

The interdependence of families on the Southside and the strong perception that it has given way to a greater familial isolation is much in the mind of the immigrant generation and its children. The widespread sentiment about the mutual attachment and support among families of the immigrant neighborhood was summed up by several informants remarking about the current nonpublic aspect of what at an earlier time had been regarded as community celebrations. Where once anyone in the community felt free to attend a marriage ceremony or other festivity ostensibly centered on a particular family, now an invitation is essential before one can participate and, consequently, informants complain, many people feel left out.

The self-sufficiency of contemporary families and their disengagement from co-operative social networks—a kind of privatization of family life—contrast sharply with the interdependence and higher degree of co-operation among the immigrant families. This difference comes to light in various examples of tension between the growing professionalization of welfare under the aegis of an umbrella organization of Jewish charities, led predominantly by established Reform Jews, and several very informal, small-scale welfare groups controlled within various "national" or "ethnic" synagogues: Russian, Polish, Hungarian, Sephardic. Of the Sephardic group, a man in his early 60s noted the following:

> There was a very strong feeling of being a very closely knit independent organization. And very strong feelings. . . . I remember during the Depression, at the Communal Building which was the Jewish Settlement House, we were sent there—my mother sent us there—and it was near the end of the holidays and we were all given new pants and new jackets and everything. . . . We were thrilled. You know, this was something. And we all put them on to show my father when he came home. He said, "Take

'em back! We will not accept charity. There are other people who need it worse than us."

And it broke our hearts and we had to bring all this back. But that was the general feeling of real pride. They did not have the same feeling within the [Sephardic] community. There was a lot of helping of each other within the community. But from outside, they had these strong feelings against charity.

This account also alludes to differences in a single family regarding charity—"my mother sent us there"—but the critical point remains the emphasis placed on informal interfamilial assistance. In the Sephardic case, the latter kind of aid preserved a father's sense of honor by not exposing his children's needs to strangers such as professional social workers.

The boundaries defining various Jewish immigrant groups were most apparent among The Sephardim, who stood out culturally and linguistically from the various Ashkenazic Jews originating in one or another area of Eastern Europe. Except for minor variations of dialect or custom, the Ashkenazic immigrants were bound together by Yiddish language and culture. Yet the nicknaming complex—conferral, dissemination, usage—growing out of Southside life cut across the Ashkenazic/Sephardic divide. The permeability of boundaries grew out of social circumstances virtually compelling the acculturation of Ashkenazic and Sephardic youth both to a broader Jewish collectivity and to American culture. Accordingly, the shared knowledge of a common corpus of nicknames among Ashkenazic and Sephardic young men points up the clear development of continuing social relationships, especially among the first American-born generation, who used English as a common medium and forged friendships in public school and in the activities centered in the Jewish Communal Building.

Types of Nicknames and Their Sources

The many nicknames currently in use are not easily categorized, although informants generally agree that most were originally conferred as part of the regular needling that occurred among boys and young men. The unflattering quality of many nicknames is immediately apparent in those that obviously mock particular character traits. Gimme regularly sought handouts, and Stingy was tightfisted. Physical characteristics also lent themselves to permanent enshrinement through nicknaming. Thus Bulldog frowned in such a way as to gain his distinctive moniker, the brothers Shrimp and Short Spoke were diminutive, Captain Keister had a big behind, and Fat Sam was heavy. Black Jack received his nickname, built on his first name, because of his dark complexion. Puggie had a snub nose.

Some of these names, while commenting on particular physical or character traits, have assumed a quality of admiration, although the ultimate derivation of the name may not have been flattering. Cob, for example, is very respected for his principled outspokenness, and gained his nickname for his youthful toughness and daring—"rough as a cob." Some narratives of the youthful adventures of this generation sound almost mythic: "Cob was the first man in our group to run the entire 1100 block of Illinois Street without touching the ground." The exploits of this seeming Jewish Mercury appeared only slightly less awesome to the narrator's audience when he explained that Cob ran the course by jumping from steeply gabled roof to roof. But despite their admiration of his various activities and their continuing regard for him over the years, Cob's friends humorously point out how the phrase "rough as a cob" also alludes to the use of corncobs in the days before toilet paper.

Other nicknames played on radio or movie characters during the 1920s and 30s with whom individuals themselves actively identified or were so connected by others. Tarzan, Tito, Zarkov, and Sabu, for example, all figured in various matinee adventures at the neighborhood movie house, and each one inspired a nickname for a once-youthful admirer. In some instances, a physical resemblance also prompted the identification, as in the muscular physique of the local Tarzan. Tom Mix, the famous cowboy, was the source of the nickname of a young gambler, known as Tom, or sometimes Big Tom, because of his notable size. The name developed because he wore a large, prominent, white hat resembling the one worn by the cowboy hero. Similar identification occurred with sports figures of the 1930s, when their first names were adopted as nicknames by some young men.

Some nicknames represent deliberate efforts to mask Jewish identity by assuming non-Jewish, often Irish surnames, especially for those with particularly Jewish sounding names, such as Cohen. The motivation here seems to have been to court Irish and other non-Jewish girls when a young man's Jewish affiliation would have been a liability in mixing socially with girls beyond the neighborhood. Young men were also concerned about keeping these activities from their immigrant parents, which was made easier if they did not use actual surnames. All of this occurred, it is now said, in an extremely light-hearted vein. One informant indicated that "these nicknames were like aliases. If there was trouble [pregnancy?] we couldn't be traced." Thus, the following changes occurred: Mordoh to Murdock, Pardo to Dugan, Calderon to Calhoun, Glazier to Gallagher, two Nahmiases to Morgan and Norman, and two Cohens to Carns and Quinn.

The last examples illustrate an important quality of nicknames; the individualizing of particular persons, which has also been described by anthropologists including Antoun (1968:160), Brandes (1975:140), and Cohen (1977:106). In the present context, the uniqueness of each nickname not only specifies the distinctive individual but also serves to differentiate him from others who may share the same given name. Amid many cross-cutting ties of kinship and a desire to honor the memories of deceased kin among Ashkenazim or to honor living kin in the case of the Sephardim, it is not unusual for cousins to share a first and last name and, in the latter case, to share names with a living person so honored. Common names may also be held by nonkinsmen. Members of several unrelated Cohen families, for example, thus share first names. By virtue of nicknames, then, Cob and Carns are distinguished, although they share identical first and last names.

Nicknames are unique and nonrecurrent—immediately tied to the distinctive individual in ways not characteristic of first and last names given within the family. Family names are not usually unique within the community. The nickname, on the other hand, is based on a characteristic quality of the individual, a distinct experience in his life, or some other singular personal feature named by peers and ultimately informing an important part of the individual's identity. But unlike the identities that are, in a sense, received from involuntary associations such as the family, nicknames mark an achieved recognition shaped through voluntary associations and not through ascribed criteria such as kinship. In this respect, no parallels exist to the inherited nicknames associated with households that Brandes (1975) and Barrett (1978) describe, although Iszaevich (1980:323) has challenged the designation of household appellations as nicknames.

Word play, linguistic elision, or other contractive forms may also shape the nickname. Mordoh, in addition to his Irish nickname, has periodically been known as More Dough, which, in view of his various business ventures and financial endeavors, is apposite. The salutation, "Hey, Mo!," evolved into the nickname Amos, which is much more widely known than the individual's given first name, Morris. Similarly, some people cannot recall Mickey's given name and a few are surprised to learn that the latter is in fact a nickname. It is based on his Hebrew name, Avraham, which in its Ladino diminutive form is Avrahamico; the last two syllables of the latter name were transformed into Mickey.

The origin of nicknames built on linguistic play, like others based simply on nonsense syllables (e.g., Bulu or Yobo), may be lost, or incorrectly interpreted. One informant, for example, noting the nickname Loda, said that for a long time he thought this name was simply a Yiddish derivative. Only in adulthood did he learn that the nickname was short for "Load of Shit." The ludic quality of nicknames is not restricted to those based on word play. Each name has an important entertainment value, often amusing in its own right but always evocative of the playfully aggressive speech of the bearers and users of nicknames.

Nickname Usage

With few exceptions, distinctions between nicknames as terms of reference or address are not relevant. I found only one nickname that informants restricted to referential use; Chaim Putz (Chaim Prick). Although there may well be others that escaped my notice, generally nicknames are suitable appellations in direct address. One informant explained that nicknames were generally affectionate designations and their common needling quality was essentially good-humored, thereby, blunting the sharper points in this usage. Of course, this commentary was elicited from an individual in his late 50s, long after the community that spawned the names was transformed and dispersed. This particular informant, like most of his contemporaries, played down the aggressive or competitive quality of nicknaming and emphasized instead its joking value. But given the nature of many of the nicknames and the context of their development among male youth of growing independence and assertive selfhood, aggression and joking represent closely related features of the same sociolinguistic phenomenon.

The names I collected and heard contextually in direct address or in reference to a third party—however sharp they sound—take on a benign quality owing to a diminished social distance between the bearers of nicknames and those who regularly use them in discourse. Their combative edge is probably more relevant to their original bestowal and has faded in significance as the name gained currency within the community. At the same time, the easy use of a seemingly insulting name presupposes a sufficiently high level of trust and fellowship to permit the free expression of what otherwise might be construed as insult or condescension. In 1945, for example, one of the city newspapers printed a story headed, "Local Fighter Pilot in Raids on Reich" and reported how "Lt. Cohen has flown sorties against oil refineries." A childhood friend living next door then began calling the returning pilot "Surtie," which plays on a Ladino expression for having diarrhea. As it turned out, this nickname did not "take," probably due to social reasons (e.g., the subject left the city for college, and greater residential mobility after World War II rapidly changed the character of the neighborhood) rather than to any personal animus at the usage. Also, the would-be Surtie already possessed a nickname, Quinn. Generally, established nicknames that originally chided or criticized their bearers for unendearing qualities are now amiably accepted by them. Stingy G. quite literally wears his nickname proudly, as one can see from the initials, SG, on his diamond ring.

The attitudes of women toward male nicknames differ from those of men who use them and/or are known by them. While recognizing the friendly quality of the names and the ways these are intimately bound to male friendship and association, many women regard the system of nicknaming as somewhat disreputable. This attitude is particularly characteristic of the wives of men who are known by obviously critical names or names that appear childish. These women, consequently, will address their husbands and refer to them by their family names. Moreover, a woman's attitudes and preferences are generally known among her husband's friends; her expectation, not always realized, is that her husband's family name will be used in her presence. Stingy's wife thus always addresses and refers to her husband by his actual first name, Morris. Pancake's wife similarly distances herself from her husband's nickname and wants his friends to call or refer to him by his given name. (Pancake earned his name as a youth when he played near a steamroller and friends warned him that he might be flattened like a pancake). One difficulty, however, is that nicknames so infuse the identity of men in the social networks of their generation that given names are not easily remembered by their friends. Women nonetheless tend to be the custodians of familial respectability, which nickname usage, in their view, undermines.

Discussion

Among the immigrants and their children, community life was solidified by a pervasive consciousness of common economic struggle as well as by the more circumscribed bonds of culture and religion defining the Ashkenazic and Sephardic groups. All families sought an economic foothold in their new home, and my older informants' picture of the immigrant community is limned in images of a ubiquitous struggle against deprivation. Economic mobility eventuated in the demise of the immigrant neighborhood and the climb out of poverty. Although the cultural distance traversed is immense due to manifold pressures for assimilation (Glazier n.d.), nicknames remain a powerful reminder of humble beginnings so close in space and time.

Friends will occasionally remark in the presence of especially successful peers, "I knew him when he was poor." This wry comment usually elicits pleas from the person named that he has not changed, despite his success. Like the nickname, such remarks are leveling devices, exercising a certain control as if to say, "No matter how wealthy or successful you become, your friends will always know your origins on the Southside and you shouldn't forget them either. And if you do, we'll remind you." In all likelihood, people do not wish to forget their origins, their friendships, the community of nicknames, and the complex interplay of diverse circumstance—social, economic, cultural, and religious—shaping their generation. The nickname, with its humorous undercurrent and evocation of youthful play, thus serves a controlling function, reminding people that however wealthy or successful an individual becomes, any effort to put on airs ultimately cannot succeed among peers. As a mnemonic of the original settlement, nicknames bring the past into the present, at once identifying the unique person and locating him within an unchanging social context preserved in the memory of his friends.

But contemporary suburban life, the atomization of families, and the preoccupation with economic gain insure that there is at least the appearance of indifference about the past owing to the stark discontinuities between the dense social life of the immigrant neighborhood and the present isolation of nuclear families. In addition, community functions ranging from welfare to burial, that once were controlled by various small-scale community groups defined by synagogue membership or country of origin, have been assumed by professional, bureaucratic organizations. Consequently, what were once activities informed by varied bonds between actors have become much less personal, friendly and, in the view of the older generations, communal.

The exclusive appearance of the nicknames among men and differing attitudes toward them on the part of men and women point up important patterns in family organization and gender roles in the immigrant community. For the generation coming of age in the years between the 1920s and 1940s, young men and women experienced very different sets of expectations, both within their own families as well as within the urban community they inhabited. The independent access of young women to a world beyond the family was severely limited and their developing social identity was very much a function of family membership; first as daughters and sisters and subsequently as wives. The European experience of immigrant parents, their religious values, and the general cultural pattern of the time emphasizing a double standard of behavior for young men and women—and thus limiting the possibilities of female independence—insured that young women would by and large comport themselves in more decorous ways. Their access to social opportunities beyond the home or neighborhood, moreover, was certain to be severely constrained. Young men, on the other hand, enjoyed much greater latitude for independent activities with peers, well beyond the knowledge or supervision of the family, including such disreputable pursuits as gambling, drinking, shooting pool, and meeting girls outside the faith living in other parts of the city.

The currency of nicknames thus became emblematic of a male world existing beyond the domestic and religious domains. In a sense, the negative connotation of nicknames and their usage might be seen as an aggressive counterpoint to the orderly world of home and religious institution, and from their combative negative quality nicknames drew some of their particular power to evoke laughter or mildly to reproach their bearers. Yet I do not want to push this point further, for it is very clear that the negative connotation of nickname usage in the present case pales before the various examples of mordant naming in the Mediterranean, that Gilmore (1982:697) aptly characterizes as "symbolic castration." Still, nicknames sound an agonistic and competitive tone, however muted, and contrast with the ideals of the protected, ordered sphere of religion and especially family where mothers and sisters embodied without ambiguity the values of respect and honor. Nicknames thus developed in a context sharply juxtaposing home life and street corner society, and this opposition accounts for both their nearly exclusive occurrence among men and the generally held belief that they are slightly disreputable and, in the view of some spouses, simply inappropriate for adult men.

But if nicknames developed and were disseminated in an exclusively male society, their usage occurs in a very wide range of circumstances. Except for the constraints felt by those wishing to respect the sensibilities of spouses, nicknames are used in a variety of social settings. These include events in which solemnity or ritual formality is expected. During a synagogue service, for example, when a Bar Mitzvah was being celebrated, the Rabbi called a member of the family (the father's brother) to the pulpit in order to offer customary blessings attendant to the reading of the Torah. After the Rabbi's invitation to the Torah, uttered in Hebrew, met no response from the man named, the boy's father simply called out to the Rabbi for all to hear, "Better ask for Tito." This remark, not a contretemps even in this setting, brought the individual to the pulpit, while eliciting light laughter from the congregation during these otherwise formal and decorous proceedings.

Nicknames, Nostalgia, and the Shape of Identity

Nicknames, besides their obvious identifying qualities, locate persons in a particular time and place shared by those who are part of this community of nicknames. Unlike a given personal or legal name that establishes a universal persona transcending time and place, the nickname is parochial in its origin and uses, defining as it does an individual in a highly circumscribed manner. But given the physical disappearance and social transformation of the urban community that engendered nickname development, the anthropologist still confronts the problem of accounting for the persistence of youthful identities embodied in nicknames.

The boundaries of the immigrant neighborhood now represent mental constructions that provide fixed references amid the swiftly changing patterns of residence and association. Upward mobility and its many economic and social correlates constitute some of the significant changes in Jewish social life, now entering the third generation removed from the immigrant experience. Nicknames and a detailed knowledge of the life histories of those so designated symbolize male bonds of association in a particular neighborhood and weave their way through the memory of older men recalling their coming of age among peers. Despite the few compunctions surrounding nickname usage and the social and ecological transformations of the immigrant neighborhood, these highly personal tags persist, reminding people of their social origins and one phase of their maturing process among neighborhood youth with whom they have maintained lifelong bonds of friendship.

But more than this, nicknames signal a continuing evocation of a transitional period. On the one hand, the nicknames represent a bridge in the formation of male identity as young men took on a sense of self based on their extrafamilial bonds with peers. Nicknames emerged as young men moved beyond the confines of their families and assumed identities derived from purely voluntary social bonds within the old neighborhood. On the other hand, the nicknames speak to more than changes in the life cycle, for they also recall the particular urban community which lay poised between two worlds. The domestic circle, steeped in European custom and Yiddish or Ladino, continued to some extent the familiar old country practices of parents and grandparents; but the wider community with its many influences of the new country, especially the public school, promised an American future very different from the immigrant past. At the least, Jewish youths might hope to enter the American mainstream, but only if they would break away from European influence (Glazier n.d.). Moreover, these transitions are even more dramatic than they otherwise might have been since they generally coincided with the two great historical watersheds in the lives of all people of this generation—the Depression and World War II.

In such dramatic shifts, both psychological and sociological, Davis (1979) claims to have located one of the elusive sources of nostalgia. While the anthropologist objectively can infer from the data important contrasts between family and neighborhood on the immigrant Southside and the suburban patterns of the last thirty years, informant perceptions of the discrepancy are even more important, especially in provoking diffuse feelings of dissatisfaction and a certain uneasy sense about the present and future. The subjective opposition of contemporary experience to a constructed past, which takes on qualities superior to those of what is perceived as an uncertain and anxious present, is the stuff of nostalgic yearning (Davis 1979:141). According to Davis (1979:101), nostalgia is born of psychological discomfort in the perceived disjunction between a putative happy past and a troublesome present; its roots lie in the "perceived threats of identity discontinuity." In that discontinuity nostalgia is important "in engendering *collective* identities among people generally, but most especially among members of the same generation." Nicknames, which cluster among men of the first American-born generation, are symptomatic of the transitional states, both in the lives of individuals and in the community. Like nostalgic recollections in personal narratives, nickname usage implicitly establishes social and personal bearings, orienting participants toward a valued history in the face of the major changes the first American-born generation has confronted.

These changes constitute a significant break with the European past, including the wholesale adoption of English at the expense of Yiddish and Ladino, the replacement of informal immigrant institutions (welfare funds, burial societies, etc.) by professional organizations, increasing rates of interfaith marriages by their children, and economic mobility. One Sephardic informant put it very succinctly when he said, "the Sephardim maintained its existence as a tightly knit, developing entity for 400 years in Turkish Macedonia ... and it was almost wiped out in the U.S. in one generation." Certainly, the same dramatic pace of change and discontinuity with the European past also shaped the experience of Ashkenazic Jews from Eastern Europe. The latter group, while lamenting some cultural losses, by and large does not share the generally favorable views of old country life held by the Sephardim, whose experience of anti-semitism was considerably less than that of the Eastern European Jews. Of course, the various changes coursing through the lives of American Jews are intimately bound together. Most important, the effort to transcend poverty required mastery of English and participation in mainstream culture when obstacles to full Jewish participation in American life fell away, including barriers to interfaith marriages.

But besides poverty, informants also recognize other less savory aspects of the recent American past that confronted the immigrant families—anti-semitism, discrimination, and the harsh realities of deprivation—and hence nostalgic feelings are highly selective. The collective nostalgic memory beckons people only to recall familial cooperation, dense neighborhood networks, the sense of sameness born of common economic circumstance, the ubiquitous occurrence of old country languages, and the warm familiarity of a less isolated, more interdependent social life. Paradoxically, these emotional states of longing assume their distinctive power in securing identity and in evoking highly positive sentiments precisely because they are selective and not recoverable. No informant would exchange the present for the past because, despite only rudimentary stratification of the neighborhood and minimal economic differentiation ("It didn't seem so bad at the time since we were all poor"), the immigrant world still connotes harsh struggle and brings forth diverse feelings that it was something to leave behind. It is as if a sharper cognitive grasp of the least agreeable aspects of life in the immigrant neighborhood balances the positively charged sentiment for what they believe was superior, at least in personal and social terms, to present circumstances.

Nicknames as mnemonics of community thus play a unique role in suffusing personal identity with complex meanings and emotions arranged around a set of common themes; generational bonds, economic sameness, family interdependence, informality, and an absence of what is regarded as the pretense often accompanying rapid economic mobility upward. Selectively and positively described, these themes represent touchstones of community authenticity, much superior to present familial individuation. Likewise, these themes underscore the immigrant settlement as interdependent and pervaded by mutual support and solidarity. They embody the nostalgic remembrance by a generation feeling acutely the personal transitions of maturing and the diverse social changes that pivoted around their peer group, at once transforming their generation and the community in which they came of age. This group experienced a shared departure from a selectively valued past and entered a very different world only partially of their own making. In short, nostalgic themes embodied in narratives of community and nickname usage serve as expressive palliatives for an ambiguous present markedly discontinuous with their youthful lives. The much vaunted value on progress is thus implicitly questioned. Otherwise, why doubt at all the present in favor of the past? At the same time, youth remains a major reference point for nickname usage, no matter how dramatically a life has been altered by age and experience. Although an individual's various selves are socially constituted over time, a nickname can distinctively preserve one of them—that of timeless, optimistic youth—by symbolically inscribing the maturing, newly independent self in the collective memory of friends.

Nostalgia thus proves a useful device for resolving the ambivalence surrounding economic success and participating in the American mainstream, goals that could be won only at the expense of the early community. It represents an important emotional response to the realization that allaying economic anxieties, especially on the part of the first American-born generation, has incurred considerable costs, not least of which has been the end of a way of life deeply rooted in the European past and selectively perceived as deeply satisfying. The generation coming of age in the neighborhood, yet choosing to leave it in their effort to achieve economic mobility, can now expressively recreate that community and their youthful place therein through its narratives and nicknames, sentimentalizing the past and using the bulwark of memory to deflect a deficient present and an uncertain future.

Conclusion

Although nicknames occur in cities and manifest characteristics deviating from what they are in European or Latin American villages, they still should command anthropological concern for several reasons. In the present case, although they operate only partially in terms of social control functions, nicknames reveal much about urban structural features and their changes. Important as the functions of social control are in the existing literature on nicknames, they do not tell the entire story, especially within an urban framework, and an exclusive interest in social control can divert attention from more revealing aspects of urban nicknaming. They are also laden with expressive value, containing as they do stable, highly condensed symbols of personhood amid the changing currents of individual and collective experience.

Part of the problem of discussing urban nicknaming is how best to deal with the perennial topic of structure. The anthropology of city life has customarily lacked its own characteristic designations for distinctively urban structural features that might be taken as basic principles or building blocks of urban society. One would thus be hard-pressed to think of urban conceptual counterparts of unilineal descent groups, age-sets, dyadic contracts, closed corporate communities, *campanilismo* or any number of other well-defined models of tribal or peasant social structure. Urban life is, of course, different but its familiar depictions in terms of social differentiation and attenuation of the collective conscience in Durkheim's parlance (Brandes's [1975] "moral unity" is a latter-day version) or multiplex social relations (Gluckman 1955:19) provide little grist for the mill of those attempting to build elegant models of urban social structure. A phenomenon such as nicknaming, then, intimately associated in the anthropological literature with small-scale peasant villages where it serves a vital purpose in checking the interpersonal behavior of those who are bound together by the need for co-operation or male solidarity may seem merely an amusing curiosity in the urban area. In the conventional view, the city is bereft of the well-integrated structural features and multi-interest social relationships conferring functional significance on nicknames.

Yet another difficulty in dealing with the seeming dissonance between urban living and a form of behavior anthropologists associate with the social order of villages derives from the concept of community, which usually has a spatial referent like a neighborhood. More important, the concept also refers to a particular quality of social relations that are primary, face-to-face, and multifaceted. In other words, it is the kind of setting where anthropologists have established that nicknames are spawned and contrasts sharply with the usual views of the impersonal city. One definition of community might simply be a place where everyone is a celebrity; that is, where each person in the community is widely known and, in turn, knows in considerable detail many aspects of the lives of other members, to whom he or she is connected in multiple and diffuse ways. This image again opposes the usual characterizations of the city as inimical to widely ramifying personal ties. But settlements or neighborhoods within cities can approximate these multiple views of community, as various anthropologists and sociologists have long recognized. Gans's (1962) well-known work, *The Urban Villagers*, on Italian-Americans in Boston's West End, is one of several examples; the title thus represents a distinct sociological reality rather than merely a clever oxymoron. And like the larger urban world they constitute, these communities can be altered or can disappear entirely either through social or spatial demise. People migrate out or urban ecology is reshaped by urban planning, or other radical physical and social alterations of the city.

But a community as an idea or a memory disembodied from its original physical representation can persist. In somewhat idealized form the community without a spatial aspect is in fact what Turner (1969:96) suggests with his important concept of communitas. If such symbols—embedded as they are in memory, emotional state, or some other equally elusive locus—do not readily lend themselves to model-building or other positivist enterprise, they remain no less vital as interpretive keys for unlocking the important meanings of nostalgia and similar sentiments expressing a particular emotional disposition and personal relationship toward a now vanished community.

NOTE

1. I gratefully acknowledge the generous assistance of the National Endowment for the Humanities and the Wenner-Gren Foundation for Anthropological

Research which made possible my fieldwork during 1980–81. I also thank Oberlin College for several grants supporting my continuing research.

BIBLIOGRAPHY

Antoun, R. 1968. On the Significance of Names in an Arab Village. Ethnology 7:158–170.
Barrett, R. 1978. Village Modernization and Changing Nicknaming Practices in Northern Spain. Journal of Anthropological Research 34:92–108.
Bott, E. 1971. Family and Social Network. New York. (First published 1957.)
Brandes, S. H. 1975. The Social and Demographic Implications of Nicknames in Navanogal, Spain. America Ethnologist 2:139–148.
Cohen, E. N. 1977. Nicknames, Social Boundaries, and Community in an Italian Village. International Journal of Contemporary Sociology 14:102–112.
Davis, F. 1979. Yearning for Yesterday. New York.
Gans, H. 1962. The Urban Villagers. New York.
Gilmore, D. D. 1982. Some Notes on Community Nicknaming in Spain. Man 17:686–700.
Glazier, J. n.d. Stigma, Identity, and Sephardic-Ashkenazic Relations in Indianapolis.
Gluckman, M. 1955. The Judicial Process among the Barotse of Northern Rhodesia. Manchester.
Iszaevich, A. 1980. Household Renown: The Traditional Naming System in Catalonia. Ethnology 19:315–325.
Turner, V. W. 1969. The Ritual Process. Chicago.

Strangers Who Settle Among Us
>>> <<<

Those who follow college football cannot help noticing the appearance of Samoan players in recent years. Where do these Samoan football players, with their odd names, come from? For older Americans, the name Samoa may stir dim memories of Pacific atolls and of 1940s vintage movies featuring Dorothy Lamour and Jon Hall. Do boys on these specks of paradise play football using coconuts? Do they kick field goals barefoot? Perhaps the world is indeed changing rapidly into a global village if Americans drive Yugoslavian and Korean cars, Japanese play baseball, Jamaicans field an Olympic bobsled team, and Nigerians become professional basketball and football stars.

Samoans are an American immigrant group. Tens of thousands of them live on the West Coast, and even more in Hawaii. Between the midwestern family reunion described by Ayoub and the Samoan funeral described by Ablon, readers will sense some basic similarities. Both events bring together widely separated members of the group who rarely meet otherwise, and provide the opportunity to meet new members. Attendance on these occasions is an affirmation of membership; repeated absences are taken to mean a desire for dissociation. To some extent, identification with the group depends on maintaining a voluntary association.

There are also differences. The American midwesterners must sometimes choose between attending different family gatherings, potentially as many as four; that is, one for each parent of the husband and wife. Sporadic attendance at any of these, or the disinclination to attend at all, does not carry the moral burden entailed with negligent Samoans. The Americans can still retain good relations with smaller circles of kin and ephemeral ties with select members of the wider kindred. But for the Samoans there is little freedom of choice; one's ethnic identity and the social supports derived from ethnic membership are contingent upon responding properly to a Samoan funeral. This is a duty.

Thus, the Samoan funeral serves not only to commemorate the deceased, but also as a rite of ethnic solidarity and an occasion for Samoans to reaffirm their national identity. The question arises as to what benefits individual members derive from this identification and group cohesiveness.

Assistance in times of need is a significant benefit. When a Samoan dies, the social network of the group is quickly activated and donations for the bereaved family arrive from relatives, friends, and other Samoans. Amounts in the thousands of dollars are collected. Although difficult to compare with material assistance, which is not trivial, the social and psychological benefits of membership in good standing may be even greater.

The mobilization of the community upon the death of a member extends beyond California to Samoa. From there come relatives for the memorial services as well as important representatives of traditional Samoan culture and society. These include family chiefs who traditionally serve as orators at public gatherings. The presence of these participants, and the use of items with symbolic value such as finely woven mats, creates a Samoan cultural frame around the elaborate and extensive memorial activities and emphasizes the primordial nature of ties among Samoans.

But being a Samoan in California is not the same as being one in Samoa. While the solidarity and support of the group for its members has been strong and has helped the immigrants to adjust to their new circumstances, there are signs, familiar to the history of other immigrant groups, that the bonds are loosening. The extent to which Samoan ethnic solidarity will wane under modern urban conditions remains to be determined. How the development of this group will compare with that of other ethnic communities in American will be of interest to scholars of American society and to all of us who wonder about the future of American cultural pluralism.

In the midst of American society are newcomers from such diverse places as Cuba, Mexico, Haiti, Jamaica, Southeast Asia, Turkey, and the Philippines. Most other Americans pay them little attention, perceiving them as inhabitants of cultural worlds all their own. Yet how different are these newcomers in their adjustments to American life from the eastern and southern Europeans, the Irish and Chinese who arrived here a century ago? If they are all fated to eventually be assimilated and Americanized, which is a dubious proposition, what do they do in the meantime, before they are melted in the vast pot? How, before achieving success as solid, middle-class citizens, do they draw from their native cultural baggage to create familiar social environments that lend support and assist in survival and adjustment, that give life its satisfactions, rewards, and meaning?

Humans are social animals; they are happiest in a cultural community that nourishes and appreciates its component members. Okamura's description of immigrant Filipinos in Hawaii may be unfamiliar to most Americans, but in general terms the description is applicable to most immigrant groups in contemporary and historic America.

Like other immigrant groups who came as strangers to a strange land, the Filipinos formed ethnic fraternal associations, called here *hometown associations*. To some extent these societies link the immigrants with their original home areas and help to maintain these channels of communication, by remitting funds to assist with infrastructural and other improvements. Sending money home is an act of loyalty, but it also serves to underscore the success of the immigrants and to justify their departure. It makes members feel important and good.

Such groups provide material assistance in times of need, but equally significant for members is the knowledge that they are appreciated. If death benefits are useful to defray funeral costs, there is also comfort in knowing that one will be memorialized. It is good to join with familiar others on festive and convivial occasions like picnics and dinner dances in order to celebrate unity and to express pride in shared origin.

Leaving home for better conditions elsewhere is always bittersweet no matter how great the contrast between the disadvantages left behind and the advantages gained. One leaves the place of upbringing, where one first learned the joys of social life in love and friendship and the pleasures of culture in food, song, dance, play, and so forth. The latter are not lightly tossed aside and replaced with equivalents in the new milieu because the functional substitutes can never be quite the same. So the hometown association picnics and banquets, offering traditional Philippine cuisine, and other sponsored social occasions with traditional dances and songs, help maintain a continuity with cultural origins that stir deep and powerful sentiments. Thus immigrants try to extract the best from both worlds while incompletely belonging to either.

How an ethnic group mobilizes its members for concerted action and how it comes to be viewed as a political force is the substance of Wells's article on ethnic movements. Her case study is that of Mexican-Americans (Chicanos) who settled in a central Wisconsin town as low paid, industrial workers. Although actually few in number, the group of 140 constitutes a sizeable minority relative to the town's heterogeneous population of 5,400. The manner in which this group adjusts to its new surroundings, then gathers strength and confidence to assert itself for its own interests, provides a microcosmic model of the process other immigrant groups underwent in shaping their portion of the American stage.

The Chicano newcomers to Riverside (a pseudonym) found the setting as unfamiliar as did the eastern European immgrants to New York or Chicago. Refuge is sought in the familiarity of fellow ethnics. Like other immigrants, they came for employment advantages. This still leaves them poor and relatively powerless by comparison with others. They seek help but are either unaware or distrustful of the institutions that might provide assistance because the institutional regulations and decisions often seem to lack reason or predictability. So they turn to what is familiar, a patron-client relationship with someone who comes closest to being one of their own.

What is sad about the case of the Riverside Chicanos is that their champion, a "Hispano" from Arizona, was, and could only have been at that time, in a position that would ineluctably unfold like the drama of a Greek tragedy. Unbeknown to the players, the situation held the certain promise of its own destruction.

When immigrants form a community on foreign soil, there is a social vacuum of leadership that must be filled by someone who will serve as a liaison between the group and the institutions of the host society that most affect it. The position demands uncommon skills and carries conflicting demands. The broker, as he is referred to, must hold the trust and loyalty of the group he represents, which sees him as its protector and champion. At the same time, the broker must gain recognition as the immigrant group's *bona fide* spokesperson from the authorities of the host society, who view him as the medium through which they communicate and hope to control the group.

The Mexican-Americans were recruited to Riverside by a foundry to fill bottom-level positions that others shunned. At that time, the foundry employed a highly assimilated Mexican-American as a personnel manager who assisted in the increase of the Chicano labor pool and worked to ensure its satisfactory performance. As a middle-class person who mixed well with Anglos, the man who came to serve as the Chicanos' broker was perfectly suited for the undertaking. He gained the workers' trust and initially succeeded in interceding on their behalf. But eventually the differences in social class interests (whether defined in the Marxian sense of conflicting and irreconcilable interests or in the Weberian sense of status groups) between the Chicano workers and the personnel manager became salient and irreconcilable. The workers perceived him as a tool of management and, as far as the company was concerned, he became a tool that no longer satisfactorily performed its function.

The model of this case study has striking parallels with other

American minorities whose members achieve middle-class status and are thrust into, or deliberately seek, brokerage roles. They face the chronic problem of being torn between ethnic loyalty and self-interest, if their principal base of support is outside the group. Who pays the piper matters.

The Samoan Funeral in Urban America[1]
Joan Ablon

>>> <<<

CULTURALLY PRESCRIBED RITUALS relating to death function in significant ways to serve the living. Mandelbaum (1959:215) has noted that "Rituals for death can have many uses for life. And the study of these rites can illuminate much about a culture and a society ... the melancholy subject of funerals may provide one good entryway to the analysis of cultures and to the understanding of peoples." The way a Samoan community in a new urban environment deals with death points to the significance both of continuing tradition and of adaptive modifications that have developed in the urbanization of a village people.

The Samoan funeral in West Coast cities of the continental United States dispatches the dead with elaborate Christian propriety and at the same time serves the living by reinforcing the social and economic security of relatives, friends, and the entire Samoan community. This paper will describe the ceremonies and ritual behavior that occur at the time of a death, and will examine the social and economic implications of these for family and community.

During the past two decades an ever-increasing stream of immigrants has come to West Coast cities from American Samoa. Some 15,000 to 20,000 Samoans now reside in Los Angeles, San Diego, Oceanside, and the San Francisco Bay area.[2] Samoans have adjusted with relative ease and poise to an environment that could hardly be more different from that of their native islands. Most have little difficulty in getting and keeping jobs. A large proportion of the men work in shipyards or in heavy industry, and the women are often nurse's aides in hospitals and nursing homes. Many families are buying their own homes and they live comfortably, although not extravagantly. They lead full and active lives centered about their families, their jobs, and their churches.

This new mainland ethnic group has retained many features of Samoan life and custom. One of the most significant aspects of *fa'a Samoa*, Samoan tradition, that is carried on with ever-increasing vigor is a modified traditional pattern of funeral observances. Not only do these observances reify community solidarity, but the ritualized patterns of donations of money from relatives and friends provide an outstanding example of people helping one another, of mutual aid in an urban area where the cost of living and dying is very high.

The following discussion is based on field research in one of the above-mentioned cities of California, where there is a Samoan population of some 4,000 to 5,000 persons. Virtually all families are attached to one or another of the many all-Samoan Christian churches representing Congregationalist, Methodist, Pentecostal, Mormon, and Seventh Day Adventist congregations. Catholics attend various parish churches in the city but unite in their own choir and Benevolent Association. Samoan funeral rites are carried on within the rituals and belief system of the Christian church. The accompanying social and economic activities are quasi-independent of these religious ceremonies and are prescribed by a developing modified Somoan cultural tradition.

Chronology of Family Activities Following a Death

Immediately following a death, the local minister of the church to which the family belongs is contacted, and he begins making plans for the various services to be held, as well as counseling the family of the deceased.

Telegrams are sent and telephone calls made to extended family members in Samoa, Honolulu, and any mainland cities where relatives reside. A number of these relatives prepare for the trip to attend the services. If there is no *matai*[3] (family chief) living in the urban area, a *matai* may come for the occasion to represent the extended family in Samoa.

During the days following the death, members of the nuclear family, close bilateral kin, and local *matai* or older and respected relatives meet to make the practical decisions for burial arrangements and for religious services and to decide the amount of money needed for necessary items. A spokesman for the family of the deceased is selected to speak on all occasions. If there is no *matai* (in this case, a talking chief, the recognized family orator) in the area, or one who can come from Samoa, an older relative or one who is respected and eloquent in speech is designated.

Soon after the death is announced to relatives and friends, a complex network of money-collecting activities goes into motion. The *aiga*,[4] the extended family—the parents, grandparents, children, siblings, aunts, uncles, and cousins of the deceased, the adopted kin within these categories, and the affines of all of these—are expected to contribute money from their respective households to the household of the deceased. The closer relatives contribute from $100 to $200 in cash. There is organized planning for these donations. For example, a group of siblings holds a meeting and decides how much they as a group should contribute. Arguments sometimes occur because one person might not feel that his household is able to contribute his proportionate share of the total at that time, but a consensus is finally reached. Probably $1,000 to $2,000 will be collected from the immediate bilateral kin. More distant relatives, such as cousins, take responsibility for gathering money from their relatives and affinal kin. Donations from each of these households range from $10 to $50, and are presented to the household of the deceased by the persons who organized the collection. Churchmates, friends, and other Samoans also contribute in smaller sums, from $5 to $20, as they are able and are inclined, depending on their relationship to the deceased. An intimate friend may in some cases donate more money than a close relative. Collections also come from other Samoan church congregations and usually are presented by the choirs of these churches during the funeral rites.

Complementing money donations from relatives and ritually even more significant is the custom of donating old fine mats, long a traditional item of economic and ritual exchange at weddings and funerals in the islands.[5] The fine mats, which are about 4 by 5 feet in size and made of the finest grade of pandanus, are no longer woven. The number in existence is limited, and the Governor of American Samoa in 1969 issued a declaration stating that they may no longer be taken out of American Samoa. Thus they are circulated in a closed and traditional manner in the United States. The closer relatives are expected to give two to five fine mats with the presentation of money. If a person has no fine mats to present, he tries to procure them from relatives or he may be able to buy them locally from others who might have a few extra. The set price of a fine mat (passing from Samoan to Samoan—they are rarely sold to non-Samoans) is $10 on the mainland and in American Samoa.

From the day of the death until the funeral and burial are completed, the immediate family and close relatives and *matai* who have come from other areas remain at the home of the deceased and receive callers who bring money and fine mats. Callers may also bring items of food such as chickens or turkeys. These gifts are presented with a formal speech to explain their purpose or the route or direction through which they come and why; that is, the relationship between the giver and the deceased or between the giver and various members of the family through whom the donations are directed. At that time, individual relatives representing both their own affinal kin and donors who are more distant kin make presentations for these kin groups as a unit. For instance, one representative may journey from San Francisco to San Diego at the time of death of his mother's cousin and take with him money and fine mats donated by his extended family and their affinal kin who reside in San Francisco. Those who come from Samoa bring a donation from their relatives there. Formal acceptance speeches are made by family spokesmen to the donors, and food is served to them. In the past, in this California city, money and fine mats were brought to the funeral services, but the formal presentations required a great deal of time; therefore, the ministers decided the giving of money and mats must take place in the household rather than at the public ceremonies.

A family may expect to receive from $2,000 to $10,000 or more in total financial gifts, depending on the social position of the deceased and his family and their standing in their church and the Samoan community, as well as the actual number of their relatives. Fine mats collected may number from 50 to 150 or more, usually in proportion to the money received. Gifts of money and mats are carefully recorded by certain family members who serve as secretaries. Mats are tagged with the giver's name, and following the funeral each fine mat is returned to the home of the person who presented it. This differs from the pattern in Samoa, where mats received by the family *matai* are redistributed to various other *matai* and family members. In the United States, because it is difficult to obtain these mats, the system of return of mats has developed. Some mats are especially prestigious and have been handed down in families; therefore, people may want the exact mats that they donated. The family of the deceased spends much time in the days and weeks following the funeral returning these beautiful mats to their donors.

Finances are carefully managed to pay the expenses of funeral and burial services. The cost of the casket (very handsome and ornate caskets often are chosen by the family) and mortuary services may amount to as much as $1,500. One mortuary official stated that most Samoan funerals handled by his establishment average about $1,200 in cost, somewhat higher than the average for his total client population. However, another stated that his experience has shown a broad range in the prices of caskets and services selected. The burial plot usually costs an additional several hundred dollars.

Several mortuaries customarily are used by the members of the various church groups. Funeral directors in these mortuaries are knowledgeable about Samoan preferences for arrangements, such as additional ceremonies held in the mortuary or church, and the holding of the body for a relatively long period of time before burial. The body is usually held in the mortuary for at least four days, and in some instances up to ten days, especially if the death is sudden and unexpected, to allow relatives to make the trip from Samoa. Samoans prefer to hold services on the weekend, because many persons do not work on these days.

A significant expenditure of money is made to provide food for relatives who have come from Samoa and other areas. Provisions for these relatives, who stay either in the home of the deceased or with other family members, may amount to $500 or more. Money is presented to ministers who participate in the memorial and funeral services. A donation of money and fine mats may be given by the family to the sponsoring church, as well as a special gift of money and a fine mat to the presiding minister. Another significant amount of money is expended on the elaborate feast that traditionally follows the funeral.

The money that remains after all the expenses are taken care of is then distributed between the immediate family and the bilateral kin. If, for instance, a man dies leaving a wife and small children, there is an obvious financial need for their support and they merit a larger share of the total. Cash may be distributed to more distant relatives from the core bilateral kin groups. One informant reported that her household and those of her five siblings each gave $100 for the collection at the death of her adopted mother. Some $6,000 was collected, and after the expenses were defrayed, there was enough left so that in the redistribution each of the six siblings received $300. Each made $200 above the return of his original donation. It is doubtful that such profits are frequent, because expenses and transportation costs are high. For example, many airplane fares may have to be paid for. The bank in Pago Pago has ready arrangements to finance travel in such emergency situations, suggesting that there is little problem about the loans being quickly repaid.

Ceremonies

The pattern of formal and informal services varies according to the church with which the family is affiliated. The following description portrays a generalized ideal pattern common to most of the church groups.

The body lies for viewing in the mortuary awaiting the formal services that may not begin for several days following death. Extended family, church members, and friends come in small numbers to sit with the casket, which usually is open, and hold informal services with prayers and hymn singing.

The first formal ceremony is held in the mortuary chapel, frequently on a Saturday evening two nights preceding the funeral and interment. This service is regarded as the family service. The details of all services are worked out with the family by the minister of the church to which the family belongs (henceforth in this description called the host minister and the host church). The chapel usually is adorned with many large and elaborate flower sprays, and frequently fine mats are draped over the bier on which the casket rests. Larger weave, though handsome, utility mats may be used to carpet the aisles and platform area of the chapel. The family service generally is attended only by the extended family, the church members, and the church choir, in all some 50 to 100 persons. However, friends and acquaintances also may attend. The minister conducts the services, and prayers are said. All the services are conducted in the Samoan language. Speeches by siblings, parents, or children of the deceased concerning his life or Christian works, and by the *matai* or representatives of the family, are presented. Hymns are sung by the church choir. Those present file by to view the dead.

The largest of all of the funeral observances is usually the public service held the night before the funeral. This service is sometimes called the "opening service." It frequently is held on Sunday afternoon or evening in the mortuary or possibly in the church, and may be attended by as many as 400 persons, who represent most of the Samoan churches in the city and surrounding areas.

The minister of the host church arranges this service and may invite other ministers who represent all congregations. If the deceased held an important position in church affairs, ministers of that denomination come from the more distant California cities to represent their congregations. These ministers may hold a brief meeting immediately before the service and the host minister decides what parts each will take. Certain of them sit on the platform area and are honored with duties of presenting various parts of the service, such as the invocation, scripture reading, prayers, and sermon. These components are interspersed with hymns sung by the choir of the host church. Various speeches of gratitude for the participation of those attending are offered by the host minister and family spokesman. The formal public service lasts about an hour. The minister closes this service by turning over the second part of the evening, the choir singing, to his choir director.

The choir director of the host church then gives instructions concerning the order of singing to visiting choirs, who represent most of the Samoan churches of the area. There may be as many as twelve choirs in attendance, and rarely fewer than seven. The choirs then begin singing in rotation, in the order prescribed by the host choir director.

Representatives of the various churches all sing and constitute ad hoc choirs even though some may not be members of the official choirs of these churches. Each choir may sing one hymn only, or may be given the opportunity to sing a second, in rotation. After each finishes its choral contribution, its choir director offers a short speech and presents an envelope containing money for the family, as the financial donation of that church. The amounts vary; larger churches whose choirs number 30 to 50 persons contribute as much as $25 to $50, while the smallest choir made up of 10 to 20 persons ordinarily gives $15 for the death of an adult and $10 for the death of a child. A monthly collection may be held for these funeral funds.

After the seated choirs have completed their alloted turns, they frequently leave the building, with the exception of the host choir, which sings a closing hymn at the end of the service. The choirs which have been standing in the corridors enter and take the vacated seats. If there are more than seven or eight choirs the process may take two rotations until all have had their opportunity to sing. The rotations are necessary because there is always a problem of seating room at the choir service. Chairs are barely available for the family, church members, the host choir, and two or three other choirs at a time. One mortuary uses two connecting chapels when possible (a rarity for their non-Samoan services), but the crowd generally is such that there is still insufficient seating. Usually the family and church members of the host church are the only non-choir persons present.

The Congregational churches, which characteristically have more members in the area, always have the largest choir participation.[6] Some of the smaller denominations such as the Pentecostals and Seventh Day Adventists are sporadically represented. All churches take pride in their choirs, and generally hold choir practice at least one evening a week. The music is strong, with a uniquely moving quality and tone. With the exception of the Pentecostals, who frequently sing common American hymns in English as well as Samoan, the choirs all sing old Christian hymns translated into Samoan appropriate for this occasion.

After the last choir has had its turn, the host choir may sing once more, and then a closing speech of gratitude is presented by the *matai* or family representative and a closing prayer is given by one of the ministers. As the crowd disperses, members of the family of the deceased frequently pass out foodstuffs, such as tins of coffee or crackers, to the departing guests as they leave the building.

The following morning, frequently a Monday, the funeral service is held. This service usually is not as long nor as well attended as that of the evening before. Family, friends, church members, and the host church choir are present. Again, various ministers representing the churches of the area sit on the stage and take part in the service, which consists of prayers, exhortations, and hymns. A member of the family speaks about the personal life of the deceased. The minister or members of the various church associations or of the choir of the church attest to the dedication of the deceased individual to the church and to Christian life. Customarily, those attending file by the casket to view the dead, and then warmly embrace or kiss the immediate family sitting near the casket. The funeral service is brief, no more than one hour in length. When it closes, people quickly go to their cars and follow the hearse for the last ride to the cemetery.

Of the many cemeteries in the area, several are chosen most frequently by Samoans for the burial of their dead. Large plot areas often are held by one religious denomination in common for all of their members regardless of individual church (Mormons or Catholics, for example), and Samoans of these religions are buried in the general plots. However, some Samoan churches have chosen sites bordering one another in one large cemetery.

The graveside service is a brief one. The family members are seated by the waiting open grave. The presiding minister conducts the service, the other ministers standing behind him. He presents several prayers and farewell statements to the dead, and hymns are sung by the crowd assembled around the burial site. The minister and relatives throw flowers on the casket symbolizing the proverbial "from dust to dust...." Flowers, and the gloves worn by the pall bearers, are lowered with the casket. Sometimes relatives and friends bring cameras and take pictures of the casket with relatives encircling it. A family spokesman then offers the goodbye to the deceased and expresses his gratitude to the ministers and crowd for their participation. He invites them to a reception immediately following burial.

The cars then head for the announced site of a traditional reception or dinner. This may be held in the church fellowship hall, in which case the food is prepared and served by family and church members. The meal features traditional Samoan foods such as chicken, pork, taro, bananas, salt-corned beef, a specialized dish called "chop suey," and potato salad. Enormous amounts of food are served and guests are expected to take home what they cannot eat. Additional wrapped packages of salt-beef, pork, or chicken may be distributed to each guest to take home. Often, however, the dinner is catered and held in the banquet room of a large restaurant. In this case the food is of American style, but it is also served in great abundance. Guests are seated at long tables, with a special table for ministers or honored guests (aside from *matai*) at the head of the room. One of these ministers gives the blessing for the food.

When the diners are some 30 minutes into their meal, an exchange of oratory begins. The chief family spokesman, often a *matai* from Samoa, asks permission from the families and other high-ranking chiefs to speak for the family of the deceased. He gives thanks to God, then thanks the ministers who have taken part, relatives who have come from long distances, and local relatives and friends for their attendance. He prays for the safe journey of those who must return to Samoa or elsewhere. Then, local talking chiefs who have the right to represent the public thank the families of the deceased for the dinner and their courtesies. At times there is competition by title for this honor, and various talking chiefs may dispute the prerogative of one who rises to speak. The family may prefer that no such speech to be given, and the spokesman indicates this to those who rise to speak.

During the course of the dinner the family presents envelopes with money to each of the ministers as a token of appreciation, and to thank them for their participation in the various services. The amounts of money range from $10 to $50 for the participating ministers and from $50 to $100 for the host minister who arranged and conducted the service.

The feast lightens the occasion somewhat, and the immediate family as well as friends may be seen talking and laughing during and after the meal, whereas lighter conversation is not so much in evidence during the preceding days. The crowd disperses and guests leave carrying bags, cartons, or boxes of food.

The old custom of observing a year of mourning is rarely followed now either in Samoa or the mainland cities, although the custom was recently observed in the case of the death of a prominent minister's wife. A graveside service and sumptuous dinner were held to close the mourning period.

Contrast with Contemporary Funeral Activities in American Samoa

Today in Samoa, immediately following a death, the family assembles and decides how long it will take relatives living outside of Samoa to arrive and how soon other necessary preparations can be made. If persons coming from the mainland or Hawaii will be delayed, there are facilities for the body to be kept at the hospital in Pago Pago. Otherwise, the whole funeral procedure is carried out within 24 hours. Embalming is not practiced, and burial is accomplished as soon as possible. All services as well as family exchange activities are centered in the home rather than in the mortuary.

Relatives and friends throughout the islands are alerted, and relatives gather to decide what each will contribute for the occasion. Contributions consist of fine mats and food. The need for cash is minimal, and only the closest of kin contribute money, which is used to pay for the food needed to serve the relatives who come. These relatives begin arriving soon after the death, or after the body is returned to the house from the hospital if there is a delay before the rites begin. Careful consideration is given to the number and kinds of mats given, depending on the status of the deceased and his relationship to the giver. Food donations vary also according to these criteria. Food is given in the form of large items such as kegs of salt-beef, pigs, and cases of sardines or biscuits. The mats collected by the family are then distributed to chiefs who may or may not be related to the deceased. Food collected is distributed to the bilateral kin in much the same fashion as cash is in the mainland cities.

Whereas in the United States the church is central in almost all the activities, there is a sharper dichotomy in Samoa between religious functions and family activities dictated by traditional cultural patterns at the time of death. The minister presides only in a set number of relatively short formal Christian services. He may say last rites before death and counsel with the bereaved following death. If death occurs at the hospital, the minister performs a short service there before the deceased is brought to the house. Only the family and church choir are present at the hospital. The body is then taken to the home, and another service is held, with a few church people and possibly ministers from several other villages. If the person who died was a minister, deacon, or lay preacher, all of the ministers of his district may participate in all of the services. Less often, ministers of other denominations may attend. The ministers and choir then leave, and the exchange of goods occupies the remainder of the day.

When evening comes, the minister and choir perform another service. Choirs come from other villages and sing the same kinds of traditional songs for the occasion as are sung at the public choir service here. When these choirs depart, they are given food by the family to eat after their return to their home villages. Following the singing of church choirs, the titled and untitled women's associations of the village of the deceased arrive. Throughout the night, these groups sing songs that have as their purpose the removal of the sadness of death and the return of the household to joy, while the family cooks and prepares for the next day's activities.

The following morning, the largest crowd at any of the services is present for the funeral. The body, which has been on public view on mats or in an open coffin, is then carried by family members to its resting place on family ground near the house or on the plantation. The plot is prepared by the young men of the family or of the village. A short service similar to the one described above for the mainland city is held at the grave, and the crowd returns for the dinner that follows burial.

Matai and their wives in attendance who are related to the family dine in the house of the deceased. Other *matai* not related to the family are assigned another house for their meal. Untitled relatives and guests are served outside. Formal speeches are made at this time in the houses where the *matai* are dining.

Historical Background of Contemporary Customs

Contemporary ritual elements, such as the presentation and redistribution of food and mats, the choir rotations, and even bookkeeping to identify goods presented can be traced from earlier accounts of Samoan funeral observances. The account by Turner (1884) of death and burial generally describes customs which have since disappeared. He does state that all who came to the burial brought presents which were all distributed again so that each person received something in return for what he had brought (Turner 1884:146).

Mead reported that at the time of her 1925–26 research the old Samoan death chants had been displaced by Christian hymns, and that Christian choirs had taken the responsibility from the untitled men's and women's groups for the customary singing in shifts at the time of an important death. Mead also documented the giving of food, fine mats, and tapa offerings. The food was consumed at the funeral feast, while goods were either returned to their donors or redistributed (Mead 1930:99–100).

A vivid and poignant description of a funeral is presented by Copp (1950), who also describes the choir singing, ritual exchange, and keeping of accounts of donations.

The History and Modification of Funeral Activities in the United States

Interchurch and community-wide interest in funeral activities is said to have developed in the West Coast cities in the early 1960s. The migration of Samoans to the mainland that began in the 1950s was rapidly increasing, and many older people who were knowledgeable about Samoan custom and who wished to perpetuate it in their new homes had arrived. Before that time, when only a few of the many Samoan churches that now flourish in the area existed, the death of a Samoan aroused little interest or activity outside of his extended family.

Informants have suggested the key years of development of the present funeral customs were 1963 and 1964. Mats first were used as a covering for the casket, and later the traditional ritual exchange of mats began. In 1964 many Samoans died in a catastrophic fire that occurred at a Samoan community-wide dance. Concern over relatives and friends led the Samoan population and all churches to reach out in a co-operative endeavor to aid those families touched by the fire with services, money, and personal consolation. One Catholic informant reported that her husband, who was critically burned in the fire, requested that he be given a traditional funeral with many choirs present. She took this plea to church officials and Samoan Catholic laymen. Over some opposition she did arrange such a funeral, and this appears to have set the precedent for the coming together of all denominations for a Catholic funeral. Such an ecumenical movement was unknown before that time. Informants state that funeral customs in mainland cities are becoming more elaborate each year.

Some Samoans have observed that the customs now prevalent in the United States make use of familiar traditional elements, but that they have been confounded through purposeful modification or through ignorance of tradition. In contrasting funeral activities carried out in the California city with contemporary practices in Samoa, modifications in four areas will be pointed out: (1) changes in protocol concerning prerogatives of chiefs; (2) emphasis on collection and redistribution of money rather than goods; (3) centrality of the church; and (4) extension of the network of involved persons.

Changes in Protocol Concerning Prerogatives of Chiefs. In Samoa, traditionally, the funneling of donations of mats has been through talking chiefs who represent their family groups in presenting mats to the family of the deceased or in receiving mats in the redistribution. In the United States all categories of relatives individually present mats.

In the United States, the family spokesman, or the persons representing other families who choose to speak at events may not be talking chiefs, and in fact may hold no *matai* title at all. A chief may speak here, although traditionally the chief could only speak on certain specified occasions. Formal oration was the prerogative of the talking chiefs, as is still the custom in Samoa. Breaks such as these from traditional protocol can occur only in a geographic area far from the homeland, where there is an absence of the controls imposed by the total structural hierarchy, and where there is a genuine shortage of legitimate *matai*, a factor that must be a realistic consideration. Thus, "pretenders" may appear, through necessity or opportunism.

Emphasis on Collection and Redistribution of Money Rather than Goods. The emphasis on the donation of money in the United States recognizes the great expense of funeral and burial procedures in the mainland cities in contrast to Samoa, where an inexpensive coffin is used and there is no need to purchase a burial plot. A mutual aid function has developed in the United States to meet a practical need for immediate cash. However, it may be observed that in almost every instance the money accumulated far exceeds that needed for actual expenses. This overgiving might be explained in several ways. There appears to be a ritual need for a redistribution of surplus of a commodity that has the most practical value in this country, that is cash instead of corned beef. Also the "overgive" serves to reemphasize the cultural value placed on generosity of the greatest extent that a family can manage in this country, where living costs are high. In other words, in the United States, a conspicuous display of money is more impressive than a conspicuous display of food, although importance is still placed on great quantities of food being served and taken home.

Centrality of the Church. The church has become the focal point not only of religious but also of social life for Samoans in the United States. The church is the institution that supports and encourages and is itself supported and encouraged by the maintenance of traditional Samoan customs. In the absence of the traditional village, district, and island hierarchies of family chiefs, the church and its officials fill a structural vacuum. It should be noted that many persons migrated to the United States specifically to escape the strictures that the traditional *matai* system placed on their personal, social, and economic aspirations. In Samoa the *matai* still to a great extent dictate the daily activities of family members and may divide and distribute family resources. Frequently, *matai* are presented with family members' paychecks, which they then apportion as they see fit. A very small amount may be returned to the actual recipient of the check. Although there was a desire to escape these more personal controlling aspects of traditional social structure, there also was a need for certain familiar supports of the culture. Church structures quickly developed to meet the needs of the individual for religion and the fellowship of other Samoans, while allowing him and his family the same basic freedom to strive for social and economic mobility that has lured immigrants to the United States from all over the world.

Extension of Network of Involved Persons. In Samoa at all times, but especially at the time of death, the individual has not only large family groups to count on for practical and emotional support, but also the potential aid of a total village. There is a strong interpersonal network in a small circumscribed geographic area. In the large and alien metropolis, where one's neighbors are not known and can hardly be expected to give substantial aid in time of crisis, a sense of cultural and social unity has enlarged the network of persons that one can rely on and, conversely, that one feels responsibilities toward, to include all Samoans. The church choirs have served as actual and symbolic vehicles of this strengthening community feeling among Samoans. Although weddings also evoke community attention, it is significant that the coming together of churches of all denominations developed only at the time of death, the ultimate life crisis.

The Social Uses of Samoan Funeral Activities

Anthropologists have demonstrated that funeral rites are a particularly good area in which to examine the social functions of ritual (Mandelbaum 1959; Firth 1961; Vallee 1955; Nadel 1951). Firth noted that "a funeral rite is a social rite par excellance. Its ostensible object is the dead person, but it benefits not the dead, but the living." Firth suggested that funeral rites as he witnessed them in Tikopia served a variety of social functions. They provided a social symbol of finality, wherein the death was publicly acknowledged by family and community. Furthermore, he observed, as had Radcliffe-Brown before him, that such ritual reinforces the system of social sentiments of the group. This reinforcement is in part exhibited in the economic activities that take place at the time of death, e.g., the passage of goods between specified persons serves as a concrete expression and reinforcement of social forms and expectations (Firth 1961: 63–64).

The social uses of Samoan funeral activities fall in interlocking ways within the functions Firth defined. The social and economic elements are almost inextricable. But, in addition to these functions which Firth observed in the stable cultural tradition of Tikopia, Samoan customs, when viewed within the dynamic contextual situation of a migrant group in the process of developing a new life style, take on a greater significance. They perform a critical function of aiding in the social and economic survival of a village people in the most complex of metropolitan settings.

These social uses of the Samoan funeral can be summarized under four headings: (1) reinforcement of family and community solidarity; (2) reiteration of basic Samoan cultural themes; (3) reaffirmation of the significance of the Samoan Christian church; and (4) mutual aid for survival in the city.

Reinforcement of Family and Community Solidarity. The immediate rallying of kin and friends around the household of the deceased is both spontaneous and expected. The gathering of the closest bilateral kin who reside in the area and the arrival of relatives from Samoa and mainland cities contributes with studied efficiency to take the burden of decision and arrangement-making off the lone shoulders of spouse, parents, or children. There are many minds and hands to help with the numerous practical matters that must be attended to, to console the grieving, and to take care of children who suddenly may be left without a parent. Likewise the planning and conferencing necessary for the intricate money collection activities reinforce the cohesion of the family. Nadel (1951: 167) has noted that individuals participating in common activities may in the course of these activities share emotional experiences which develop a bond between them, a predisposition to work together more effectively in other contexts. The more emotionally charged the experience, the greater may be the strength of such bonds that develop.

Indeed, the coming together of the Samoan community at the time of death fosters an esprit de corps which serves them well in a new urban situation. One funeral director commented that he feels a chief reason that Samoans manage their grief so well is that they have "extraordinary financial and moral backing." He pointed out that many of his clients have only one other person to rely on for practical matters, and to comfort them, but Samoans have a whole "colony."

The Samoan identity establishes imperatives of responsibility to one's fellows. Death clearly evokes support not only of relatives but of other Samoans who may have been friends of the deceased, who migrated from the same village, or who had only a bare acquaintance with him. Because the Samoan population of the area is so large, people may know only relatives, friends, and persons attending their church. However, because of early village ties, schools attended in the islands, and wide affinal involvement, they know of other people. The feeling exists that one should contribute money and should attend the funeral services because the person who died was Samoan. It is said that the family of the deceased would be ashamed if only a handful of people or a few choirs came, or if their closing meal had few guests. However, given the number of relatives and affinal kin that any Samoan is bound to have in the area, and the fact that others come to show respect for the relatives and affines of the deceased, as well as for the deceased, a sizable crowd is always assured. If a relative cannot attend the services, he will at least stop by the house of the deceased to make his presentation and offer consolation. One comes to show respect; and if a person does not meet the needs of others, they may not meet his in similar circumstances. Indeed, this practical consideration may be more effective than the threat of having one's face blackened with soot, the punishment Mead (1930: 100) recorded for those who failed to appear to sing for the dead.

Having to work is often the only legitimate excuse one might have for not participating in the choir singing. As one informant put it: "Well, if I had to work, that's all right. You could be excused to work, but if somebody saw you going to a show instead of going to sing, then you or they would feel badly about it."

Samoans are ingenious in their ability to find ways of being excused from their jobs to attend funeral functions. Many women work in nursing homes where there are other Samoans on the staff, and they are able to trade shifts or days off. Also, many persons work swing or night shifts, and are thus free for morning activities. (Churches often arrange to have their main Sunday service in the morning or afternoon depending on the work shifts of the majority of members.)

The number of funerals each year in this area varies from five to fifteen. Most funerals are for older persons who die from natural causes. Younger persons usually represent traffic fatalities. The potential for depressive feelings at attending so many funerals was probed in interviews. It became apparent that even this suggestion reflected imposed cultural bias on the part of the investigator. The effect of melancholy is subordinated to the social obligations of attendance. Unless the person who died was a close relative or friend, an attitude of uninvolvement with the situation or the obvious grief of relatives seems to prevail. A woman who attends almost every funeral service held in the area was asked:

Q: How do you feel about being present at so many sad occasions? Does it make you feel sad?
A: I don't know too many people here except my relatives. I left the island in 1948. Unless it is someone you know, in this case you do feel sad, then you just sort of sit there.
Q: What do you think about?
A: Well, you sit there and you are curious. You wonder what is going to happen next on the program, or you just look around and see the people that are there. That is the way you spend your time.

Samoans view death as one of the natural events in the experience of the living. In contrast, death in the United States is a subject that is hidden away, or at least ignored as much as possible. As a commentary on this, there is little ritual at the time of death, and most persons attend only the funerals of those with whom they have had close interaction. Indeed, by age fifty, a person may only have attended a half a dozen funerals. For Samoans, death has little of this mystique.

Mead (1961: 105–106) has discussed the way in which birth and death are presented matter-of-factly to the Samoan child. She vividly described the mode of primitive autopsy at the grave to determine the cause of death, and the postmortem Caesarean operation customary for women who died in pregnancy. Children routinely viewed these events.

Mead stated that these "horrible but perfectly natural, non-unique occurrences" were presented as a legitimate part of the Samoan child's experiences. In contrast, the American child whose circle of intimates is much smaller, may only experience the death of one close relative in his years of growing up. All of the negative affect surrounding one highly charged emotional experience may be carried over to all other deaths that he encounters in his later life (Mead 1961: 158). The fact that Samoans, in contrast to mainland Americans, tend to view death as an aspect of the daily reality of life, allows the funeral rites and accompanying activities to provide a positive area for social interaction.

Reiteration of Basic Samoan Cultural Themes. Central themes of Samoan life are generosity, hospitality, reciprocity, and helping one another. This applies to the stranger in the path, as well as the relative in one's home; hence the importance of the ritualized presentations of money, fine mats, and food, and the expected attendance at ceremonies. Through his generosity, the donor honors himself and his extended family in the United States and in Samoa, as well as the recipient.

The giving of fine mats is a ritual documented by early chroniclers of Samoan life. In the United States, at the time of a funeral, mats must appropriately accompany the money presentations of relatives. Several informants expressed the opinion that the exchange of mats is an antiquated custom that still might "make sense" in Samoa, but one that they consider as useless (as contrasted to the very functional donation of money) in the United States. Yet these same persons feel their responsibility to contribute mats as long as the custom continues, and they unfailingly follow the elaborate protocol attending the presentation of the mats.

Generosity and hospitality are strongly evidenced by the supplying of food to visitors and the preparing and sponsoring of the elaborate dinner that is a requisite ending to the funeral ceremonies. The large crowd, the great quantity of food consumed and taken home—all honor and maintain the prestige of the family of the deceased, as well as serving to express gratitude to those who participated in the last rites. In discussing the social and symbolic significance of food for Samoan ceremony, Keesing (1956: 80) noted that a successful feast insured that the occasion and its business purpose would be publicly validated and would hold a place in the memories of the guests, a most significant consideration in an oral culture. Samoan mainland custom has indeed maintained the tradition of elaborate feasting at funerals and weddings, as well as at other less formal ceremonial occasions held in the household or church.

Reaffirmation of the Significance of the Samoan Christian Churches. Reaffirmation of the daily importance of Christianity—whatever the particular denomination—in the life and death of parishioners is effectively accomplished in the course of the funeral observances. All of the formal rites are couched within Christian form and dogma. Since the advent of the London Missionary Society and other Christian churches in Samoa, there has been an effective integration of the Christian religion with the traditional social structure. The church today remains a center of Samoan village life, and church attendance and household family prayer are routine. In the United States, the churches developed upon the mushrooming of Samoan settlement and quickly became the centers of social activity for individuals and families. It is fitting, therefore, that the churches take on the responsibility for the last rites of their members and elaborately dispatch the dead, while drawing the living even closer to the bosom of church security in an alien environment.

The development and elaboration of Samoan churches assume a special significance when examined within the context of the migration process of a non-Western village people entering an impersonal metropolitan area. The integration of a religious dimension with as many life activities as possible may serve to recapture some of the sacred nature of Samoan life, as opposed to the secularism of daily life in urban America. Other ethnic migrants have likewise turned to intensive organized religion in their attempts to reestablish the sacred quality of life that their small communities had provided for them.

At the time of death, religion appears to be the chief consolation for the mourners. In the very act of withstanding the sacrifice of their loved one, they are able to show their dedication to God and Jesus, much as Abraham was privileged for the opportunity to sacrifice Isaac (this parallel was drawn by a minister in speaking to a congregation about the recent loss of a much-loved member). The continual reaffirmation of their faith allows some survivors to speak of this time of death as their happiest hour, of sacrifice accompanied by understanding and blessing.

Frequently the speakers at the services are the choir director and representatives from the men's or women's associations of the deceased individual's church. They talk about the contributions of the deceased as a member of these groups. The dead one may be pointed to as an example of Christian conduct or as the exemplary Christian mother or Christian father. The significance of the person's relationship to the church is stressed. If a person was especially active in the church or was a member of the minister's family, the services are more likely to be held in the church rather than the mortuary, and there may be additional special prayer services in the church to honor the family.

A Force for Survival in the City. The prospering of a new ethnic group in a metropolitan area is influenced by many complex factors, one of the most significant being the cultural heritage its members bring with them to their new environment. Their valued attitudes and forms of behavior greatly affect their economic and social adaptation in numerous and complex ways. A key cultural characteristic that has contributed to Samoan success in the city is that of family and community cohesion and loyalty. The responsibilities of loyalty extend in varying degrees to all Samoans. The time of death offers the opportunity for this loyalty and adhering mutual aid obligations to prove their most functional when kin and community are mobilized to aid and console a family in the throes of the ultimate life (death) crisis.

For many Samoans, the sympathy and desire to help are naively spontaneous responses, and they little question the obligation to give money, despite the continual drain on finances of large households. Some, in fact, comment on the security that the reciprocal nature of the cash exchange offers them for their own times of crisis.

> When my son died, my relatives paid for the whole funeral—you know, I didn't have anything, any money. Look, if your husband should die, for instance, you would just have to sweat it out yourself—you wouldn't have any money. I was given $2,000 right away by the relatives that paid for all the expenses. It is very important that you have someone to help you at a time like that—to help with money. People come and give. Everybody helps. The thing is that you are giving and giving, but you know that you get it all back. There will come a day that it will all come back to you. If you don't give to anybody else, then when you have a death, when you have a wedding, when you have that time of trouble when you need money, you won't have anything. And it's like everybody is related. You know somebody and you just have to help them.

Nonetheless, ambivalence about giving is created by a conflict of cultural dictates and practical considerations of household finances in homes where there are many mouths to feed. Informants often refer to this conflict:

> That's one thing with the Samoan people—when anything happens, other Samoans help you. Not just relatives, but other people care about you. Not like Americans here. Where no one cares and the people don't help you. You know—I might want to refuse.

> Q: What do you mean?
> A: Well, when we get our pay checks—my husband works hard to pay for us and our children and our house, but every month we always must help someone when there is a wedding or funeral, or someone goes back to Samoa. There is always this thing—we always have to pay money—$50, $100, $200, and so on.
> Q: What do you do? Do you ever refuse?
> A: No, I never refuse. We can never refuse. We always help. And it just means that we don't pay some of our bills then. But we can never refuse this.

And another comment:

> Some people would like to cancel out that custom to give. They just don't want to have to give all that money. I have a lot of bills here just to pay for my house and to pay for my family, and then I am slapped with a bill to pay for somebody who needs it. But there are too many people around, and there is nothing you can do about it. You can't get away from it.

One informant, when asked if there are people who do not give, replied:

> Yeah, there are a lot of people who won't give anything, but some people can't give at one time because it just hits them at a bad time when they don't have money or something ahead, and they can't give. But another time of trouble will come and they will give. You don't just have one trouble in your life, you have many troubles. And when the next time of trouble comes, then they will give. So it will be all right. People know. Maybe if you can't help someone this time people know you would help them next time.

Other Samoans are more cynical about the necessity to give. One very active church member expressed his reservations as follows:

> Nobody has to play that political game and particularly over here, and people don't realize it. What can they do to you? Like, people are always complaining to me. You have to give money, have to give this, have to chip in, have to help. I say to them, "You're crazy, you don't have to do anything. What are they going to do to you?"
>
> Well, everyone's so afraid people are talking about them. I say, so let them talk. That's not going to harm you because you know they're not giving you your job or you're not dependent on them anymore. I don't give anything unless I want to.

However, this same informant was himself ambivalent; he makes it a point to attend every funeral, and commented on how badly a family would feel if "nobody showed up."

Every Samoan family contacted in the course of this research was asked what they most disliked about life in the United States, compared to Samoa. In response, most commented on the fact that people just do not care or feel responsible for others and their welfare. The Samoan, by contrast, has to care, has to help, has to be there. Persons in temporary need are aided by family or church. Informants generally disclaim knowledge of any family in chronic financial distress, but several stated that if it were known that a man could not support his family and his alternative was to receive public welfare, his relatives would collect money to send the family back to Samoa. The receiving of welfare benefits is considered shameful for a family; thus the fact is usually concealed from other Samoans. The number of families receiving public welfare appears to be very small proportionate to the size of the community.

Conclusion

Samoan funeral rites in urban America display a remarkable blending of Samoan tradition, elaborate Christian ceremony, and practical consideration and planning for the realities of a new environment. Differences from contemporary island practices reflect efforts to meet these realities as well as shifts that occur as a result of opportunities for deliberate changes in those aspects of the culture that Samoans wished to escape by their migration.

Funeral customs in this California community represent a rich area for the analysis of social process and cultural change. The ritual patterns described here have developed during less than a decade and have become more elaborate each year as the process of cultural reorganization takes place. Indeed, the occasion of death is an event that reflects the continuing reinforcement of the cultural and social identity of the individual, and the regirding of Samoan cultural and Christian tradition to meet the demands of urban life.

NOTES

1. The field research for this paper was supported in part by the National Institute of Mental Health, U.S.P.H.S. Grant No. MH–08375 to the Community Mental Health Training Program, Langley Porter Neuropsychiatric Institute; General Research Support Grant No. FR–67–23 (awarded to Langley Porter Neuropsychiatric Institute), from the General Research Support Branch, Division of Research Facilities and Resources, National Institutes of Health; and Ford Foundation Grant No. 690–0231 (administered through the Urban Research and Public Service Program, University of California).

I would like to thank Faatui Laolagi for assisting in the collection of the data on which this paper is based, and for his criticisms of the manuscript.

2. There are no accurate census figures for the California Samoan population. The figures given here are estimates by Samoan ministers who travel widely between these cities.

3. The *matai* is the family title holder who bears the responsibilities and privileges of leadersliip of the extended family. *Matai* are classified as chiefs and as talking chiefs or official orators.

4. Mead (1930: 40) thus defined the term *aiga*: "Aiga means relative by blood, marriage and adoption, and although no native actually confuses the three ways by which the *aiga* status is arrived at, nevertheless a blanket attitude is implied in the use of the word. An *aiga* is always one's ally against other groups, bound to give one food, shelter and assistance. ... No marriage is permitted with any one termed *aiga* and all contemporary *aigas* are considered as brothers and sisters. Under the shadow of these far-flung recognized relationships children wander in safety, criminals find a haven, fleeing lovers take shelter, the traveler is housed, fed and his failing resources reinforced, property is collected for a house building or a marriage; and a whole island is converted into a series of cities of refuge from poverty, embarrassment, or local retribution." This functional definition is especially relevant for the understanding of the practical value of the retention of extended family bonds in the urban setting.

5. Mead (1930: 73) offered a detailed discussion of the making and economic value of the fine mat, and noted: "Fine mats (i.e. *toga*) have often been called the Samoan currency. Their economic value is ceremonially enhanced by their age, by high lineage of the ladies who plaited them, and by the exchanges in which they have played a part. Some mats come to have the same sort of almost fictitious value which is attached to stamps or coins with us. Such mats have names, their history is well known, and is conventionalized into a formal account how and where the name was given."

6. The London Missionary Society, which Christianized the Samoan Islands in 1830, constituted the first of the many Christian missionaries to Samoa. The majority of Samoans still attend LMS churches both in Samoa and in the mainland cities, where these churches frequently have affiliated with their American counterpart, the Congregational churches.

BIBLIOGRAPHY

Copp, J. D. 1950. The Samoan Dance of Life. Boston.

Firth, R. 1961. Elements of Social Organization. Third edit. Boston.

Keesing, F. M., and M. M. Keesing. 1956. Elite Communication in Samoa: A Study of Leadership. Stanford.

Mandelbaum, D. G. 1959. Social Uses of Funeral Rites. The Meaning of Death, ed. H. Feifel, pp. 189–217. New York.

Mead, M. 1930. Social Organization of Manu'a. Bulletins of the Bernice P. Bishop Museum 76: 1–218.

———. 1961. Coming of Age in Samoa. Third edit. New York.
Nadel, S. F. 1951. The Foundations of Social Anthropology. London.
Turner, G. 1884. Samoa. London.
Vallee, F. G. 1955. Burial and Mourning Customs in a Hebridian Community. Journal of the Royal Anthropological Institute 85: 119–130.

Filipino Hometown Associations in Hawaii[1]

Jonathan Y. Okamura

>>> <<<

HOMETOWN ASSOCIATIONS have proliferated among Filipino immigrants in Hawaii since the arrival of increasing numbers of Filipinos after the liberalization of United States immigration laws in 1965. These organizations either have been started anew or represent revivals of previously inactive groups. Awareness of their growing numbers seems to have given rise to a desire on the part of immigrants who share a common specific locality of origin to establish and to maintain ties with one another through formal organization. From a review of various lists of Filipino voluntary associations compiled by the Oahu Filipino Community Council (a federation of Filipino organizations on Oahu), the Filipino 75th Anniversary Commemoration Commission,[2] and the Philippine Consulate General in Hawaii, it seems that there were 62 Filipino hometown and provincial organizations on the island of Oahu in 1981. These associations comprise a little more than half of the total number of voluntary organizations represented on these lists. Yet, despite the significant increase in the number of hometown associations since 1965, most of these organizations are not especially active and are no longer necessary to meet the mutual aid functions for which they were originally established during the plantation period of labor recruitment. This paper seeks to determine the factors that account for the continued existence and establishment of hometown associations and the purposes they presently serve.

Bases of Membership

The bases of membership of Filipino regional, that is, hometown or provincial organizations reflect the nature of both the historical and present processes of immigration to Hawaii. The more intensive plantation labor recruitment during the 1920s in the Ilocos region in northern Luzon[3] and the continued predominance of Ilokanos among Filipino immigrants to Hawaii are evident in the greater number of Ilokano associations. That is, 39 associations, or almost two-thirds of the total number of regional organizations, base their memberships on communities in the Ilocos region. Because of the substantial numbers of Ilokano immigrants in Hawaii, 34 of these associations represent hometowns, while the remainder are provincial or wider regional organizations. There are also nine associations whose memberships are drawn from Pangasinan province, which is adjacent to the Ilocos region, and eight of these are hometown associations.

The earlier arrival and the lesser numbers of plantation workers from the Visayas region are reflected in the few organizations which represent that area. Significantly, these are not hometown but provincial associations for Bohol, Siquijor, Samar and Leyte, and the Visayas in general.

In the past, there was only one association that drew its membership from the Tagalog area around Manila, but it later changed its name so that non-Tagalogs could also join. However, since the post-1965 immigration of Filipinos to Hawaii there are several organizations that represent provinces in the central Luzon area including Bulacan, Tarlac, Cavite, Batangas, and Nueva Ecija.

The basis of membership in Filipino regional organizations is common locale of origin, either a town or a province, in the Philippines. Associations also extend membership to the spouses of members if they are not from the community in question and to local, Hawaii-born Filipinos whose parents are from that community. However, few local Filipinos join hometown associations or participate in their activities. Most associations are not very restrictive about membership and, in some cases, have provisions for honorary membership to persons, usually officers of other associations, who would otherwise be ineligible to join. However, in one association an individual who is not from the town or related to someone from the town can only become a member by first being declared an adopted son or daughter of the town by resolution of the municipal council in the Philippines.

Annual membership dues in Filipino hometown associations are generally between $2 to $5 per person. Some associations, aware that their members have more pressing economic obligations, charge only an initial membership fee. It is not uncommon for hometown associations to have fairly large memberships, between 200 to 400 persons, although active members comprise a minority of the total membership. In some hometown associations the leaders emphasize that their activities, especially the larger social gatherings, are open to all persons from the town, whether or not they are association members.

Entitlements and Benefits of Membership

Filipino hometown associations provide various benefits for their members. In most cases, it is stated in its constitution and by-laws that one of the objectives of the organization is to provide assistance to members in times of illness, emergency, or death. In the event of the latter, members may be assessed a specified amount, generally between $2 and $5, or the association contributes a prescribed sum of money to the family of the deceased. Such death benefits are not inconsiderable, and the deceased's family may receive anywhere from $200 to $500, depending on the size of the membership of the association. In one especially large organization, the deceased's beneficiaries could receive up to $850. This money is often presented to the family at the wake for the deceased by the association's president who may also deliver a short eulogy. In addition, some associations donate a floral wreath in its name, and one organization also pays for the announcement of the death on a Filipino radio station. Association members are expected to attend the services for a deceased member.

Some hometown associations provide small monetary amounts to members when they are hospitalized or when a member takes a trip to the Philippines. Several associations award scholarships to the children of members.

In addition to these benefits which are specified as entitlements of membership, members may receive additional benefits through informal interaction with other association members. Friendships may develop, and contacts can be made with persons who may be sources of information on jobs and housing or who can provide introductions to persons who are able to furnish such assistance.

Most hometown associations hold at least one large social gathering during the year, usually a dinner and dance or a potluck picnic. Some organizations appear to compete implicitly with one another for prestige in terms of where they hold their social affairs, and for these associations Waikiki hotel banquet rooms have become the standard. These social functions are generally for the installation of new officers, the coronation of the association's beauty queen, to commemorate the anniversary of the founding of the organization or, less frequently, to honor municipal officials or other distinguished guests from their hometown. The proceedings at these affairs are very similar; the keynote address, one of several speeches, is delivered by a Filipino politician or government official, and officers are inducted by an official from the Philippine Consulate. In some of the more traditional associations, the Philippine national anthem along with the "Star Spangled Banner" are sung at the beginning of the program.

The souvenir programs for these social affairs are also very similar in format and are modeled after the program booklets which are prepared for town fiestas in the Philippines. Their contents include congratulatory messages from the president of the Philippines (fabricated in some instances), the provincial governor of Ilocos Norte or Ilocos Sur, the governor of Hawaii, the mayor of Honolulu, and the consul-general of the

Philippine Consulate in Hawaii. These messages seem intended to enhance the prestige of the association. Also included in the souvenir program are advertisements and congratulatory remarks from Filipino travel, real estate, and insurance agents, restaurant owners, and other businessmen, many of whom are association leaders, and from other Filipino voluntary organizations. These advertisements are a significant source of funds for associations and establish reciprocal relationships with other voluntary organizations that can be expected to make similar appeals for advertising when they hold their annual social gatherings.

In only a few cases are these social functions of hometown associations held to coincide with their town fiesta in the Philippines or include aspects of a typical fiesta. One association does hold an annual *Fiesta ti Kailokuan*, or fiesta from the Ilocos, that comprises some of the more traditional elements of the town fiesta. It includes the presentation of a standardized drama or *comedia Ilokana*, song and dance numbers, and the coronation of the fiesta queen. The latter follows Philippine tradition as the queen, dressed in a formal gown with a long train, promenades with an escort to her throne where she is presented with a sash, crown, and trophy by different Filipino politicians and community leaders.

Almirol (1978:82) maintains that in California, Filipino voluntary associations "provide a social framework for interpersonal relations within the ethnic community." This generalization as it stands is also valid in Hawaii, especially since many hometown associations draw their memberships from Honolulu and widely scattered plantation towns, and members may not have the opportunity to see each other regularly. It must be noted, however, that most hometown associations in Hawaii do not have regular and frequent activities that bring their members together. In most organizations, meetings are supposed to be held every three months but usually are held irregularly, and the majority of members do not attend anyway. The infrequency of meetings is essentially because associations have few ongoing activities that require discussion or participation by members. Most members of Filipino associations seem content to limit their participation to the purchase of fund-raising tickets, to the payment of dues and death benefits, and to attendance at the annual banquet or Christmas party. It is a commonly heard expression among Filipino immigrants that they are "too busy" with work, family, and other social obligations, and this factor may also account for their lack of participation or nonmembership in hometown associations. It might also be pointed out that there are other, perhaps more frequent, social occasions within the immigrant Filipino community for "townmates" (immigrants from the same hometown in the Philippines) to renew their ties with one another and with other immigrants. Whenever a family celebrates a rite of passage, such as a baptism, wedding, birthday, or graduation, townmates are generally invited, whether or not they are members of a common hometown association.

Nonetheless, although large social gatherings such as installation or anniversary banquets or potluck picnics are generally held only once a year, association members still appreciate these opportunities to see each other and to renew their relationships. Similarly, while meetings do not attract most of the members of an organization, for those who do attend regularly they are occasions for convivial fellowship before and after association matters are discussed. Meetings are commonly held at the homes of members rather than at more formal settings, and refreshments are served afterwards. On special occasions such as the election of officers that attract more than the usual number of members, the association may pay for a pig to be prepared for everyone's enjoyment.

Ties with the Hometown

Most Filipino regional associations in Hawaii have made monetary or other charitable contributions to their home communities in the Philippines, and this activity is often stated as one of the primary objectives in the constitution and bylaws of organizations. In the recent past, associations have donated money to their hometowns for the construction of health centers, a water tank, an electric power plant, for repairs to the municipal building and town plaza, to assist schools, churches, and hospitals, and for walkie-talkies and uniforms for the town police. For the more costly projects, plaques are commonly erected in the hometown which note the name of the contributing association. Besides these enduring kinds of projects, monetary and material assistance are sent to home communities on occasions of natural disasters such as floods or fires. It should be noted that in the great majority of cases these contributions are not regular organization activities but were given either at the request of the hometown or at the inclination of the association. Only a few organizations have annual fund-raising projects, such as popularity beauty queen contests, banquets, or the sale of foodstuffs, to raise money for their hometowns.

Once a hometown association has donated money or material goods to its home community, it can expect to be besieged with continued requests for assistance. In one case, the administrators of an elementary school in the Philippines sent a copy of a resolution which expressed their gratitude to the association of their townspeople in Hawaii for its contribution towards the purchase of playground equipment. Accompanying the resolution was yet another which formally requested their donation of a typewriter. The latter was a rather modest request because previously the association had been asked to purchase a station wagon for the municipal government. These contributions seem to have enhanced the perception on the part of people in the home communities that the United States is a veritable land of plenty where even immigrants have easy access to material wealth.

Donations to their hometown are a means for former residents in Hawaii to demonstrate their continuing concern for their home communities and to signify to townspeople that they have attained a measure of economic success as immigrants in their adopted country. In return for their charitable contributions, association members are accorded social prestige as civic minded and prosperous individuals by their home communities. Such recognition can be enjoyed at a distance; for example, chairs that were donated to a public school in the Philippines each bore the name of the individual donors in Hawaii. The relation between the home community and the hometown association would seem to be of greater benefit to the former than to the latter since the hometown gains substantially more in tangible terms than do association members. Certainly, it is more common for the home community to request assistance than for the association to offer it. Also, while townspeople in Hawaii do have a desire to assist in the development of their hometowns, they are sometimes suspicious if money sent to the town is actually spent on the project for which it was intended. Municipal officials and association officers are the usual objects of these suspicions.

Some of the more active associations organize *balikbayan* (returnee from abroad) trips to the Philippines for their members, usually to coincide with the fiesta of their hometown. These organizations also commonly sponsor popularity beauty queen contests in conjunction with their trips home so that the association's queen, along with her attendant princesses, can be crowned during the town fiesta. Proceeds from the popularity contest are sometimes presented as a contribution to the hometown during the fiesta. Popularity queen contests are generally decided on the basis of the sale of raffle tickets, the prize sometimes a trip to the Philippines, and the winner is the young woman who has sold the most tickets.

A few of the hometown associations that organize popularity queen contests have revived the social box dance as another means to raise funds. In the past, this practice was commonly observed on the plantations in Hawaii among Filipino laborers and is still held in the Philippines. At a box dance, each of the queen contestants brings three wrapped boxes which usually contain some food item or alcoholic beverage. During the evening's proceedings, the master of ceremonies announces that the next dance is for the box of a particular candidate "to the damage of $25." The young men present then begin bidding at that amount for the privilege of dancing with the young lady and also for the box. As a higher bid is made, a young man steps forward to dance, and the winner of the box is the gentleman who has made the highest bid by the end of the song. The money he is thus obliged to pay is contributed to the monetary tally of the candidate in question.

During the plantation era, social box dances were occasions for eligible young men to distinguish themselves in order to gain the attention of a young woman or her parents. The winning bid for a box was then about $10, while at present it may be $50 to $100. However, during the "last canvassing" when the final tally will be made and the queen declared, winning bids may be in excess of $1,000, although this money is not from a single individual but from close relatives and friends of a candidate who pool their resources. Besides money that is received from the winning bids, supporters of a contestant also place envelopes of money collected from the sale of raffle tickets into a ballot box. At the end of the evening's proceedings, a final tally is made of the money raised by each candidate and the young lady who has raised the most money is declared the association's queen. Social box dances and popularity queen contests in general have the potential to raise substantial amounts of money for an association, depending on the number of candidates, and gross proceeds of $15,000 to $20,000 from such events are not uncommon.

The officers and other members of a hometown association can expect to be treated as special and honored guests of their hometown when they return for its town fiesta. For example, in the case of one such association that has organized annual trips to their hometown since 1975, the party in their rented bus is met at the municipal boundary by townspeople, and they proceed in a motorcade to the town. Upon their arrival, they are honored guests along with other *balikbayans* at a lavish party hosted by the town mayor at which they are individually recognized. During the town fiesta, one of the evenings is sponsored by the hometown association and is highlighted by the coronation of its queen and princesses and by the presentation to the town by the association president of a monetary contribution, $1,000 in recent years.

Voluntary Associations as Adaptive Mechanisms

Much of the social anthropological literature on voluntary associations has focused on their role as adaptive mechanisms in situations of social and cultural change (see Kerri 1976 for a review). Functional analysis has resulted in a decided emphasis on the positive aspects of voluntary associations such that all manner of activity in these associations is viewed as being of eufunctional significance for their members. Nonetheless, the literature from Africa in particular (Banton 1956; Little 1957, 1965; Parkin 1966) has clearly demonstrated the part that voluntary associations play in the adjustment of migrants from rural areas to towns and cities. However, this adaptive role of voluntary associations is not as appropriate to an understanding of Filipino immigrants and their hometown associations in Hawaii.

For example, Little (1957:593) maintains that in West Africa voluntary associations facilitate adjustment for the urban migrant by serving as a substitute for the extended family and thus satisfying many of the same needs as this traditional grouping. This support and assistance are provided in the form of companionship, legal counsel and protection, and sickness and funeral benefits (Little 1957:593). In the past, Filipino laborers on the plantations were provided with such familial aid and support by joining a *saranay* or mutual aid society. These associations were formed among townmates or the wider Filipino plantation community to provide various social and security benefits. For their one dollar monthly dues, members were entitled to attend picnics, dances, and social gatherings hosted by another member. In the event of illness or death of a member, the club made a contribution to his family through assessments on its members (Alcantara 1981: 58). Hospitalization and death benefits were also provided through another form of mutual aid society, the *inanama*, although since its members did not assemble it lacked the social functions of the *saranay* (Alcantara 1981:58). Mutual assistance was also available through membership in a *kumpang* (*amung* in Ilokano) or rotating credit association in which a number of men contributed a prescribed amount of money each month and received in turn the entire sum that was collected.

At present, hometown associations no longer perform a surrogate role of the extended family for Filipino immigrants in Hawaii because of the fairly extensive kinship ties of most immigrants since the 1965 changes in United States immigration laws. It is on his kin that the newly arrived immigrant depends for assistance in finding his first job and for his initial accommodation, which is usually provided at no expense (Okamura 1983:163–164). Even after he has been settled in Hawaii, he continues to rely on his kin for advice and assistance, for example, in petitioning other members of his family, learning to drive a car, or buying a house. It might be noted that certain kinds of security provisions, such as health and unemployment insurance, retirement benefits, and welfare assistance, are provided through one's employer or by the state government, thus also lessening the dependence of immigrants on hometown associations.

In the absence of close relatives, it is true that the recently arrived immigrant may turn to townmates for assistance, but the basis for expecting aid is not common membership in a hometown association but the townmate relationship itself. In the immigrant setting in Hawaii, townmates look upon each other as quasi-kin and are considered as potential sources of assistance. Thus, in the event of the death of a townmate, one would not refrain from the customary paying of respects at his wake or funeral and a monetary contribution to his family simply because the deceased, although a townmate, was not a member of the hometown association. A distinction must be maintained between townmates and members of a common hometown association. Although both relationships derive from common origin in the same town, many of the familial functions that Little (1957) assigned to voluntary associations in West Africa are observed by immigrant Filipino townmates in Hawaii whether or not they share mutual membership in a hometown association.

Little (1957:593–594) also contends that in West Africa voluntary associations serve as substitutes for traditional agencies of social control and for the resolution of private disputes. In the past on the plantations, the association president may have admonished members not to bring shame to their fellow members by unsociable behavior (Alcantara 1981:58). At present, however, hometown associations do not have that degree of authority over their members. At the individual level, sanctions against improper behavior originate in the family and extend to the larger Filipino community through informal neighborhood gossip networks. Similarly, domestic disputes can be settled within the family and need not be taken to association leaders.

What should be clear at this point is that Filipino hometown associations in Hawaii do not facilitate the adjustment of immigrants by serving as surrogates for the extended family. The essential reason for this is because the social circumstances of Filipino immigrants at present differ considerably from the plantation period of labor recruitment. Furthermore, Filipino immigrants have a more viable adaptive mechanism, the presence of real kinsmen, to assist them in their adjustment to the wider Hawaii society.

Little (1957:593) also implies that in West Africa voluntary associations facilitate adaptation for rural immigrants into the towns by functioning as acculturative mechanisms insofar as they instill new standards of dress, etiquette, hygiene, and punctuality. In particular, he notes that the "traditional-modernized" association acts as a "cultural bridge which conveys ... the tribal individual from one kind of sociological universe to another" (Little 1957:593). He also remarks that by encouraging the migrant to socialize with persons from outside his lineage and tribe, the association assists him in adjusting to the more cosmopolitan atmosphere of urban life (Little 1957:593).

Filipino hometown associations in Hawaii do not serve this acculturative role for immigrants because they do not exert that degree of influence or control over their members. Filipino immigrants experience acculturation processes more through their daily work situation, where they usually must speak English, interact with non-Filipinos, observe interpersonal norms of behavior appropriate to such relationships and become acquainted with aspects of local culture in Hawaii, than through their membership in hometown associations. While members may be exposed to such association practices as parliamentary procedures, organizing fund-raising and social activities, and seeking office, these are not activities that are of instrumental use in an immigrant's daily life. Furthermore, hometown associations tend to maintain certain cultural traditions and social relations rather than serve as instruments of social or cultural change. That is, Ilokano is the common medium at meetings, links with the home community are continued, hometown traditions are perpetuated, and social ties with townmates are reinforced. While hometown associations cannot be said to encapsulate an immigrant in a network of social relationships solely with other immigrants, they also do not promote interactions with other ethnic groups since non-Filipinos are rarely present at association activities and affairs except for politicians seeking Filipino votes.

Despite the inapplicability of some of Little's (1957) notions of voluntary organizations as adaptive mechanisms to the case of Filipino hometown associations in Hawaii, one of his West African findings is quite appropriate. He observes that voluntary associations serve an adaptive role through the new criteria of social achievement they set up and through the opportunity they offer for the "ambitions of the rising class of young men ... who have been to school" (Little 1957:592). A similar observation is made by Banton (1956:365) who notes that Temne companies in Freetown allocate new leadership roles in a context where the traditional authority structure based on age is inappropriate with urban life and where prestige lies in acquiring western technology and culture. Since the post-1965 immigration of Filipinos to Hawaii, the leadership positions in many hometown associations have passed from oldtimer plantation recruits or longtime members of an organization in general to these more recent immigrants. However, the presidency is an exception to this trend since it often continues to be held by an oldtimer out of the members' sense of respect for his longtime contributions to the association. In other cases, post-1965 immigrants have started a regional association if there was none before or it had become inactive.

While it would be incorrect to depict these newer association leaders as young in an absolute sense, they are relatively younger by at least a generation from the oldtimers. They also differ from their predecessors in being far better educated; in many cases they were college graduates and professionals in the Philippines before immigrating to Hawaii. They also hold more prestigious occupations than the oldtimers in management, administrative, or clerical work. While the younger leaders have a greater command of English than the oldtimers, this ability is not necessarily an advantage in the internal affairs of the association since those are generally conducted in Ilokano.

Schism in Hometown Associations

The proliferation of voluntary associations in Hawaii is commonly perceived by Filipinos as evidence of divisiveness and disunity within their community. For the 1930s Cariaga (1974:85) also noted the same observation being made of the Filipino community: "It is often said that one of the unfortunate features of life among Hawaii Filipinos is their lack of leadership and of unity. Disputes occur between factions and their leaders. Often organizations with the same objectives compete, as it would seem, unnecessarily." However, the increase in the number of Filipino voluntary associations is not necessarily the result of disharmony but is a reflection of the numerical growth of the Filipino community since the 1965 changes in United States immigration laws and of the diversity of interests of Filipinos. Furthermore, organizational divisiveness within the Filipino community is not manifest between associations as much as it may be within the same association. Most organizations, through their officers, are supportive of the activities of other associations (Okamura 1981). Association officers sell fund-raising tickets for each other, pay for advertisements in souvenir banquet programs, donate trophies and door prizes and are invited to attend each other's social affairs. While they must pay for their own tickets to these social functions because they are fund-raising activities, they can expect that other leaders will reciprocate and attend their social affairs. Also, many association officers occupy positions in several organizations since they were invited to join as honorary members. Furthermore, in only a few cases does more than one hometown association represent a particular group of townspeople. While it is true that Filipino regional associations have proliferated since the post-1965 immigration to Hawaii, they have not done so necessarily as a result of segmentary schisms from other organizations or because they represent rival associations to ones already in existence.

Internal discord was characteristic of Filipino hometown associations in the past. Alcantara (1981:147) notes that retired plantation workers generally considered these clubs, as they called them, to have been status-oriented, divisive, proliferative, and short-lived. He maintains that associations were used by their officers as avenues for status competition since holding office in a club, particularly the presidency, was a means to distinguish oneself from the general rank and file of common laborers (Alcantara 1981:150). Not surprisingly, the most common complaint against officers was that they used the association for their personal self-glorification. Meetings were conducted in English rather than a Philippine language and were occasions for the demonstration of oratorical skills through interminable argumentation over such matters as the interpretation of charter rules (Alcantara 1981:150). Alcantara (1981:150) contends that such discord and divisiveness were inherent in Filipino voluntary associations because they were organized by various partidos, or alliances of kinsmen and friends, that sought ways to assert their relative prestige rather than by individuals who desired membership benefits. Thus, the defeated faction in an election would lose interest in association affairs and withdraw its support or might start another club. At present, hometown associations can be credited with bringing together all the various groupings of first generation Filipinos in Hawaii, that is, former plantation laborer oldtimers, 1946 plantation recruits and other post-war immigrants, and post-1965 newcomer arrivals. However, cleavage appears to be present between the oldtimers, or longtime members of an association in general, and the more recent immigrants. The former resent the latter "taking over" the association and "telling us what to do." After they had been in charge of the organization's affairs for many years, the oldtimers do not appreciate the changes that the newer members would like to introduce. In one association, the oldtimers resisted the attempts to start a scholarship fund because there had been no provision for such when their children were younger. On their part, the post-1965 immigrants complain that the oldtimers "want to do the same old things," prefer to have social activities rather than civic projects and engage in endless arguments over trivial matters.

Yet despite such internal cleavages within Filipino hometown associations between the younger and the older members, the more active members from among the latter are often accorded positions as advisers or as members of the board of directors. While these positions are somewhat honorific in nature, oldtimers are often asked to offer their opinions (if they have not already taken an active part in the meeting up to that point) during discussions of association matters. Kinship norms such as respect for elders continue to be observed in hometown associations despite a general emphasis on achievement criteria of status for election to office.

Factionalism continues to be the organizational basis of divisiveness within Filipino hometown associations in Hawaii. Opposing factions tend to coalesce over differences with the officers of an association, most commonly over their disbursement of association funds. Members are often suspicious that the officers have used the organization's assets for their personal benefit rather than for their intended purposes. During meetings, the treasurer's report is inevitably followed with questions as to the reasons for particular expenditures by the club or its officers and whether receipts are available to prove that such monies were actually spent.

Leadership in Hometown Associations

The primary function of Filipino hometown associations in Hawaii is no longer to provide mutual aid as was the case during the plantation period essentially because most immigrants have close kinsmen who can be depended upon for moral and material support in times of need. Although many associations continue to provide death benefits, such security provisions would seem to be of absolute necessity only for the destitute and elderly without any relatives. Furthermore, as stated above, retirement plans, medical insurance, and unemployment benefits are available through employers or from the state government, and life insurance policies can be purchased on one's own.

The question thus arises why do Filipino hometown associations continue to exist since they no longer serve the functions for which they were originally established. Necessary for an adequate understanding of this question are two perhaps contradictory processes. First, the arrival of substantial numbers of Filipino immigrants in Hawaii since 1965 has led to an increase in the number of regional organizations, either through the revival of inactive ones or the establishment of new ones. Second, most of these associations have few regular activities for their members, and the majority of members do not take an active participatory role in them. Thus, despite the widespread proliferation of Filipino regional organizations, they seem to exist in somewhat dormant form. Selznick's (1952:96) description of a typical voluntary association as "skeletal in the sense that they are manned by a small core of individuals—the administration, the local sub-leaders, a few faithful meeting-goers—and around whom fluctuates a loosely bound mass of dues-payers" is a fairly accurate description of most Filipino hometown associations in Hawaii. Nonetheless, hometown associations evidence a remarkable capacity for perdurance despite their general periods of inactivity.

The more general question as to factors that lead to the emergence of voluntary associations has been addressed by a number of anthropologists. While Kerri (1976:34) claims not to have the answer to the question that he poses for himself, "What causes individuals and/or groups to resort to the use of common interest associations as mechanisms for dealing with adaptive problems?," he does note that the introduction of common interest associations has been in some cases the result of efforts "to deal with problems for which existing pathways had been found ineffective." From a similar adaptive perspective, Little (1957:594) contends that the two factors that are primarily instrumental in the "growth" of African voluntary associations are the existence of an urban population which is predominantly "immigrant, unstable, and socially heterogeneous," and the "adaptability of traditional institutions" to urban settings. On the other hand, Banton (1956:367) argues from the viewpoint of the cultural background of the immigrant group and maintains that "the more devolution of authority there is in tribal societies the more rapidly do contractual associations like companies emerge" in the urban area.

Of these generalizations, Kerri's is perhaps the most relevant to an explanation of the initial emergence of Filipino voluntary associations in Hawaii during the period of labor recruitment since they were clearly started to mitigate the insecurities of the harsh living and working conditions on the plantations. For the most part, these mutual aid associations represented adaptations of traditional barrio practices to the social setting in which immigrant workers found themselves.

Filipino voluntary associations seem to have proliferated during the plantation period. Cariaga (1974:84) noted that "A widely reported fact is that Filipino organizations 'spring up like mushrooms and die away as quickly', giving rise to the apt aphorism of a Filipino pastor of Honolulu who remarked that 'The inauguration of an organization, with all its pomp and ceremony, serves likewise as its funeral ceremony'." Cariaga implicitly accounted for the emergence of these associations in terms of leadership within the Filipino community. He noted that the usual leaders in the barrios whence came the plantation workers, that is, the elders and the *caciques*, or landowners, did not migrate to Hawaii. Thus, in this fluid situation in which everyone shared peasant origins and a common socioeconomic status as unskilled laborers, until a new basis for leadership could be firmly established, "Every migrant Filipino is likely to feel himself about as fine and worthy of being the head of any current enterprise as his fellows. When a society is formed, there are plentiful candidates for the position of officers, but not many ordinary members" (Cariaga 1974:87).

At present, community leadership is also relevant to an understanding of the question that was initially posed as to why Filipino hometown associations continue to exist and to be newly established if they are no longer necessary to meet the mutual aid purposes for which they were originally intended. The essential factor in the continued existence of most Filipino hometown associations are their officers, particularly the president, and a few of the more active members who maintain the continuity of the organization, if in name only. If it were not for their leaders, associations would fall, as many have, into various states of inactivity. Leaders are the members who attend meetings faithfully, organize fund-raising projects, banquets, dances, picnics, and other activities for members, and represent the organization at gatherings of other Filipino associations. Officers assume this greater participatory role not only because it is their expected duty but also because they have the most to gain from such activity. While leaders may have attained a measure of economic success through their occupations, they and other members of hometown associations are generally denied social recognition and leadership positions in the wider Hawaii society. Therefore, should they wish to assert claims to superior status within the Filipino community, they may do so by serving as officers in a voluntary association.

Association officers and other members who desire prestige can seek distinction in commonplace settings such as at association meetings. They do so through ways that are intended to impress the general rank and file of members, for example, by demonstrating their knowledge of parliamentary procedures, using flamboyant expressions in English, engaging in drawn out arguments over trivial points, and generally by speaking out much more than most of the other members. Officers address the assembled group as *gaygayyem ken kabkabsat* (friends and siblings), an expression commonly used by politicians in the Ilocos region. Members address officers with the honorific title *apo* (sir) or *apo presidente*, as the case may be.

The hometown association itself confers recognition through its multitude of elective and appointive offices open to members. For example, there are often two vice-presidents, not only a secretary, treasurer, and auditor, but also assistants for these offices, several sergeants at arms, and numerous advisers and members of the board of directors. Recognition awards for outstanding achievement and service to the association are presented to members at the annual banquet. In addition, the Philippine Consulate General in Honolulu bestows "Presidential Gold Medal" awards and trophies, supposedly from the president of the Philippines, to the leaders of its favored organizations.

Officers of hometown associations are also accorded recognition in their home communities in the Philippines. Their annual messages of greetings to townspeople are included in the town fiesta souvenir booklet along with those sent by more illustrious dignitaries such as the president of the Philippines and the governor of the province. The list of officers of the association is also included in the fiesta booklet. Should an association organize a trip to their hometown, the leaders can expect to be treated as honored guests of the town. Municipal officials fete them at lavish parties, and they "rub shoulders" with the social elites of the town.

Association officers also gain prestige and recognition in their home communities as resourceful leaders for organizing monetary contributions to the hometown. These donations are an indication of the significance of achievement of status in hometown associations. In this striving among officers and members to attain status, there seems to be an orientation to the Philippines rather than to Hawaii for validation of their claims. Association officers organize fund-raising projects such as popularity queen contests not only because of the considerable amounts of money that can be raised, but also because through their presence in the hometown for the presentation of the contribution to the town and the coronation of the queen and princesses the officers can thereby assume a greater role in the town fiesta proceedings.

Social recognition and prestige are the rewards for association leaders in keeping the organization functioning. Officers speak of the sacrifices they must make in money and time spent away from their families in order to organize association activities. Yet there are tangible rewards for association leaders who through their positions come into contact with a wide segment of the Filipino community in Hawaii. Many of these leaders are in the insurance, real estate, and travel business, occupations that depend on "good public relations" with the community as Almirol (n.d.: 24) noted for Filipino leaders in California. Filipino community leaders in Hawaii are especially noticeable in the travel agency business, either as owners or as sales representatives. Their contacts with association members and the larger Filipino community prove beneficial when those persons decide to visit their hometowns or to petition their relatives to Hawaii. These contacts prove even more rewarding if the association regularly sponsors *balikbayan* trips to the hometown or beauty queen contests with travel arrangements for the queen, princesses, and their accompanying families handled by the leader's agency.

Thus, through the organizing efforts of their leaders, Filipino hometown associations in Hawaii provide a corporate representation of townmates and thereby afford an organized means for the maintenance of social relations, not necessarily interpersonal relationships, with one another. By collective reinforcement of the townmate relationship through formal membership, hometown associations foster a sense of group identity and loyalty for members as immigrants who share a common locality of origin.

Thus, the hometown association becomes the focus for the mobilization of townmates when their support and participation are required. Association members and townmates alike are appealed to through the hometown association on such occasions as to honor a distinguished visitor from their town, to recognize the achievements and contributions of a townmate, to render assistance to a townmate in times of need, to contribute aid to the hometown, or when the United Filipino Council of Hawaii (a statewide federation of Filipino voluntary organizations) or the Philippine Consulate requests the participation of the larger Filipino community for a special event. While these activities represent some of the functions of hometown associations, any one of them cannot be said to be the primary purpose of associations in general because organizations vary in the extent to which they sponsor these various activities. That is, not all hometown associations serve these purposes on a regular basis because many associations are not especially active. However, what is common to all hometown associations once they have been established, even though they are relatively inactive and have been for some time, is that they provide a formal means for the organization of the above functions as the need arises or as members decide to implement them. As stated earlier, Filipino hometown associations are quite tenacious despite lack of interest and participation by their general membership. Thus, in their corporate form (Smith 1975:177), they represent the potential for mobilization of townmates for association activities.

Conclusion

While the proliferation of Filipino hometown associations since the post-1965 immigration to Hawaii would appear to indicate their significance for immigrants, the general low level of participation by members in association activities and the infrequency of these occasions would denote otherwise. Nonetheless, hometown associations afford various benefits for their members. They provide members with moral and material support in times of need, in particular, death benefits. The occasional social gatherings and meetings are opportunities for members to renew their relationships with one another. Organized donations to their hometowns are a means for members to contribute in a substantial way to the development of their home communities and thereby to gain recognition and prestige as civic minded and economically successful individuals. Since leadership positions in the wider Hawaii society are generally denied to Filipino immigrants, those persons who would like to assert their claims to superior status within the Filipino community can do so by holding office in a hometown association. In particular, associations provide an avenue for the ambitions of the younger, educated post-1965 immigrants who would like to establish themselves as leaders in the Filipino community.

Despite these varied functions, hometown associations do not serve as adaptive mechanisms for Filipino immigrants, except in a very general sense, as they did during the plantation labor recruitment period because the post-1965 immigrants have kinsmen to assist them in their adjustment process. Also, because hometown associations do not exert a significant degree of influence over their members and tend to maintain certain cultural traditions, they do not foster the acculturative adjustment of Filipino immigrants to Hawaii society through familiarization with local norms of interpersonal behavior or the use of English. However, although hometown associations serve various functions, it cannot be claimed that these activities are their primary purposes in general since most associations do not implement these enterprises on a regular basis because of their common inactivity. Thus, Filipino hometown associations in Hawaii provide a corporate mode for townmates to maintain their social relations with one another and thereby foster their potential mobilization for association activities.

NOTES

1. I would like to thank M. G. Smith for his comments on an earlier draft of this paper.
2. This was an appointed state body whose task was to coordinate activities planned to mark the anniversary of Filipino immigration to Hawaii in 1981.
3. The Ilocos provinces include Ilocos Norte, Ilocos Sur, La Union, and Abra.

BIBLIOGRAPHY

Alcantara, R. R. 1981. Sakada: Filipino Adaptation in Hawaii. Washington, D.C.
Almirol, E. B. 1978. Filipino Voluntary Associations: Balancing Social Pressures and Ethnic Images. Ethnic Groups 2:65–92.
———. n.d. Filipino Ethnicity and Voluntary Associations. Unpublished ms.
Banton, M. 1956. Adaptation and Integration in the Social System of Temne Immigrants in Freetown. Africa 26:354–368.
Cariaha, R. R. 1974 (1936). The Filipinos in Hawaii. A Survey of Their Economic and Social Conditions. Master's thesis, University of Hawaii. Reprinted by R and E Research Associates, San Francisco.
Kerri, J. N. 1976. Studying Voluntary Associations as Adaptive Mechanisms: A Review of Anthropological Perspectives. Current Anthropology 17:23–47.
Little, K. 1957. The Role of Voluntary Associations in West African Urbanization. American Anthropologist 59:579–596.

———. 1965. West African Urbanization: A Study of Voluntary Associations in Social Change. London.
Okamura. J. Y. 1981. Filipino Voluntary Associations and the Filipino Community in Hawaii. Paper presented at the Second International Philippine Studies Conference, Honolulu.
———. 1983. Immigrant Filipino Ethnicity in Honolulu, Hawaii. Unpublished Ph.D. dissertation, University of London.
Parkin, D. 1966. Urban Voluntary Associations as Institutions of Adaptation. Man 1:90–95.
Selznick, P. 1952. The Organizational Weapon. New York.
Smith, M. G. 1975. Corporations and Society: The Social Anthropology of Collective Action. Chicago.

Brokerage, Economic Opportunity, and the Growth of Ethnic Movements[1]

Miriam J. Wells

>>> <<<

THE FLORESCENCE of ethnic interest groups in the United States and elsewhere raises important questions concerning the social factors promoting ethnic solidarity. Central among these are the impact of the changing structural positions of minorities on public ethnic identification and their position in the wider society. Understanding of these changes requires study of fluctuations in the political and economic conditions constraining minority activity and of alternative linkage roles connecting minority and majority groups.

The mainstream of American scholarship on ethnicity has provided little research on these issues. For years, scholars assumed the disappearance of ethnic contrasts over time (Park and Burgess 1924; Park 1952; Eisenstadt 1954). Those who did examine ethnicity generally focused on the characterization of cultural traits or on the psychological functions of ethnic identification (Linton 1940; Spiro 1955; Herskovits 1958; Naroll 1964; Isaacs 1975). These approaches did little to clarify the conditions under which action groups based on ethnic relationships would emerge. They implied the discreteness of minority groups as social systems while neglecting features of the broader environment which might encourage changes in ethnic identification. They assumed the congruence of cultural heritage and behavior, rather than inquiring into the ways that group members might transform and manipulate traditional symbols for present purposes. And they suggested a stability of group structure and congruence of interests between leaders and followers which often do not exist.

The use of decisive-action models in the study of ethnicity, following Firth (1951) and Barth (1956), has directed much needed attention to the role of individual choice in ethnic group formation but has tended to underplay the role of structural limits on activity. While conflict models of ethnicity (e.g., Wallerstein 1973; Hechter 1974) have interjected valuable consideration of environmental constraints, they have frequently concentrated on the macro level, failing to make the connection with local-level structures and activity.

It is argued here that understanding of the fluctuations of ethnic movements may profit from a perspective which considers the broad political and economic contexts within which minorities operate, the intermediate structures which link them with the wider society, and the alternative courses of action which group members pursue in particular situations. Under certain conditions, ethnic minorities may be linked to majority individuals and institutions by mediators or brokers (Wolf 1956; Foster 1961) who control communication between the two. It is suggested here that brokers may significantly affect the public management of ethnic identity and the formation of ethnic action groups. They may also influence the future place of a minority in society, as well as the integration of local communities into the wider social system.

This article aims to clarify the historical conditions underlying the growth of a particular ethnic movement and describe the contrasting roles played by two sorts of brokers in that process. It traces the development of a Chicano ethnic organization in a midwestern town.[2] Particular attention is given to the impact of traditional patron-brokers whose intervention provided individual, nonethnic means of obtaining resources, and of innovative ethnic brokers who encouraged the collective ethnic demands. Contrasts in the success of these two types of brokers in attracting clients, and differences in the cumulative impacts of their mediation, are attributed to changes in the political and economic opportunity structure and to differences between the brokerage sets in terms of their positions, functions, goals, and numbers.

The case presented here involves Mexican-Americans who have recently left the Texas-midwestern agricultural labor stream to settle permanently as industrial workers in a small central Wisconsin town. It is of particular interest because we have little information on Mexican-Americans in nonmetropolitan northern contexts, and even less on the impact of radical ethnic politics on such populations. The town of Riverside has an established population of about 5,400, consisting primarily of Americans of Polish, German, and British descent.[3] Although British-Americans dominated political, educational, and economic institutions in the first generation after settlement, the three groups are currently distributed rather evenly within these institutions (Wells 1975). The town's newest settlers, the Mexican-Americans, occupy no formal positions within the educational or political institutions. As industrial laborers, they are confined almost exclusively to the lowest economic stratum.

Riverside's economy rests on manufacturing and on the retail trade of the surrounding grain and dairy region. The largest employer and taxpayer in the town is a foundry, whose approximately 600 employees include most of the resident Mexican-Americans. Numbering about 140 individuals at the time of study, Mexican-Americans began to settle in Riverside in the mid-1960s in response to the availability of industrial employment.

Structural Conditions of Mediation

Brokers in Riverside mediated transactions between individuals and sectors of society differing in power. These mediators were not merely "cultural brokers," translating between the idioms of two segments, but were also "power brokers," wielding power at each of two levels and deriving their power at one level from their success at the other level (Adams 1970). In this sense brokerage was a structural element of part-whole relations, not simply a social role.

Brokerage was made possible by particular features of the local context, most importantly by a discontinuity in the power and communication systems of majority and minority segments and by the possibility of resource allocations by a broker. In Riverside, the major sources of goods and services sought by Mexican-Americans, such as the foundry, the welfare department, and the consolidated school, were local branches of institutions whose major power centers were situated outside the community. All these branches exhibited considerable structural flexibility at the local level; that is, they were not strictly regulated from above in their daily operation. Several examples illustrate this flexibility at the local level. State law bans employment discrimination on the basis of age, race, creed, color, handicap, sex, national origin or ancestry (Wisconsin, State of, 1975). In practice, however, employment decisions were made in the private offices of local firms, with only cursory policing by government. While the city welfare director had general instructions to provide emergency aid to needy families, she alone made the actual determination of need. Of pivotal importance in such decisions were the uninstitutionalized judgments of the local community.

Latitude for local discretion was considerable even within the county welfare system which had written regulations prescribing qualifications for assistance. The welfare rules were worded very abstractly and decisions regarding need, employment, levels of benefits, and the moral status of recipients were made by local officials. Moreover, because the caseworker system was geared to respond flexibly to individual family needs, the element of discretion was built into the system. Caseworkers in Riverside sometimes failed to tell clients about programs for which they might qualify. Their like or dislike of a client seemed in several cases to have been the deciding factor in granting or denying aid.[4]

Other public service programs available to Mexican-Americans in Riverside had similar features. For example, according to fieldworkers with federal public housing progams, local discretion determined an individual's qualification for public housing rental and financing. In short, there was ample leeway within the formal system for the operation of brokers who could influence decision-makers towards potential recipients of goods and services.

Another structural feature encouraged the operation of brokers: the gap between the Mexican-American and Euro-American sectors in terms of power and communication. Since almost all local Mexican-Americans were manual laborers in the foundry, they had minimal material resources and few sources of personal influence or information that could link them to the higher echelons of institutions. By contrast, local Euro-Americans were dispersed within economic, political, and educational institutions and could negotiate for resources by relying upon intra-ethnic networks. In addition, the Mexican-American population had low social status because of their occupations, poverty, and the negative stereotyping of their ethnic identity by the dominant population. Their recent arrival in the region not only reduced the legitimacy of their claims on resources in the eyes of Euro-American powerholders, but also limited their knowledge of available benefits and of the courses of action necessary to obtain them. Finally and importantly, over half of the Mexican-American population spoke English very poorly or not at all.

All the Mexican-American families but one could be thought of as occupying a single stratum within which individuals had roughly equivalent and subordinate power. In terms of socioeconomic status, language, information, and, to some extent, cultural values, there was a marked discontinuity between the Mexican-American and Euro-American populations. Mexican-Americans suffered multiple disadvantages when they attempted direct confrontations. This disparity created a niche for power brokers with skills to operate in both segments, mediating exchanges across the gap between strata. In performing this task, brokers created a status for themselves and, ideally, met the needs of participants in both segments.

When this study began, almost all Mexican-Americans sought the involvement of a broker in their approaches to local and outside institutions, both because of their inability to operate effectively in the broader society and because of the demonstrated efficacy of mediated transactions. Their choice of either traditional or innovative brokers influenced the public management of Mexican-American ethnic identity and the evolving structure of minority-majority relations.

Traditional Brokers

The brokers most frequently employed during the first years of settlement are termed "traditional" here because their relationships with their clients mirrored patron-client bonds familiar in Latin cultures and previously experienced by these particular clients. Like Mexican and Spanish patronage relationships, brokerage in Riverside involved a code of deferential behavior on the part of clients and was reinforced by generalized relationships of reciprocal responsibility such as *compadrazgo* (co-parenthood) (Foster 1961; Wolf 1966; Kenny 1969). From another perspective, these brokers may be seen as "traditional" because their mediation preserved the status quo of power distribution.

Only two persons in Riverside served as traditional brokers at the time of study: a Mexican-American couple, the Garcias, whose socioeconomic and cultural backgrounds were quite different from those of the rest of the Mexican-American population. As upper middle-class "Hispanos" from Arizona, their identification with their Mexican and Spanish ancestry was largely intellectual. Their accents, grammar, and vocabulary clearly distinguished their spoken Spanish from that of the ex-farmworkers. They were the only local Mexican-American family for whom English was the language of the home. In terms of cultural values and behavioral styles, they shared much more with the local Euro-Americans than with the Mexican-American foundry workers. They were, however, equipped both linguistically and culturally to communicate with both.

Examination of the traditional brokers' motivations for mediation and their placement within the socioeconomic structure lends insight into the conditions and limitations of their brokerage. This discussion is confined to Mr. Garcia's position, which was also the principal basis of Mrs. Garcia's mediation. Mr. Garcia occupied a formal position as assistant personnel manager within the town's major source of economic benefits, the foundry. Brokerage was a means of consolidating that position, but the position in turn placed constraints on the extent to which he could mediate to the advantage of both employer and employee. His ability to satisfy both parties was highly dependent on the structure of economic opportunity.

In the economic climate in Riverside in the late 1960s and early 1970s, the interests of Mexican-Americans and Euro-Americans were complementary with respect to employment. During this period the county had one of the lowest unemployment rates in the state. Since local Euro-Americans were refusing to take the bottom-level foundry positions, the foundry's management recruited Mexican-Americans, though voicing a preference for Euro-American workers.

In this period, Mr. Garcia was recruited from Arizona as assistant personnel manager. The foundry managers hoped that he would both expand the foundry's hiring pool and provide some guarantee that Mexican-American employees would be industrious, steady, and uncomplaining workers. Mr. Garcia's establishment of personal ties with Mexican-American employees accomplished these ends. Mexican-American workers were anxious to perform well in order to reciprocate what they perceived as the favor of being hired. They also valued other types of mediation that Mr. Garcia provided, such as interceding on their behalf with public-service agencies, accompanying them to court or the police station, and assisting them in writing letters and filling out forms in English. During the early years of Mexican-American settlement in Riverside, almost all Mexican-Americans sought employment at the foundry and attempted to establish patron-client bonds with Mr. Garcia. They encouraged friends and relatives to leave the migrant agricultural stream in order to work in the foundry. When these individuals were given employment, the established workers exerted pressure on newcomers to perform well.

An additional consequence of the connection between Mr. Garcia and his employee-clients, and one that was valued by foundry management, was the resolving of employee grievances. Union leaders complained that Mexican-American workers were extremely cautious about voicing grievances against management, and that when they did so, it was in a conciliatory manner in private conversation with Mr. Garcia. The author observed a number of instances in which Mexican-American employees failed to complain either to the union or to Mr. Garcia about what they felt to be violations of seniority rules in distributing preferred positions or promotions within the foundry. They gave as their reason for silence a fear of disrupting their relationships with Mr. Garcia. In this economic environment, then, Mr. Garcia was able to satisfy both foundry management and Mexican-American employees by operating as a mediator.

Brokerage also served certain social ends for the Garcia family. Accustomed to equal-status association with Euro-Americans in Arizona and distant from local Mexican-Americans in terms of socioeconomic and cultural background, the Garcias were shocked and angered to find that they were treated by the general populace in Riverside "like any other Mexican." The Garcias thought of themselves as Americans and declared that this was the first time in their lives they had been made to feel they were "ethnics." They explicitly praised assimilation as the ideal form of intergroup relations. Presenting themselves to the larger society as Americans, they also encouraged their clients to downplay evidence of ethnic identity in public. For the Garcias, brokerage was a means of establishing their distinctness from the rest of the minority population and of gaining acceptance into majority groupings. As mediators and spokepersons they had ample opportunity to demonstrate publicly their facility in Euro-American cultural idioms and to build relationships with Euro-Americans. Increasing social acceptance diminished this important motivation for the Garcias' brokerage. Eventually the Garcias began to voice the majority view that "most Mexicans" were irresponsible, deceitful, and lazy.

The bonds between Mr. Garcia and his clients were eroded both by the limitations inherent in his own structural position and by changes in social conditions changing the relationship between minority and majority. The Garcias' goal of social incorporation into the majority sector meant that they were reluctant to mediate to the advantage of Mexican-Americans in any situation involving conflict or competition between the two sectors. Initially, although there were situations in which the interests of management and Mexican-American workers diverged, the issue of employment was paramount. Mr. Garcia was bound to side with the company in conflicts of interest, however, since his own economic security was dependent on management's perception that he represented the foundry's welfare. In time, a number of issues arose which made it clear to Mr. Garcia's clients that he was an unreliable broker.

Foundry laborers were exposed daily to the possibility of serious burns, cuts, and torn or strained muscles. The foundry wanted to minimize work-related injury claims in order to avoid paying higher premium rates for Workman's Compensation Insurance. Moreover, a high accident rate could lead to investigation by enforcers of the federal Occupational Safety and Health Act, with possible adverse publicity and orders for expensive safety measures. As a result, on repeated occasions when Mexican-American workers asked for Mr. Garcia's assistance in obtaining accident insurance and disability benefits, he refused to acknowledge that they might have been injured on the job. He tried to persuade them, sometimes successfully, to sign disclaimers of company responsibility. In one instance a young woman with a severe abdominal rupture signed what she later discovered to be a disclaimer, simply because Mr. Garcia had represented it as trivial but unavoidable paperwork. "I trusted him," she lamented. "I thought he was one of our people." This accident ended forever the young woman's ability to do hard work. The injuries to the others were also serious and resulted in long periods of unemployment. Since the Mexican-American population viewed these particular claimants and their grievances as legitimate, they considered Mr. Garcia's behavior as a betrayal of loyalty.

These events might not have been so critical, and indeed might have been ignored by clients, if other changes in the economic structure had not rendered his brokerage less critical and advantageous. First, a downturn in the local and national economic climates meant that there were fewer jobs and more Euro-Americans competing for them. The turnover rate for Euro-Americans in foundry positions began to fall, diminishing the relative advantage of hiring Mexican-Americans. Although the locally prevailing image of Mexican-Americans as transient, unreliable outsiders had been disregarded when their labor was needed, foundry management now pointed to it to justify the renewed employment of Euro-Americans. This change brought no corresponding increase in union activity by Mexican-Americans. In fact, union leaders labeled these as hard times for labor: jobs were scarce, union meetings were poorly attended, and the threat of layoffs always hovered in the background. The foundry discontinued efforts to recruit Mexican-Americans and no longer viewed Mr. Garcia's mediation as critical to company welfare. As the complementarity of interests between Mexican-American workers and the foundry diminished, so did Mr. Garcia's ability and willingness to mediate to the advantage of his Mexican-American clients.

New Brokers

At this same time the local political climate was altered by the advent of a new set of brokers, who challenged the Garcias' exclusive control over the broker role between minority and majority. They strengthened the interconnection between the locality and the broader society. These new brokers were situated differently with regard to local economic and social structures and were guided by a different vision of ideal interethnic relations.

Economic and ideological developments in the larger society formed the broader context for the growth of an ethnic movement in Riverside. While presumptions of assimilation had dominated popular and academic consideration of ethnicity for most of American history (Gordon 1964) and still prevailed as a description of social reality and a prescription for approved public behavior in Riverside (Wells 1975), new formulations were gathering force in the country.

In academic circles, pluralist models of American social structure represented the country as composed of competing interest groups rather than of unaffiliated individuals or social classes (Dahl 1967; Rose 1968). While proponents of assimilation claimed that it provided maximum individual social mobility along with minimum social conflict, advocates of pluralism pointed out that assimilation had not provided minorities with equal opportunities. In the America of the 1960s and 1970s, opportunities for individual economic mobility had greatly diminished. Not only had the demand for unskilled labor decreased relative to the growing work force, but mechanization, the opposition of established unions to newcomers, and the upgrading of job requirements for more formal education also restricted the traditional avenues of economic mobility open to minorities. By the mid-1960s some observers were predicting the continued growth of an "underclass" of poverty—unemployed individuals marginalized by mechanization and lacking the minimal training necessary to break into the increasingly competitive work force (Myrdal 1969).

It was American blacks, large numbers of whom had sought industrial employment in northern cities after World Wars I and II, who presented the most visible challenge to the ideology of assimilation and social mobility. Black spokepersons pointed out that many Euro-American ethnic groups had in fact used ethnic organizations to represent their own needs within the larger society (Carmichael and Hamilton 1967:44–45). Young black leaders argued that in an increasingly competitive economic climate, persons disadvantaged by discrimination and low initial economic position should band together as political interest groups. In a political system committed to equal opportunity for all and at a time when liberal welfare legislation had increased the number and diversity of resources that could be directed to disadvantaged groups, ethnic organizations promised substantial rewards. The success of black Americans in obtaining special consideration provided other minorities with a provocative example.

The new brokers who appeared in Riverside in the early 1970s were activists in a Chicano ethnic organization, La Raza, which advocated a pluralist model of social relations and brought outside values and resources to bear on the local scene. These brokers were Mexican-Americans who were fluent in English and familiar with the institutions and customs of the broader society. While many were middle-class members with college educations, others arose as leaders from the farmworker union movement of the 1960s. Still others were clergymen and nuns who regarded the Chicano movement as one of the important human-rights causes of the times. While none of the new brokers lived in Riverside, La Raza set up an office in the town in 1974, staffing it with two fulltime workers.

The pool of skills, information, and influence offered by the new brokers was by no means limited to those who served Riverside directly. La Raza was part of a broader network of members and sympathizers who could mobilize other brokers with valuable professional skills (doctors, lawyers), powerful position-holders (congressmen, committee heads, officials in public institutions), and free-floating advocates whose power derived largely from evidence of the movement's following. Brokers allied with the Chicano movement provided clients with recommendations, special services, and detailed information concerning legal rights and procedures. The availability of movement brokers increased clients' alternative means of obtaining benefits and reduced their dependence on a single benefactor. It provided them with a diverse array of mediators whose skills and influence exceeded those of the traditional patrons. It expanded clients' ability to tap resource networks beyond the bounds of the local community and improved their competitive position within the local opportunity structure.

Traditional brokers had accepted the locally prevailing norms and balance of power, whereas movement mediators challenged them. The first sued for favors; the latter demanded rights. Movement brokers did not aspire to social acceptance in Riverside and were not constrained to accept disparaging judgments of Mexican-Americans. On the contrary, the Chicano movement constituted a social sphere whose guiding purpose was to change Mexican-American ethnicity from a social stigma to a basis for solidarity, respect, and personal status. Movement brokers urged their followers to engage openly in ethnic behavior—to speak Spanish, to wear colorful clothes, to hang Mexican posters in visible places, to hold and attend Mexican fiestas and church services. The brokers themselves openly emphasized ethnic identity and tried to change its assessment in the broader society by making the negative stereotype of Mexican-Americans the object of overt re-education. As avowed Mexican-American advocates, they attempted to obtain benefits for clients who identified themselves as Mexican-Americans, whether or not this advocacy involved competition with Euro-Americans. In fact, movement activists tended to assume that competition and conflict over resources were inevitable but that the bargaining position of Mexican-Americans could be improved by new tactics.

While traditional brokers insisted on strict behavioral protocols of superordination and subordination between patron and client, movement ideology discouraged such distinctions. The director of La Raza leveled harsh criticism against the Garcias for this reason. La Raza did not accord generalized high status to a person with brokerage skills. Instead, it maintained that all Mexican-Americans were equals in an ethnic community.

Although some movement brokers held positions within resource-allocating institutions, their appeal to extralocal authorities and their mobilization of allies within and outside of formal institutions reduced dependency on local authorities. Movement brokers tried to channel the allocation of resources toward persons of Mexican descent by appealing to the charters of publicly accountable institutions. They pointed to the formal ideal of equal consideration for all citizens and the reality of unequal treatment. They used persuasion and the threat or actuality of exposure to the public and to organizational superiors to convince local authorities that more services should be extended to Mexican-Americans. They also argued that past and present discrimination against Mexican-Americans should be redressed by creating special policies and programs to serve them.

Under statewide pressure from La Raza and similar groups, Wisconsin printed Spanish-language versions of numerous state regulations: a summary of Wisconsin's labor standards; Wisconsin's non-discriminatory contracts law concerning equal opportunity in housing, employment, and access to public facilities; information on how to present a complaint of illegal discrimination in employment; and the procedure to follow to obtain workmen's compensation, to mention a few. La Raza disseminated this and other information to Mexican-Americans in Riverside.

Largely in response to Raza lobbying, English classes for the Spanish-speaking and driver education classes in Spanish are now offered in Riverside. A special health clinic for Mexican-Americans has been established in a town 30 miles away, and a job training and placement program and free or low-cost legal services have been made available to Mexican-Americans in the area. As a direct result of La Raza's activity in Riverside, a program of special tutoring for Mexican-American students has been initiated to provide immediate assistance to the many students who have serious problems in school. The program is aimed also at refining evaluation of these problems and determining the need for a permanent program that would deal with the special problems encountered by children with bilingual/bicultural backgrounds.

Several of the injured foundry workers who had initially turned to Mr. Garcia were visited by Raza leaders. Whereas Mr. Garcia had been skeptical of the workers' claims, movement brokers immediately assumed their legitimacy. They assisted the workers in obtaining and filling out compensation claim forms, provided them with free legal assistance, and accompanied them to court. They complained of Mr. Garcia's behavior to the foundry manager and to officials in the state Department of Industry, Labor, and Human Relations. The La Raza newspaper published a feature story on the contribution of Mexican-American workers to the local economy and on Mr. Garcia's failure to look after the welfare of foundry employees. Printed in both English and Spanish, this paper was distributed to Riverside's Mexican-Americans, as well as to regional and state political leaders. It publicized the efficacy of Raza mediation, while engendering official scrutiny of foundry procedures.

It is important to note that the power of movement brokers, both in influencing particular decision-makers and in obtaining special services for Mexican-Americans, depended on evidence of minority need and concern. Flanked by numerous other petitioners for public resources, movement brokers represented their clients as a political following. In point of fact, many of the Mexican-Americans in the Riverside area who sought out mediation and services sponsored by the Chicano movement did not necessarily share the movement's ideology. Although clients were constrained to present themselves as ethnics, their motives were often purely instrumental. Some movement ideals, however, struck a strongly sympathetic note. Many found the ideal of ethnic brotherhood much more satisfying than the status asymmetry of traditional patronage. Although patron-client relationships were a familiar part of their cultural heritage, most clients also shared the egalitarian ideals of American society. They had chafed under, but endured, the subservient stance required by the Garcias.

Alliance with movement brokers was not without its costs on the local scene. To a community whose Polish and German members had long practiced and advocated public masking of ethnic distinctiveness (Wells 1975), explicit ethnic displays were seen as confrontations. Ethnic alliance made Mexican-Americans more visible in a decidedly negative sense. Movement attempts to alter the negative stereotype of Mexican-Americans were not successful in the short run, and demands made in ethnic terms intensified local sentiment that Mexican-Americans were a "problem," "outsiders," and unpleasantly "different." Mexican-American clients tried to minimize this cost to themselves by allowing movement brokers to make public demands. The benefits offered by movement advocacy were attested by the ongoing alliances with movement brokers.

Structural Impact of Mediation

The continued operation of these different linkage mechanisms combined with fluctuations in the economic and political environment to shape the evolving structure of minority-majority relations. The traditional patrons played a conservative role. They vaunted assimilation as an ideal, but their own activity relied upon and preserved the separation between Mexican-American and Euro-American segments. By insisting that clients go through them for sources of benefits, these brokers diminished the likelihood that clients would directly negotiate for resources, either separately or in alliance with others. By obtaining resources for clients as individuals, rather than as a category of disadvantaged citizens, the traditional brokers maintained the inferior bargaining position of Mexican-Americans.

At the same time, the economic environment of the early period served to modify the stratifying impact of these brokers' activity. Given ample economic opportunity, Mexican-Americans were included within the economic stratum which also contained Euro-American manual laborers. Confrontations between the two populations were rare, since jobs were available for all. That situation permitted some Mexican-American mobility and blurred intralevel ethnic distinctions. With the contraction of economic opportunity, however, Mexican-Americans were thrown into competition with Euro-Americans for scarce jobs. In this climate, ethnicity was activated to discriminate among employees, forcing Mexican-Americans, in effect, into a lower social stratum. Given local preference for Euro-Americans and the traditional brokers' acceptance of that ranking, alliance with traditional brokers brought diminished returns.

This context conferred a particular advantage on collective ethnic activity. Movement brokers aimed to change the relative placement of Mexican-Americans within the local social structure by increasing the social, economic, and political resources of the Mexican-American population as a whole. Some movement activity was aimed at changing the broader society to meet the needs of the minority by eliminating the negative Mexican-American stereotype and by redirecting existing programs and developing new services to serve them.

Unlike the traditional brokers, the ethnic brokers also served as change agents by preparing their clients to participate directly in the larger society. Rather than monopolizing communication between minority and majority, the ethnic brokers encouraged direct involvement by clients themselves. This involvement was facilitated by English-language classes, introductions to pivotal decision-makers, and lessons in the operation of public institutions, as well as by increasing the sensitivity of public agencies to Mexican-American needs. Clients who participated in movement meetings and in various demand-making activities such as demonstrations, conferences with officials, radio and television programs, and preparation of the Raza newspaper, gained familiarity with the broader society and confidence in their ability to operate within it. Some participants gained personal recognition and employment in government programs.

Movement brokers attempted another innovation. They tried to change what Mexican-Americans thought they could and should obtain. They communicated values of the dominant society that best served their purposes, such as "equal opportunity for all" and "the government exists to serve the people." They asserted that Mexican-Americans should not be content with the low level of societal benefits they had received in the past. These desiderata were the rights of all American citizens, not charities which should be granted or withheld according to the personal inclination of a local official.

In short, the new brokers aimed to weaken the boundary between

Mexican-Americans and Euro-Americans in terms of access to resources, while maintaining overt ethnic distinctions. They attempted to increase their clients' social mobility by providing them with a variety of conduits for obtaining resources, by increasing the integration of the locality and the broader society, and by working to change both the minority and the majority. The long-term outcome of movement activity would be a different relationship between minority and majority social systems, involving direct participation without mediation. Most movement activists acknowledged that they were working themselves out of their jobs as brokers. The ideal outcome from the movement's point of view would be a society in which Mexican-Americans did not require the movement, but continued to ally with it because of shared values and sentiment.

Some Mexican-Americans are responding to the improvement in their bargaining positions by opting for individual rather than collective strategies of resource mobilization. As their facility in English and familiarity with the procedures and staffs of public institutions improve, some former clients are attempting to obtain benefits on their own, or with the help of friends and relatives. This is probably a consequence of the costs of allying with a confrontive ethnic movement in a small community where social, political, and economic contexts have been dominated by Euro-Americans. While all Mexican-Americans continue to benefit from the collective efforts of the movement, some individuals are withdrawing their participation and are striking out on their own. The net effect is an increase in the number of unmediated transactions and a blurring of ethnic boundaries.

Conclusion

Understanding of the growth of ethnic movements requires examination of the interplay between minorities and the constraining and permissive aspects of their operating environments. It also requires understanding of the structural articulation between the subunits of a society and the broader system: most particularly between minority and majority, and between locality and nation. In this case, changes in the linkage roles between a Mexican-American population and Euro-American individuals and institutions shaped the development of an ethnic movement, the interconnection of community, state, and national systems, and the placement of the minority in the social structure. In this sense this study pursues the time-honored inquiry into the relationship of localized social phenomena to wider social systems (Redfield 1941; Steward 1955; Wolf 1956). It reinforces studies (e.g., Geertz 1960; Silverman 1965; Adams 1970; Stuart 1972) which pinpoint brokerage as a fruitful concept for understanding part-whole relationships. It indicates that brokers may not only communicate between levels but may actively intervene to alter their interconnection.

Power brokers are shown here to be crucially linked to the rise of an ethnic movement. Two sorts of brokers were available: traditional mediators, who discouraged overt manifestation of ethnicity, and innovative ethnic brokers, who encouraged public ethnic demandmaking. Brokerage relationships differed significantly in four ways: (1) in terms of the specific functions which brokers performed; (2) in terms of the numbers of alternative mediators available; (3) in terms of the structural positions of the brokers themselves and their degree of integration into the local system; and (4) in terms of the immediate purposes and more pervasive ideologies that guided their activities. Traditional brokers preserved the economic and social stratification between minority and majority and observed local Euro-American judgments in their mediation. The new brokers attempted to decrease the disparity between Mexican-Americans and Euro-Americans in terms of access to resources and to reinforce voluntary social separation along ethnic lines. They also aimed to increase the adherence of local decision-makers to state and national standards.

This case indicates that the growth of an ethnic movement may not reflect substantial identity change by members or complete agreement on goals. Rather it may be an epiphenomenon, the outcome of an increase in the number of contexts in which individuals adopt ethnic identification in order to obtain scarce resources. In this instance, the goals of mediators and those of their clients did not necessarily coincide. Since improved access to material resources was a major motivation for client alliance with a broker, the changing character of economic and political opportunity had a marked impact on ethnic group formation. Fluctuations in local economic opportunity combined with changes in national political orientation toward ethnicity to alter the relative advantage of ethnic identification.

NOTES

1. Fieldwork for this project was carried out between January, 1973 and January, 1974. Financial support was provided by grants from the National Institute for Mental Health (Predoctoral Fellowship Award), the Ford Foundation (Ford Area Fellowship), and the National Science Foundation (Doctoral Dissertation Research in Anthropology on Problems of Poverty).

2. Following local usage, Americans of Mexican background are generally referred to as "Mexican-Americans." The term "Chicano" is used here, as it is in

Riverside, to refer specifically to those involved in the movement to enhance Mexican-American ethnic legitimacy and public power.

3. Riverside and all other identifiable names of persons and places in the immediate area are pseudonyms.

4. In an exhaustive study of the system of Wisconsin's welfare administration, Handler and Hollingsworth (1971) found this decentralization and discretion to be characteristic of the entire Wisconsin welfare system. They added that overwork on the part of caseworkers also contributed to their failure in providing services to deserving clients.

BIBLIOGRAPHY

Adams, R. N. 1970. Brokers and Career Mobility Systems in the Structure of Complex Societies. Southwestern Journal of Anthropology 26: 315–327.
Barth, F. 1956. Ecologic Relationships of Ethnic Groups in Swat, North Pakistan. American Anthropologist 58: 1079–1089.
Carmichael, S., and C. Hamilton. 1967. Black Power. New York.
Dahl, R. A. 1967. Pluralist Democracy in the United States: Conflict and Consent. Chicago.
Eisenstadt, S. N. 1954. The Absorption of Immigrants. London.
Firth, R. 1951. Elements of Social Organization. New York.
Foster, G. M. 1961. The Dyadic Contract: A Model for the Social Structure of a Mexican Peasant Village. American Anthropologist 63: 1173–1192.
Geertz, C. 1960. The Changing Role of a Cultural Broker: The Javanese Kijaji. Comparative Studies in Society and History 2: 228–249.
Gordon, M. 1964. Assimilation in American Life. New York.
Handler, J., and E. J. Hollingsworth. 1971. The "Deserving Poor": A Study of Welfare Administration. Chicago.
Hechter, M. 1974. The Political Economy of Ethnic Change. American Journal of Sociology 79: 1151–1178.
Herskovits, M. J. 1958. Acculturation: The Study of Culture Contact. Gloucester.
Isaacs, H. R. 1975. Idols of the Tribe: Group Identity and Political Change. New York.
Kenny, M. 1969. Patterns of Patronage in Spain. Anthropological Quarterly 32: 14–23.
Linton, R. 1940. The Distinctive Aspects of Acculturation. Acculturation in Seven American Indian Tribes, pp. 501–520. New York.
Myrdal, G. 1969. Challenge to Affluence: The Emergence of an "Under-Class." Structured Social Inequality, ed. C. S. Heller, pp. 138–143. London.
Naroll, R. 1964. On Ethnic Unit Classification. Current Anthropology 5: 283–291.
Park, R. 1952. Human Communities. New York.
Park, R., and E. W. Burgess. 1924. Assimilation. Introduction to the Science of Sociology, pp. 734–783. Chicago.
Redfield, R. 1941. The Folk Culture of Yucatan. Chicago.

Rose, A. 1965. The Power Structure: Political Process in America. New York.
Silverman, S. F. 1965. Patronage and Community-Nation Relationships in Central Italy. Ethnology 4: 172–189.
Spiro, M. E. 1955. The Acculturation of American Ethnic Groups. American Anthropologist 57: 1240–1252.
Steward, J. 1955. The Theory of Culture Change. Urbana.
Stuart, W. T. 1972. The Explanation of Patron-Client Systems: Some Structural and Ecological Perspectives. Structure and Process in Latin America: Patronage, Clientage, and Power Systems, eds. A. Strickon and S. M. Greenfield, pp. 19–42. Albuquerque.
Wallerstein, I. 1973. The Two Modes of Ethnic Consciousness: Soviet Central Asia in Transition? The Nationality Question in Soviet Central Asia, ed. E. Allworth, pp. 168–175. New York.
Wells, M. J. 1975. Ethnicity, Social Stigma, and Resource Mobilization in Rural America: Re-examination of a Midwestern Experience. Ethnohistory 22: 319–343.
Wisconsin, State of, 1975. Fair Employment Law, Section 111. 31, Dept. of Industry, Labor, and Human Relations, Madison.
Wolf, E. 1956. Aspects of Group Relations in a Complex Society: Mexico. American Anthropologist 58: 1065–1076.
―――. 1966. Kinship, Friendship, and Patron-Client Relations in Complex Societies. The Social Anthropology of Complex Societies, ed. M. Banton, pp. 1–22. London.

Seeing and Understanding
>>> <<<

All people, even those of the simplest societies, engage in the practice of contrasting their own cultural customs and practices with those of their differing neighbors. This curiosity about strangers and the exotic was raised to the level of formal practice by early chroniclers like Herodotus and ibn-Khaldun, but it first became a standard disciplinary procedure within anthropology, which makes use of cross-cultural comparison. Nowadays anthropologists and practitioners of other social sciences regularly employ a variety of sophisticated, mostly statistical, methodologies for cross-cultural analyses. Rarely, however, do anthropologists deliberately contrast the customs of exotic societies with the practices and institutions of their own culture in their professional publications, except when writing textbooks. But when they teach, particularly with introductory courses, anthropologists love to contrast examples of cultural exotica with cultural analogues familiar to the class members, not just to season their lectures, but to expand their students' provincial horizons and provide them with a means for viewing themselves and their own society more objectively.

Anthropologists profess that the purpose of anthropology is to better understand the essence of human nature. Their way of contributing toward this quest is to see and understand how human nature is expressed through the great variety of societies and cultures, and that is why all known examples of human society are equally worthy and necessary materials for investigation and contemplation. If anthropologists rarely make explicit comparisons between the people they study in the field or in the archives and their own culture, it is only because of professional convention. Comparisons are always made implicitly by the researcher. This cannot be avoided, for the researcher is a cultural product, albeit trained to be sensitive to ethnocentric influences, not all of which can be controlled.

Sometimes anthropologists make deliberate comparisons between exotic *others* and the familiar *ourselves* because an introspection cannot otherwise be fruitful. While not common, this practice holds a venerable position. It first appeared with the founding ancestors of anthropology, who partly justified anthropological endeavors as a means for better appreciating Victorian society, especially its purportedly elevated evolutionary status above other societies.

We all know the ancient fable of the naked emperor displaying his new clothes. Centuries later, social scientists discovered the truism that people believe what they want to believe and see what they expect to see in consonance with their cultural conditioning.

Errington addresses this fundamental human characteristic by looking at the situation of ranchers in Montana, a state which has long suffered economic depression. The ideals of friendly competition and neighborly assistance prevail, but the contradiction between these values, normally not in the foreground, is exacerbated by the recent failing economy that has sent many ranches into bankruptcy and threatens the viability of others. Errington's question concerns how the ranchers perceive their condition. Do they, as others might, regard the larger economic system as fundamentally flawed or, given the basic American values of self-reliance and effort-optimism, do they view failure as self-deserved or caused by a string of poor luck?

When Montana ranchers go belly up, their neighbors benefit. There are fewer conflicts over the allocation of irrigation water; additional land is available for purchase at bargain prices; there is less competition for bank loans and mortgages; and the market for stock animals increasingly favors the surviving ranchers. The virtue of good neighborliness, however, requires that people downplay the competitive nature of their relations and stress instead compassion and assistance.

When economic reserves run dry and a ranch folds, Montana ranchers come face-to-face with the contradictions of their existence. The defeated rancher is forced to sell his equipment and household belongings at a public auction held at the home he must leave. The auction, like a funeral without eulogies, marks the humiliating end to a personal career for a member of the local community. Errington does not tell us what those bidding on the spoils may be thinking, nor may we ever know. Do they think, "There but for the grace of God go I," or is it, "His loss is my gain"? Perhaps both.

Errington focuses on the auction as the quintessential event marking the inherent contradictions, and highlights the role of the auctioneer as critical for masking them. The auctioneer helps to preserve the ideological equilibrium of the participants by framing the situation in a manner that encourages the bidders to see themselves not as vultures and cannibals, but as good neighbors and as folks just doing what is right and natural for people to do.

The auctioneer removes the discomforts of dissonance. Through him events appear congruent with basic values. The world is made to look right, and people can continue to believe in it, seeing perhaps not so much what they wish as what they must hold on to. But they may have no choice. Disbelief is too threatening.

Hatch's comparison of New Zealand and California ranchers makes an important theoretical point: even in societies that are apparently the same, conceptions of wealth are culturally relative. He also shows how the anthropologist, ideally a neutral medium of objective observation and research, actually is conditioned by his or her own cultural assumptions and unwittingly manipulates information to construct data. The underlying point of the articles in this section is that our perceptions are culturally conditioned, so that what we appear to see is refashioned in a manner that makes sense with our cultural expectations.

Before turning to study New Zealand sheep ranchers, Hatch had conducted research with California grain and cattle ranchers. With the latter, as any American rightly expects, social standing is associated with income, and wealth is objectively measurable in the size of land holdings, the head count of stock, the amount and types of mechanized equipment, the size of the rancher's home, the quantity and quality of the home's appliances and furnishings, the number and kinds of vehicles possessed, and so on. Wealth, income, and social status are of one piece; the measure of one trait predicts the rest. But when Hatch questioned New Zealand ranchers regarding the relative wealth and standing of their neighboring ranchers, he became disturbed at their apparent equivocating and prevaricating. Why could they not be straightforward and come forth in confirming what was to Hatch so obvious?

Hatch's persistence in extracting the New Zealanders' admission of his correct assessments finally paid off, but in an unexpected manner, as so often happens in anthropological fieldwork. He came to realize that wealth and social status are not perceived similarly in the eyes of different beholders. Nor is it that New Zealand ranchers are less rational in economic matters than Americans. They hold different assumptions and they operate under different economic constraints. Therefore they apply different measures of evaluating wealth and social standing. In New Zealand, the size of holdings must be assessed in terms of stock management, mortgages, and household composition, and income must be measured against taxes. All of these, in turn, are related to anticipated future needs of the ranch and to the generational life cycles of the ranchers before a New Zealander is comfortable in sizing up how well his neighbor is doing.

Goodman's research is within the anthropological tradition of comparative analysis. It also illustrates an eclectic practice of anthropologists and other social scientists, that of mutual borrowing and cross-disciplinary influence. To compare the cognitive styles of Japanese and American children, presumably culture-influenced, she uses an instrument called *story recall* that had been employed by another anthropologist, Nadel, some thirty years earlier among Nigerian peoples. Nadel, in turn, got the technique from psychologists.

If readers expect that Goodman's analysis of the mental characteristics of Japanese children might help explain the rapidity with which Japan modernized since Commodore Perry's unwelcome visit to Tokyo in 1853 and the country's phenomenal industrial and commercial success since World War II, they will be disappointed. She shows that Japanese and American children are in many respects similar and that the differences between them move in directions contrary to our expectations. Japanese children are less accurate than American children in recalling details of a story, they are "less systematizing in conceptual habits," and a "scientific-technical" theme is pervasive with the Americans but not with the Japanese. Clearly, the explanations for the Japanese success in public education and industrial development do not lie in any advantages they hold in cognitive conceptualization.

The Cultural Evaluation of Wealth: An Agrarian Case Study[1]

Elvin Hatch

>>> <<<

IN SOCIETIES THROUGHOUT the world wealth confers prestige. Other factors are also involved in defining social standing but, in general, wealthy people rank higher in the social hierarchy than the poor. Even the famous exceptions seem to confirm the rule. The examples that come to mind are the *nouveaux riches* of both the American South and nineteenth-century England, in which people representing "new money" stood lower in the social scale than less well-to-do families representing "old money." One assumes that the influence of economics is inexorable and that it is only a matter of time until the *nouveaux riches* will move into the ranks of the old-moneyed families. Similarly, the spectacle of an impoverished family of high social standing is regarded as a curiosity because wealth and social position seem to be so intimately linked.

The principle that the distribution of wealth and prestige tend to be isomorphic seems to lead to another, which is that once a person understands the economic facts of a district, such as the system of production and distribution of material goods, the pattern of land ownership, and the organization of economic labor, it should be possible to predict where people stand in the prestige heirarchy of that community. In other words, it seems that the essentials of the prestige hierarchy (which is a system of subjective evaluations on the part of the members of a social body) are immediately deducible from the objective, or directly observable, features of the economic order. Similarly, if two communities are characterized by identical economic features, they should exhibit fundamentally similar prestige hierarchies.

This paper examines the relationship between ostensive economic facts and subjective evaluations of prestige in two rural, predominantly Anglo, farm communities, one in California, the other in New Zealand; and it suggests that wealth is given different cultural definitions in the two districts. Even if the two locales were to exhibit the same objective economic features, they would not exhibit the same subjectively perceived social hierarchies. What is more, a full understanding of the economic organization of the two communities would not enable a person to infer the social hierarchies that exist there.

This analysis views the economic system of a district as a complex of etic factors. In language, a phonemic system is based upon a limited number of phonetic elements, for a few speech sounds are selected from the entire range of possibilities. Similarly, in assessing wealth for the purpose of ordering local families, some selection is made from the total gamut of economic facts. Not all of the ostensive economic features of a community are culturally significant in making judgments about who is wealthier than whom, and two communities that exhibit the same economic facts may conceivably employ different economic features in defining wealth and, so, may exhibit different culturally defined social hierarchies. Put briefly, the same economic facts are compatible with more than one prestige hierarchy and, in order to understand the social hierarchy of a community, it is not enough to attend to economic facts alone.

The Comparative Farm Communities

The California community is located in the Central Coast region of California and is devoted primarily to dry-land grain and cattle (Hatch 1973, 1975, 1979). Research was conducted in the mid-1960s, one focus of which was to understand how the social hierarchy had changed since the 1920s as a result of technological and economic developments. For example, the range of differences in wealth had increased considerably, greater capital was needed to begin farming, and it had now become impossible for the farm hand to acquire a farm through savings. The social implications of these changes are patent; the social distance from top to bottom of the local hierarchy had widened and the social cleavage between farmers and most others in the district had grown as well.

Economics provide a comprehensive, linear, hierarchical ordering of farmers. At the top are two millionaire families, both engaged in cattle ranching, whose holdings are by far the largest in the district; at the bottom are several farmers who do not have enough land to support their families and who therefore must hold part-time jobs to augment their incomes. The other landholders are distributed along a continuum between these extremes. Community members do not always agree on the relative economic and social standing of a particular farmer but the disagreements are never fundamental. In any event, it is a relatively simple (and interesting) exercise for local people to list farm families according to what they consider to be their relative economic and social standing.

This social and economic hieararchy also constitutes a dominant idiom for thinking about social relations, for a farmer's placement in this hierarchy is probably the most important feature of his local social identity.

The New Zealand community is located on South Island, on the outer fringes of Canterbury, and the land is devoted primarily to sheep.[2] I lived in the community for over nine months in 1981 and one of the key findings of the study has to do with the shape of the local hierarchy among landholders, which is comparatively flat. In part this reflects the narrow range of differences in wealth among the New Zealand farmers, a point to which I return, but it also reflects the fact that wealth is only one of several principles employed by farmers in assessing one another's social position.

The local standing of farm families rests on at least three principles. First is farming ability. The topic of who are good or bad farmers in the district, or in what respects a particular farmer is good or bad, stimulates considerable interest among local people. This is one of the first things they discuss when they comment on one another in private. The range of differences here is considerable, in part because the New Zealand system is so forgiving. A farmer whose fixed expenses are low and whose mortgage is paid can survive almost indefinitely with a minimum of effort. Yet those who enjoy the reputation of being particularly good farmers— whose sheep are especially healthy, whose paddocks are particularly green and show better care than their neighbors', whose fences and buildings are in excellent repair, and the like—enjoy considerable local esteem.

The second factor is cultivation or refinement, which produces a gradation from what I call the local genteel families on one hand to the rough on the other. Like the evaluation of farming ability, this is not an absolute distinction inasmuch as a person can be judged as more or less refined, or more or less rough. The markers of each category include features such as speech patterns, "presence," dining hahits, home furnishings, and so on. By all accounts, the elite members of the community are identified by these criteria and by where they went to school; they attended one of the prestigious boarding schools in Christchurch or elewhere. On the other hand, the truly rough farmers are described as exhibiting the kind of coarseness in appearance and behavior that one associates with manual workers in contexts like the pub.

The third factor is wealth. All else being equal, the more prosperous farm families enjoy higher social standing than the less prosperous ones.

The application of these three factors does not produce a comprehensive, linear hierarchy within which all farmers can be placed. Some people clearly stand higher than others overall but the community does not think in terms of a comprehensive continuum. In part this is because none of the three factors is clearly dominant over the others and each produces a different ordering of farm families. A given individual may be considered an excellent farmer and have a sizable farm in good financial condition yet he may also be considered very rough in his personal style. Another may be less prosperous, considered only fair in farming ability, but regarded as highly refined.

The New Zealand Conception of Wealth

The typical view in the New Zealand community is that the farmers there are all at about the same level of wealth. Landholders in other areas, including some nearby, with very sizable properties and larger incomes, are described as well-to-do. But this is a district of medium-sized farms that are only moderately profitable. The reason why differences in wealth do not play a prominent role in the community (according to local thought) is that these differences are so small.

The relative unimportance of wealth as a factor in distinguishing farmers was a consistent theme in interviews.[3] For example, in one interview I stated that I thought wealth played a role in distinguishing between farmers of higher and lower social standing. The person responded, "Yes it does, a little bit—yes, it would. But it's not a really significant role. Really. Just because you've got a lot of land doesn't mean you're wealthy. You might have an enormous mortgage. This could be the case with anyone just starting or shifting."

Indirect evidence also suggests that wealth is not the chief basis for distinguishing among farmers in the New Zealand community. In particular, when people are pressed to name the especially wealthy farmers, they often stray from the point. In this respect they are unlike the people in the California community, to whom wealth is a particularly interesting topic on which they have little difficulty focusing. The most common issue that diverts a person's attention in the New Zealand community is farming ability; this subject first springs to mind when farmers are asked to comment on one another and it sustains their interest in the way that wealth does among the California farmers.

I was initially frustrated by the local insistence on the flatness of the hierarchy of wealth among farmers in the district, for it was obvious to me that significant differences did exist. Some farmers lived in old, inadequate houses that they admitted they could not afford to improve, whereas others had recently built new homes or remodeled their old ones. Some could afford late model automobiles, others could not. Some could afford to take a trip abroad, others could not, and so on. Similarly, some farms were comparatively small, requiring only the labor of the farm family itself (except for shearing and perhaps a few other seasonal jobs), whereas others hired a substantial amount of casual help throughout the year, and some farmers employed full-time hired help the year-round. Several farmers had progressively enlarged their holdings until they had the equivalent of three, four, or even five farms, which would soon be (or were presently being) taken over by their sons, whereas other farmers' sons struggled to maintain nothing more than the father's original holdings. I raised these issues with people in the community and was given explanations for why they did not constitute genuine differences in wealth among farmers on every count. I will consider the points separately.

1. Why can we not use differences in personal income (as manifest in degrees of affluence) for sorting farmers into a comprehensive, linear hierarchy of wealth? (In order to facilitate the discussion I assume that we are comparing farmers whose holdings would be roughly similar in productive potential if operated at maximum efficiency; the reasons for doing so will become clear.)

The main reason why differences in personal income are rejected by local people as a basis for sorting farmers into a hierarchy is that differences in income are primarily a function of the developmental cycle. When a young man starts out on his own, he is very heavily burdened with debt because he has to purchase the farm. This is true even for a farmer's son because inheritance taxes are so high that he, too, has to acquire the land through purchase (although he enjoys substantial advantages in doing so over the sons of those who are propertyless). Consequently, a young farmer has a very high mortgage payment, which leaves little to be spent on the family itself.

The response of the young farmer to the economic pressures he feels is to increase production, for the more sheep and cattle produced the easier it is for him to pay the mortgage bill. In order to increase productivity he is likely to engage in a program of farm improvement: augmenting the application of fertilizer to increase the growth of grass and therefore to facilitate an increase in stock numbers; adding fences to reduce the size of paddocks and thus to improve the management of his animals; draining swampy sections to increase their productivity, and the like. These improvements are expensive and require considerable labor, so they are done in piecemeal fashion over a period of years.

Typically, as the farmer reaches his mid- to late-forties, the mortgage payment is no longer a serious burden, so an increasing percentage of the farm income is diverted to personal income. What is more, the pressure to maintain a high level of production is no longer severe and, consequently, the farmer is less likely to continue making farm improvements that are expensive, time-consuming, and laborious. His personal income is reasonably high at this stage and his work load comparatively light. This is often the point at which the farmer remodels his house or at which he and his wife take their first trip abroad.

Yet as the farm approaches this mature stage of its developmental cycle the income tax bill becomes prominent. The young farmer typically pays little, if any, income tax because both the mortgage payment and the cost of farm development are deductible. As these deductions diminish (eventually almost to the vanishing point), the tax bill increases. For example, one of the highest annual incomes among the farmers of the district I studied in 1981 was about $NZ20,000 (then worth about $17,000 in American dollars). This person probably had some deductions but not enough to move him into a lower tax bracket; consequently, he was almost certainly taxed at the highest rate, 60 per cent.

The income tax system has crucial implications for the farm operation and the farmer's income. Once the mortgage bill largely disappears and farm improvements have largely been achieved, the farmer no longer has a strong incentive to maintain a high level of production. He is inclined rather to reduce production: if he maintains high stock numbers he risks having more sheep or cattle than can be fed in the event of a drought or a severe winter; and a majority of his personal income is going to be taken in taxes anyway. Besides, the more stock he has, the heavier is his work load. Consequently, while it is true that the mature farmer exhibits the signs of a higher personal income than his fledgling neighbor, he certainly is not rich by local standards. He probably is no more affluent than a local school teacher of similar age.

To summarize, the beginning farmer is heavily burdened with debt, has a very small personal income, pays relatively little income tax, and works very hard to increase the productivity of his holdings. The mature farmer has comparatively little debt, a significantly greater personal income but is relatively heavily taxed, and does not work as hard or have as productive a farm.

An important implication of the developmental cycle of the farm is the amount of elasticity or variation in its productivity. Two farms of equal potential produce very different gross incomes depending on the stages of the respective farmers' careers. Similarly, the same farm varies considerably in productivity over time.

2. Farmers do not have equally productive farms, some properties are larger than others. Some are also better situated: they are flatter, slightly lower in elevation, slope more toward the sun than away from it, have better soil, and the like. Why, then, can we not use differences in size and quality of farms as a measure of wealth? To simplify the discussion, I will

hold the developmental cycle constant and consider farmers without regard to the stages of their respective careers.

Differences in farm size and quality produce two distinguishable measures that may be used in assessing wealth; income and market value. Regarding income, the larger and better properties can potentially make more money. For example, a person who has a two-man farm and needs a full-time hired man to help him has a larger turnover or gross income than another man who owns a one-man property.

According to local opinion, one reason why this kind of difference among farms does not result in a hierarchical ordering of farm families is the levelling effect of the income tax; another is the great expense of hired labor. The farmer must pay the worker's salary and provide the man and his family with a house, which has to be maintained, as well as mutton and such other incidentals as firewood. Most farmers contend that they could probably earn as much from a one-man farm as they could from a two-man operation. Not all fully agreed with this, however, and I was not able to resolve the issue satisfactorily. It is clear that if a person with a two-man farm does enjoy a greater personal income than someone with a one-man unit, the difference is not substantial. One point on which all agree is that it does not pay to buy land for the purpose of adding additional labor units; the worker's salary and other costs associated with maintaining his family, combined with the cost of the mortgage payment on the new property, are greater than the income the land could produce.

The elasticity in a farm's productivity also leads farmers to minimize the importance of income differences among property-holders. The farmer with a larger property is able to maintain larger stock numbers than the smaller farmer when they start out, but once their operations reach maturity the larger farmer no longer has an incentive to keep his stock numbers high. Rather, at the mature stage, both farmers tend to drift toward similar levels of production in spite of the differences in their holdings. The smaller farmer has to work harder; he has to move his sheep more often to get more feed out of his paddocks, for example, and he has to be more diligent at lambing time to ensure a high survival rate among the lambs. But the income from both properties would not differ greatly at the mature stage.

Differences in the size and quality of holdings could in principle result in the second measure of wealth; the larger and better properties have higher market or book values than the smaller and poorer ones. This notion of wealth was tacitly expressed in one farmer's statement that "There are several farms around [the district] that are worth a million." This is literally true; some farms could bring at least that much, and probably more, if they were sold. According to an official in the Ministry of Agriculture (personal communication), $NZ326,000 was the minimum that a person would have to pay in 1981 in order to purchase a farm (including stock, plant, land, and working capital) that would be adequate to support a family and, indeed, several farms in the district were about that size. I infer that this represents the bottom end of the range of differences in farm value in the district. Consequently, by this measure, the largest and best farms are worth at least three times the value of the smallest and poorest.

The principal reason people give in rejecting this as a measure of wealth is that the concept of book value has little significance in everyday life. While it is true that the market value of the farm was increasing through inflation, and had been doing so fairly regularly since shortly after World War II, the farmer would have to sell the property for his assets to have any value to him and his family. In any event, he makes roughly the same dollar amount from the production of the farm whether it is worth a third of a million dollars or three times that figure.

Size and quality of holdings is considered a poor measure of wealth for still another reason. Some of the largest property-holders are farmers who have reached the mature stage of the developmental cycle and who have recently acquired additional holdings. For example, if a small parcel of 200 or 300 acres near their farm were to come on the market, they might buy that as insurance against a dry year or a particularly bad winter. If they have more than one child, they try to acquire enough land to allow each of the children to have a farm to purchase from the family estate. Each parcel of the additional land that the farmer buys requires that he refinance his holdings and thus that he go back into debt, and such a person is thought to slip backwards economically. Consequently, a larger landholder is often considered less wealthy than a smaller landholder who is at the same stage of the developmental cycle.

Two considerations seem to be involved in this evaluation of the mortgage bill. First, the new mortgage has a retrogressive effect on the farmer's income; he is now less likely to travel abroad, rebuild the shearing shed, remodel the house, and the like. Yet the effect on his standard of living need not be dramatic if his farm, home, and automobile are in good condition. He and his wife might not be able to travel, and they will certainly have to cut back on expenses in general, but they are not forced to sacrifice to the extent that is typical for the young farm family.

Second, in local thought, a well-to-do person does not owe large amounts of money, he is not encumbered with debt. In one interview, a husband and wife were discussing who they thought were wealthy farmers. The wife turned to her husband and asked, "What about Kenneth O'Reilly?"[4] (O'Reilly has sons who were interested in farming and to assist them, over a period of years, he has purchased the property of several neighbors as they retired. His original farm and each of the new holdings have sizable mortgages.) The husband replied that he did not think of O'Reilly as a particularly wealthy farmer because he had "bought an awful lot of land over the years." O'Reilly's name was mentioned in another interview with a retired farmer and his wife. The couple I was speaking to had two sons, one of whom had taken over the farm, which had been mortgaged in order to purchase a second property for the other son. The wife first mentioned O'Reilly as an example of a person she would consider wealthy "because he's bought a lot of land." Her husband quickly commented, "but not Kenneth, he's put [his sons] all in the same way we put [our son] into [his farm], by mortgaging his own place. I wouldn't put Kenneth among the top. That is not what I would class as wealthy." The man then named another farmer as an example of "one of the most well-heeled chaps in the district." This other farmer has a much smaller holding than O'Reilly's—a two-man unit that he and his son work together—but his property carries a very low level of debt. The discussion continued for several minutes, when the husband commented that several local farmers, like himself, "have bought farms, and they have done quite well on them, and they've put their sons onto farms. But likes of James O'Connor, [when] he'd bought the place for [his son], he said to me, 'Well, Alister, you and I are both back to square one.'" By acquiring new mortgages to purchase additional land, both farmers went backward in their economic position.

The Cultural Definition of Wealth

My initial skepticism about the claims of local people that differences in wealth are not marked was stimulated primarily by the wide differences in the size of their farms, as I noted. I suspected that the community members either were not entirely truthful or that they were not fully aware of the role wealth played in their assessment of social standing. I therefore decided to put their claim to the test by asking a variety of people to name the ones they thought were the wealthiest in the district. I was looking for some consensus in people's responses which would suggest that wealth was indeed more important in local thought than the people realized or admitted and I hoped to discover the grounds on which the selections were made.

People did not find this an easy question to answer but, when pressed, they could name a handful of farmers whom they thought were more well-to-do than others. Several patterns emerged from their responses. First, two farmers were named more frequently than any others. Even if these two names were not volunteered, the person interviewed usually recognized this as an oversight if I proposed the names myself. Here unquestionably were the wealthiest people in the district. On the other hand, these were equivocal cases, both of the holdings were located on the outer fringe of the community and these two families did not interact much within it. Their properties were also somewhat remote and were not easily seen. Equally important, both men engaged in a different type of operation from a large majority of those in the district. These were high-country runholders, not sheep farmers, strictly speaking. Like many of the high-country runs in New Zealand, these had lower operating expenses (particularly lower labor costs) and therefore greater income potential than the more intensively farmed properties that made up the great bulk of the holdings in this locality. These two runs were associated in people's minds more with the large and more lucrative properties in the adjacent high country than they were with the moderate-sized and somewhat less profitable farms that predominated within the local community.

If these two runholders are excluded from consideration, another pattern emerges. I discovered a fair degree of repetition in the other names proposed as well-to-do farmers, although none of these names was put forward with the same confidence as the first two. This larger group of farmers had several things in common. One is that they had reached the mature stage of the developmental cycle; their level of debt was comparatively low and they enjoyed relatively high personal incomes. Another is that they were all considered to be excellent farmers. Not only did they drive late-model cars and live in houses that were more modern and more comfortable than the average, their fences were in good order, they produced excellent stock, and the like. Their prosperity was reflected in their personal affluence as well as in the condition of their farms.

Although the names of this category tended to reappear in interviews with different people, the consensus was hardly complete, but here again there seems to have been a pattern behind the variations that occurred. When people gave me the names of individuals they considered to represent the well-to-do members of the district, they tended to select from among their own, immediate personal network, including friends, neighbors, relatives, and the like. Consequently, if I only considered the responses of farmers who were related to or socialized with one another, I discovered considerable overlap in the names they offered as examples of prosperous community members. But if I shifted my attention to people who represented a somewhat different network, a different set of names tended to appear.

This provokes a comparison with the California community, in which everyone offers the same names in pointing out the wealthiest local families. The reason for this contrast surely is that the range of differences in wealth is so much greater in the California community; the ostensive features setting apart the truly wealthy community members are more manifest there and the wealthiest families stand out more clearly.

When people in the New Zealand community are pressed to name the farm families they consider to be well-to-do, what criteria do they use in making their choices? Size of holdings is mentioned on some occasions, although this is always done with considerable equivocation, coupled with a denial that these differences are very great within the district. This denial itself casts doubt on the importance of size of holdings in judgments about wealth, however. We have seen that the book value of farms at the mature stage of the developmental cycle ranges from about a third to over a million dollars, which surely is sufficient to serve as the basis for a hierarchy of wealth among landholders. Another consideration leads one to be suspicious about the importance of farm size. I indicated earlier that a point made repeatedly by farmers is that although they are worth a lot "on paper," this means very little to them unless and until they sell their land. These statements not only imply that the assets of their farms are fairly inconsequential in their everyday lives but, more important, that income is the true measure of wealth; the reason they feel that differences in assets are relatively unimportant is that these differences do not directly result in significant differences in income.

While size of properties is mentioned, differences in income play a very prominent role in most people's judgments. For example, I asked one farmer if it was true that some landholders in the district are wealthier than others and his response was peppered with such phrases as "people I look up to as being pretty comfortable," "farmers which have pretty good bank balances," those who are "pretty well to do," who are in a "comfortable position," "are pretty well heeled," and have "never really been too short of a bob." Size of holdings entered into his comments as well. For example, he remarked that one farmer "has a very big farm. Never a big spender, but [he] doesn't really do without anything." Yet size of the property is not the essential differentia for it is easily overridden by signs of affluence. For example, at one point this person compared three families with adjacent farms, each of which was relatively large. He considered two of these families as well-to-do, while the third was not; the latter, he noted, is "A pretty young guy, and he's taken over in pretty hard times with not very much money, but he's got equally as big a place but isn't in as comfortable a position. He started from scratch." To paraphrase, although these three farmers have equal amounts of land, one has a larger mortgage, which means (among other things) that he does not have as much money to spend.

A very well run farm in very good condition is a sign of prosperity and wealth whereas a poorly run property in poor condition is not, regardless of its size. A particularly telling case is that of Brian Johnson. Johnson's farm is at the mature stage of its developmental cycle and he has bought several additional parcels with the goal eventually of placing each of his sons on the land. Since he had purchased his property in increments over a period of years, at the time of my research he was not carrying a heavy burden of debt. Judging by size of holdings and the book value of farms, he ranked among the top landholders in the district. Yet he was virtually never mentioned in interviews as one of the well-to-do farmers and this was clearly no oversight. Instead of investing to improve his stock and the land he already had, he spent relatively large amounts on the domestic side of the ledger—he had recently remodeled his house—and he bought additional land. One person commented, "the Johnsons have a fair block of land now. They personally think they are a big landowner, one perhaps above the rest. But they're not utilizing the land they've got to its ability. ... They think they're big landowners and think they might be the apple of everybody's eye, but knowing them as well as I do it's not very satisfactory. ... They've got a beautiful home, but the way they're operating their property leaves a lot to be desired. An interesting quote was made by him—he said he'd rather buy more land than spend the money on getting his existing land into shape. Which is a stupid attitude, I think." In another interview with a different person I asked why Johnson had not been mentioned as a wealthy farmer. He said, "Possibly I might be judging a little on farming ability." Later in the same interview he said, "They've got quite a large area of land, and their stock and stock management is probably some of the poorest."

I asked another farmer to name the wealthiest farmers in the area. He said, "There are two brackets in this." First are the middle-aged men who have increased the productivity of their farms and whose "costs have disappeared into the background." He offered the names of two farmers, and said, "They would be some of the better farmers in the district. They're doing very nicely." The other category, he said, "are probably very wealthy farmers, the likes of our neighbors, the Johnsons, who live over in the next gully, who have a lot of land, a lot of sheep, but their performance is disastrous. They don't spend anything on development. They suck everything they can out of the place. Their biggest bill would be the tax bill. And they would be getting a handsome living out of it, but they're spending nothing back on the place. So which is the best farmer? They [the Johnsons] probably make the most money, but [the other category of landholders] would be the better farmers."

Further light is shed on this case by a comment made by yet another person. The context was a free-ranging discussion of farmers in the district, and I asked, "What about the Johnsons?" He said, "He's not too good a farmer, but I wouldn't criticize him too much all the same. He bought a lot of land. He'll have good properties to hand on to his sons." This statement tacitly acknowledged that Johnson is widely criticized in the district for his poor farming practices; this was the first issue that sprang to mind in commenting on him. The fact that Johnson has acquired considerable land was the second issue. Yet what was worth comment was not the significance of this land as a measure of Johnson's wealth or social standing, but rather that this property will make it relatively easy for each of his sons to become independent landholders.

Another farmer, Richard Wood, provides a telling contrast with the Johnsons. Wood is among those frequently named as one of the wealthy landholders in the community. He is also considered one of the best farmers and, above all, has produced some of the best sheep. Although his mortgage payment is relatively low, he continues to spend large sums on improving the farm, and its appearance is nearing perfection. His house is sub-standard, however; it is repaired and painted but very old, damp, disintegrating, and (in his opinion) badly needs replacing. Wood's mortgage payment has diminished to the point that he is about to build a new house at a more favorable spot on the property.

Wood's is hardly a large farm. He runs the place as a stud operation and so has greater labor requirements than if his sheep were raised strictly for their meat and wool. As he operates it, this is a one-and-a-half man farm but if it were run as a normal operation it would be a one-man unit. His land is about as fully developed as it can be, so an infusion of capital will not expand its production or labor requirements by a significant amount.

Thus Johnson is considered to be one of the largest landholders in the district but one of the worst farmers and most people explicitly exclude him from the list of the most well-to-do. Wood's is an average-sized farm but he is considered one of the best farmers and he is generally counted among the wealthiest in the district.

I can now summarize the cultural definition of wealth in the community, or the grounds by which some are judged to be wealthier than others. The critical factor in assessing wealth is income or, rather, its ostensive manifestation, affluence. The well-to-do farmers are those who can afford to rebuild or remodel the house if needed or build a new shearing shed, add additional fences and repair old ones, maintain the quality of the paddocks by top-dressing, and the like. The single most important factor in determining level of income (and affluence) is the mortgage bill; consequently, to be well-to-do, one has to be at the mature stage of the developmental cycle. Thus the son of a wealthy farmer moves down the hierarchy of wealth once he buys his own farm and goes into business on his own account.

Achieving the mature stage of the developmental cycle does not automatically place one among the most well-to-do in the district, however, for there are several disqualifiers. First is to be considered a poor (inept) farmer. The person whose farm is rundown, whose stock are poorly cared-for, and whose paddocks are not properly managed does not produce all that he can from the property. By contrast, the truly good farmer raises healthier, heavier, woollier sheep in greater numbers, so the turnover on his farm (or its gross income) is greater. Yet the family of a good farmer is not necessarily more prosperous in their personal lives than the family of a bad farmer, for a larger percentage of the gross income of the good farmer is spent on the farm itself. This leads to the paradox that some inept farmers actually show greater signs of affluence in the personal sphere than the very good farmers who are considered to be among the wealthiest.

Another disqualifier is the mortgage bill. A farmer who is at the mature stage of the developmental cycle and who has acquired additional land by mortgaging his property is thought to slip backward in wealth, for the status of being wealthy and the condition of indebtedness are conceptually incongruous.

Discussion

The New Zealand farmers regard their ideas about wealth and about the way it does or does not sort farm families into a hierarchy to be a matter of common sense. If the question were put to them, they would say that the difference between their hierarchy of wealth and the one in the California community is a matter of economics. If the California farmers were confronted with the same economic facts as the New Zealand farmers (such as the high cost of labor and the very steeply inclined income tax system) and if the California farms exhibited roughly the same range of differences in size and quality, among other things, then the differences between the social hierarchies of the two districts would vanish.

An alternative view is that wealth is defined according to conventional criteria and that the criteria that are employed in the California and New Zealand communities cannot be reduced to economic principles. Before explaining this, however, I need to enter a caveat; my material on the California community is not as full as it is for the one in New Zealand because this issue had not occurred to me at the time of the California study. When I did my research there, I took the hierarchy of wealth to be as much a matter of common sense as the New Zealanders did when I worked among them.

One major difference in the way the California and New Zealand farmers evaluate wealth is that the former use size and quality of land as the principal differentia. "Large farmer" and "wealthy farmer" are synonymous. A California farmer, stepping into the New Zealand community, would initially "see" a different social hierarchy from the one the New Zealanders see, for whereas the California farmer would tacitly assume that the larger landholders are wealthier, the New Zealand farmer does not. An illustration is my own perplexity when the New Zealand farmers refused to confirm what I saw with my own eyes—that some farmers are significantly wealthier than others because they have significantly larger and better holdings.

Yet this difference in the evaluation of wealth in the two communities may be explained by reference to differences in the respective economic systems. In the California case, family income is closely associated with the size and quality of a person's holdings; a family whose farm is twice as large as another's derives a good deal more from the land. It is conceivable that if this characteristic of the California system were to change in the direction of the New Zealand pattern, so that the size of a farm is not a reasonable gauge of a family's income, then the criterion of farm size and quality would no longer be the primary basis for sorting landholders into a hierarchy of wealth. The reverse might also be true. If the New Zealand economic system were to change in such a fashion that the larger and better farms made significantly more money for their owners than the smaller and poorer ones, then size and quality of farms could become the standard measure of wealth. This argument does not necessarily deny that the cultural definition of wealth plays a significant role in structuring community members' perceptions of social hierarchy but it does suggest that the cultural definitions ultimately are reducible to purely economic facts.

Is it possible, however, that there are other differences between the two sets of ideas for evaluating wealth besides the fact that the one group of farmers focuses on income and the other on property? Is it also possible that these other differences in assessing wealth cannot be fully reduced to economic principles?

It seems that the concept of property operates somewhat differently as a measure of wealth in the two communities. In the California case, property is evaluated not only for the income it provides but also as a form of collateral, in that bank financing is an indispensable part of the operation of the farm, like the use of the tractor or the application of fertilizer. The farm loan is used for living expenses in a bad year, to cover operating expenses virtually every year, and for the purchase of additional land or other business interests when the opportunity arises. Land is considered to be too good an asset not to use in this fashion. What is more, the value of agricultural land has been rising in the California community since World War II and every increase in property values means that the farm would bring more money if it were sold and that the amount of money the farmer can borrow increases. Even if the farmer does not make a suitable return on his investment from the production of the farm, he still is able to convert the inflation of land values into usable cash by virtue of the property's borrowing power. Of course, the larger and better farms have greater borrowing capacity.

Some farmers are also in a better economic position than others to buy additional land. Obviously, the greater the amount of land a farmer has to borrow against, the easier it is for him to acquire the financing to buy property that happens to come on the market. In New Zealand, property is not regarded in the same light. One piece of evidence for this is the relationship in the New Zealand farmers' thought between poor (inept) farming on one hand and judgments about wealth on the other. Not only are the inept farmers excluded from the ranks of the most well-to-do in the district, the bad managers are privately criticized for buying additional land at the expense of improving existing property.

It is difficult to compare California and New Zealand farmers with respect to the distinction between good and bad farming. A California farmer has to be reasonably good merely to survive; consequently, judgments about good and bad farming are not pronounced there. Nonetheless, it is clear that the California farmers evaluate the purchase of additional land in different terms from their New Zealand counterparts. In the California case, crucial to assessing a purchase of this kind is whether or not it is a wise financial investment in the long term and the implications that acquisition might have for the quality of farming on the home place is quite irrelevant. I suspect that the California farmers would offer a positive evaluation of Brian Johnson, the New Zealand farmer who increased his holdings considerably while he ignored the development of the land he already had. With each new purchase, he increased his capacity to borrow and therefore to buy even more land. In 20 or 30 years,

Johnson's sons will be at a considerable advantage over the sons of the other farmers (some considered the best in the district in 1981) who are much slower to expand their holdings.

A second piece of evidence that property is conceived differently in the two communities concerns the evaluation of indebtedness in the New Zealand community. The notion that a man who mortgages his farm to buy additional land slips backward in wealth is much less pronounced in the California community. There, to increase one's holdings, even by raising the level of indebtedness, is considered an advancement. The statement quoted above, in which one farmer in the New Zealand community rejected another farmer as one of the wealthy people in the district "because he's bought a lot of land," makes little sense to the California farmers.

Yet it may be that these differences in thought about the acquisition of additional land and about indebtedness are themselves explainable in economic terms. In particular, land may not be as valuable an asset in New Zealand, and the benefits of the inflation of land values for property-holders may not be as great there. This is an extremely complicated matter and the solution is not altogether clear; yet it seems doubtful that the California community in the mid-1960s was significantly different in this regard from the New Zealand community in 1981. Land Boards were set up in New Zealand during World War II to restrain the inflation of land values and to inhibit land speculation (Wise 1943). They continued to operate through the period of my research, although their role was much reduced. Land Boards were not considered by farmers in the district to be an impediment to farm amalgamation, and they no longer were empowered to control the price of farmland. The value of farms in New Zealand had risen slowly but fairly steadily since World War II and had increased dramatically beginning in 1972 (New Zealand Valuation Department 1981). According to an official in the Ministry of Agriculture, the value of farmland in the district of my research had gone up 40 per cent the year before my study. What is more, unlike the United States, capital gains tax was not levied on farmland in New Zealand, so farm property should have been a highly desirable investment there.[5]

Tentatively, the New Zealand economic environment appears highly favorable for the development of the kind of ideas about property and wealth that obtain in the California community and therefore that the evaluation of wealth in the two places reflects differences in cultural ideology and values as much as economics. Should the California farmers operate in an economic environment identical to that in New Zealand—or vice versa—the two groups would continue to evaluate wealth differently.

Conclusion

In both communities wealth is but one of a complex of factors upon which a person's social identity and social standing are based. Wealth is perhaps relatively more important in the California community than in New Zealand, where judgments about a person's refinement or coarseness, or about a man's ability as a farmer, assume considerable prominence. But wealth remains crucial in both places. While the New Zealanders tend to minimize the importance of wealth in the district, the landholder whose property is at the mature stage of the developmental cycle—and who is thought to be an excellent farmer—is considered well-to-do by local standards and this is a highly significant part of his family's social identity.

In pursuing the social role of wealth in these communities I am led to the question of the bases of people's judgments when they assert that one person is wealthier than another. What do they look for in deciding? We have seen that the two communities differ on this point, yet the salient features to which people attend in making such judgments are similar in at least one respect. This is that these features are directly observable and open to public view. Property size, the quality of a farmer's sheep, a family's financial capacity to remodel the house or to build a new shearing shed—these facts are all available to the senses of anyone who cares to look and, of course, who knows how to look. It is possible for a person who knows the cultural code to "read" the local hierarchy of wealth by discovering the significant facts concerning each farm household. It is not necessary to ask who is wealthier than whom, or who stands higher in the local hierarchy; one can interpret the facts for oneself.

This analysis of people's judgments about wealth bears some resemblance to Leach's (1954) discussion of ritual in *Political Systems of Highland Burma*. To Leach, ritual serves to express a person's social status or position; it is a "symbolic statement which 'says' something" about individuals within a structural order (1954: 10–14). In a Kachin *gumsa* community, for example, the marriage of a man and woman signifies the relative standing of their lineages, inasmuch as women in theory marry into lineages that are inferior to their own. A person who understands the *gumsa* code also knows the relative standing of the lineages of a community by observing who is married to whom.

A difference between the California and New Zealand communities is that they employ somewhat different codes for assessing wealth, for they look to different ostensive economic facts in doing so. The contrast between the two goes yet deeper. We have seen that the New Zealand farmers present very rational justifications for rejecting size of holdings as the chief criterion for assessing wealth. They argue that a large farm may be more heavily burdened with debt than a small one and in any event that the family income that can be derived from a large farm is severely limited by the income tax system and by the high cost of labor. The argument, at bottom, is that a family with a decidedly smaller farm can enjoy a standard of living equally as high as that of a family with two or three times as much property. By contrast, the California farmers argue that land is an investment and that the larger the property, the better is the family's financial condition in the long-term.

We may say that the two systems for assessing wealth rest on different rationales and a key question raised by this paper regards the basis of those rationales. Do the differences between the conceptions of wealth reflect differences in the objective economic facts of the two locales or are they a matter of differences in *a priori* cultural assumptions? I have suggested the latter. In the California case, a key assumption is that the increasing market value of land is an economic asset that can be put to good economic use by increased borrowing. In the New Zealand case, however, it is assumed that the bank loan is something to be gotten rid of and that land is an economic asset to the extent that one makes a living from it by selling the commodities it produces.

One reason these differences in conceptions of wealth are significant is that they result in different social hierarchies as conceived by the community members. The hierarchy in the New Zealand case is flatter than the one in California and in part this is due to the objective economic fact that the range of differences in wealth—as measured in absolute dollar terms—is greater in the California community. In addition, the definition of wealth that prevails in the New Zealand community, a definition that minimizes the importance of differences in property size in assessing who is wealthier than whom, contributes to the apparent flatness of that hierarchy. A member of the California community, using his or her own cultural code to interpret the economic facts of the New Zealand community, will see greater hierarchy there than do the New Zealanders.

NOTES

1. I thank David Pearson for comments on an earlier draft of this paper. The California portion of this research was supported by a Public Health Service fellowship (5 F1 MH–29,955–02 [BEH]) from the National Institute of Mental Health, and the New Zealand research was supported by a grant from the National Science Foundation. A version of this paper was presented at the annual meetings of the American Anthropological Association, November 16, 1984, in Denver, Colorado.

Throughout this paper I write in the present tense, yet one should keep in mind that the economics of farming recently have undergone drastic changes in both New Zealand and California. Many of the economic details reported here have almost certainly been modified.

2. The principal community studies in New Zealand are Chappel (1976), Pearson (1980), and Somerset (1974). The principal surveys of class and stratification in New Zealand are Bedggood (1980), Collette (1973), Pearson and Thorns (1983), Pitt (1977), and Vellakoop (1969). Very little systematic work has been done on rural New Zealand; the publications I have found most useful are Gill and Gill (1975), Hall, Thorns and Willmott (1983), and Wilkes and Willmott (1976).

3. These were conducted in private, normally in the person's home, and were open-ended. Normally they lasted from a half hour to over two hours. The interviews were tape-recorded and later transcribed verbatim. I spoke to 159 people in a total of 133 interviews in the course of the research (some people were seen more than once, and sometimes I interviewed husband and wife, or close relatives, together). The question of wealth and social standing occupied a prominent place in 46 interviews with 57 people.

4. This and other personal names used here are pseudonyms.

5. An adequate comparison of the value of land as an asset between the two communities would have to take account of a variety of factors in addition to land inflation. Among these would be interest rates and changes in the consumer price index (see New Zealand Department of Statistics, 1981:923).

BIBLIOGRAPHY

Bedggood, D. 1980. Rich and Poor in New Zealand: A Critique of Class, Politics and Ideology. Auckland.

Chapple, D. L. 1976. Tokoroa: Creating a Community. Auckland.

Collette, J. 1973. Social Stratification in New Zealand. New Zealand Society: Contemporary Perspectives, eds. S. D. Webb and J. Collette, pp. 34–43. Sydney.

Gill, H., and T. Gill. 1975. New Zealand Rural Society: A Framework for Study. New Zealand Agricultural Science 9:60–68.

Hall, B., D. Thorns, and B. Willmott. 1983. Community Formation and Change: A Study of Rural and Urban Localities in New Zealand. Department of Sociology, University of Canterbury, New Zealand, Working Paper No. 4.

Hatch, E. 1973. Social Drinking and Factional Alignment in a Rural California Community. Anthropological Quarterly 46:243–60.

———. 1975. Stratification in a Rural California Community. Agricultural History 49:21–38.

———. 1979. Biography of a Small Town. New York.

Leach, E. R. 1954. Political Systems of Highland Burma. Cambridge.

New Zealand Department of Statistics. 1981. The New Zealand Official Yearbook. Wellington.

New Zealand Valuation Department. 1981. The Rural Real Estate in New Zealand. Research Paper 81/2.

Pearson, D. G. 1980. Johnsonville: Continuity and Change in a New Zealand Township. Sydney.

Pearson, D. G., and D. C. Thorns. 1983. Eclipse of Equality: Social Stratification in New Zealand. Sydney.

Pitt, D., ed. 1977. Social Class in New Zealand. Auckland.

Somerset, H. C. D. 1974. Littledene: Patterns of Change. (enlarged edition). Wellington.

Vellakoop, C. 1969. Social Strata in New Zealand. Social Process in New Zealand: Readings in Sociology, ed. J. Forster, pp. 233–71. Auckland.

Wilkes, C. D., and W. E. Willmott. 1976. Class in New Zealand Rural Society. Paper presented at the annual meetings of the Sociological Association of Australia and New Zealand. Melbourne, August, 1976.

Wise, H. L. 1943. Stabilization of Land Values in New Zealand. Economic Record 19:225–30.

The Rock Creek Auction: Contradiction Between Competition and Community in Rural Montana[1]

Frederick Errington

>>> <<<

VIRTUALLY EVERY OBSERVER of America since de Tocqueville (1969 [1835]) has commented on the tension that exists, particularly in small towns, between the values of individuality and those of community, a tension shaped and exacerbated by a competitive economic system. On the one hand, individuality that takes the form of economic competition is regarded as desirable since it encourages individuals to display their best efforts by pursuing their self-interest. On the other hand, although neighbor competes against neighbor, community relationships that are warm and supportive are also regarded as important. Significantly, as observers have also frequently noted, Americans show little recognition of the essential tension and the dissonance between the principles on which their socioeconomic system is based. Indeed, much of the often reported complacency and boosterism expressed by small-town Americans stems from their conviction that the free enterprise system and neighborliness are entirely congruent bases of the best possible way of life (Lynd and Lynd 1929; 1937; Warner 1953; Vidich and Bensman 1958; Slater 1976; Varenne 1977; Bell 1978; Lasch 1984; and Bellah, et al. 1986).

The intent here is not to document the obvious fact that residents of small towns throughout America have managed to deal with this conflict in such a way as to preserve their faith in the integrity of their system. Rather, it is to treat what is much less apparent: namely, how people have been able to do so, not only in good times but in bad.

The Community of Rock Creek

This issue is addressed in the context of a small, economically peripheral area of southcentral Montana. Located at the junction of the plains and the Rocky Mountains, Rock Creek (a pseudonym), a town of 2,000, is the principal settlement and county seat of a county with a population of 5,000. In recent years the struggle for economic survival has become intense and the success of one neighbor is likely to come at the cost of the failure of another. When this conflict between free enterprise and neighborliness is exacerbated by these circumstances of economic constriction, how do the residents of Rock Creek avoid the recognition that theirs is a socioeconomic system based on and flawed by a fundamental contradiction? How in this situation do those who view each other as competitors continue to interact on a friendly and cooperative basis and, more important, continue to regard their socioeconomic system as so highly satisfactory?

To address these questions, I examine the Rock Creek response to actual business failures, since it is on these occasions that the conflict between the values of an economic system based on individualism and a social system based on mutual support becomes objectified, if not embodied, in the neighbor who is forced to sell out. I will argue that the local auction, by which the failed competitor liquidates his commercial and personal holdings, is the mechanism that enables Rock Creek residents to resolve the crisis in the system without acknowledging that it has even taken place.

The Rock Creek auction should not, therefore, be regarded as a "performance" (Bruner 1984; Schechner 1985; and Turner and Bruner 1986). It is not a time (frequently described as one of liminality) when "performers—and sometimes spectators too—are changed by the activity of performing" (Schechner 1985:4). The Rock Creek auction serves to obscure the conflict between free enterprise and community precisely because it is not viewed as special occasion of reflexivity in which members of a group are compelled to explore and reformulate their collective identity.

The auction also differs in an important respect from the mechanisms usually described by anthropologists for the resolution of crisis. Unlike courts and rituals, which are extraordinary measures designed for the resolution of serious conflicts (Turner 1957, 1968; Bateson 1958; Hamnett 1977; and Comaroff and Roberts 1981), the auction regulates by diminishing recognition of the extraordinary and the serious. Employed precisely at those times in which economic failure threatens to rend community relationships, the auction appears an inseparable part of common sense, daily experience. Because the auction is of the same piece of ordinary life, the regulation it effects is not perceived as such and, in consequence, recognition that a serious contradiction exists between the essential premises on which social life is based is suppressed.

Neighborliness and Economic Competition

The residents of Rock Creek and the surrounding area explicitly believe (as do rural Americans elsewhere) that they embody the American way of life. They believe that they have been able to maintain the distinctive values of competition and community that originally characterized America. Local cars, for instance, bear bumper stickers with the slogan, "Montana is the Way America Used to Be."

Life in the Rock Creek area is based on the assumption that economic competition between individuals is good since it encourages achievement and rewards those who are able to exercise clear judgment, self-control, and common sense, and who can get along with their neighbors. Thus in a discussion of why an unpopular local bar owner had failed in business, Rock Creek residents enumerated with satisfaction some of the various mistakes he had made: he had ordered far more beer than he could sell on the Fourth of July, subjected his customers and employees to outbursts of ill temper, charged more for drinks than any other Rock Creek bar owner, and proclaimed that the people of Rock Creek were too unsophisticated to appreciate the kind of music played by those bands he hired.[2]

The inhabitants of the Rock Creek area are quite aware that their general level of prosperity is affected by national economic forces. Nonetheless they are convinced that the free enterprise system is the appropriate economic basis of life and that those who fail do so because they are unsuccessful competitors. This perspective is illustrated in the following letter to the editor in the local paper under the caption, "Disaster is Not Imminent" (Carbon County News 1986:4).

> Dear Editor,
> I would like to take exception to statements made in your last week's paper by Mr. ... in the article which detailed his reasons for closing the ... Motel in [Rock Creek]. Mr. ... stated, "There isn't a motel in [Rock Creek] that's not in trouble," and "some have taken out disaster loans. ... "
> I don't speak for the other motels in town but I am confident that there is no imminent disaster approaching our town. I feel that perhaps Mr. ... was not informed enough to speak for the other motels, either. Our motel has enjoyed an approximate 23 percent increase in revenue over each of the past two years and we are enjoying living in [Rock Creek] and working with the [Rock Creek] community.
> I do agree that regional and national economics are a factor for all business in [Rock Creek]. However, we feel that this can be overcome by giving our visitors good value for dollar, promoting our business with the community as well as individually, and by trying very hard for repeat/return business.

Thus, entrepreneurial skills are viewed as particularly important during times of national or regional recession. For instance, when interest rates and energy prices are high, when commodity prices are low, and when tourism is in decline, the competitive struggle is intensified and individuals must be at their best to survive.

Despite the fact that Rock Creek is a small town, most businesses have at least one local competing enterprise (and many in neighboring towns). There are seven motels, two large grocery stores, several convenience stores, three hardware stores, three drug stores, two car agencies and ten saloons.

Although ranchers in the surrounding county are sellers to a distant commodity market and thus do not compete as directly as, for instance, do the owners of the local hardware stores, they nonetheless are in competition with each other over land and over water to irrigate that land. One old rancher, in response to my question of how he and his father got on with their neighbors, said that they either drove them out or bought them out. Today, as well, according to a local lawyer who is not only a specialist in land transactions but a rancher himself, the most likely purchaser of a ranch will be a financially more solvent neighbor. This process of competition between neighbors is reflected by statistics: in this county the average ranch of 1,000 acres (see Neu and Holm 1983:9-1) represents the consolidation of six homesteads.[3]

Ownership of land does not in itself confer rights to the water flowing through that land. No one in this county has access to as much water as he would like to be able to use for the irrigation of hay and other cash crops. Although water rights are registered and indicate the priority and amount of access a rancher may have to water in streams flowing through his land, it is difficult to know how much water a property owner is in fact diverting. Ranchers are frequently thrown into conflict with their neighbors when one diverts more than his entitled amount of irrigation water from the local stream or is thought to have done so. Indeed, in one instance, elderly sisters who lived on adjacent ranches along a stream fought with their shovels when they encountered each other while irrigating. Each believed the other was claiming more water than she had rights to. Comparably, a recent barroom confrontation led a man to seek a court order restraining his neighbors from diverting water he claimed as his and, in addition, prohibiting "them from carrying firearms and [keeping] them away from [him] and his family" (Carbon County News 1985:1).

Under these circumstances, ranchers perceive that they are in competition with each other since one is likely to benefit when his neighbor goes out of business. In addition, ranchers recognize that they compete with each other to obtain the low interest loans and other forms of support from finite state and federal sources that may assist them in covering their operating expenses. He who can through his entrepreneurial efforts weather hard times may well profit from the failure of his neighbor.[4]

However, locals believe that business rivals can remain friends; if they follow fair business practices, competition between them will not become so direct as to be cutthroat. It is in fact an important aspect of Rock Creek thought that competition is not only good as an appropriate expression of individualism but that it can exist without producing such expressions of self-interest as would be a source of dissension within the community. I have on several occasions observed an entrepreneur direct business away from himself by suggesting that a potential customer repair rather than replace a broken implement or by advising that the cost of purchasing a specialized tool would make a do-it-yourself repair uneconomical.

That Rock Creek and environs are composed of individuals who share a sense that social relations are personal rather than impersonal is a source of collective satisfaction. One rancher told me, for example, that this was a great place to live. Even when he went on business to the county court house in Rock Creek, he was among friends. On a similar theme, locals describe their community as a place where you can dial a wrong number and still talk for twenty minutes.

Thus in the local view, the free enterprise system needs to be linked with a sense of concern for others; people must be able to "stand on their own two feet" yet they should be sociable and obliging. Personal relationships that acknowledge the importance of demonstrating both autonomy and willingness to cooperate take the form of neighborliness. One rancher, for instance, judged another in his vicinity as "a real good neighbor" because he had gone out of his way to inform him that his cattle were loose and because he always ungrudgingly loaned his tools. Although grateful, the rancher did not feel beholden; circumstances would arise when he could reciprocate. (See Vidich and Bensman 1958 for comparable examples.)

The same generalized reciprocity characterizes relationships in town, even between those who are direct competitors. For example, while I was conversing with a saloon proprietor, the owner of a rival and neighboring establishment presented him with a bottle of whiskey. This was in return for the ice he had willingly provided when his rival's ice machine was out of service. Help is given in these instances since such misfortunes "could happen to anybody." Comparably, help will be freely given and accepted in response to such virtually unavoidable catastrophies as flood, fire, and major illness.

Neighbors are sometimes torn between curtailing another's autonomy and wishing to help. To illustrate, a seasoned rancher told me that a younger neighbor was not using his water efficiently to get the maximal production of hay during the short Montana growing season. He wanted to give the younger man some advice but did not see how he could without causing offense as a meddler.

Neighborliness, as the practical and moral basis of life in a community of essentially autonomous equals, is reflected in the local expression, "If you live right, folks will treat you right"; that is, if you are neighborly to others, others will be neighborly to you. The difficulty encountered by those who attempt to combine free enterprise and community through advocating neighborliness as a dominant and pervasive value is that in the economic competition between sellers, especially when the market is limited, some neighbors are likely to fail. Although most in the Rock Creek area claim that they would not want to live in any other place, many eventually do move because they can no longer support themselves locally.[5] When bills cannot be paid, the enterprise goes under. No one can rely on neighbors for extended help lest his neighbors' own economic survival be threatened.

When an entrepreneur in the Rock Creek area does lose economic viability, his failure provides a potential threat to the validity of those economic and social values of the community which are explicitly identified with the American way of life. Under these circumstances of economic failure, social life threatens to become subtly but significantly transformed. As long as competition is based only on the possibility of failure, neighborliness appears entirely feasible as an essential form of social life. However, neighborliness appears less feasible when competition has resulted in the actuality of failure. When the success of one person drives another out of business, competition may no longer appear as an abstract and socially beneficial principle but instead as the immediate and socially discordant assertion, "I win, you lose." Moreover, not only for those whose competition is direct, but also for those, such as ranchers, whose competition is in major degree indirect, the equally immediate and socially discordant assertion of "you lose, I win" may emerge when a neighbor sells out.

Such a view of competition would threaten the reciprocity that constitutes neighborliness, a reciprocity conveyed in the expression "If you live right, folks will treat you right." This challenge to neighborliness is a challenge to the possibility of achieving a harmonious balance between the economic and social bases of life. (It should be noted that unneighborly treatment is the appropriate response toward someone such as the overweening saloon keeper mentioned earlier. For such a person to go out of business conversely validates the proposition, "If you live right, folks will treat you right.")

However, rather than perceiving that someone's economic failure establishes an incongruity between the economic and the social bases of their life, the people of Rock Creek are able to reaffirm their belief that economic competition will not disrupt the relationship between those neighbors who live right. This incongruity is obscured by the very process through which someone relinquishes an active economic role in the Rock Creek area.

The Auction: Obscuring the Implications of Failure

According to local sources, many ranchers in this area have already or will soon exhaust their credit. Because of factors including high interest rates and operating expenses and low commodity prices, their rate of indebtedness has been steadily increasing, in many cases up to the limit provided by their collateral, which includes not only land, equipment, and livestock but personal and household property as well. Indeed, many banks now find that they have overextended themselves, since the value of land they have as collateral has fallen sharply. Consequently, some ranchers have been told that they will not be advanced credit for their operations during the forthcoming year. Without this credit, they will have no chance to earn the money necessary to service their existing debt. Faced thus with foreclosure, most of these ranchers decide to sell virtually everything. Thus, in the advertisement for a local auction, a financially strapped rancher listed for sale all his heavy farm equipment, a pickup truck, his pack saddles, two Nubian goats, and "Household items, tools and miscellaneous items too numerous to mention" (Carbon County News 1983:4).

Through arranging such sales ranchers avoid the humiliation of a bank auction; moreover, they hope that if their sale appears voluntary they will receive slightly higher prices for their goods—perhaps enough to leave them a bit of capital after they pay their debts—than they would if their distress were entirely manifest. Nonetheless, since the agricultural crisis is general, the prices they can expect to receive will be low. Since few would choose to sell out under such circumstances, all ranch auctions at this time are regarded as forced by economic distress.[6]

At the time of economic failure in which the "American Way" as a viable model for small-town life is most likely to be scrutinized, the auction effects a temporary but, as we will see in a moment, crucial shift in the usual relationship between buyers and sellers. The significance of this shift derives in major part from the fact that no one engages in activities that he experiences as extraordinary.

A public auction in Rock Creek is simple in its structure. It takes place out-of-doors on the premises of the seller. Anyone can attend and anyone who has the money can buy. No credit is offered. Goods are worth whatever someone is willing to pay for them. The goods are sold on an "as is" basis without guarantee. During the auction all buyers are in potential and visible competition with each other. In these aspects, the auction seems to have the form of pure and transparent market exchange.

Unlike the usual competitive situation that led to a neighbor being forced to sell out, it is the buyers during an auction who are in competition. Given the nature of mass production and retail selling, buyers ordinarily do not compete with each other. A retail purchase does not affect the opportunity of another to make a similar purchase. In fact, as normal consumers, Rock Creek buyers ordinarily can readily regard a shopping trip, especially on Saturday morning, as a particularly suitable occasion for socializing with neighbors.

Hence, at a time when the competition between sellers has become so strong as to force one of these entrepreneurs out of business, the auction defines the realm of economic competition as existing between those who as buyers regard their essential relationship to be that of neighbors. Within the context of the auction, therefore, competitive buyers become defined as neighbors. As we shall see, the auction is fairly redolent with neighborliness. As we shall also see, the buyers who compete at a time of another's economic failure are able to present themselves not only as superior neighbors but as superior competitors.

This definition of competitive buyers as neighbors is effected by the seller, the person who is having his possessions auctioned off. Because the person selling out does not engage in the competition to acquire his own goods, he does not conform to the definition of neighbor as established by the context of the auction. Indeed, during the auction, the seller is either absent or very much in the background. And, as his goods are redistributed among those defined as neighbors, he disappears as seller. Furthermore, after the auction, he frequently must leave the community in order to find work in a more prosperous metropolitan area. Thus, the seller whose very failure has raised the possibility that competition has become so strong as to compromise neighborliness—after all he has been forced out of business—comes, in major part through both the form and the fact of the auction, to be excluded from the system as neighbor and as competitor.

In this process by which competitors become neighbors, all the ingredients of everyday life are present although partially rearranged. In the auction, there is a shift with the primary effect that one of the attributes of a seller—that of competitor—is added to those of a buyer. However, since everyone has had experience as a buyer and most, as a seller, individuals as they participate at the auction are still enacting the familiar themes of everyday life. The auction, hence, is experienced as essentially consonant with, and thereby a part of, everyday life rather than as an extraordinary event.

Through effecting the conjuction of competitors with neighbors, the auction resolves the conflict embedded in everyday life between, on the one hand, the values and forms of an economic system based on impersonal competition between sellers and, on the other, the values and forms of a cultural system based on friendship and cooperation. That this conjunction occurs virtually without notice prevents the public from recognizing that a serious conflict has ever existed. Thus, during an auction members of the community experience personal validation as good neighbors rather than crises of conscience, and experience cultural vindication rather than anomie, when they strive to offer the lowest possible prices at a time when a neighbor struggles for continued physical survival by liquidating his personal possessions and those of his family, as well as the assets of ranch, farm or business.

The Auction as Marketplace

Those who attend a local auction are likely to know most of the others who attend, as well as the person who is selling his goods. Consequently those who attend looking for bargains not only receive as buyers structural definition as neighbors but are likely actually to be neighbors. Although there is quite a bit of socializing during an auction, these neighbors also make consistent efforts to demonstrate simultaneously that they are astute entrepreneurs.

In the auction individuals compete as individuals. There are no alliances; each must exercise judgment on his own behalf. People know that individuals sometimes solicit advice, that husbands and wives discuss business problems and strategies with each other. Still, a person needs to give the appearance of being strong and shrewd enough to go it alone. Any advice sought is sought quietly and from a confidant.

Because goods are generally in used condition and are always sold without guarantee, the prospective purchasers must exercise care in appraising their condition, in estimating whether or not repairs are needed, and, if needed, how extensive and expensive they will be. In addition, the purchaser must estimate how much such an item would normally bring at an auction. Not only must everyone make up his own mind but must as well expose his judgment to the appraisal of others. Indeed, bystanders frequently provide running commentary on each sale appraising whether a good or bad price was paid.

The proper attitude while engaging in the bidding is one of inscrutability since opponents should not know how high one is willing to go. Moreover, one should create the impression that feelings are under control. Thus, if one does engage in high bidding, it is supposed to follow from recognition of the real value of an item. Given that full control and rational appraisal are the only patterns of proper conduct during an auction, then not bidding at all, or dropping out of the bidding, are also approved modes of participation. Often, someone who drops out may remark to a companion that the bidding is going crazy, or that so and so must really want the item.

Men sometimes announce that they would not take a particular item at any price. One such instance at a ranch auction concerned a snowmobile coming up for bid. A man remarked to a friend that its track was no good and that it would cost more than the machine was worth to fix. The bidding was indeed very slow in this case, perhaps because his comment had been heard, perhaps because others had made comparable judgments. The auctioneer seemed aware of this collective appraisal and did not challenge it. Rather than claim this machine was "in just dandy condition," as he had for many previous items, he said only, "it would be a lot of use for someone." He then recognized someone in the crowd and, after identifying a young man by name and by occupation as someone who fixed snowmobiles, he began urging him to bid. This person eventually did buy the machine for $50.00 after making clear through his remarks that he was acquiring it only as a source of used parts; i.e., that it was to him of genuine, although limited, value.

The auction is consistent with the Montana variant of the free enterprise system. In both contexts, one must have the capacity to exercise the common sense and self-control necessary to make and follow good judgments. In an auction as in a business—whether a ranch, shop or store—practical, immediate decisions must be made and implemented. All realize that imagination and emotion must be harnessed; fancy plans and dreams, people say, don't pay the rent, don't put food on the table, don't provide the basis of survival, much less, of success.

At an auction, those who compete as buyers are thus able to justify and demonstrate their own economic viability, especially, relative to the seller, through a display of their own economic competence. In some cases the judgment of relative competence may be explicit. For instance, one auction was of the stock and tools of a construction firm that had just gone out of business. Afterwards, I heard the auctioneer talking in a bar. Among other comments about the auction, he said that the company had invested far too much money in equipment because the number and kind of tools owned were excessive for the size of the business. Others during the auction itself had expessed a similar judgment.

The auction is tied into the free enterprise system and its values of individuality and common sense in other ways. Many auctions provide the opportunity for locals to appraise the material resources of one another. This is not to imply that the property of a rancher or the inventory or the supply of tools of a small businessman are regarded as matters to be kept secret. Tools and equipment are loaned between neighbors and everyone has a pretty good idea of whom to seek for a product or service. But there is rarely a chance except at an auction to appraise an entire inventory. One of the problems inherent in a system of small private enterprises is the absence of guidelines about how to reach decisions. How much inventory is appropriate; how extensive should the stock of specialized tools be; how much is a labor-saving device worth? Businessmen and ranchers seek this information. I have heard ranchers put very pointed and perceptive questions to an implement dealer, requiring him to make a good case for how a new bailer—and this dealer's bailer in particular—will make money for them. Ranchers talk among themselves about how someone is liking his new piece of equipment. The need for comparing notes clearly exists and the auction provides valuable supplementary information about why a business has failed. Auctions thus provide occasions for post-mortems on the victims, the entrepreneurial failures, of the free enterprise system.

Auction and the Restoration of Society

Because of the shift in the usual patterns of competition, with buyers rather than sellers in competition with each other, and because of the economic individualism of appraisal and bidding, the auction by its very structure demonstrates that good neighbors can also be astute, dispassionate, and successful businessmen.

The auctioneer himself, as a neighbor whose business is to bring neighbors together to dispose of another's business, may make these themes additionally explicit. Certainly, the most popular and successful auctioneer in the county acts as both the essential neighbor and businessman and in so doing exemplifies and conjoins the two. In addition, because he is skilled at defining bidding as a neighborly activity, he establishes during the auction the context which gives these roles of neighbor and businessman their full meaning. By first binding the participants to him, he is then able to bind them to each other to form, for the duration of the auction, a community.

This auctioneer, recently elected to his third six-year term as one of the county's three commissioners, is the best known individual in the area. He comes from an old ranching family and has a large ranch some ten miles outside of Rock Creek. Extremely outgoing, with an excellent memory for names and faces, he is never at a loss for words and is always able to produce a greeting and a bit of badinage.

During the period of an auction when the items to be sold are on display for inspection, he circulates, chatting with prospective customers, engaging often in banter and backslapping. His humor might include accosting a man and telling him not to go around talking to other folks about the two of them, since they are both such bad characters, and then sealing this alliance with a hearty laugh and a clap on the shoulder. And members of the crowd reciprocate. A bystander might call out to him that he should have been with him last night and then add, but if he had been, he wouldn't be auctioneering today. The mutual acceptance of mild insults shows that friendship exists because no offense is given or taken. Furthermore, the insults often concern traits which are at least covertly admired, such as the capacity to engage in heavy drinking or moderately rowdy and boisterous behavior. As he circulates and chats, he makes each of the prospective purchasers feel welcome. And he is at the same time recognizing each as his social equal. This in turn enables them to be comfortable with each other. In short, he makes them feel like neighbors whose competition will be entirely friendly.

Once the auction begins he goes to pains to describe the circumstances of the sale so that nothing mars the appearance of neighborliness. As a preamble to one auction, he said that members of the family having the sale had been good neighbors and we (those present) were sorry to lose them. They were moving to California but probably some other good folks would come in after them. "That is how things are right next to the mountains, and if the new people weren't good folks," he added, with enough of a laugh so that it was not clear whether he was being entirely serious, "then we probably won't let them stay very long." The family members, he was indicating, were leaving to seek other economic opportunities and would in fact no longer be neighbors; moreover, it was those who remained and attended the auction who were the arbiters of neighborliness. On this occasion of social depletion, he was expressing confidence that Rock Creek would regenerate and remain a community of good folks.

Although he occasionally employs classic auctioneer's patter during the bidding—in order, he says with a laugh, to show that he knows how—he prefers to use ordinary speech which he employs to establish and maintain social relationships. He continually defuses any tension between competing buyers that might make the bidding unpleasantly competitive and unneighborly. At the same time he also often identifies those who are engaged in bidding for an item as neighbors. He may announce the name and occupation of a bidder, particularly if that person is engaged in business. For example, if a bank officer is bidding, he might joke that if anyone needs money for his bidding he should go to so and so at the such and such bank. Then he might add with an apparently self-deprecating comment that he hopes that person's credit is better there than his own. On another occasion, after he had encouraged a man to remain in a three-way bidding competition, he thanked him when he dropped out for having helped get the price "up to where it should be." He then gave the man's name and said that we should all eat at his restaurant. He followed this with a laugh, asking the man, in rhetorical fashion, whether his continued bidding had been worth the free advertising with which the auctioneer had just provided him.

Comparably, when a man appears to hesitate in bidding and stops to consult his wife, one of his favorite lines is to joke, "Why are you asking her? She doesn't run your business too, does she?" Or, when a woman hesitates, he may say, "What is money to a person like you? You have a great big husband; just work him a little harder."

He continually makes jokes not only at the mild expense of others but of himself and his family. He often says that he may be a crooked county commissioner but is an honest auctioneer, or say just as frequently that he may be a crooked auctioneer but is an honest commissioner. I heard him vouch for the sturdiness of a chair offered for sale by calling attention to the fact that it had managed to support his wife. And, during the brief lull when items for bid are being brought forward by an assistant, he may sing a few bars of a country and western song and do a cowboy dance step.

Many of the jokes have to do with the auction itself as an event and serve as reminders that it is he who is in charge of this event and that it is his business. Anyone who makes a gesture during the bidding may be taken facetiously by him as having bid. "It can be expensive to have itchy hair at an auction," he may remark. Or he may address a certain member of the crowd suggesting reasons why that person should bid. On hardware items, he might suggest to the owner of a hardware store that he should buy these so that he would then be able to sell merchandise in his store at a reasonable price. Once when a baby carriage was up for bid, he singled out a young, unmarried man in the crowd by name and said that from what the auctioneer was hearing about him, he should be bidding on this—followed by a booming laugh. Sometimes he simply looks at someone and, giving his name, teases, "Aw, come on, it's just a buck."

This auctioneer is then, in his pleasantry, banter and allusions to minor delicts, an embodiment of the friendly, entertaining and rather gossipy neighbor. He also makes clear in his remarks that he is no better than anyone else. His commentary is acceptable because it is not self-righteous and, indeed, virtually as many of his barbs are directed at himself as at others. He shows that to be good neighbor is to have the strengths, weaknesses, and idiosyncracies characteristic of ordinary, fundamentally decent, people. He is, in this context, defining virtually everyone present as meeting these qualifications.

Through these exchanges he is thus able to reinforce the definition the auction gives to those who attend as buyers: since all are good neighbors, their actions in bidding against each other to acquire goods as cheaply as possible from a former neighbor in economic distress can still be regarded as entirely neighborly. In fact, given the personal relationships which he establishes or renews, to bid is to help him out; not to bid is to remain aloof and unneighborly. During the auction, neighborliness is demonstrated as thoroughly pervasive.

While this auctioneer engages as a neighbor and creates a community of neighbors, he demonstrates impressive business skill. However much he may banter, he never acts incompetently; he never begs, hesitates, or appears foolish. In addition, through his continual references to what he is doing as an auctioneer, he not only conveys the idea that he knows his business but that his business, that of the auction itself, is entirely transparent and reasonable. That there is no real disjunction between neighborliness and the free enterprise system is thus given additional reinforcement by the fact that the auction is not only a context in which goods are bought and sold in a neighborly fashion but is itself a business run in neighborly fashion.

Conclusion

The auction is a microcosm that exemplifies and shows as consonant the values of critical importance to those in the Rock Creek area. The question of whether competition and community are seriously opposed values is resolved even before it is explicitly raised by a model in which the competition is fair, open, and above board and the participants—the competitors—remain friends. Those who cannot successfully compete, leave, dropping out of the system and out of public awareness.

This view of the auction as a microcosm is supported by a cartoon that appeared recently on the editorial page of the local newspaper (Carbon County News 1984:4). It depicts an auction taking place under a banner that reads, "Another Ranch Family Bites the Dust." On display are the contents of an old ranch kitchen, including a wood-burning cook stove and a venerable refrigerator. The crowd includes a cross-section of the Rock Creek community. Significantly, in a part of the country where men take great pleasure in outdoor pursuits such as fishing, the item up for sale at that moment is the rancher's fishing rod. One of the two men bidding appears embarrassed, but the embarrassment seems entirely a product of confrontation with the other bidder. The only dialogue that is presented refers to a transaction that is characteristic of the relationship between neighbors; a man in the crowd is shown remarking to another that he has come to watch the sale so that he will know from whom he can borrow specific items.

Thus, according to this cartoon, although there is recognition that times are hard,[7] the community gathers with the expression of neighborly values to participate in the liquidation of an entire estate in which even the man's fishing rod is sold. The only expression of discomfiture is between the buyers and not between the buyers and the disadvantaged seller.

There is evident here a process of regulation; the circumstance that threatens to make dominant local values appear inconsistent triggers the mechanism that affirms their consonance. Even the losers in this local socioeconomic system have little choice but to support these values. Although an auction in this area is the only feasible way to liquidate a large and diverse estate, holding an auction is nonetheless regarded as an act of choice, as a manifestation of individual economic autonomy. To return to an earlier example, the man who sold virtually everything including his two Nubian goats, through deciding to hold an auction as well as through the auction itself, acted in a way that embodied and sustained the values and experiences of everyday life. In this way the patterns of everyday life are endorsed even by those who have least reason to do so.

That this view of the world is sustained has important consequences. Area residents can continue to think that they have achieved and indeed validated a remarkable and distinctively American synthesis that allows them to engage each other in their everyday lives as neighborly entrepreneurs through employing a mechanism that results in the periodic (and unneighborly) sacrifice of community members.

Furthermore, by regarding an economic failure as the consequence of an individual proving unable to sustain himself in the competition, they not only support the value of individual autonomy but simultaneously perpetuate their vulnerability to outside economic forces. Although the auction may in a limited way contribute to the viability of the remaining competitors through giving them access to inexpensive goods, it does little to alter the economic constraints of life or the likelihood of future economic failure. It certainly does not augment their control over the major economic forces that affect them. Indeed, by regarding economic failures as personal failures, these rural Montanans are unlikely to engage in any sort of action that might increase their influence over, or change the nature of, the regional or national economic system.

Because the auction is consistent with everyday life it does not appear to be a regulating mechanism and, in consequence, nothing appears in need of regulation. Through it, the residents of the Rock Creek area can, despite the increasing frequency of failure, remain committed to their everyday world of economic competition and neighborliness.

NOTES

1. Earlier versions of this paper were delivered at Yale University and Bates College. I am grateful for the comments received on those occasions and also thank Mary Catherine Bateson, Deborah Gewerts, and Michael Lieber for their suggestions and Carolyn Errington for her editorial assistance. The data are from work during the summers of 1980–1982, 1985–1986.

2. Many have noted that the small-town ethos in America includes a considerable measure of social conformity, and distinctions implying that someone considers himself better than another are greatly resented (Blumenthal 1932; Lynd and Lynd 1937; Atherton 1954; Vidich and Bensman 1958; Billington 1966; and Varenne 1977).

3. In 1974, there were 662 ranches in the county with an average size of 979 acres; by 1978, there were 613 ranches with an average size of 1,017 acres. Local ranchers are subject to the same economic pressures, especially stemming from the high rates of interest and the high cost of equipment, that force agriculturalists in other parts of the country to either sell out or expand their holdings (Kramer 1980).

4. Since virtually all local entrepreneurs and most of those who bid at auctions are male, I use, without implying prejudice, male pronouns throughout.

5. The county has long fallen behind both state and national averages with respect to important economic indicators. In 1970, annual per capita income was $2,720 in the county, $3,379 in Montana, and $3,921 in the nation; moreover, 19.2 per cent of the county residents, in contrast to 13.6 per cent of Montana residents, lived below the poverty level (Obermeyer et al. 1974:2–8). More recent statistics support this pattern: in 1981, per capita personal income in the county was 80.2 per cent of the national average, while in Montana it was 89.7 per cent of the national average (Neu and Holm 1983:6–4). Forecasts for recovery are grim because of the "current instability of the primary sectors of the Carbon County economy. Agricultural prices and markets, national and international policies on energy, and the effects of a host of variables on tourism all combine to result in an air of insecurity that seems to permeate the economic future" (T.A.P. 1979:132).

6. There is clear local recognition that many in this area are experiencing considerable economic distress. According to my survey, fifteen ranches—and, in

addition, four other businesses—were sold in the county at auction between August 1984 and July 1985.

7. Not only have Montana ranchers been subject to the same problems in obtaining credit as have other American agriculturalists, they have in addition experienced severe drought from 1983–85. Nonetheless, they have not engaged in collective action comparable to that of Midwestern farmers who have, for instance, marched in protest to their state legislatures or have physically prevented bidding at bank auctions. (See, for example, Magnuson 1985.) The only explanation I was given for this regional difference in response to economic pressure was that "Montana ranchers were just too independent" to engage in collective action. According to this formulation, Montana ranchers are too independent to organize in order to defend their independence. Clearly, the American values of individuality and community can result in a variety of behaviors.

BIBLIOGRAPHY

Atherton, L. 1954. Mainstreet on the Middle Border. Bloomington.
Bateson, G. 1958. Naven. Stanford.
Bell, D. 1978. The Cultural Contradictions of Capitalism. New York.
Bellah, R., et al. 1986. Habits of the Heart. New York.
Billington, R. 1966. America's Frontier Heritage. New York.
Blumenthal, A. 1932. Small-Town Stuff. Chicago.
Bruner, E., ed. 1984. Text, Play and Story: The Construction and Reconstruction of Self and Society. Washington.
Carbon County News. 1983. Advertisement. June 2, 1983:7.
———. 1984. Cartoon. June 14, 1984:4.
———. 1985. Irrigating Dispute Lands in Court. July 4, 1985:1.
———. 1986. Disaster Is Not Imminent. May 8, 1986:4.
Comaroff, J., and S. Roberts. 1981. Rules and Processes: The Cultural Logic of Dispute in an African Context. Chicago.
de Tocqueville, A. 1969 (1835). Democracy in America. New York.
Hamnett, I., ed. 1977. Social Anthropology and Law. London.
Kramer, M. 1980. Three Farms. Boston.
Lasch, C. 1984. The Minimal Self. New York.
Lynd, R., and H. Lynd. 1929. Middletown. New York.
———. 1937. Middletown in Transition. New York.
Magnuson, E. 1985. Real Trouble on the Farm. Time 125:24–39.
Neu, D., and R. Holm. 1983. Montana County Profiles. Helena.
Obermeyer, D., et al. 1974. Carbon County Housing Survey. Unpublished manuscript, Carbon County Planning Office.
Schechner, R. 1985. Between Theater and Anthropology. Philadelphia.
Slater, P. 1976. The Pursuit of Loneliness. Boston.
T.A.P. 1979. A Focus on the Economy of Carbon County. Bozeman.
Turner, V. 1957. Schism and Continuity in an African Society. New York.

Turner, V., and E. Bruner. (eds.). 1986. The Anthropology of Experience. Urbana.
Varenne, H. 1977. Americans Together. New York.
Vidich, A., and J. Bensman. 1958. Small Town in Mass Society. Princeton.
Warner, W. L. 1953. American Life. Chicago.

Culture and Conceptualization:
A Study of Japanese and American Children

Mary Ellen Goodman

>>> <<<

THE STUDY REPORTED here deals with the cognitive functions and with the influence of culture upon them.[1] Cognitive functions, and the conscious mental processes as determinants of behavior, constitute an important emerging field of study. As Siegel (1958) has pointed out, there is increasing concern for "the individual's beliefs, frames of reference, major orientations, role perceptions, ideas and values." This field is being rediscovered by psychologists and by social scientists as well; the fact is evident in such recent work as that by Bruner and his associates (1957), and in such publications as those of the Social Science Research Council (1960) and of the Merrill-Palmer Institute (1960). Anthropologists can hardly be content, however, with the noncomparative study of these phenomena, with studies focused on the individual and on developmental stages, or with studies concerned with the psychological dynamics of cognition to the exclusion of cultural aspects.

It is appropriate that anthropologists develop, on the basis of their distinctive concerns and methods, their own ways of cultivating this intriguing field of inquiry. This cultivation should be, moreover, more systematic than in the past, and more focused on culturally patterned "styles of thinking." Such inquiry promises important insights of both practical and theoretical significance.

Statement of the Problem

Both Kroeber (1948: 604–606) and Nadel (1937; 1937–38) have shown interest in this type of inquiry (though the one called it "cultural psychology" and the other "racial psychology"). Taking leads from their work, the writer has searched for conceptualizing habits in a sample of 681 American and 239 Japanese urban middle-class children (of the fifth and sixth grades), using the method of "story recall."

This study is a large-scale replication of Nadel's investigation focused on groups of youth in the west African Yoruba and Nupe societies (twenty subjects, twelve to eighteen years of age, in each). Nadel tested the hypothesis that a people will develop thoughtways which reflect and accord with the implicit premises, emphases, and values patterned in their culture. He assumed that one could sample—in a systematic fashion—the thoughtways characteristic of a given people by use of a simple device borrowed from the psychologists (e.g., Bartlett 1932) and their studies of memory. This device is the story recall: one tells a story and later asks the subjects to reproduce it; discrepancies between the original and the recalled versions are then examined for regularities from which culturally patterned conceptualizing habits can be inferred.

Nadel's use of this method with the Yoruba and Nupe produced convincing and interesting results. He found certain marked modalities among the discrepancies, and these were strikingly different as between the two groups of subjects. Moreover, these modalities were of the sorts to be expected in view of Nupe and Yoruba cultures with which he was thoroughly acquainted.

Discrepancies between the original and recalled versions, of course, result partly from individual differences in memory, interest, or attention. But in the Yoruba and Nupe recalls there was ample evidence of culturally determined conceptualization of the events and sequence in the story. This was predicted; the two cultures are in sharp contrast in many ways. For example, Yoruba culture is intricately organized with respect to social structure, law, and beliefs. Nupe culture is much simpler; e.g., it lacks a hierarchy of gods. Where Nupe art is purely ornamental, Yoruba is representative and symbolic. It was reasonable to suppose that the bearers of these cultures would have been differently conditioned to attend to— and hence remember—certain kinds of material; to differently distort, by under- or overemphasis in recall; to differently enhance, by addition or expansion; to differently order events, by reorganizing and regrouping.

Kroeber (1948:604–605) commented with interest on the Yoruba-Nupe findings and on other scraps of evidence relevant to "cultural psychology." To him the significant implication was that cultures differ markedly in the extent to which they are "systematizing." By this he meant that in some societies people are culturally habituated to "recognizing and dealing in relations," to generalizing (though this might be by feeling or guessing as well as by reasoning). In other and polar cases the mode is to "take each fact of experience as separate; it is a matter-of-fact attitude of detailed sensory accuracy as compared with the more imaginative and constructive one of seeing significance." In a systematizing culture its bearers are given to the "rational" (and/or "feeling" or "guessing") mode of conceptualization. In a nonsystematizing culture they are given to the "sensory" mode of conceptualization.

The Kroeber-Nadel view of shared conceptual habits within a society contrasts with views set forth by A. F. C. Wallace (1961). Wallace concludes that "cognitive sharing" is not even a functional prerequisite of society; quite the contrary perhaps. Wallace's conclusion follows on his observation that human beings rarely or never actually achieve "cognitive communality," i.e., fully shared sets of "cognitive maps." Rather, each lives in his own "uniquely private cognitive world." However, these generally articulate, in a complementary fashion, to an extent which makes social life possible, though interaction is a highly uncertain and inefficient affair. The type of cognitive communality with which Kroeber and Nadel are concerned, as is the writer, is for Wallace not a reality.

Nadel found Yoruba subjects more inclined than Nupe to systematize and to reason. Hopi children are reported (by Kroeber) to be rather like Yoruba, and Navaho to resemble Nupe in their "sensory" mode. Kroeber suggests, too, that Pueblo and some Plains tribes would tend to the systematizing-rational mode, while California, Northwest Coast peoples, and Eskimo would incline to the sensory.

It is Kroeber's view that "all advanced cultures are relatively systematizing." "Advance" is in fact evidence of and dependent upon systematization, as well as productive of it. He suggests that the great world religions are major elements in a complex of systematizing factors of which science (a "de-facto religion") is another: "The great world religions are obviously strong agencies of organization in that they provide a basic philosophy, with a scheme of causality and motivation. ... It may well be that the degree to which science has of late become ... a de-facto religion, or equivalent of religion, is due to the fact that with all its intricacy it possesses a coherence, a master plan that organizes innumerable items" (Kroeber 1948: 606).

The cross-cultural comparison in the present study involves data from two advanced cultures.[2] In line with Kroeber's hypothesis we would expect to find, in both of these, more "systematizing" than in either Yoruba or Nupe. Findings do not consistently bear out this expectation, but the fact that Nadel's subjects were, on the average, somewhat older may be relevant.[3] There is reason to believe that Japanese culture is less systematizing than American (assuming an urban middle-class base in both cases). For example: a well-knit system of religious thought is not a feature of Japanese culture; this fact is illustrated by Dore (1958: 362) who writes of a Tokyo ward: "Most of the residents ... are uncommitted to any particular religious doctrine ... Few subscribe to any coherent religious doctrine and few are members of any religious association." Nor is Japanese culture significantly affected, to date, by a pervasive scientific ethos (as distinguished from considerable dependence on a scientific technology). Goodman (1957: 997), in content analysis of compositions by Japanese and by American children, found no "scientific-technical" theme pervasive in the compositions by the Japanese as it was in those by American children.[4] The present study proceeded on the assumption that the data would show Japanese children to be, on the whole, less systematizing in conceptual habits than the American, and hence reminiscent of the Nupe vis-à-vis the Yoruba. The findings in general support this hypothesis, though some unexpected tendencies do appear.

Research Design

In this study we used Nadel's story (prepared by him for his African study) with minor modifications. Our story goes as follows:

> Long, long ago there was a king, and this king had two children—sons.
> When these sons had grown up, they saw a beautiful girl. She was the daughter of a farmer. They both made friends with her, and loved her very much. Both of them loved her from the bottom of their hearts.
> But the girl did not love the elder brother. She only loved the younger.
> Thereupon the elder brother went to the younger and told him to give up the girl. He said: "I am the one to marry the girl, for I am your elder brother."
> Thus he spoke. But the younger refused. They quarreled a great deal until the elder brother became furious. When night fell he went to a magician and said: "Please change my younger brother into a toad."
> The magician did so. He did so that very night. And the younger brother remained a toad forever.
> When the people heard the news they said: "The elder brother did an evil deed; God will punish him."
> But the girl cried. She cried for twenty days and her heart was full of pain. When she had finished crying she left and went to another place. Nobody saw her again.

This story was read to the children by their teachers. Four hours later the subjects were asked to write the story as they remembered it.[5] The recalled versions were checked, item by item, against the original (which for analytical purposes was broken into 40 items; see Table 1). Each recall was coded and card-recorded. Responses were then tabulated, by subjects' grade, sex, and nationality, for: (1) items exactly recalled, i.e., verbatim and in proper sequence; (2) items recalled, but in modified form

TABLE 1
Frequency of Recall

		Exact Recall		Exact Plus Modified Recall	
Item No.	Story Item	Am. Chil.[1] %	Jap. Chil.[2] %	Am. Chil. %	Jap. Chil. %
5	Long, long ago	51	96	95	99
6	There was a king	88	80	92	83
7	This king had two children	88	65	91	73
8	Sons	75	63	100	88
9	When these sons had grown up	22	16	27	17
10	They saw a beautiful girl	10	18	55	64
11	She was the daughter of a farmer	57	48	74	58
12	They both made friends with her	6	13	9	19
13	And loved her very much	11	6	26	19
14	Both of them loved her	57	11	83	52
15	From the bottom of their hearts	22	1	25	4
16	But the girl did not love the older brother	10	22	25	32
17	She only loved the younger	55	46	90	75
18	Thereupon the older brother went to the younger	14	12	15	21
19	And told him to give up the girl	14	11	41	38
20	He said	33	56	47	62
21	I am the one to marry the girl	12	8	42	50
22	For I am your elder brother	34	27	36	36
23	But the younger refused	16	41	57	54
24	They quarreled a great deal	2	0	28	28
25	Until the older brother became furious	6	3	26	33
26	When night fell	1	1	43	62
27	He went to a magician	73	54	96	93
28	And said	14	4	87	91
29	Please change my younger brother into a toad	34	77	90	87
30	The magician did so	34	22	59	68
31	He did so that very night	19	1	36	17
32	The younger brother remained a toad	6	9	32	16
33	Forever	19	16	33	16
34	When the people heard the news	5	5	21	19
35	They said	19	14	33	23
36	The older brother did an evil deed	5	3	30	10
37	God will punish him	17	6	26	12
38	But the girl cried	6	21	16	26
39	She cried for twenty days	52	54	73	77
40	Her heart was full of pain	1	0	6	2
41	When she had finished crying	5	0	22	8
42	She left	6	9	71	32
43	And went to another place	5	0	17	51
44	Nobody saw her again	17	63	72	73

1. N = 681; Boys 51%, Girls 49%
2. N = 239; Boys 57%, Girls 43%

and proper sequence; (3) items recalled (exact or modified) but out of sequence; (4) items omitted; (5) items added.

Results of the Study

The findings are summarized in terms of general accuracy of recall and of certain qualitative features of recall. Nadel's categories of response are utilized, with modifications.

General Accuracy of Recall. Except on a few items, American and Japanese children do not differ greatly in the frequency with which they recall story items (in modified if not in exact form). The Americans tend, however, to a somewhat higher level of accuracy, and increasingly so as the story moves through its middle phases. In giving exact reproductions the Japanese are conspicuously more accurate with respect to the opening and closing items (i.e., "Long, long ago" and "Nobody saw her again"). On two other items the Japanese children are notably the more accurate (again as measured by exact reproductions); these are: (a) "But the younger refused" (to give up the girl), and (b) the request by the elder brother: "Please change my younger brother into a toad." Relative accuracy is high among the Americans on the following items: "This king had two children"; "Both of them (the brothers) loved her"; "From the bottom of their hearts"; "He went to a magician."

Set Phrases and Formulas. In this category of items Nadel treats mainly the formulistic opening and closing and the sentence "God will punish him." (In Nadel's original this phrase reads: "God will revenge it.")

The Japanese do not fail (except in 4 per cent of cases) to reproduce the opening phrase verbatim, while about half (51 per cent) of the American children reproduce it in any form, and most present modified versions. The majority of Japanese (63 per cent) reproduce the closing phrase verbatim, while fewer than a fifth (17 per cent) of the Americans do so. However, many Americans (55 per cent) present a modified version of the closing, and these versions include a wide range of imaginative variations.

In the item "God will punish him" we find neither Japanese nor Americans much given to recall (12 and 26 per cent, respectively, counting exact and modified), though the latter are stronger on the item. Nadel reports his subjects, especially the Nupe, much more given to recall of the item. (Exact recall by Americans, 17 per cent; by Japanese, 6 per cent; by Yoruba, 25 per cent; by Nupe, 50 per cent.) Both Japanese and American children tend toward modifications which serve, as did those supplied by the Yoruba, to introduce a "rational" explanation. (Nadel says that only two Nupe supplied this additional rational link which turns a stereotyped phrase, quoted almost automatically, into a logically sound judgment.) For example: "The older son was sure to get punished by God" (A); "God knew what he did and would curse him" (A); "God will punish one who does such a thing" (J); "Surely God will get angry" (J).

Rational Aspects. These points, at least, are "rational aspects" in the sense that they are logically essential to the development of the narrative: "When these sons had grown up"; "But the girl did not love the elder brother"; or the inverse point: "She only loved the younger"; "But the younger (brother) refused (to give up the girl)"; "They (brothers) quarreled a great deal"; "The magician did so (changed the younger brother into a toad)." Nadel classifies two more and Goodman an additional ten of the story items as being primarily appropriate to the "rational" category.

We find, curiously enough, that reproductions by both Japanese and American children include these rational aspects less frequently than those by Yoruba (but more frequently than those by Nupe). The difference is major with respect to the item "When these sons had grown up" (17 of 20 Yoruba include it; 27 per cent of Americans and 17 per cent of Japanese do so). This discrepancy may have little to do with rationality, however. Quite possibly the Japanese and American children simply take it for granted that the triangular love affair would have occurred only after "the sons had grown up," and hence neglect to mention the item. However, it may be significant that, relatively speaking, the Americans do recall this rational aspect.

Present subjects differ little from Yoruba with respect to the items stating the girl's preference (i.e., she "did not love the elder brother" or "she only loved the younger"). All Yoruba recalled one or the other of these, and nearly all Japanese and Americans do so too (on the former item, 25 per cent of the Americans and 32 per cent of the Japanese; on the latter, 90 and 75 per cent, respectively). The Japanese, as compared with the Americans, more often make the point through the item stating the girl's negative sentiments toward the elder brother. Conversely, the Americans are more inclined than the Japanese to recall her positive sentiments toward the younger. For Japanese the matter of negative sentiments toward the older brother should be memorable, since in traditional Japanese terms[6] the elder brother has distinctly more prerogatives and more important status.[7]

With respect to another item which one might suppose memorable in Japanese terms (because of the power of elder over younger brother in the traditional Japanese family) we find almost no difference between the two groups of children. This is the item on the younger brother's refusal to give up the girl to his elder, recalled by 57 per cent of the American and by 54 per cent of the Japanese children. Yoruba do not fail to mention this fact.

In view of the culturally patterned expectation that the younger will be submissive to the elder brother, one might suppose that the brothers' quarrel would stand out in the recollections of Japanese. In fact it does not, either relatively or absolutely, being mentioned by 28 per cent of Americans and of Japanese alike. More than half the Yoruba recall it, as against about a fourth of the present subjects. Possibly the quarrel, like the growing up, is taken for granted in view of the rivalry of the brothers and in view of ensuing events.

A substantial majority of Japanese (68 per cent) and somewhat fewer Americans (59 per cent) do recall the crucial fact of the younger brother's magic and tragic transformation ("the magician did so," i.e., changed him into a toad). We have no data for Yoruba or Nupe on this item because it does not appear in the original version, which had the elder slay the younger brother with his sword. Japanese educators cooperating in the study balked at exposing their pupils to a story containing such violence and fratricide. They suggested the substitution (magic and permanent transformation of the younger brother, at the instigation of the elder), which was adopted for the present study.

On other logically significant items—the fact that the brothers "loved her very much," the elder telling the younger to give her up, and why, the elder's charge to the magician, the permanence of the transformation, the girl's departure when she had "finished crying"—there is either little American-Japanese difference or the frequency of recall by the Americans is greater. There is but one exception: the Japanese are relatively (19 against 9 per cent) given to recall of the fact that both the boys "made friends" with the girl. This seems appropriate in cultural terms, as the more delicate Japanese way of describing development of a romantic interest.

Situational Aspects. Situational aspects are those which, though of no great importance to the logical progress of the narrative, supply specifics, e.g., of time, place, or circumstances. These may be logically irrelevant, but they contribute to the concrete and vivid qualities of the narrative. For example, "When night fell" (the elder brother went to a magician) is a situational feature of importance to the Nupe, while to the Yoruba it is a minor detail which is often slighted or ignored. We find neither Japanese nor Americans so indifferent to the point as the Yoruba, but the Japanese are considerably more inclined to recall this circumstantial fact (Americans 43 per cent; Japanese 62 per cent).

On one situational item the Japanese show marked superiority of recall (51 against 17 per cent); this is the statement that the girl went to another place. This follows the logically significant item "she left," on which the Americans show marked superiority (71 against 32 per cent). To the Japanese it is of interest that the girl went somewhere else, and this, rather than the stark fact of her departure, apparently strikes them as the significant consideration. Their focus is the more specific and detailed, and it is reminiscent of the Nupe.

Other situational items are recalled by American and Japanese children with about equal frequency or by Americans with somewhat greater frequency. In the latter category we find: "There was a king"; "This king had two children—sons"; "She was the daughter of a farmer"; "He (magician) did so (changed the younger brother) that very night."

Emotional and Esthetic Aspects. Items which refer to emotional states may be recalled in either of two quite different ways, as Nadel points out. They may be recalled in the rational context, as by the Yoruba. In this case they are dealt with as reasons or motivations for subsequent human events. Or they may be recalled in the situational-specific context, as by the Nupe. In this case they are dealt with as discrete facts, of interest and importance in themselves rather than because they produced some action. This latter mode of recall does not preclude a notable degree of interest in emotional aspects; Nupe in fact pay considerable attention to such items.

The emotional aspects of the story have to do with love, anger, and sadness. On items having to do with love—"And (they) loved her very much"; "Both of them loved her"; "From the bottom of their hearts"—the American children show a consistently higher frequency of recall, as is expectable in view of American cultural emphasis on love and romance. Both groups show relatively high frequency on the item "Both of them loved her," but with the Americans far in the lead (83 against 52 per cent). Moreover, among Americans the recall is, in a majority of cases, verbatim; among Japanese it is seldom so.

The item concerning anger—(they quarreled) "until the elder brother became furious"—shows an expectable trend, but weakly. The Japanese, who might be expected to be more sensitive to the matter of fraternal quarrels (since intrafamily solidarity and harmony are highly valued) and to the importance of an elder brother's fury,[8] do in fact recall the item with greater frequency than the Americans (33 against 26 per cent). The differential, however, is surprisingly small. This fact may be partly accounted for by the Japanese inclination to lower rates of recall for items in the body of the story.

Sadness is expressed in the story by three items having to do with the girl's unhappiness: "But the girl cried"; "She cried for twenty days"; and "Her heart was full of pain." The expression "Her heart was full of pain" was perhaps strange, unchildlike, and difficult to remember; in any case it was omitted by most Americans and nearly all Japanese (recalled by only 6 and 2 per cent respectively). The majority of both Japanese and Americans recalled, often verbatim, the fact that "she cried for twenty days." Japanese recall is somewhat the more frequent (77 against 73 percent). The unadorned fact that "the girl cried" is recalled with greater frequency by Japanese (26 against 16 per cent), who largely reproduce it verbatim. Sadness is apparently an emotion to which the Japanese are somewhat the more sensitive.

The mention of personal beauty (i.e., "They saw a beautiful girl") is also somewhat more frequently recalled by the Japanese (64 against 55 per cent). Though the Japanese recall the item verbatim more frequently than the Americans, the modifications which they introduce are numerous and distinctive. They often supply additional facts, e.g., she is not just "a girl" but "a daughter"; she "lived near the brothers"; they "met her in the field" or "in the street"; she "came to them" or "passed by," coming "from a certain place." Elaborations of these sorts, none of them important to the logic of the story, exhibit much greater variety in Japanese than in American reproductions. The Japanese show interest, not just in the fact that the girl was beautiful, but in the specifics concerning how this girl came into the lives of the brothers. Like the Nupe, they are moved to supply detail and circumstantial specificity.

Moral Aspects. Only one moral judgment occurs in the story, i.e., "The elder brother did an evil deed." The Americans who reproduce this item generally do not do so verbatim. They utilize synonyms but otherwise stay close to the original. The Japanese reproduce the item less frequently (10 against 30 per cent), but they, too, generally modify the statement. Their modifications, however, more often shift the judgment from the deed to the man, e.g., "How evil he was." And one Japanese faithfully illustrates the traditional sensitivity to opinion sanctions by writing that the elder brother was "ill spoken of."

Sequence. Of the two African groups, it was the more "rational" Yoruba whose reproductions nearly always preserved the order of events in the original story. Among the subjects of the present study it was the Japanese who best preserved the sequence. Their margin over the

Americans is not large, however, either when measured in terms of percentage of responses which are out of sequence (16 for the Japanese against 23 for the Americans) or in terms of the number of whole-story-in-order reproductions (8 Japanese; 0 American). In regard to the number of items on which the Japanese had a lower percentage of out-of-sequence responses than the Americans (29 of the 40 items), the Japanese superiority appears still more marked. In keeping with other evidence that the Japanese memory is strongest for the early and late phases of the story, we find that it is middle-story items that they are most likely to reorder.

In the matter of order the Japanese resemble the "rational" Yoruba, of whom only two out of the twenty rearranged the order of events in the story, while eleven of the twenty Nupe did so. It seems likely, however, that Japanese superiority of recall in this respect springs from a conceptualizing habit which differs from the rational habit of the Yoruba. It may result from the Japanese interest in form, as expressed, for example, in both the arts and interpersonal relations, as against the Yoruba interest in the logical flow of events.

Summary and Conclusions

Japanese and American children were studied and compared with respect to their conceptualizing habits. This investigation replicates, on a larger scale, Nadel's study of Nupe and Yoruba children, and utilizes Nadel's story-recall method. Conceptualizing habits are deduced from the forms in which the children reproduce, after a time lapse, a short dramatic story.

The Nupe and Yoruba studies by Nadel showed modal thoughtways (conceptualizing habits) of sorts consistent with the respective cultures. Yoruba culture is relatively systematizing (Kroeber's term), i.e., generalizing, recognizing and dealing in relations. Yoruba subjects showed more inclination than Nupe to reproduce story material in an organized and rational fashion. Nupe reproductions showed more specificity. Kroeber suggests that these types, which are identified as "rational and sensory" respectively, are recognizable also among American Indian peoples.

Data from the present study indicate that Americans are somewhat more systematizing than Japanese. This finding is in accord with what was anticipated in view of the nature of the two cultures, e.g., the systematizing influence stemming from American cultural emphasis on ideologies both religious and scientific-emphases not paralleled in Japan. However, there are unanticipated findings as well.

It is surprising, for example, that Yoruba appear to be more systematizing in their conceptual habits than either Americans or Japanese. Kroeber supposes all "advanced" cultures to be of the systematizing type relative to less advanced cultures. We seem to have, in the Yoruba, an exception to the generalization. Whether this is true, and whether this case is unique, can only be determined by further studies and by more refined comparative analysis of data drawn from Yoruba, Japanese, American, and ultimately other societies.

Among unanticipated findings we note also that the Japanese, as compared with the Americans, are somewhat less accurate in reproducing story items, particularly with respect to the body of the story. However, when interpreted in the light of other findings, this fact supports an inclination which was anticipated for Japanese, i.e., the inclination toward recall of a nonsystematized type, through attempted rote memorization of specifics. The supporting findings are: high Japanese accuracy at the beginning and end of the story; stronger inclination of Japanese to reproduce verbatim or nearly so; less inclination to add, modify, or paraphrase; less inclination to depart from the original sequence of events.

Certain other trends in Japanese reproductions are less easily interpreted, e.g., that the Japanese are no more given than Americans to recall the fact of the younger brother's refusal to give up the girl; or the ensuing violent quarrel between the brothers. In the light of the traditional Japanese emphasis on family solidarity and harmony, on the prerogatives of the elder brother over younger brothers, and, at least ideally, on the submissive attitudes of younger toward older, somewhat greater emphasis on these points might have been expected. Relative to Americans, the Japanese do give some emphasis to items of this sort, however, e.g., the girl's failure to love the elder brother and the elder brother's fury at the younger's refusal to give her up, as well as the elder's statement: "I am the one to marry her." We conclude that the Japanese show, in these respects, no striking departures from the anticipated.

Recall of the emotional and moral aspects of the story coincides with culturally plausible expectations. The Americans tend to lead in recall of items having to do with love (except the item noted above, "The girl did not love the elder brother"). The Japanese tend to lead in items having to do with sadness. The Americans lead in recall of the moral judgment item, containing reference to the elder brother's "evil deed."

This study points up the difficulties inherent in analyzing and interpreting data collected by the story-recall method, and provides a basis for refinement of both the data-gathering device and the analytic categories. But the investigation supports Kroeber's and Nadel's views concerning the potentialities of the study of conceptualizing habits and the usefulness of the type of approach developed by Nadel. Differences in the conceptualizing habits modal among bearers of Japanese and of American cultures have been shown to be inferable from the story-recall data.

NOTES

1. A preliminary form of this paper was prepared for presentation at the annual meeting of the American Anthropological Association in November, 1961.

2. The Japanese data presented herewith were collected during the writer's tenure as Fulbright Research Scholar in Japan, 1954–55. For invaluable assistance the writer wishes to acknowledge gratitude and indebtedness to Mr. K. Ikenaga and Miss A. Saito, distinguished Japanese educators, and to administrators and teachers in a number of schools in the Osaka-Kobe area. For opportunities to collect American data the writer is indebted to administrators and teachers in the schools of Brookline, Massachusetts, and of Chevy Chase, Maryland. The work of data analysis was accomplished under a grant from the Public Health Service, National Institutes of Health.

3. Nadel's subjects were 12 to 18 years; present subjects were fifth and sixth graders, hence 11 or 12 years old.

4. "Underlying and cross-cutting all our findings we see evidences of the vitality of strongly contrasting cultural themes in Japan and in the United States. ... American children exhibit strong inclinations suggesting such themes as may be identified by the labels scientific-technical, urban-sophisticate, pragmatic-humanistc, and individualistic. The inclinations of Japanese children suggest themes which we might label commercial, sentimental-humanistic, and others-oriented" (Goodman 1957: 997).

5. These instructions were given by the investigator:

The teacher reads the story aloud, just once (no repetition or review, no questions concerning its content to be answered after it is read to the children). The teacher reads at her usual rate for story material and in her usual fashion.

Four hours later (as nearly as possible) the children are asked to write the story just as they remember it, from beginning to end.

Before reading the story to the children the teacher explains to them that they will he asked to write it after four hours, and that this is a special kind of exercise. They should of course be given no assistance or prompting as they write.

This follows Nadel's procedure except that he took recalls orally (each subject alone). He also took a second recall one week after the first. This step was omitted from the present study, since it apparently added little of significance to his findings. In this paper all comparisons with his data are based on his first-recall findings.

6. In this and subsequent references to "traditional" aspects of Japanese culture we follow a practice which is widespread among observers both Western and Japanese, as Caudill and Scarr (1962) have pointed out, namely, the practice of implying a certain dualism in contrasting "traditional with nontraditional or "modern" values in contemporary Japanese culture. With Caudill and Scarr (1962: 54), we recognize that "Japan is not moving evenly [nor are its people moving uniformly] in all spheres of behavior toward individualism" (and other modern values). In fact, findings reported here which are identified as suggesting traditional" values and practices point to certain areas and degrees of cultural conservatism.

7. Haring (1949: 847–851) reports: "At the age of sixty a man retires from the family headship in favor of his eldest son. ... At maturity younger sons leave the household to enter the Army, business or a profession, or to work in factories. ... A boy must obey his father and elder brothers." The practice of primogeniture, though officially halted by postwar legislation, remains prevalent.

8. Norbeck (1954: 49–51) reports: "There is a strong feeling of unity among members of a household.... Quarreling between members of the same sex, except among young children, is uncommon." Though this observation pertains to rural Japan, it undoubtedly illustrates cultural modalities.

BIBLIOGRAPHY

Bartlett, F. C. 1932. Remembering. Cambridge.
Bruner, J. S., J. J. Goodnow, and G. A. Austin. 1957. A Study of Thinking. New York.
Caudill, W., and H. A. Scarr. 1962. Japanese Value Orientations and Culture Change. Ethnology 1: 53–91.
Dore, R. P. 1958. City Life in Japan: A Study of a Tokyo Ward. Berkeley and Los Angeles.
Goodman, M. E. 1957. Values, Attitudes and Social Concepts of Japanese and American Children. American Anthropologist 59: 979–999.
Haring, D. G. 1949. Japan and the Japanese 1868–1945. Most of the World, ed. R. Linton, pp. 814–875. New York.
Kroeber, A. L. 1948. Anthropology. Rev. edit. New York.
Merrill-Palmer Institute. 1960. Some Current Research and Thinking about Cognitive Processes in Children: A Symposium. Merrill-Palmer Quarterly 6: 245–284.
Nadel, S. F. 1937. Experiments on Cultural Psychology. Africa 10: 421–435.
———. 1937–38. A Field Experiment in Racial Psychology. British Journal of Psychology 28: 195–211.
Norbeck, E. 1954. Takashima: A Japanese Fishing Community. Salt Lake City.
Siegel, A. E. 1958. The Influence of Violence in the Mass Media Upon Children's Role Expectations. Child Development 29: 35–55.
Social Science Research Council. 1960. Intellective Development in Children. Items 14: 25–30.
Wallace, A. F. C. 1961. Culture and Personality. New York.

# *Pollution and Purity*
>>> <<<

As we saw earlier with the Amish, Oneida, and Shakers, one of the fundamental problems faced by religious communities is that of maintaining, in the face of environmental realities, the purity of the ideals that brought them into existence. Endogenous strains and exogenous forces constantly threaten to erode or pollute that purity. Because it is the fate of almost all religious sects to experience early extinction, it is a wonder how some religious communities survive and a greater wonder still how a few of them succeed to become world religions like Christianity, Islam, and the Church of Jesus Christ of Latter-day Saints (Mormons). Equally astonishing is how some religious sects, like the Amish and the Lubavitch Hasidim, so apparently anomalous and anachronistic in contemporary American society, and so intent on preserving centuries-old modes of existence, actually thrive.

Berger-Sofer's analysis of the kinship and marriage links of the Lubavitch leadership is intended as a political study. It shows how succession to the office of principal rabbi from fathers to sons (or to sons-in-law) tied the generations and connected the founder to all subsequent leaders. Like a royal lineage, especially with cousin marriage, the mode of succession helped distinguish a leadership core from all other members of the devout community. Thus, Berger-Sofer's study can also be appreciated for its contribution to understanding the importance of maintaining charismatic purity in the leadership line.

The structure of succession and organizational leadership invites comparison with similar phenomena. The caste-like endogamy that preserves the charismatic purity of the rabbinical line parallels the way Islamic sects trace their origins to the Prophet and his closest kin. Perhaps religious charisma is like lineage wealth: to marry out is to invite its dissipation.

But with succession to high office the Lubavitch face a demographic threat opposite to that of the Shakers. As a consequence of their religious beliefs, the Hasidim, as Orthodox Jews, must follow God's command to be fruitful and multiply. What does a royal lineage do with surplus sons, particularly those showing less ability for organizational leadership?

The Lubavitch solution is to balance ascription with ability, to avoid the rigidity of linear succession and primogeniture by allowing talented younger sons to be chosen over older sons, or even by picking a nephew, but to make the nephew like a son through marriage with the leader's daughter. While advantageous, this system creates other problems. What does one do with potentially disgruntled brothers or sons? They can be disruptive forces for divisiveness and factionalism. A solution that has worked in history employed by the Lubavitch is the notion that those who cannot have the kingdom can go out to colonize. Thus an expanding core of lineage leaders is absorbed in the process of proselytizing and expansion. As long as the movement experiences continuous growth, as long as new branches are founded and membership increases, the contradictions inherent in maintaining successional charismatic purity when choosing among many offspring are avoided.

The article by Katz, also treating a concern with purity, is deliberately provocative. How dare we speak of one of the most evolved examples of scientific and technological development—modern medical surgery—and of the rituals of primitive peoples in the same breath, except to contrast them as extreme opposites? Yet Katz does, and we should pay attention. The comparison is not intended to confound primitive ritual, religion, or magic with science, but to suggest that a homology is present; that both modern surgery and primitive ritual have a similar underlying mental structure, that there exists a similar logic basic to each. Katz uses the startling device of viewing modern surgery as "ritual" to demonstrate a shared humanity between all peoples, even those at widely different levels of sociocultural evolution.

She compares hospital surgical procedure with a generalized pattern of the ritual process of simple societies as outlined by anthropologists; that is, how people undergoing ritual move through distinctive phases (or stages) in time and place, how they avoid the dangers of pollution, and how they exaggerate differences in ritual states or conditions. Katz wishes us to regard the design of the operating rooms area of a hospital like sacred ground, like a temple with increasing degrees of inner *sancta*. The purpose of this design is to protect against the dangers of infection. The religious analog in primitive societies is to protect participants from the dangers of ritual pollution.

Katz does not intend to press her analogy beyond the observation that when people treat the ultimate matters of health and illness, life and death, they think and act alike, but her vivid description of surgical procedures stimulates my choreographic imagination to use the metaphor of the modern dance theater for the operating theater.

With apologies to the modern medical profession, picture the performers scrubbing before an operation, turning tap water on and off with hip movements. Imagine the prescribed motions governing the meticulous washing of arms, hands, fingers, and nails. Proper hip movements open the door to the operating room and with a twirl of the body the surgeon enters. Arms, bent at the elbow and aloft, are dried with a towel, which is then flung away. Arms still held away from the body, the surgeon moves into a green gown held by an assistant and the hands are then thrust into rubber gloves, after which the gown is secured with a quick pirouette.

Well, anthropology does not always have to be serious.

Political Kinship Alliances of a Hasidic Dynasty[1]

Rhonda Berger-Sofer

>>> <<<

THIS PAPER EXAMINES and offers an historical analysis of the political kinship alliance network of the Lubavitcher Hasidic leadership family, the Schneersohns. The political alliance network of this family represents an interesting example of a group's reaction to historical exigencies and its analysis provides an unusual application of genealogical kinship studies.

A kinship alliance network can be understood as "a relevant series of linkages existing between [kin-related] individuals which form a basis for mobilization of people [kin] for specific purposes under specific conditions" (Whitten and Wolfe 1973:720). The analyses of kinship systems in general, and alliance networks in particular, have focused on the processes of political and social organization (e.g., Dumont 1957; Fortes and Evans-Pritchard 1950; Fortes 1969; Lande 1973; Radcliffe-Brown and Forde 1950), economic and political strategies (e.g., Davis 1973; Schneider and Schneider 1976), and cultural organizations (Campbell 1964; Witherspoon 1975; Wylie 1957). A group's kinship structure or alliance network both affects and is affected by its interaction and relationship with various wider social and historical circumstances. Therefore, a study of a kinship system or a political kinship alliance network which ignores wider social and historical influences and emphasizes only genealogical factors would impede complete understanding of that system or network. A purely historical approach to a group which ignores the political, social and economic dynamics of genealogical structures or kinship alliances is similarly limiting.

This paper analyzes the political alliance network of the Lubavitcher leadership family genealogically and historically, and shows how the dynamics of the family's kinship alliances affected and were affected by its social and historical experiences. The power positions of the movement have been kept within the originating Lubavitcher's rebbe's family through a combination of leadership succession from fathers to sons (or sons-in-law who were also family members) and through parallel and cross-cousin marriages, which enabled noninheriting sisters' and noninheriting brothers' children to ascend to positions of leadership within the movement, including that of rebbe.

The first section of this paper provides some background and a general overview of the Lubavitcher Hasidic leadership's alliance network. Then I analyze how the genealogical dynamics of the kinship alliances of the Schneersohns relate to their historical circumstances. Finally, I discuss the trends of the kinship alliance network.

The Kinship Alliance Network

The Lubavitcher movement developed from the general Hasidic movement that spread rapidly through Eastern Europe in the eighteenth century (Katz 1958; Mahler 1971; Rabinowicz 1970; Rabinowitch 1971; Weinryb 1972). Schneur Zalman (1746–1812), a disciple of Dov Baer, "The Maggid" of Meseritz (d. 1772) who was the disciple of the founder of Hasidism, settled in Lubavitch, a town in White Russia, in 1777 (Rabinowitsch 1971 :33).[2] He became the leader of the Hasidim there and founded the Lubavitcher movement. His branch of Hasidism is known as *Chabad*, whose Hebrew letters stand for wisdom (*Chokmah*), understanding (*Binah*), and knowledge (*Da'at*) (Mindel 1947:17).

The genealogy of the Lubavitcher rebbes (Figure 1), beginning with Schneur Zalman (A1), shows that the position of rebbe has always remained in the family, with each new rebbe being a descendent of Schneur Zalman. In the seven generations of *Chabad* rebbes, the position has been handed down from father to son on four occasions (in generation B, E, and F) and from father to son-in-law on two occasions (in generation C and G). These sons-in-law, however, can also trace their ancestry back to Schneur Zalman (A1).

The Lubavitcher rebbes are all considered *zaddikim* (righteous holy men). Like all Hasidic communities, the Lubavitcher community is formed around a *zaddik*, its rebbe, who is its spiritual supervisor and practical leader.[3] The Lubavitcher rebbe is revered by his followers, who usually attribute divinely inspired powers to him. Many of the *Chabad* Hasidim consult the rebbe regarding all types of problems, ranging from the spiritual to personal and business, and often ask the rebbe to provide divine intercession in resolving the most serious of these problems (Weiner 1969:156–157, 175).

In addition to their spiritual duties, the Lubavitcher rebbes, like rabbis in general, have always performed a practical role in giving actual material aid to Jews. To provide this aid, the leadership family has had at its

A Hasidic Dynasty 261

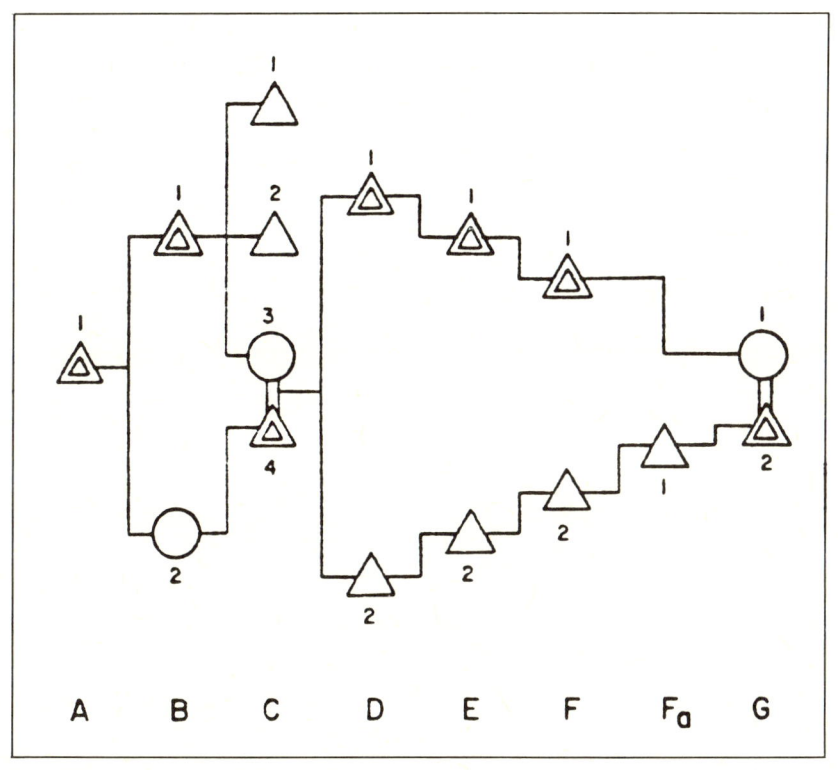

FIGURE 1. *Lubavitch Hasidic Leadership*

disposal financial resources, usually donated by Lubavitcher Hasidim and sympathizers. The rebbes have set up *yeshivas* (religious academies) and schools for training Jewish artisans and farmers, even buying land for Jewish development and settlement. They have fought for Jewish rights in national and international arenas. In effect, following the example of traditional Jewish communal organization, the Lubavitcher rebbes have developed an efficient organization to help the Jews (Goldberg 1979; Mindel 1947, 1969; Schneersohn 1962; Weiner 1969).

The genealogy of the Lubavitcher Hasidic rebbes may be compared to the characteristics of a modified ancestor-focused, restricted, cognatic descent group (Fox 1967). Both male and female descendents of Schneur Zalman are considered members of the group if they follow the life-styles, rules, and obligations of the Lubavitcher Hasidim.

Lubavitcher Hasidim abide by the matrilineal definition of a Jew as anyone who is born to a Jewish female. In addition, the Lubavitcher

Hasidim abide by the patrilineal definition of whether a Jew is a Cohen, Levy, or Israelite. Both rules are followed by all traditional Jews. The official power and authority of Lubavitch is patriarchal.

Like groups with cognatic descent, *Chabad*'s leadership family is endogamous. Out of approximately 115 marriages over seven generations, at least 25 marriages (or 22 per cent) are endogamous. This is a conservative figure as all marriages of Schneur Zalman's descendants whose spouses I could not trace genealogically (about 40) were counted as exogamous. The endogamous marriages of the Schneersohn family are shown in Figure 2. The endogamous marriages occur almost randomly and do not follow any rule like mother's-brother's daughter or father's-sister's daughter system of marriage.

Endogamous Marriages

The kinship links between a man and his wife, shown in Table 1, include four possible ways of being related to spouses. The mother's sister (MZ)

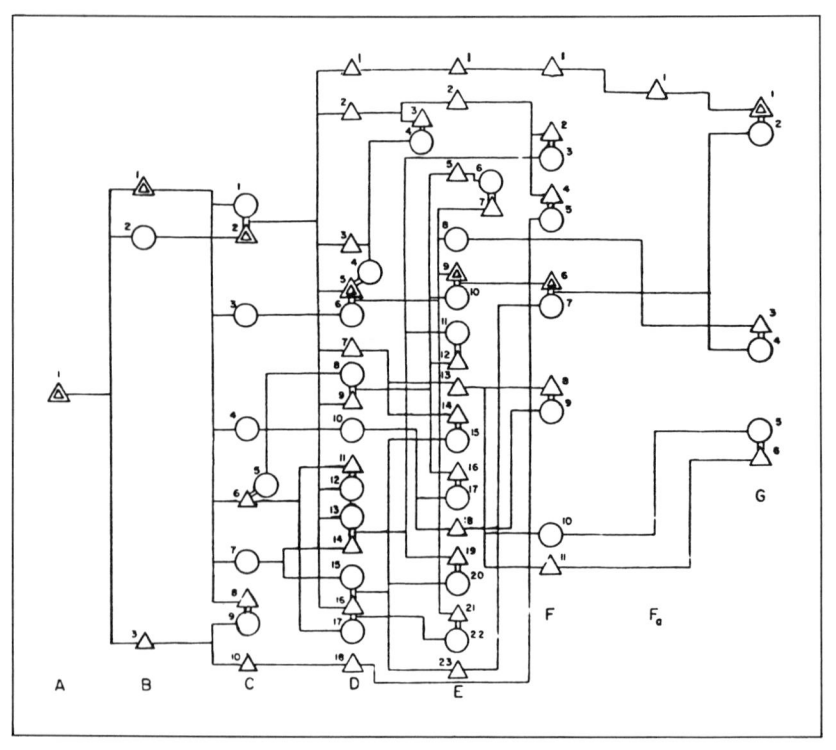

FIGURE 2. *Endogamous Marriages of the Schneersohn Family*

TABLE 1
CONNECTING LINKS BETWEEN SPOUSES
(a man to his wife)

MB	7	(17.5%)
MZ	16	(40.0%)
FB	11	(27.5%)
FZ	6	(15.0%)
	40	

is the most frequent connection (40 per cent of the cases). Table 2 depicts endogamous marriages that occurred in each generation of leaders. Out of 25 total marriages, 52 per cent of the husbands can trace their connection to their wife through their MZ. Moreover, in the three generations in which most of the family endogamous marriages occur (D, E, F), most of the kinship links to the wife are through the MZ (thirteen out of nineteen marriages or 68 per cent of the marriages). The data appear to suggest that the MZ is of greatest significance connecting kin-related spouses. Yet, when only the closest relation to the spouse is traced, as shown in Table 3, the frequency of endogamous marriages is practically random between the MZ, MB (mother's brother), FZ (father's sister) and FB (father's brother). Therefore, any endogamy rule for the leadership family should be stated in the widest or most general fashion. Even so, we must still explain why a high percentage of men can trace some relationship to their wives through the MZ connection.

Table 2 shows that the MZ connection begins to become important for marriages occurring in generation D. The connection to the MZ endogamous marriages occurs in generation C. Figure 2 shows that in

TABLE 2
INDIVIDUAL MARRIAGES ACCORDING TO GENERATION

Generation	Total Marriages	MB	MZ	FB	FX
C	3	1	0	1	0
D	7	2	5	0	2
E	8	2	5	4	2
F	4	1	3	2	1
G	3	1	0	1	1
Total	25	7 (28%)	13 (52%)	8 (32%)	6 (24%)

TABLE 3
Closest Connecting Link

MB	5
MZ	6
FB	8
FZ	5

Note: The appendix table, The Consanguinal Relationship Between Spouses, presents the raw data which are the basis of Tables 1–6.

generation C there are four daughters of the second rebbe of the Lubavitcher movement (B1, Dov Baer). It is the offspring of these four daughters of Dov Baer who account for 21 out of 22 endogamous marriages that occurred in generations D through G. Only F5 is not a descendant of one of these four sisters in generation C.

The leadership in generation C was not inherited by a son of Dov Baer (B1), but by a son-in-law and uterine nephew, Menachem Mendel (C2). The offspring of Dov Baer's daughters were continually drawn back into the lineage in order to contribute potential leaders to the, group and to keep Dov Baer's direct descendants in authority positions. Figure 3 plots the leadership marriages, and shows that each of the daughters of Dov Baer have daughters who marry three sons of their brother-in-law, the Rebbe of generation C (Menachem Mendel C2). In generation D, the leader marries an offspring of Hayyah Sarah (C3), a daughter of Dov Baer. In generation F, the leader marries an offspring of both Hayyah Mushka (C1) and Frieda (C4). In generation F, the wife of the leader is an offspring of Bella (C5) and Hayyah Mushka (C1).

This patrilineal definition of family membership is in line with Jewish rabbinic tradition in general, and especially Hasidic dynastic tradition. It is almost always the sons who inherit their fathers' positions and statuses and perpetuate their father's name (through their own sons). Although daughters of rabbis are indeed members of their father's family, they adopt, as do most Jewish daughters, the family name of their husband at marriage, and their children become members of their husband's line of descent. Therefore, unless there are family intramarriages in rabbinic lines that bring the descendents of rabbinic daughters back into the family, these descendents tend to become lost to the rabbinic (natal) line of their mother. That the daughters of Dov Baer form the core of endogamous marriages may be seen as an arrangement to draw the offspring of Dov Baer back into the power structure of the movement. In this way, daughters of sisters are not lost but are important contributors providing potential leaders to the group. In addition, it appears that the males of generation C,

A Hasidic Dynasty 265

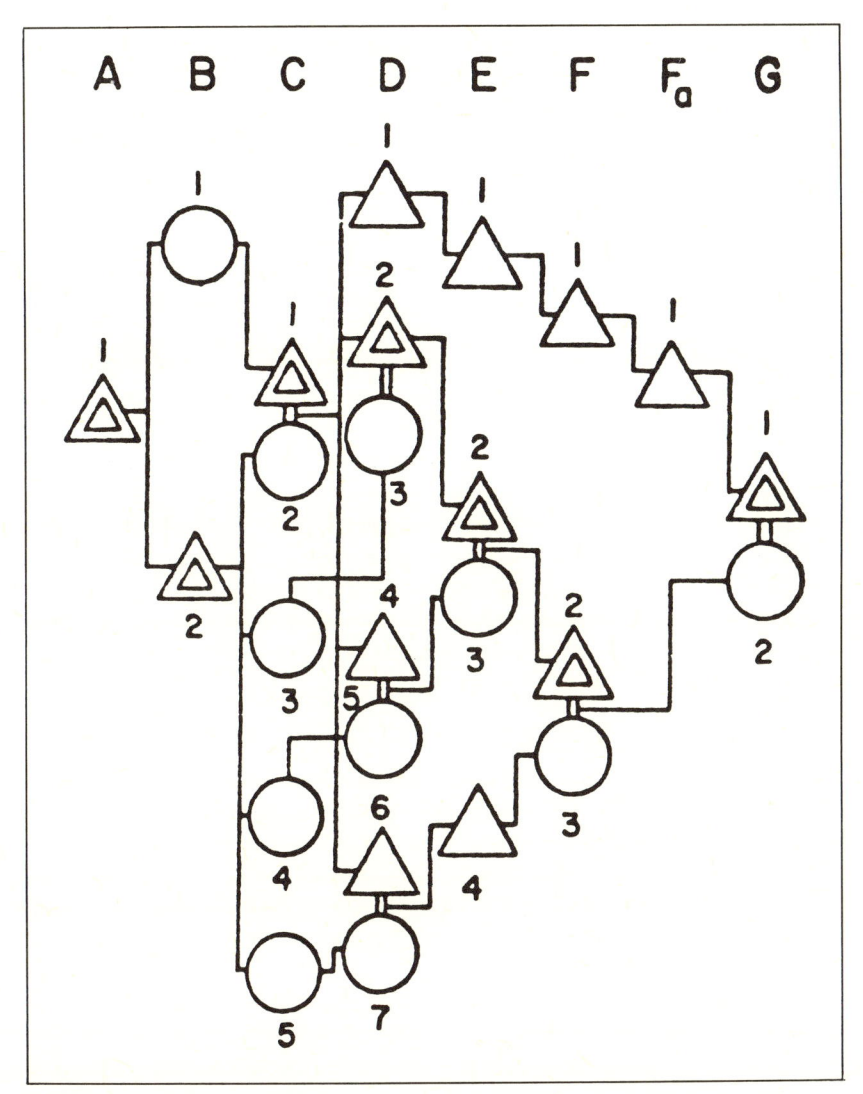

FIGURE 3. *Leadership Marriages*

Menachem Nachum (C6 of Figure 2), Baruch (C8), and Dov Baer (C10), did not provide enough offspring for endogamous family marriages.

Finally, an explanation is necessary to clarify why Menachem Mendel (C2), a son-in-law and nephew of Dov Baer (B1), inherited the position of rebbe, while Dov Baer's two sons (C6 and C8 of Figure 2), did not. According to a *Chabad* historian, Nissan Mindel (1969:101), Menachem Mendel's mother, Deborah Leah (B2), died to save the life of her father, Schneur Zalman, who was very ill. Deborah Leah beseeched God to take her soul in place of her father's. After she died, Schneur Zalman adopted her only son, Menachem Mendel (Mindel 1969:161). Therefore, Menachem Mendel was both a grandson of Schneur Zalman, and his adopted son.

From an early age, Menachem Mendel's learning abilities and organizational capabilities were so amazing that he was soon viewed as being "destined to succeed Rabbi Schneur Zalman's son, Rabbi Dov Baer to the third generation of leadership of the *Chabad* movement" (Mindel 1969:98).

Menachem Mendel's marriage to a daughter of Dov Baer was Dov Baer's expression that his nephew should succeed him as the third leader of *Chabad.* In addition, it assured Dov Baer that his direct descendents would be close relatives of the Lubavitcher Rebbe's family. As Menachem Mendel possessed all the spiritual requirements of being a rebbe—he was a son of a "woman of valor" and a grandson and adopted son of Schneur Zalman, the founder of *Chabad* Hasidim—and also was capable of handling all the practical requirements of the position, it was easy for the followers of Dov Baer to transfer their loyalty from Dov Baer to Menachem Mendel.

Social and Historical Contexts

We now address the question of how the dynamics of a restricted cognatic kinship alliance network relate to the social and historical experiences of the group. Jewish opposition to the Hasidic movement peaked in 1772 and 1781, when the leader of the *Mitnagdim* (people who have been skeptical or even antagonistic towards Hasidim), Elijah of Vilna, declared a *herem* (ban) against the Hasidic community, excommunicating the members as heretics and forbidding intermarriage with them (Rabinowitsch 1971:24). Although the *herem* was never fully implemented, marriages between Hasidim and *Mitnagdim* were socially discouraged (Rabinowitsch 1971:168). In addition, over the years, divisions arose among the various different Hasidic sects themselves. This restricted marriages even further to within each Hasidic sect.

Lubavitcher Hasidim were established in White Russia, the stronghold of the *Mitnagdim.* In this hostile environment, *Chabad* Hasidim had to choose from alternative strategies for its survival. At one extreme, *Chabad* Jews could have chosen to isolate themselves physically or socially from non-*Chabad* Jews, similar to Wilson's (1970) category of the introversionist sect. Or, at the other extreme, they could have chosen to adapt to their locality almost completely and lose their distinctiveness as a group. Instead, *Chabad*'s leader, Schneur Zalman, chose to develop a philosophy and belief system that would not be totally dissonant with the environment and social atmosphere of the Jewish community of White Russia, while not compromising the group's distinctiveness.

The Lubavitcher Hasidic movement from its inception was a missionary movement.[4] Zalman developed a philosophy and established a sect that appealed to the Jews living in Lithuania and White Russia. Like most Hasidic groups, he welcomed unlearned Jews. Unlike other Hasidic groups however, *Chabad* also adapted to the learned and scholarly atmosphere of the learned Jews of Lithuania and White Russia by integrating an intellectual approach to its brand of Hasidim. In appealing to this wide range of Jewish social strata, Zalman was able to gain some support against the *Mitnagdim* attack. Despite Zalman's success in recruiting new members, marriages to his offspring and descendants tended to remain family endogamous.

Relatives of Zalman filled important positions in the Lubavitcher organization. For example, he appointed as his assistants his brother, Yehuda Leib, and his eldest son, Dov Baer (B1 Figure 2). These men and an unrelated disciple, Aharon Hurvitz, aided him in his various inter-Hasidic duties which included practical and spiritual guidance; e.g., distribution of charity, counseling Hasidim, etc. Schneur Zalman's youngest son, Moshe, was in charge of studying the economic problems of the Jews, and under his father's direction he organized (with the approval of the Russian government) a program of buying land in the district of Kherson for Jewish families to settle and develop (Mindel 1969:219; Zalman 1967:249). To aid the Jews dislocated from many communities by the Napoleonic Wars, Zalman sent his two sons, Dov Baer and Chaim Abraham (B1 and B3 of Figure 2), to several towns to raise money (Mindel 1969:258–259).

Each rebbe of *Chabad* needed people to contribute to the movement's educational, missionary, and economic goals. By keeping sisters and daughters as members and as producers of future members, the power and other resources of the Lubavitcher leadership family were concentrated among kinsmen. This gave the rebbe a greater number of family members to choose from to fill important positions in his organization. In this way, the Schneersohn family maintained tight control over its financial and spiritual resources. Restricted cognatic tendencies also provide a large selection in the choice of leadership, as any male descendent of Schneur Zalman is a potential candidate, if he or she lived according to the ideals of the group. Indeed, the transitions of leadership from generation to generation have occurred relatively smoothly.[5]

Each rebbe proved his organizational capabilities well before he became the leader by engaging in assigned missions and various other responsibilities ordered by the previous rebbe. It is fair to assume that each new Lubavitcher rebbe was chosen by the previous rebbe on the basis of the following qualifications: descent from Schneur Zalman, personal charismatic qualities, and demonstrated organizational and administrative abilities. The rebbe usually indicated in his will who his successor should be. The right to choose his successor gave each rebbe great power over his sons, sons-in-law, and nephews. These latter, if they had ambitions to leadership, had to demonstrate skills in their positions, as well as loyalty to the rebbe and to the general philosophy and goals of *Chabad*.[6] The restricted cognatic tendencies supplied many potential leaders and therefore heightened the competition among these members of the family. The endogamous marriages provided one way of restricting the competition for leadership candidates.

The Lubavitcher Hasidic group can be compared to corporate groups. Like corporate groups, the members come and go while the group continues. In addition, the Lubavitcher Hasidic group has a definite ideology, policy, and numerous resources. It has financial assets, and provides many services for its members: e.g., welfare, charity, counseling, etc. In addition, the group has a well-defined belief system that gives its members faith and purpose in their daily lives. Any policy decisions made by the leader and his advisors are acted upon and implemented by the whole group. These include various aspects of their expansionist missionary policy which often sends potential leaders to out-lying areas to set up new centers.[7] This policy prevents intrafraternal disputes, as only a few potential rebbes remain at the major center of *Chabad*, while the others are kept busy elsewhere. That the leader himself chooses his heir also lessens the potential for intrafraternal disputes. Finally, such disputes are inhibited by a gradual transition of power, with the incoming rebbe slowly accumulating power and experience.[8]

Endogamous marriages among the Lubavitcher Hasidic leadership family show that the genealogical links merge back towards the four daughters of generation C (Figure 2). Table 4 suggests that the more distant the relationship is between the spouses, the greater is the tendency to trace the genealogical relation through the father. Table 5 indicates that there is no difference in tracing the genealogical links between either the mother or the father, or through a brother (B) or sister (Z). Therefore, the only general characteristics we can state are: (1) there is a tendency to trace the linkage of endogamous marriages up through the male line the more distant the relationship is between the spouses; and (2) the endogamous marriage linkage is made more or less randomly through the mother or father, and brother or sister.

Table 5 also suggests the lesser importance of the mother's lineage

TABLE 4
Consanguinal Connections to Spouse until Link

F	10	M	9
FF	2	MM	5
FM	4	MF	2
FFM	4	MMM	0
FFFF	2	MMF	0
FFFM	1	MFM	1
	23		17

and the greater emphasis or importance placed on the father's lineage in finding spouses for the leadership's family. It may be that the group, over the past 100 years, is gradually moving away from restricted cognatic tendencies—both male and female descendants being considered as candidates for intrafamily marriages if they follow the life-style, rules, and obligations of the group—to more sex-restricted cognatic characteristics: i.e., both male and female descendants being considered intrafamily marriage candidates if their fathers are members of the group and they live up to its ideals.

Possibly, the lessening of importance of the mother's line is due to the increased importance of the male line connected specifically to the sons of Menachem Mendel (C2 Figure 2). Menachem Mendel had seven sons who lived to adulthood. Out of fourteen intrafamily marriages that have occurred in generations E through G (Figure 2), eight were between offspring and descendants of Menachem Mendel's sons (Figure 4). Perhaps, as the sons of rebbes did not produce enough offspring for intrafamily marriages in the beginning of the movement, offspring of daughters of *Chabad* rebbe were tapped to fill this important need. Once there were enough sons of a Lubavitcher rebbe who propagated enough children for family intramarriages however, the intramarriages that did occur, were

TABLE 5
Connections to Spouse

	Closest Connection	*All Connections*
M	11	23
F	13	17
B	13	18
Z	11	22

among the children or descendants of these sons. This trend does complement Jewish *Yichus* (lineage) ideology, according to which a child's family affiliation is usually through the father.

There was a great expansion of *Chabad* Hasidim during generation D, and it is necessary to analyze what may have stimulated this expansion which, as we shall see, affected the process of change and transition of the Lubavitcher rebbe's kinship alliance network. Three factors may be postulated as causes or influences of this expansion: (1) the internal Hasidic quarrels beginning in the mid 1800s; (2) a reaction to the spread of *Haskalah* (Jewish Enlightenment) movement; and (3) external conditions.

Inter-Hasidic Quarrels. From 1860 onward, internal civil strife divided Hasidic families and splintered communities (Dubnow 1916 Vol. II:120–125). It appears as if modified ultimogeniture occurred during generation D, as the rebbe's youngest son (Samuel D5 of Figure 2) inherited his father's position as the rebbe of Lubavitch. The year before Menachem Mendel's death (C2), he assigned his responsibilities to his sons as he was unable to fulfill them (Heilman 1903 Part III:23–32). Several sons were sent, prior to Menachem Mendel's illness, to outlying areas to establish Hasidic centers there (Heilman 1903). Other Hasidic, non-*Chabad* sects were perhaps seen as competition to the Lubavitcher movement, especially since these sects had differing ideologies from those of Chabad. Therefore, the establishment of Chabad centers outside the Lubavitch lessened the possibilities that *Chabad* Hasidim in those outlying areas would leave the fold.

In addition, the establishment of several branches of *Chabad* Hasidim can be seen as an attempt by the movement to influence non-Hasidic Jewish people towards their brand of Hasidim before being exposed to other groups. Finally, as many of Menachem Mendel's sons were sent to establish *Chabad* centers in outlying areas, perhaps the expansion may be viewed as preventing competition among his sons by dispersing them.

Although Menachem Mendel's sons were sent to various areas to establish Lubavitcher Hasidic centers, they arranged endogamous marriages for their own children. Each Lubavitcher rebbe (as shown in Figure 4), from generation D through G, has married a descendant of one of these brothers of generation D who did not inherit the position of rebbe. In generation D, the rebbe marries a daughter of his brother, Hayyim Schneur Zalman (D2). In generation E, the rebbe marries a daughter of Joseph Isaac, (D5). In generation F, the rebbe marries a granddaughter of another brother, Israel Noah (D7). The present rebbe is married to a great-great-granddaughter of yet another brother of

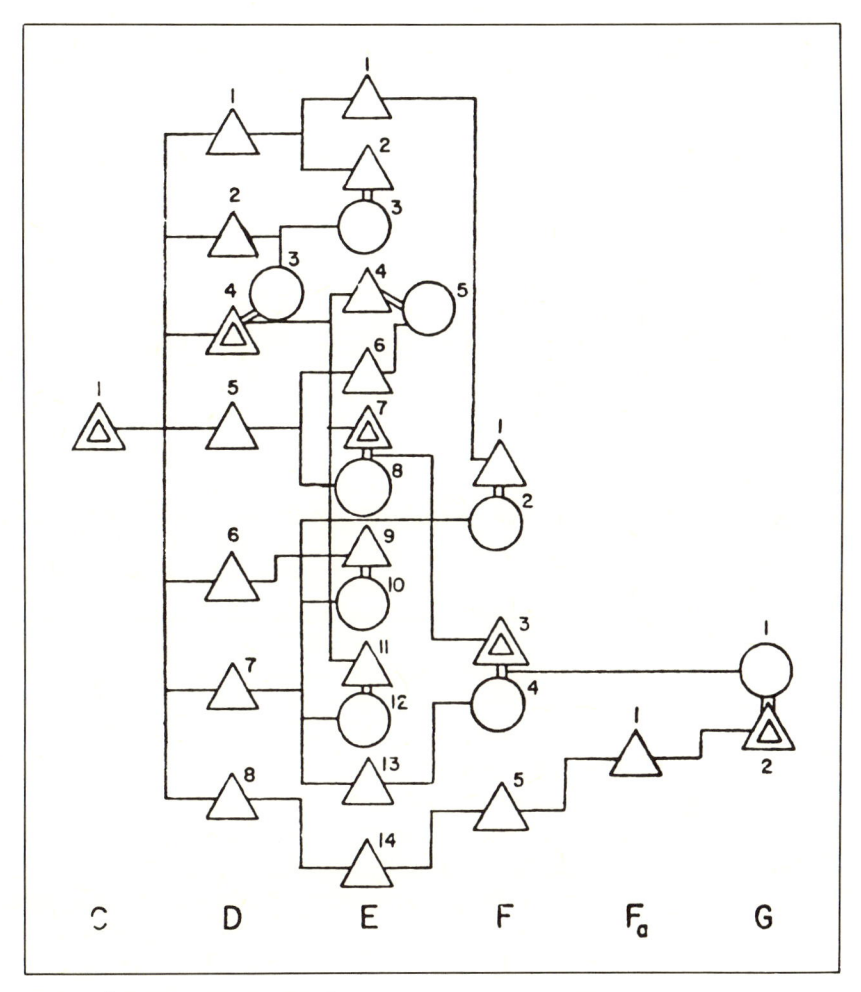

FIGURE 4. *Alliance Among Brothers*

generation D, Baruch (D8). So, four out of the six brothers who were excluded from the leadership position have descendants who have married one of the following Lubavitcher Rebbes. This suggests that any animosity among these brothers that may have emerged was eventually resolved by having a descendant become the rebbe.

Haskalah. The growth of the *Haskalah* movement (the Jewish Enlightenment) in the nineteenth century affected the expansion of Chabad. Its influence was especially great during the last half of the nineteenth century. Hasidic books were subject to censorship by the governments through pressure exerted by the *Haskalah*, and rebbes were forbidden to visit their followers in their parishes for the purpose of performing miracles, giving advice or soliciting funds (Dubnow 1916 Vol II:211; Rabinowitsch 1971:125–127). Perceiving the *Haskalah* movement as a threat to Jewish tradition and identity, Chabad endeavored, by expansion, to influence as many Jews as possible (Schneersohn 1962:12–15). I suggest that the strife within the Hasidic movement and the growth of the *Haskalah* during that period acted as catalysts in the spread of the *Chabad* movement.

External Conditions. By the end of the nineteenth century, of the approximately six million Jews living in Eastern Europe, 94 per cent were confined to the Pale of Settlement (Rabinowicz 1970:156). In 1880/1881, over 160 communities in Eastern Europe suffered pogroms. Perhaps the expansionist policy of *Chabad* should also be viewed as providing a network of centers in several areas to aid not only those who remained in communities where pogroms occurred, but also those refugees who migrated from the decimated areas.

Once Lubavitch expanded, however, endogamous marriages declined from 28 per cent during generations C through E to 15 per cent during generations F through G. Table 6 provides a precise breakdown of the percentage of endogamous marriages over the five generations. The trend indicates a shift from endogamous family marriages to exogamous marriages, but endogamous within Hasidic groups generally.

Trends of Lubavitch's Kinship Alliance Network

Historical circumstances during the leadership of Shalom Dov Baer, Joseph Isaac, and Menachem Mendel (E7, F3, and G2 in Figure 2), motivated

TABLE 6
PERCENTAGES OF ENDOGAMOUS MARRIAGES

Generation	Total Marriages	Endogamous Marriages	Percent
Third Generation C	9	3	33%
Fourth Generation D	15	5	33%
Fifth Generation E	33	8	24%
Sixth Generation F	45	7	16%
Seventh Generation G	13	2	15%
Total	115	25	22%

the movement's continued expansion and influenced the trend away from kin-endogamous marriages. Under the leadership of Shalom Dov Baer (E7) (1866–1920), the fifth Lubavitcher rebbe, the first Hasidic *yeshiva*, "Tomchei Temimim," was founded in an effort to provide a more organized and effective religious education for the *Chabad* movement. He also established *yeshivot* in Georgia, Russia, and was the first Hasidic rabbi to open his branch of Hasidim to non-Ashkenazic Jews (Encyclopedia Judaica Vol. 14:1434–5). Joseph Isaac (1886–1950) (F3), the sixth Lubavitcher rebbe, set up a network of *yeshivot* all over Europe, the United States, and Canada. In 1940, he moved the center of *Chabad* to New York and established there a modern organization. A printing press and publishing society were founded for the purpose of printing newspapers, magazines, books and news about *Chabad* philosophy and history. In 1948, he founded Kfar *Chabad* in Israel as a settlement for his followers who survived the concentration camps.

Under the leadership of Menachem Mendel (G2), (1902-   ) the seventh and present rebbe of Lubavitch, *Chabad* adopted even more modern organizational techniques and succeeded in expanding to North Africa. He founded the Lubavitcher Youth Organization in 1955 and established regional offices all over the world. Under his leadership, between 1950–1974, the number of followers and sympathizers with the *Chabad* movement increased to an estimated 500,000 (Schultz 1974:34; Refael 1977:40–47; Rivkin 1978:39–41).

The expansion of Lubavitch to many different areas resulted in the spreading of the family over these areas. A geographic review of the locations of family members during this period (1882–1950), shows some family members to be in Western Europe (i.e., Paris and London), Eastern Europe (i.e., Riga, Warsaw, Moscow, and Leningrad), and in the United States. Being dispersed, the family could control resources from various sources for the survival of the group. For example, after his arrest and conviction by the Russian government for counterrevolutionary activities, Joseph Isaac was eventually released from prison in 1927 because Hasidim in America were able to elicit the sympathy of members of Congress and the Coolidge administration, who exerted international political pressure upon the Soviet government. Without the numerous centers throughout Europe and America, the news of the rebbe's arrest would most likely have had little impact on any government.

Many factors contributed to the drop in endogamous marriages. Most important, the availability of marriageable family members in Europe declined because many were murdered during the holocaust of World War II. Second, those who survived were scattered throughout the world to establish new centers.

Summary

By utilizing both genealogical and historical data in analyzing the kinship alliance network of the Lubavitch Hasidic leadership family, we have been able to understand the relationship of these alliances to broader social and historical circumstances. Genealogically, the kinship alliance network can be understood as a process in transition. The kinship network appears to be gradually moving away from endogamous marriages. The endogamous marriages that have occurred have their genealogical linkage connection to the four daughters of Dov Baer (B1 in Figure 2), in generation C. The more distant the relationship is between spouses, the more likely marriage links will be traced through the father. This indicates a weakening of the mother's important position over the generations. The position of leadership has been handed down from father to son or sons-in-law. Parallel and cross-cousin marriages kept noninheriting sisters' (and brothers') children as direct contributors to the position of rebbe and other leadership positions within the movement. These endogamous marriages lessened sibling rivalry over the power positions of *Chabad*.

Historically, the kinship alliance network contributed to having the resources remain within the control of the family. These alliances permitted the expansion and the establishment of diverse centers, kept competition among potential leaders at a minimum, and are viewed as being influenced by numerous factors ranging from internal competition, to inter-Hasidic rivalries, the growth of the *Haskalah* movement, and the pogroms of the late nineteenth century.

APPENDIX
CONSANGUINAL RELATIONSHIPS BETWEEN SPOUSES[1]

Third Generation (C)
C2 =[2] MBD (B2 B1 C1).[3] C6 = ZD (C4 C5). C8 = FBD (B3 B1 C9)

Fourth Generation (D)
D5 = BD (D3 D4). = MZD (C1 C3 D6)
D9 = MZD (C1 C4 D8), FMBSD (C2 B2 B1 C6 D8)
D11 = MMZD (C5 C3 C1 D12), FZD (C6 C4 D12)
D14 = MZD (C7 C1 D13), MFZSD (C7 B1 B2 C2 D13)
D16 = MBD (C1 C6 D17)
D16 = MZD (C1 C7 D15)

Fifth Generation (E)
E3 = FBD (D2 D3 E4). E7 = FBSD (D5 D9 E5 E6), MMZDSD (D6 C3 C4 D8 E5 E6)
E9 = FBD (D5 D9 E10), MMZDD (D6 C3 C4 D8 E10), FMZDD (D5 C1 C4 D8 E10)

A Hasidic Dynasty

E12 = FZD (D9 D13 E11), MMZSD (D8 C4 C7 D14 E11), FMZSD (D9 C1 C5 D14 E11)

E14 = FBD (D7 D16 D15), FMZDD (D7 C1 C7 D15 E15)

E16 = MZD (D8 D10 E17)

E19 = MBD (D13 D16 E20), FZD (D14 D15 E20)

E21 = FBD (D5 D16 E22), MMBDD (D6 C3 C4 D17 E22)

Sixth Generation (F)

F2 = FFZD (E2 D2 D13 F3), FFMZSD (E2 D2 C1 C7 D14 F3)

F4 = FFFMBSSD (E2 D2 C2 B2 B3 C10 E18 F5), FFMFBSSD (E2 D2 C2 B1 B3 C10 E8 F5)

F6 = MFBSD (E10 D9 D16 E23 F7), FFBSD (E9 D5 D16 E23 F7), FFMZDSD (E9 D5 C1 C7 D15 E23 F7), MFMZDSD (E10 D9 C1 C7 D15 E23 F7)

F8 = FFMZDSD (E13 D7 C1 C4 D8 E18 F9)

Seventh Generation (G)

G1 = FFFFBSSD (Fa1 F1 E1 D5 E9 F6 G2) FFFFBDSD (Fa1 F1 E1 D1 D9 E10 F6 G2)

G3 = MBSD (E8 E9 F6 F4)

G6 = FZD (F11 F10 G5)

---

1. This table includes the closest and varying ways of being related to one's spouse and not all possible ways (e.g., D5 also is related to his wife through his FMBDD (C2 B2 B1 C3 D6).
2. (= Married)
3. Specifies the direct connection according to Figure 2.

NOTES

1. I would like to thank Professors J. Robin Rox, B. Kirsenblatt-Gimblett, and H. Rosenfeld for their constructive comments on an earlier published paper (Berger 1977). I am also grateful to Mr. S. Gorr, curator of the Central Archives and Research Institute for the History of Gedolei Israel, for allowing me access to its genealogical charts.

2. For an account of Israel ben Eliezar (the Besht), the founder of Hasidism and his main disciple Dov Baer, see Mahler (1971).

3. The Hasidic rebbes were believed by their followers to be capable of performing miracles, unlike the non-Hasidic scholar-rabbis whose authority was based mainly upon scholarly attainment and had almost absolute and unchallenged authority over their followers (Dresner 1960:116–141; Mahler 1971:448–454).

4. Its mission was towards non-*Chabad* Jews only, not gentiles.

5. Elior (1979:166–186) describes the conflict over the leadership in the second generation of the movement, that between Schneur-Zalman's son, Dov Baer, and his other disciple Aaron Hurvitz, who broke away and formed his own branch of *Chabad* Hasidim.

6. Each Hasidic rebbe has the power of choosing his successor. Lubavitch, however, is almost unique in that only one leader is chosen to succeed the Lubavitcher rebbe. Almost all other Hasidic rebbes sent many of their potential leaders (especially sons) to various areas to become rebbes and *zaddikim* in

those places. Because Lubaviteh has only one rebbe at a time, the focus of the movement is centralized.

7. From the group's inception, its motto has always been the phrase from Genesis 28:14, "Thou shalt spread forth to the West, and to the East, and to the North and to the South."

8. It is important to emphasize that the rebbe, until his death, is the sole ruler and leader of the community. He has absolute spiritual power. The successor would never question or threaten the authority of his predecessor.

BIBLIOGRAPHY

Berger, R. E. 1977. An Exploration into the Lubavitch Hasidic Leadership Kinship Alliance Network. Working papers in Yiddish and East European Jewish Studies: No. 27. YIVO

Campbell, J. K. 1964. Honor, Family and Patronage: A Study of Institutions and Moral Values in a Greek Mountain Community. Oxford.

Davis. J. 1973. Land and Family in Pisiticci. London School of Economics Monograph in Social Anthropology. 48. London.

Dresner, S. 1960. The Zaddik. New York.

Dubnow, S. 1916. The History of the Jews in Russia and Poland (three volumes). Philadelphia.

Dumont, L. 1957. Hierarchy and Marriage Alliance in South Indian Kinship. London.

Elior, R. 1979. The Controversy over the Leadership in the Chabad Movement. Tarbitz: 166–186. Hebrew University of Jerusalem.

Encyclopedia Judaica. 1972. Volume 7:1390–1420. Volume 14:1434–5.

Fortes, M. 1969. Kinship and the Social Order. Chicago.

Fortes, M., and E. E. Evans-Pritchard. 1950. African Political Systems. London.

Fox, R. 1967. Kinship and Marriage. London.

Goldberg, D. 1979. Education Day, U.S.A. The Uforatzto Journal 18: 18–38.

Heilman, H. M. 1903. Bet Rabi. Berditchev.

Katz, J. 1958. Tradition and Crisis. New York.

Lande, C. B. 1973. Kinship and Politics in Pre-Modern and Non-Western Societies. Southeast Asia. The Politics of National Integration, ed. J. T. MacAlister, pp. 219–234. New York.

Mahler, R. 1971. A History of Modern Jewry 1780–1815. New York.

Mindel, N. 1947. Rabbi Joseph I. Schneersohn: The Lubavitcher Rabbi. New York.

———. 1969. Rabbi Schneur Zalman. New York.

Rabinowicz, H. 1970. The World of Hasidim. London.

Rabinowitsch, W. 1971. Lithuanian Hasidim. Chicago.

Radcliffe-Brown, A. R., and D. Forde, eds. 1950. African Systems of Kinship and Marriage. London.

Refael, Y. 1977. Operation Torah Education. Uforatzto Journal, volume 4, No. 31, 40–47.

Rivkin, M. 1978. L.Y.O. Campaign for Education. Uforatzto Journal 18:39–41.
Schneersohn, J. L. 1962. The Tzemach Tzedeck and the Haskalah Movement (Translated by Zalman Posner). New York.
Schneider, J., and P. Schneider. 1976. Culture and Political Economy in Western Sicily. New York.
Schultz, R. 1974. The Call of the Ghetto. New York Times Magazine, November 10, 1974:34, 113–129.
Weiner, H. 1969. 9½ Mystics: The Kabbalah Today. New York.
Weinryb, B. 1972. The Jews of Poland. New York.
Whitten, N., and A. Wolfe. 1973. Network Analysis, ed. J. Honigman. Handbook of Social and Cultural Anthropology, pp. 717–746. Chicago.
Witherspoon, G. 1975. Navaho Kinship and Marriage. Chicago.
Wilson, B. 1970. Religious Sects. London.
Wylie, C. 1957. Village in the Vaucluse. New York.
Zalman, S. 1967. Sefer Hatoldos, Rabbi Schneur Zalman mi-Liadi, ed. Glitzenstein. New York.

Ritual in the Operating Room
Pearl Katz
>>> <<<

RITUAL HAS BEEN DEFINED as standardized ceremonies in which expressive, symbolic, mystical, sacred, and nonrational behavior predominates over practical, technical, secular, rational, and scientific behavior (Beattie 1966; Durkheim 1961; Gluckman 1962; Goody 1961:169; Leach 1968), although anthropologists have acknowledged that rational, technical acts may occur as part of ritual behavior.

The analysis of ritual has assumed various forms. One is to investigate the meanings, types, and structures of the symbols used in rituals (e.g., Turner 1967; 1969). Another is to examine the thought processes that occur in ritual, or how the actors believe in the effectiveness of the rituals (Jarvie and Agassi 1970), how the thoughts expressed in ritual reflect their social structure (Levi-Strauss 1966), and how thought processes in ritual compare with those in science (Horton 1970). Another form of analysis of ritual focuses upon the structure and function of ritual in society. Van Gennep's (1960) pioneering work describes the ways in which rituals deal with movements of people through passages in time, place, and statuses, and distinctive phases. Gluckman (1962) shows how ritual may exaggerate the distinctions between different events enacted by the same people, and explained some means by which rituals masked conflicts by emphasizing solidarity. Douglas (1966) describes the ways in which ritual resolve anomaly by avoiding the dangers of pollution.

According to these studies of ritual, behavior in an operating room in a modern hospital would not be defined as ritual because it involves predominately technical, rational, and scientific activity. By relegating behavior in an operating room to a nonritual realm, the meanings of the symbols, movements, and thought processes they reveal are not likely to be subject to the same kinds of analyses as they would if they were termed ritual behavior. Even in Horton's (1970) provocative essay, in which he compares traditional and modern thought, traditional thought is conceived as magical, religious, and expressed in ritual; modern thought as secular, technical, and expressed in scientific activity. Although Horton emphasizes the similarities as well as the differences of these two kinds of thinking, he deliberately defines the two thinking styles as embedded in two separate and different contexts.

Recently, some anthropologists (Firth 1972; Moore and Myerhoff 1977) have acknowledged that secular ceremonies may be examined as rituals because they share the symbolic and communicative functions of rituals. In the same spirit this paper examines both ritual and science in one technical context, the hospital operating room. It describes behavior and thinking in the operating room in order to understand the functions of ritual in a scientific context. Specifically, it examines the functions and efficacy of sterility procedures.

Despite the elaborate rituals, and despite the rigorous application of advanced scientific knowledge in the operating room, infections do occur as a result of surgery. In the vast majority of cases the specific cause of these infections remains unknown (Postlethwait 1972:300). In the United States each year there are approximately two million postoperative infections, causing 79,000 deaths among surgical patients (Boyd 1976:78). This paper argues that the elaborate rituals and technical procedures of the modern hospital operating room, manifestly designed to prevent infection, better serve latent functions. Ritual actually contributes to the efficiency of a technical, goal-oriented, scientific activity, such as surgery, by permitting autonomy of action to the participants and enabling them to function in circumstances of ambiguity.

The Operating Room

In most modern hospitals the surgical area is isolated from the rest of the hospital, and the operating room is further isolated from other parts of the surgical area. The surgical area may include dressing rooms, lounges, storage rooms, offices, and laboratories as well as operating rooms. Entrance to the surgical area is restricted to those people who are properly costumed and who are familiar with the rituals within. These include surgeons, anesthesiologists, pathologists, radiologists, operating room and recovery room nurses, student doctors, nurses, and ward orderlies who work in that area.[1] The major exception to these occupational roles is that of the surgical patient who, although costumed, is unfamiliar with the rituals. All of the people in the surgery area wear costumes which identify both their general role in the hospital, as well as denoting the specific areas within the surgical area which they are permitted to enter.

Ritual in the Operating Room 281

The restrictive entrance procedures and costume requirements contribute to the maintenance of cleanliness and prevention of contamination. Identification and separation of cleanliness and dirt are the most important concepts in the operating room. They govern the organization of the activities in surgery, the spatial organization of rooms and objects, the costumes worn, as well as most of the rituals.

The surgical area of University Hospital[2] has four parts: the periphery, outer, middle, and inner areas (see Figure 1). Physical barriers separate these four areas. They function to prevent contamination from dirtier areas to cleaner ones. From outside to inside, these areas are differentiated according to increasing degrees of cleanliness. The periphery, the least

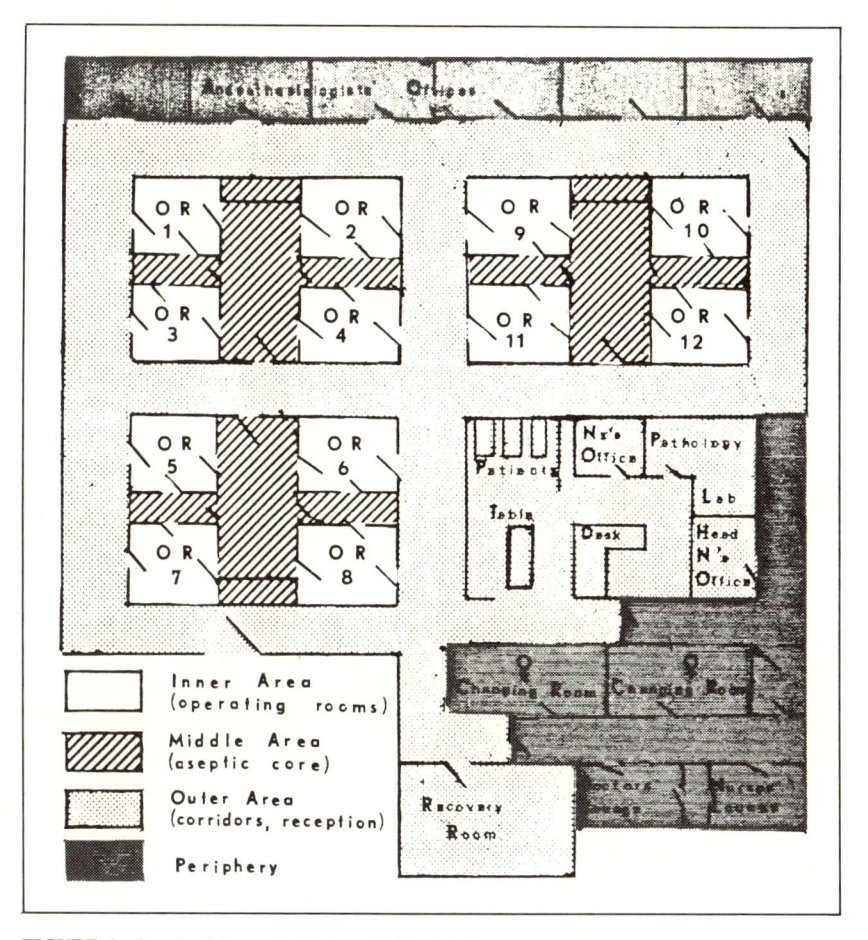

FIGURE 1. *Surgical Areas in University Hospital*

clean area, includes the offices of the anesthesiologists, a small pathology laboratory for quick analyses of specimens, dressing rooms for men and women, and lounges for nurses and doctors. To enter the periphery area a person must wear a white jacket for identification as a member of the medical staff.

The outer area is separated from the periphery by a sliding door. Within the outer area, a nurse at the main desk can prevent the door from opening if an unauthorized person tries to enter. Entrance to the outer area is restricted to patients and to those medical personnel who wear blue or green costumes. The largest and most populated part of the outer area consists of an open corridor in which the daily operating schedule is posted and a blackboard indicating the current use of operating rooms. Patients awaiting surgery lie in narrow beds lined in a single row along one wall of the open corridor. A nurse, in charge of coordinating the timing and activities in each operating room, sits at an exposed desk in the outer area. She is in continual intercom communication with each operating room. The outer area also contains a large recovery room which houses patients immediately after their surgery is completed.

The middle area consists of three separate areas called "aseptic cores." Each aseptic core contains five doors. One of them links the outer area to the aseptic core. Each of the other four doors leads to an operating room. Each aseptic core contains a long sink, three sterilizing machines (autoclaves), and many carts and shelves containing surgical equipment, sheets, and towels. In order to enter an aseptic core, a person must wear a mask which covers the mouth and nose, coverings for shoes and for hair, and a blue or green outfit.

The innermost area contains the operating rooms and small laundry rooms. In each aseptic core there are four operating rooms and two laundry rooms. Each operating room contains three doors. One door adjoins the outer area and is used exclusively for the patient to enter and leave the operating room. A door with a small glass window connects the aseptic core to the operating room. This is used by the operating room staff. The third door leads to the laundry room which serves as a depository for contaminated clothing and instruments.

Preoperative Rituals

One of the more important operating room rituals, scrubbing, takes place in the aseptic core before each operation begins. It is a procedure by which selected personnel wash their hands and lower arms according to rigidly prescribed timing and movements. The purpose of scrubbing is to remove as many bacteria as possible from the fingers, nails, hands, and

Ritual in the Operating Room

arms to the elbows. The people who scrub are those who actually carry out, or directly assist in, the surgery; not everyone in the operating room scrubs. The surgeon, assistant surgeon(s), and the scrub nurse, participate in the scrubbing ritual. Medical students and other surgical assistants consider it an honor if they are asked to scrub with a surgeon.

Before a person begins scrubbing he checks the clock in order to time the seven-minute procedure. He turns on the water by pushing a button with his hip, and reaches for a package which contains a nail file, a brush and sponge which is saturated with an antiseptic solution. For two minutes he cleans under each of his nails with the nail file. For two-and-a-half minutes, he scrubs his fingers, hands and arms to his elbows, intermittently wetting the sponge and brush with running water. Using a circular motion he scrubs all of the surfaces of his fingers on one hand, his hand, and, finally, his arm to the elbow. After rinsing that arm thoroughly under running water, he repeats the procedure for two-and-a-half minutes on his second hand. After having scrubbed for seven minutes, he discards the sponge, brush, file, and paper, and turns off the tap water by pressing a button on the sink with his hip.

After scrubbing, the surgeon and his assistant(s) enter the operating room by pushing the door with their hips. They hold their lower arms and hands in an upright position, away from the rest of their bodies. They are forbidden to allow their scrubbed hands and arms to come into contact with any object or person. The scrub nurse hands them a sterile towel to dry their hands. They dry each finger separately, and throw the towel into a container on the floor. The scrub nurse holds the outside, sterile part of a green gown for the surgeon and his assistant(s) to wear. They insert their hands through the sleeves, without allowing their hands to touch the outside of the gown. At this point, their hands, although scrubbed and clean, are not sterile. But the outside of the gown is sterile. After their arms pass through the sleeves, the scrub nurse holds their sterile gloves in place with the open side facing their hands. The surgeon, followed by his assistant, thrusts one hand at a time into each glove. They accomplish this in one quick movement, in which a hand is brought down from its upward position, thrust forward inside the glove and snapped in place over the sleeve. When only one glove is on, the surgeon is not permitted to adjust it with the other hand. However, when the second glove is on, he can adjust his glove and the sleeve of his gown and any other part of the front of the gown.

At this stage, the gown is not completely fastened. In order to fasten his gown, the surgeon unties a tie of his gown at waist level. Although this tie had been sterile, he hands it to the circulating nurse, who has not scrubbed. The circulating nurse brings the tie to the back of his gown.

The back is a nonsterile area of the gown. The surgeon helps her reach the back by a making a 360° turn, while she holds the tie. The circulating nurse secures this and two more ties to the back of the gown.

Principles of Sterility and Contamination

The rituals of scrubbing, gowning, and gloving suggest some basic principles underlying most of the rituals in the operating room.

1. In the operating room, objects, or parts of objects and people, are classified either as sterile or nonsterile (S = sterile; NS = nonsterile):

    a. Nonsterile objects are further classified as clean, dirty, or contaminated.

    b. No part of the circulating nurse or the anesthesiologist is sterile.

    c. Parts of the surgeon and the scrub nurse are sterile.

2. To remain sterile, sterile objects may only come into contact with other objects that are sterile (c = contact; > = remains, becomes, or is transformed into; therefore, S c S > S).

3. To remain sterile, sterile objects may not come into contact with anything that is not sterile (~ = not, therefore, S c NS > S).

4. Nonsterile objects may come into contact with other nonsterile objects, and both remain nonsterile (NS c NS > NS).

5. Sterile objects may be transformed into nonsterile by contact with objects which are nonsterile. This process is called contamination (S c NS > NS).

6. Contaminated objects can only be restored to sterility by either placing them in an autoclave for a specified period of time, or, in the case of a person's clothes, by discarding the contaminated clothes and replacing them with sterile clothes. If gloves become contaminated, re-scrubbing for three minutes is required before replacing the gloves and the gown.

Before the operation begins, most sterile objects are either symbolized by the color green, or are in contact with an object colored green. Sterile instruments, for example, are placed upon a green towel which lies on a nonsterile tray. Although the green towel has been sterilized, it becomes contaminated at the bottom through contact with the nonsterile tray (S c NS > NS). The towel remains sterile at the top, however, and the sterile instruments lying on the top remain sterile (S c S > S).

The surgeon, his assistant(s), and the scrub nurse wear sterile gloves and a green or blue gown which is sterile in the front from the waist to the armpits. However, the gown is not sterile in the back nor above the armpits and below the waist in the front. That is why the surgeon unties the tie at the sterile side of his gown with his sterile gloves, and the circulating (nonsterile) nurse holds the tie without touching the surgeon's (sterile) gloves, and brings the tie toward the (nonsterile) back of the surgeon's gown. The sterile tie becomes contaminated when the circulating nurse's hand touches it. It remains contaminated because it is tied in the back of the surgeon's gown.

The potentials for manipulating the overhead light in the center of the operating room illustrate some principles of sterility and contamination. Before the operation begins, the scrub nurse places a sterile handle on the huge, movable, overhead light. This permits the light to be adjusted by the surgeon, his assistant(s), and the scrub nurse through contact with the sterile handle (S c S > S). The circulating nurse and anesthesiologist, however, are also able to manipulate the light by touching the nonsterile frame of the light (NS c NS > NS).

In order for a person to move to the other side of the person next to him, as the scrubbed members of the operating team stand next to the patient's table, a ritual must be enacted. The person making the move turns 360° in the direction of his move, allowing his back to face the back of his neighbor. This movement prevents his sterile front from coming into contact with his neighbor's nonsterile back (S ~ c NS > S). Instead, his nonsterile back only comes into contact with his neighbor's nonsterile back (NS c NS > NS).

Before the operation begins each member of the operating team is busily engaged in activities that are essentially similar for each operation. The surgeon and his assistant(s) gown and glove and check last-minute details about the forthcoming operation. The anesthesiologist checks his tools, his gas supply, and his respirator. He also prepares the instruments for monitoring the patient's vital functions, and prepares the patient for receiving anesthesia. In the outer area, a nurse checks to insure that the patient is properly identified and his operative site is verified. She independently checks the preoperative instructions written by the surgeon with the administrative order written when the surgery was booked, and asks the surgeon to identify the proposed operation and the precise site of the operation. Finally, she asks the patient to identify his name and the site of the operation.

Within the operating room, the words "clean," "dirty," "sterile," and "contaminated" assume different meanings according to different stages of the operation. Before the operation begins, the operating room is considered to be clean. Dirty objects have been removed or cleaned. Instruments and clothes which have been contaminated by the previous operation have been removed. Floors, walls, permanent fixtures, and furniture have been cleaned with antiseptic solution. The air in the operating room is continually cleaned during, and between, operations by a filter system.

Fields of sterility and cleanliness within the operating room are mapped out. Everyone in the operating room, with the exception of the patient, is knowledgeable about these fields. Some of the fields, such as that surrounding the patient, are invisible. Other fields are distinguished by the use of sterile paper sheets colored green. The sheets provide only a minimal material barrier against airborne bacteria yet serve as a symbolic shield separating fields of sterility and nonsterility. They are also used to isolate the operative area of the body from the rest of the patient's body. The sheets cover the entire body of the patient leaving a small opening for the operative area, or separate the head end of the patient from the rest of his body. The head end is considered nonsterile and is accessible to the anesthesiologist and his equipment, which are also nonsterile.

After the patient is rendered unconscious by the anesthesiologist, the scrub nurse applies an orange-brown antiseptic solution (Providine) onto the patient's skin. She pours the Providine liberally onto the skin, and distributes it with circular movements radiating outward from the center of the operative site. This action is repeated at least once, using a sterile sponge on a long holder which is discarded and replaced with each action. The sterile sponges become contaminated through contact with the patient's nonsterile skin (S c NS > NS). This action, which transforms the sterile sponge into a contaminated sponge, also transforms the dirty body area of the patient into a clean area. When this act is completed, sterile green paper towels are placed on the patient's body, exposing only his aseptic, painted, operative site.

Before the operation begins both nurses lay out and count all the sterile instruments and sponges that are likely to be used. The circulating nurse obtains articles from their nonsterile storage place. When the outside of sealed packages is nonsterile and contains sterile objects inside, the circulating nurse holds the outside of the package. She either thrusts the objects onto a green sterile towel, or asks the scrub nurse to grasp the sterile object by reaching down into the package and lifting the object upwards, with a straight, quick movement. These procedures are followed for each sterile needle, thread, or vial that is wrapped in a nonsterile wrapping in order to prevent contamination of sterile parts by the nonsterile parts of the same package. The two nurses also simultaneously count items that are laid out for use during surgery. The circulating nurse records the amounts of each item that are counted. Each item must be accounted for before the operation is completed, and the last count must concur with the total of the previous counts.

Different operations are classified according to the degree of sterility and contamination likely to be present. At University Hospital there are four categories of operations classified according to decreasing sterility: (1) clean; (2) clean contaminated; (3) contaminated; and (4) dirty. Eye operations, for example, are clean. Most gall bladder operations are clean contaminated. Duodenal operations are contaminated. Colonic operations are dirty. Intestinal operations are considered dirtier than many other operations because the contents of the intestines are highly contaminated with bacteria, requiring additional measurements for vigilance against contamination during the operation. Ritual during most operations is concerned with avoidance of contamination of the patient from the outside. Ritual in operations which are classified as contaminated or dirty are concerned, in addition, with contamination of the patient and the medical staff from inside the patient.

After the completion of dirty operations, the medical staff is required to discard all their outside garments before leaving the operating room. Since the unscrubbed members of the operating team wear only one set of clothing, before the operation they don an additional white, clean, nonsterile gown over their green or blue costume. After the operation is completed they discard the gown.

The Operation

Although extensive variation exists among types of operations, as well as variations among the medical conditions of patients, there is, nevertheless, considerable similarity in the structure of all operations. Operations contain three distinct stages. Specific rituals are performed during these stages. Stage One consists of the incision, or opening. Stage Two consists of the excision and repair. Stage Three consists of the closure.[3]

The operation begins after the anesthetized patient is draped, all sterilized instruments are counted and placed in orderly rows upon trays, and the nurses and doctors, wearing their appropriate costumes, are standing in their specified places. The anesthesiologist stands behind the green curtain at the head of the patient, outside of the sterile field. The surgeon stands next to the operative site, on one side of the patient. His assistant usually stands on the opposite side of the patient from that of the surgeon. The scrub nurse stands next to the surgeon, with the pole of an instrument tray between them. The instrument tray is suspended over the patient's body. The circulating nurse stands outside of the sterile field, near the outer part of the operating room.

Silence and tension prevail as the first stage of the operation begins. With a sterile scalpel, the surgeon makes the first incision through the layers of the patient's skin, then discards the scalpel in a sterile basin. He has transformed both the scalpel and the basin from sterile to nonsterile. The transformation takes place because the sterile scalpel touches the patient's nonsterile skin. (The patient's skin, although cleaned with an antiseptic, is not sterile.) The scalpel, which has become nonsterile (S c NS > NS), touches the sterile basin and contaminates the basin (NS c S > NS). The surgeon uses another sterile scalpel to cut through the remaining layers of fat, fascia, muscle, and, in an abdominal operation, the peritoneum. The same scalpel may be used for all the layers underlying the skin because, unlike the contaminated skin, these layers are considered to be sterile.

As the surgeon cuts, he or his assistant cauterizes or ties the severed blood vessels. The patient's blood is considered sterile once the operation has begun. Before the operation, however, the patient's blood is considered to be nonsterile. This was illustrated graphically at University Hospital before a particular emergency operation in which a patient was bleeding externally from an internal hemorrhage. The nurses complained about "the man who is dirtying our clean room!" However, once the operation on this man began, his blood was considered sterile. Sterile instruments which touched his blood during the operation remained sterile (S c S > S) until contaminated by touching something nonsterile.

The rituals enacted during the first stage of the operation involve the transformation of objects defined as sterile and nonsterile, at the same time that the appropriate instruments are made accessible and are being used to make the incisions. The beginning of the first stage, in which the first incision is made, introduces new definitions of sterile and nonsterile. For example, the patient's blood and internal organs, which had been considered nonsterile before the operation, are considered sterile once the operation begins. (The surgeon's blood, however, remains nonsterile.) The patient's skin, although cleansed with antiseptic before the operation, becomes nonsterile once the operation begins and the incision is made (see Figure 2). The rituals also enforce the segregation of sterile and nonsterile objects while the initial incisions are being made. The surgeon typically utters terse commands, usually stating the specific names of the instrument he needs. The scrub nurse immediately places the requested instrument securely in the palm of the surgeon's hand. If the instrument remains clean, the surgeon returns it to the scrub nurse and the scrub nurse places it upon the sterile tray. If it becomes contaminated, as occurs to the skin scalpel after the first incision, the surgeon places it into a container which could only be handled by the circulating nurse.

As the technical tasks become routinized during the first stage of the operation, joking begins. Most of the joking at this stage revolves around

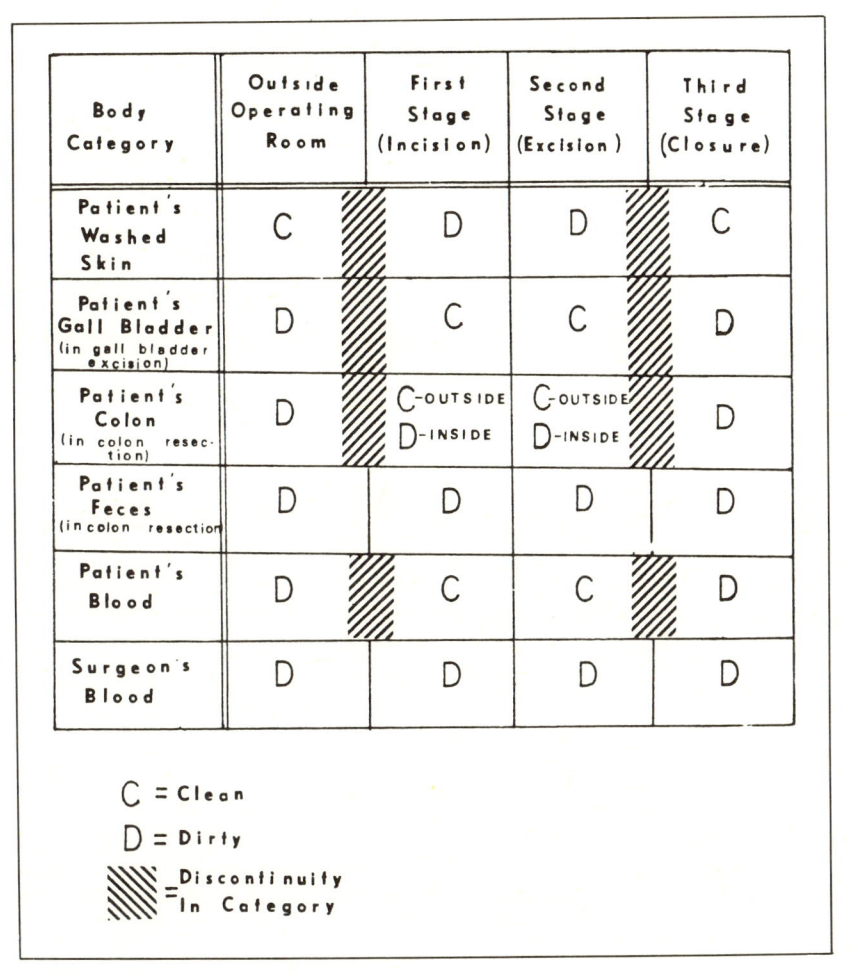

Body Category	Outside Operating Room	First Stage (Incision)	Second Stage (Excision)	Third Stage (Closure)
Patient's Washed Skin	C	D	D	C
Patient's Gall Bladder (in gall bladder excision)	D	C	C	D
Patient's Colon (in colon resection)	D	C-OUTSIDE D-INSIDE	C-OUTSIDE D-INSIDE	D
Patient's Feces (in colon resection)	D	D	D	D
Patient's Blood	D	C	C	D
Surgeon's Blood	D	D	D	D

C = Clean
D = Dirty
▨ = Discontinuity In Category

FIGURE 2. *Discontinuity Of Body Categories During Different Operative Stages And Outside The Operating Room*

the operative procedures which are to be carried out during the next stage: "I can't wait to get my hands on your gallbladder, Mr. Smith." "Okay sports fans, we're going to have some action." The first stage of the operation ends when the first incision has been completed and the organs are exposed. The joking abruptly ends just as the second stage of the operation is about to begin.

The second stage of the operation consists either of repair, implantation or the isolation and excision of the organ, and the anastomosis. (An anastomosis is the connection of two parts of the body which are not normally connected.) This stage contains the greatest amount of tension of the entire operation, and adherence to ritual is strictly enforced. It begins with the identification and isolation of structures surrounding the organ to be excised. The surgeon identifies vessels, nerves, ducts, and connective tissues, carefully pulling them aside, and preserving, clamping, severing, or tying them. The surgeon utters abrupt, abbreviated commands for instruments to be passed by the scrub nurse, structures to be cut by the assistant(s), basins and materials to be readied by the circulating nurse, and the operating table to be adjusted by the anesthesiologist. These people respond to the surgeon's commands quickly, quietly, and efficiently. A delayed, or an incorrect, response may be met with noticeable disapproval from the others.

During the second stage of the operation many of the classifications of sterility differ from those of the first stage. In a cholecystectomy (gallbladder removal), for example, the gallbladder is considered to be nonsterile before the operation begins. Yet during the first and second stages the gallbladder is considered to be sterile, before it is severed. Once it is severed, however, although it is considered to be clean, it transforms to nonsterile (see Figure 2). It is placed in a sterile container, but the container becomes contaminated by its contact with the nonsterile gallbladder (S c NS > NS). Because it is nonsterile after it has been removed, it can only be handled by a nonsterile person such as the circulating nurse. But, since the gallbladder is clean and must be examined, it must not be further contaminated from sources outside of the patient. To prevent further contamination, the circulating nurse wears a sterile glove over her nonsterile hand to examine the gallbladder and its contents. The gallbladder is not sterile, but it is not grossly contaminated. It is clean, but nonsterile. It is avoided by the sterile members of the team, yet only touched by the nonsterile members if they wear sterile gloves. The ritual surrounding its removal and examination is complex, and the removed organ is avoided by most members of the operating team because its classification is ambiguous.

Once the gallbladder has been removed, x-rays of its ducts (which remain inside the patient) are taken to determine if gallstones remain. A masked, gowned, and lead-shielded radiologist enters the operating room with a large x-ray machine that is draped with green sterile sheets. The surgeon injects a radio-opaque dye into the ducts, and everyone, except the radiologist, leaves the room to avoid the invisible x-rays. When the x-rays have been taken, the radiologist and the machine exit, the staff enter, and the operation proceeds.

Although unexpected events may occur at any stage of the operation, they are more likely to occur at the second stage because this stage contains the greatest trauma to the patient's body. If a sudden hemorrhage or a cardiac arrest occurs, the rituals segregating sterile from nonsterile may be held in abeyance, and new rituals designed to control the unanticipated event take over. If, for example, hemorrhaging occurs, all efforts are dedicated to locating and stopping the source of hemorrhage and replacing the blood that is lost. Even though immediate replacement of blood is required, rituals are enacted which delay the replacement, yet ensure accurate matching. The anesthesiologist and the circulating nurse independently check, recheck, record, and announce the blood type, the number and date of the blood bank supply, and the operating room request. They glue stickers onto the patient's record and onto the blood bank record. This complex ritual involves repetition, separation, and matching records before the blood is transfused into the hemorrhaging patient.

If a patient's heart ceases beating, a prescribed ritual is enacted by a cardiac-arrest team, whose members enter the operating room with a mobile cart, and enact prescribed procedures to resuscitate the patient. Considerations of preserving the separation of sterility and nonsterility (including most of the rituals previously described) are ignored while this emergency ritual is enacted.

Tension remains high throughout the second stage of the operation. There is virtually no joking or small talk. As the remaining internal structures are repaired and restored in place, some of the tension is lifted, and the routinization of rituals continues. The second stage of the operation ends when all the adjustments to the internal organs are finished and only the suturing of the protective layers for the third stage remains.

The third stage of the operation begins with the final counting of the materials used in surgery. Both nurses engage in this ritual of counting. They simultaneously orally count all the remaining materials, including tools, needles, and sponges. The circulating nurse checks the oral count with her written tally of materials recorded at the beginning of the operation. When the circulating nurse has accounted for each item, she informs the surgeon that he may begin the closing.

The rituals enacted during this stage of the operation are similar to those enacted during the first stage. The surgeon, or his assistant(s), request specific needles and sutures from the nurses. They sew the patient closed, layer by layer, beginning with the inside layer. Although careful suturing is an essential part of the operation, this stage is enacted in a comparatively casual manner. There is considerably less tension than there was during the second stage, and greater toleration for deviations from the rituals. Questions about the procedures are acknowledged and answered. Minor mistakes may be overlooked. If the surgeon touched his nonsterile mask with his sterile glove during this part of the operation, he would be less likely to reglove and regown than he would if the same incident had occurred during the second stage.

The silence of the second stage is replaced in the third stage by considerable talking, including jokes and small talk. Most of the joking revolves around events which occurred during the second stage and references are made to actual or potential danger during this stage. "I thought he'd never stop bleeding." "You almost choperated [sic] his spleen by mistake." "Well, I hope he has good term life insurance." Much of the small talk revolves around future activities of the medical staff. The subject of small talk rarely relates to the patient. It may involve the next operation, lunch plans, or sports results.

When the closure has been completed, the surgeon signals to the anesthesiologist to waken the patient. The staff members finish recording information, transport the patient to the recovery room, and prepare for the next case. The operation is finished.

Discontinuity and Operating Room Rituals

The observed rituals help to establish the operating room as a separate place, discontinuous from its surroundings. They also help to establish and define categories of appropriate and inappropriate behavior. This includes indicating behavior categories and their limits.

The rituals in the operating room and the meaning of many of the words used there are exclusive to that setting. The observed rituals express beliefs and values which are exclusive to the operating room. The use of the words "clean," "dirty," "contaminated" in the operating room do not correspond to their use elsewhere. This indicates the existence of discontinuity between the operating room and the outside. Discontinuity between the operating room and the outside is also reflected in the restricted entrances, the specific costumes required for entrance, the special language used, the classification and segregation of objects into sterile and nonsterile, and the dispassionate emotional reactions to parts of the human body. A person can be prohibited from entering the operating room if he were not properly dressed, if he transgressed the rules for segregating sterile from nonsterile, and he did not behave in a dispassionate manner upon viewing or touching parts of the body.

The boundaries which separate the operating room from the outside contribute to a particular mental set for the participants, which enable them to participate in a dispassionate manner in activities they would ordinarily view with strong emotion. For example, in the operating room,

Ritual in the Operating Room

they look dispassionately upon, and touch internal organs and their secretions, blood, pus, and feces. Outside of the operating room context, these same objects provoke emotions of embarrassment, fear, fascination, and disgust in the same persons. Discontinuity was illustrated during a movie shown to the surgeons outside of the surgical area of the hospital. The film illustrated different techniques for draining and lancing pus-filled abcesses. The reactions observed for the surgeons watching this movie were unlike any reactions observed for the same surgeons while they drained abcesses in the operating room. They uttered comments and noises indicating their disgust. They looked away from the screen. Outside of the context of the operating room, with its rituals and its isolation, the same events are experienced differently. In the operating room a purulent lesion is mentally linked to the rituals that are enacted during the act of lancing. The image of the lesion is embedded in the entire operating room context, including the ritual prescriptions for managing that lesion and for organizing the behavior of others in the room. In contrast, outside of the operating room, the image of the lesion is embedded in images of everyday life. In that context, the reaction to the lesion is one of disgust. Outside of the operating room there are no rituals to diffuse their concentration. Moreover, sitting in a darkened room, watching a movie, the viewers are forced to focus on the picture of the lesion. The only opportunity they have to diffuse their focus is to look away, or to make noises indicating their disgust. The operating room, with its focus upon precise rituals, permits diffusion of emotions and encourages discontinuity from everyday life.

The different stages of an operation express discontinuity of mental sets. For example, blood, internal organs, feces, and skin are classified differently during different stages of the operation, and some are different outside of the operating room. Figure 2 illustrates the transformations of the categories "clean" and "dirty" for parts of the body during different stages of the operation. For each of the parts of the body—the patient's washed skin, gallbladder, colon, feces, blood, and the surgeon's blood— the greatest transformations of dirty and clean categories occur before the first stage of the operation (the incision), and between the second and third stage (the excision and closure). For example, the patient's blood is considered to be dirty outside of the operating room, yet it is considered to be clean during the first and second stages of the operation. But during the third stage, blood is again classified as dirty. Similarly, the patient's skin, after having been thoroughly cleaned with antiseptic, is considered extremely clean outside of the operating room. However, once the operation begins, the patient's skin is classified as "dirty." It remains dirty for the first and second stages of the operation. Once closure takes place, during the third stage, the patient's skin is transformed again to "clean."

Rituals exaggerate the discontinuity in the operating room and they proclaim definite categories. An instrument is either sterile or nonsterile; it is never almost sterile or mostly sterile. A person is either scrubbed, gowned, and gloved, and, therefore, sterile, or he is not scrubbed, gowned, or gloved, and, therefore, not sterile. An operation is either in Stage One, Two, or Three, or it has not yet begun, or it has ended. It is never partially begun, nor incompletely ended.

Rituals in the operating room are prescribed for four different kinds of situations: (1) passing through the three stages of surgery, (2) managing unanticipated events, such as cardiac arrest or sudden hemorrhaging, (3) matching information, such as blood types, operative sites or instrument counts, and (4) separating sterile from nonsterile objects. In each of these situations there exists a potential confusion about the appropriate classification of events. There is danger that objects and events can be confused or indistinct or that there is danger of contact of forbidden categories: blood may not be properly matched; the wrong operative site may be selected; an instrument may remain in the patient's body; objects or events may not match or fit; or sterile objects may touch nonsterile ones. For those situations in which behavior categories are not clear, rituals clarify. In a recent textbook for operating room nurses, more than one hundred prescriptions for precise behavior are spelled out in which confusion existed about definitions of categories (Berry and Kohn 1972). At University Hospital, the head operating room nurse claimed that the rituals performed in the operating room "were introduced in response to actual mistakes, problems, conflicts that we had, when how to behave was not clearly spelled out." Rituals in the operating room not only indicate the categories which are potentially confusing, they also indicate the boundaries, or limits, for these categories. Through the use of rituals it is clear to all the participants when Stage One ends and Stage Two begins. It is clear to them which part of the surgeon's body is sterile (between the armpits and waist in front) and which part is not sterile (the remainder). Rituals, then, make salient, and even exaggerate, the boundaries of categories.

Rituals in the operating room have much in common with rituals in other contexts, sacred or secular. Rituals are enacted during periods of transition. In the operating room they are enacted during transitions of events or classifications of objects. Danger is perceived during these periods of transitions. Indeed, Van Gennup (1960) emphasizes the dangers which lie in transitional states because the classification of neither state is clear. When states are not clearly defined, ritual controls the danger. Similarly Douglas (1966) claims that pollution behavior takes place when categories are confused, or when accepted categories are not adhered to, as in anomaly.

Beyond the operating room, rituals also indicate categories and limits or boundaries for these categories. These include rituals which define passages—of time, seasons, stages of life, or passages through different lands—as well as rituals of pollution. Rituals proclaim that something is in one category and not in another. One is an adult, not a child. It is the rainy season, not the dry season. We are in the new land, not the old land. I belong to this kinship group now, not that group. Even the middle, liminal, stage of ritual, which Turner (1969) describes as a kind of limbo, has limits. Although the middle state is neither incorporated into the first stage, nor reintegrated into the last stage, its boundaries are clearly recognized and known to all the participants.

In all societies rituals take place when categories are not clearly defined and when limits of categories are not known. Gluckman (1962) suggests, for example, that primitive societies have more rituals than modern societies because different roles are enacted with the same people in primitive societies. This may be understood as exaggerating the boundaries or limits of each of their roles, precisely because they are unclear. Indeed, ritual is found in modern secular society in those situations in which boundaries are unclear, not only during changes of status, such as marriages and deaths, but also in situations such as entering or leaving a house, installing a political officer, and beginning a team sport.

The operating room observations suggest that through its elaborate, stylized behavioral prescriptions, and obsession with detail, ritual exaggerates the boundaries between categories. Rituals create boundaries because boundaries have been transgressed or are unclear. When boundaries are not precisely defined, confusion may result about which category is operative at a particular time or place. The actors do not know to which situation to respond. Knowing the limits or boundaries gives shape and definition to the categories. Ritual by defining categories and prescribing specific behavior within these categories, creates boundaries. Moreover, when the boundaries are known, autonomy to function can increase (Katz 1968).

Autonomy and Ritual

At first glance, it seems improbable that ritual, with its emphasis upon specific detailed prescriptions for behavior, may provide autonomy for its participants. To be sure, it is known that ritual exaggerates and often provides license for behavior which may be prohibited in everyday life

(Gluckman 1962). Studies by Katz (1968, 1974, 1976) suggest that autonomy increases when the limits of the system are known and implemented. On this basis one will expect that ritual, by indicating and clarifying boundaries of behavior categories—such as sterile/nonsterile or child/adult—increase the autonomy of the participants. Conversely, when the rituals have not been fully carried out—when a person is not clearly within the prescribed limits—there will be very little autonomy.

For example, when the surgeon enters the operating room after he has scrubbed, but before he has gowned and gloved, he is helpless. He has virtually no autonomy. His scrubbed, clean hands are not clearly classified as sterile, nor as contaminated (although strictly speaking, they are nonsterile). He has to exercise extreme caution lest his hands touch anything. If he touches a sterile object, that object becomes contaminated. If he touches a contaminated object, his hands become further contaminated, and he is required to rescrub. He is so helpless that he can do almost nothing. His hands are raised in a helpless position. He depends upon a nurse to give him a towel and to provide him with a gown and gloves. He is not able to put the gown on himself, nor to tie his gown once it is on. Even when he is gowned, he has no autonomy to touch anything. He cannot pull the sleeve of the gown from his hands. The nurse has to put his gloves on his hands for him. His classification of sterility is confusing because, being half sterile and half nonsterile, he does not clearly fit in either category. His autonomy is severely restricted. The autonomy of others interacting with him is also reduced. Only after he has completely scrubbed, gowned, and gloved, and become unequivocally sterile, does he attain his autonomy. He can move about within the sterile field and touch all sterile objects.

In the operating room, boundaries of categories are likely to become confused if a person is present who does not know the appropriate rituals. When this occurs, autonomy decreases, both for the uninitiated person, and for others who interact with him. On one occasion during surgery in University Hospital, the circulating nurse requested a scrubbed medical student to remove a sterile needle from the nonsterile wrapping which she held in her hand. Although the student knew that the wrapping was nonsterile and the needle was sterile, and he was familiar with many rituals, he did not know the precise ritual required for removing the needle. The ritual required him to grasp the needle between his forefinger and thumb, quickly thrust his fingers upwards, and place the needle upon the sterile tray. The circulating nurse was required to pull downward on the wrapping, discard the wrapping in a contaminated bag, and record the addition of that needle. Neither person had autonomy to deviate from this behavior.

The student succeeded in contaminating his glove and the needle by touching both with the nonsterile wrapping. A great deal of autonomy was lost through his failure to follow the prescribed ritual. The student had to reglove and regown. The circulating nurse had to aid him in regloving and regowning. The needle had to be discarded. Since the needle had contaminated the sterile green towel on the tray, the towel had to be replaced, the sterile contents of the tray removed from the contaminated towel and replaced on the sterile towel. In addition, the circulating nurse had mistakenly recorded the addition of that needle, and, near the end of the operation, it appeared that a needle was missing. All the people present searched for the needle, both inside and outside the patient. This activity delayed the completion of the operation until the circulating nurse realized the source of the mismatching. In this case, the autonomy of most of the staff was restricted because one person did not follow the ritual properly.

The surgical patient who is awake can reduce the autonomy of the operating team. The conscious patient has autonomy to express his fears and concerns about the operation. Most members of the medical staff in the operating room regard the waking patient as a hindrance to the smooth performance of preoperative rituals. The waking patient may restrict discussions which are necessary for planning the strategy of the operation. Rendering the patient unconscious deprives the patient of all autonomy, while increasing the autonomy of the staff. The staff gains the autonomy to ignore the patient's psyche, to consider only the parts of his body relevant to the operative procedure, to joke about the patient and his expressions of fear, and to discuss subjects that have nothing to do with the operation. Although the patient loses autonomy, the staff gains autonomy.

It is well known to most laymen that irreverent behavior in the form of jokes and small talk occur in the operating room. Jokes and small talk in the operating room represent autonomous behavior par excellence. They are autonomous because they are not a prescribed part of the operative procedure. They often express values which are antithetical to the serious and dangerous nature of the operation itself. Jokes differ from small talk in that jokes explicitly focus on events of surgery (whether real or imagined), whereas small talk revolves around events unrelated to surgery. Both jokes and small talk trivialize the solemnity, significance, discipline, and danger that typically accompany surgery. Although the precise content of jokes and small talk in the operating room is unpredictable, their timing is. They are not expressed while transitions take place—when stages are crossed, transformations from sterile to nonsterile occur, or when mismatching or emergencies occur. During transitions, danger is often perceived to be present. All attention becomes focused on the rituals which are enacted to restore the boundaries. Jokes and small talk are expressed during those periods in which categories—of stages, sterility, or matching—are clearly defined. They occur when ritual succeeds in restoring and bounding these categories, and activities are routinized. Once the boundaries have been restored by ritual, autonomy flourishes. When the rituals are enacted routinely, the boundaries are defined and autonomy increased.

Jokes and small talk do not occur during periods of transition, when danger is present, although they express concern about these periods. Jokes are not expressed during the times that autonomy is most severely restricted, such as during the transitions. Autonomous behavior of joking and small talk occur after the transitions pass, after the tension subsides, after the rituals have been enacted in their carefully prescribed manner.

Most of the jokes focus on events which occur during transitional or dangerous periods. Jokes about organs to be severed do not occur during the dangerous period while the organ is being severed. Jokes about the incision do not occur while the incision is being made. Jokes about the incision only occur before or after the incision is made. When jokes touched on dangerous or transitional situations, they did so only after rituals had clearly indicated that the situation was over. Only then did the surgical staff make irreverent jokes about the most dangerous and vulnerable aspects of the operation. They made jokes in the crudest terms about internal organs, external appearances, sexual organs, the personaiity of the patient, or other members or the operating team. But they did not joke about the rituals themselves. The operating room staff treated the rituals with reverence and less questioning than other surgical activities.

Many anthropologists have tried to understand the simultaneous presence of both controlling and autonomous aspects of ritual. Van Gennup (1960), and later, Firth (1972:3) emphasized the controlling and regulating function of ritual. Munn (1969) describes how ritual myths function as social control mechanisms by regulating states and bodily feelings. Turner (1969) describes the presence of elaborate autonomous improvisation within highly structured ritual. Leach (1968:526) suggests that stylization in secular ritual may be either "escetic, representing the intensification of formal restraint, or ecstatic, signifying the elimination of restraint." Gluckman (1970) describes license in ritual as reversals that express behavior outlawed in everyday life. Gluckman (1970:125) also recognizes that license is only permitted in ritual when the limits are known and agreed upon by the participants: "The acceptance of the established order as right and good, and even sacred, seems to allow unbridled license, very rituals of rebellion, for the order itself keeps this rebellion within bounds."

The rituals in the operating room, as well as those described by Gluckman, Leach, and Turner, suggest that the boundaries of behavior are not open to questioning. They are firm. However, within those boundaries there is a great deal of autonomy. In the operating room, the rituals themselves, as signposts indicating boundaries, are not open to question, nor to ridicule. However, within the boundaries considerable autonomy exists. There is autonomy to joke about everything, except the rituals. There is autonomy to question details about the rituals (e.g., how long to scrub), but virtually no autonomy to question the ritual itself (e.g., whether scrubbing was necessary).

Conclusion

In modern operating rooms rituals, as stylized, arbitrary, repetitive, and exaggerated forms of behavior, occur as integral parts of surgical procedures. Most of the rituals in the operating room symbolize separation of areas containing micro-organisms from areas free of micro-organisms, or separation of realms of cleanliness (sterility, asepsis) from realms of pollution (nonsterility, sepsis, contamination).

Most rituals considered by anthropologists, especially those in sacred settings, express and communicate values, and are linked to institutions of everyday life. Such rituals are not amenable to serious questioning of their major premises. It is different, however, with rituals in the hospital operating room. That setting is discontinuous with everyday life, and rituals there have no continuity with values or categories of thought outside of the medical setting. Inspection and introspection of their premises should be examined, but are usually overlooked. It is through the examination of rituals in ordinary settings, whether in traditional or modern contexts, that we can become aware of some of the functions of rituals that, heretofore, have largely gone unrecognized in the anthropological literature. The study of the hospital operating room suggests that ritual defines categories and clarifies boundaries between important states by exaggerating the differences between them, doing so precisely where the boundaries normally are not clear and well-defined. It is then that rituals are enacted in order to avoid the confusion that may result when it is uncertain which categories are operative at a particular time.

By imposing exaggerated definitions upon categories, rituals also serve to increase the autonomy of the participants by providing them with an unambiguous understanding of precisely which categories are operative at a certain time. Without the boundaries provided by rituals, participants do not know to which situation to respond. When the boundaries are known, autonomy is increased. Extreme license in ritual is an expression of this. In the operating room irreverent joking, as an example, is only possible after the ritual has succeeded in establishing a boundary between indistinct states. Autonomy is limited, and reverence and awe prevail during transitional states of ritual, when boundaries are not yet firm. When indistinct categories are ritually separated and given sharp definition, ambiguity of behavior is lowered and autonomy enhanced.[4]

NOTES

1. Occasionally others, such as salesmen or filmmakers, are allowed in parts of the surgical area. I was allowed free access to all surgical areas at all times, which included scrubbing and standing next to the surgeons and patient during surgery.
2. University Hospital is a pseudonym for a hospital in North America affiliated with a medical school.
3. The stages are heuristic. I have not encountered surgeons nor surgery texts which describe three distinct stages.

BIBLIOGRAPHY

Beattie, J. 1966 Ritual and Social Change. Man 1:60–74.
———. 1970. On Understanding Ritual. Rationality, ed. B. Wilson, pp. 240–268. Oxford.
Berry, E. C., and M. L. Kohn. 1972. Introduction to Operating Room Technique. Fourth Edition. New York.
Boyd, W. C. 1976. Surgical Infections. Synopsis of Surgery, eds. R. D. Liechty and R. T. Soper, pp. 78–95. St. Louis.
Douglas, M. 1966. Purity and Danger. London.
Durkheim, E. 1961. The Elementary Forms of Religious Life. New York. (1st English Edition, London 1915).
Firth, R. 1972. Verbal and Bodily Rituals of Greeting and Parting. The Interpretation of Ritual, ed. J. S. La Fontaine, pp. 1–30. London.
Gluckman, M. 1962. Les Rites de Passage. Essays on the Ritual of Social Relations, ed. M. Gluckman, pp. 1–52. Manchester.
———. 1970 Custom and Conflict in Africa. Oxford.
Goody, J. 1961. Religion and Ritual: The Definition Problem. British Journal of Sociology 12:142–164.
Horton, R. 1970. African Traditional Thought and Western Science. Rationality, ed. B. Wilson, pp. 131–171. Oxford.

Jarvie, I. C., and J. Agassi. 1970. The Problem of Rationality of Magic. Rationality, ed. B. Wilson, pp. 172–193. Oxford.
Katz, F. E. 1968. Autonomy and Organization: The Limits of Social Control. New York.
———. 1974. Indeterminacy in the Structure of Systems. Behavioral Science 19.
———. 1976. Structuralism in Sociology: An Approach to Knowledge. Albany.
Leach, E. R. 1968. Ritual. International Encyclopedia of the Social Sciences 13:520–526. New York.
Levi-Strauss, C. 1966. The Savage Mind. London.
Moore, S. F., and B. G. Myerhoff. 1977. Introduction. Secular Rituals, ed. S. F. Moore and B. G. Myerhoff, pp. 3–24. Amsterdam.
Munn, N. 1969. The Effectiveness of Symbols in Murngin Rite and Myth. Forms of Symbolic Action, ed. R. F. Spencer, pp. 178–207.
American Ethnologial Society, University of Washington.
Postlethwait, R. W. 1972. Principles of Operative Surgery: Antisepsis, Technique, Sutures, and Drains. Textbook of Surgery: The Biological Basis of Modern Surgical Practice, ed. D. C. Sabiston, Jr., pp. 300–318. Philadelphia.
Turner, V. 1967. The Forest of Symbols. Ithaca.
———. 1969. The Ritual Process: Structure and Anti-Structure. Chicago.
Van Gennep, A. 1960. The Rites of Passage. Chicago.